The Meaning of
The Holy Qur'an
For School Children

Volume 1 of 2

Presented by Yahiya Emerick

Table of Contents

Volume 2

Nature is the Proof of Allah

Practical Matters

The Beautiful Poems

The Rhythmic Chapters

The Two Chapters of Protection

Appendices

Preface

The Holy Qur'an is a book of guidance and spiritual progress. This book outlines the values and beliefs that can make you the best person you can be. It teaches a way of thinking that is positive, progressive and solution-oriented.

Any person who adopts the world-view of this book becomes a person who believes in justice for all, equality for all and personal responsibility.

The Qur'an teaches its message in a very unique way. It is not a book like other religious books that starts with the beginning of time and tells the stories of thousands of people and hundreds of nations and their ups and downs before closing with predictions about the future. It isn't a book of thousands of laws or diverse types of lectures, stories or poems, again like you would find in other holy books.

The Qur'an is more of a book of persuasion – it is a book that speaks to you like a friend. Stories of famous people are given only as a way to prove a point. Laws are few and are connected with trying to make you a better person. Poetic phrases become beautiful ways to remember sound advice and good teachings. You can open the book at any page, start reading and learn something useful.

In short, the Qur'an is a personal letter from Allah to you, asking you to become something more than you thought you could be: someone whom Allah loves and someone who loves Allah's world so much that he or she will do everything in their power to take good care of it and place their ultimate hopes in an even better one.

This translation of the meaning of the Qur'an is not the same as the original Arabic Qur'an. You can use this book to get at the meanings and message of the Qur'an, but it is the original Arabic text where the message really lives. May your search bear fruit and may the message of the Qur'an guide your way for all the rest of your days.

Ameen, let it be so.

Yahiya Emerick
New York
June, 2000

Eyes are at rest, the stars are setting.
Hushed are the stirrings of birds in their nests
and of monsters in the sea.

You are the Just Who knows no change,
the Balance Who can never swerve,
the Eternal Who never passes away.

The doors of kings are bolted now
and guarded by soldiers.

Your door is open
to all who would call upon You.

Each love, my Lord, is now alone with his beloved,
and now I am alone with You.

- Rabi'ah al Adawiyya of Basra (d. 801)

The Meaning of the
Holy Qur'an
For School Children

Hardcover Edition
Volume 1 of 2

Bismillahir Rahmanir Raheem

In the Name of Allah,
The Compassionate, the Merciful.

The Opening

1 Al Fātihah
Early Meccan Period

☞ Introduction

Muhammad (p) was frightened of the visions and words he was receiving in the first days of his ministry. At the age of forty, he had experienced a supernatural visitation while meditating alone in a mountain cave. A voice had told him that he was appointed as a messenger of Allah. Then the voice said some rhythmic words to him. (See chapter 96 for this first revelation.)

He didn't understand what was happening to him at first, but Waraqah, the old blind cousin of his wife Khadijah, later assured him that he had been contacted by an angel of the Lord.

Now, whenever he would walk in the desert outside of his hometown of Mecca, Muhammad (p) would sometimes hear the voice of that hidden spirit calling out to him, causing him to run back to the safety of his home. (See introductions to chapters 73 and 74.)

When he again told his wife's cousin Waraqah about this continuing phenomenon, he urged Muhammad (p) to stay and listen and report back to him with what he heard.

Accordingly, one day Muhammad (p) stood his ground when he heard the voice again during one his walks in the countryside. When the voice called out his name, Muhammad (p) **said, "Here I am."**

Then the voice commanded him to repeat that there was only One God and that he, Muhammad, (p) was the Messenger of Allah. After Muhammad (p) had done so, then the voice commanded him to recite yet further a new set of phrases, which were the verses of this chapter below. (*Wahidi*)

In the Name of Allah,
the Compassionate, the Merciful [1]

Praise be to Allah, Lord of All the Worlds; [2]
the Compassionate, the Merciful [3]
and Master of the Day of Judgment. [4]

To You alone do we offer service
and to You alone do we look for aid. [5]

Guide us on the straight path: [6]
the path of those whom You have favored,
not of those who've earned Your anger,
nor of those who've gone astray. [7]

The Cow

2 Al Baqarah
Early to Middle Medinan Period

☞ Introduction

The focus of this chapter, which takes its name from an incident recounted in verses 66-73, is to give us a sense of the history that exists between Allah and humanity. Allah created human beings to be the caretakers of the earth. As such, He endowed them with a capacity to learn and know that is far more advanced than any other creature He made. However, due to human weakness, our earliest ancestors lost their fellowship with Allah, and very few have tried to regain it.

Our overall failing is due as much to our own desire for worldly pleasure, as it is to the whisperings of the forces of darkness. That darkness is embodied in Shaytan, an evil creature who felt he was better than humans were, and thus he set out on a campaign to prove Allah wrong.

Allah accepted his challenge, but not because He was afraid or in need of something to do. He accepted it because, as is His way, He wanted Shaytan to understand how he went wrong *before* he was going to be defeated and punished.

Even though humans *could* be turned bad, as Shaytan **proved, he didn't realize that they were** also created with an inner nature that always moves them to notice their absence from Allah. Even though Shaytan continues to try and corrupt as many humans as he can in his foolish quest to somehow best Allah and **save himself, some humans still do look for Allah's truth.** Allah constantly holds out the offer of His forgiveness and acceptance into His fellowship, regardless of the direction that human culture or values take.

In the Name of Allah,
the Compassionate, the Merciful

*A*lif. Lām. Meem. [1]

That is the Book in which there is no **doubt**. It's a guide for those who are mindful (of their duty to Allah). [2]

(They're the ones) who believe in what they cannot see now, they establish regular prayer and spend in charity out of what We've given to them. [3]

They believe in what's being revealed to you, (Muhammad), just like they believe in what's been revealed before your time, and they're confident of the reality of the next life. [4]

They're living by the guidance of their Lord, and they're the ones who will be successful. [5]

Disbelief and Hypocrisy

Now as for those who (willfully) cover over (their inner awareness of Allah), it doesn't matter if you warn them or not, for they're not going to believe. [6]

Allah has closed up their hearts and ears and placed blinders over their eyes (because they refuse to believe). (And for all their bad behavior) they'll (be made to suffer) a painful **punishment**. [7]

Among the people (are some) who say, "*We believe in Allah and the Last Day,*" but they have no faith. [8]

They try to play a trick against Allah and those who believe, but they fool no one but themselves – *and they don't even realize it!* [9]

There's a sickness in their hearts, so Allah adds to their sickness. A severe punishment will be theirs because they covered up (their inner awareness of the truth first). [10]

When they're told, "*Don't make any trouble in the world,*" they say, "*But we're only trying to make it better.*" [11] But

they're the ones who are making the trouble - *without even realizing it!* [12]

When they're told, "*Believe (in Allah), like the (rest of the) people believe,*" they sneer, "*Faith is for fools!*" Yet, they're the fools – *and they just don't know it!* [13]

Hypocrites Try to Trick Allah

> **Background Info... v. 14-16**
>
> The leader of the hypocrites in Medina was a man named 'Abdullah ibn Ubayy. He was angry because the coming of the Prophet prevented him from assuming the kingship of the city.
>
> He used to tell his followers to flatter the Muslims as a way to mock them. He told his men, "Look at how I trick those fools!" Then he overly praised Abu Bakr and 'Umar loudly when they passed by.
>
> After the pair left, Ibn Ubayy said, "Whenever you see them, do the same."

When they meet the believers they affirm, "*We believe, too,*" but when they're alone with their devilish (friends), they take back what they said by saying, "*We're really with you. We were only playing a joke on them."* [14]

Allah will throw their joke back at them by letting them fall deeper into error until they're left wandering around, completely lost. [15]

They're the ones who've traded guidance for mistakes, and they gained nothing from the deal. They've lost all sense of direction! [16]

The Example of the Storm

> **F.Y.I...**
>
> Many Arabs made their living through trade caravans. Getting lost in the desert at night during a storm was a terrifying idea. This example likens the condition of an unbeliever to being lost in such a way. Allah's guidance comes in flashes, but if they ignore it, they will remain lost.

Their example is like the man who lit a torch (in the night). When it illuminated (the area) around (both) him (and his friends), Allah took away their light and left them (lost) in total darkness, unable to see at all! [17] They're deaf, dumb and blind and won't return to the path! [18]

(Another example) is of a storm cloud (in the sky) seething with darkness, thunder and lightning.

No matter how much they cover their ears from the **booming** thunderclaps - *fearing for their very lives* - it doesn't help them, for Allah surrounds those who cover (the light of faith within their hearts)! [19]

When a lightning bolt flashes before (their eyes), it all but blinds them, but they can at least fumble forward (in its afterglow). However, when the darkness returns, they hesitate (in uncertainty).

If Allah had wanted, He could have taken away their hearing and their sight, for Allah has power over all things. [20]

18

Why are We Here?

Background Info... v. 22-25

After explaining the differences between faith, hypocrisy and rejection of Allah, the Qur'an next gives us a summary of the main themes to be found throughout the rest of the book.

The One God (Allah) is the Creator and Sustainer of our reality. He chose a messenger, and that Messenger is true. There is an afterlife for the soul, and our beliefs and actions will determine what that future will be for us.

O you people! Serve your Lord Who created you and those who came before you so you can become mindful (of your duty towards Him). [21]

(He's) the One Who made the earth as your couch and the sky as your canopy. He sends down **WATER** from the sky and with it causes many types of plants to grow for your survival. So don't make rivals with Allah, especially when you know better. [22]

If you have any doubts about (the truth) of what We're revealing to Our servant (Muhammad), then compose a chapter similar to this.

Then call upon your witnesses - *besides Allah* - if you're so certain (of your allegations that he made it all up himself.) [23]

If in fact you find it impossible (to duplicate this message), *and it is impossible*, then beware of the Fire whose fuel is people and stone - (a blaze) that's been prepared for those who covered over (their innate ability to believe in Allah). [24]

Announce to those who believe and do what's morally right the good news that they shall have gardens beneath which rivers flow.

Every time they're served with fruit from within, they'll exclaim, "*These look just like what we had before (in our earthly life)."*

(That's because) they'll be given (their reward) in the form of what was familiar to them. What's more, they'll be joined by wholesome mates (with whom) to abide for all time. [25]

How does Allah Use Examples?

Background Info... v. 26-27

Some of the Jews of Medina started to make fun of the Qur'an because it mentioned things as small as insects in its examples.

For example, idols are said to be helpless because they can't protect themselves from a fly, as in 22:73, and spider webs are an example of how weak an argument can be, as in 29:41.

Some Jews said, "This doesn't seem like a revelation from Allah." And so verses 26-27 were revealed in response. (*Asbab ul-Nuzul*)

Allah won't hesitate to illustrate a point with something as small as a **bug** or anything bigger (or smaller) than that.

Those who believe know that (all good lessons are) the truth from their Lord, while those who cover (their capacity to believe ridicule such things) by saying, "*What can Allah possibly mean by these examples?*"

By them He allows many to fall further into error, and by them He allows many others to be guided.

However, He doesn't allow anyone to be confused by them except for those who've gone beyond the bounds (of goodness first). [26]

They're the ones who broke their (natural) bond with Allah after it had been made **strong**, and they separated (the family ties) that He's ordered to be joined together. They behave badly in the world, so in the end they'll be the losers. [27]

How can you cover over (your own natural faith) in Allah, seeing how He gave you life (when you had none)?

Then He's going to take back your life and bring you to life once more, and then you're going to go back to Him. [28]

He's the One Who created everything that's on the earth for your benefit, and then He projected Himself upon the design of the sky, making it into seven (layers). (He was able to do that) for He knows about all things. [29]

Why did Allah Make People?

Background Info... v. 30

The Qur'an now begins the story of people, and it starts at the very beginning with the first human being of our kind – Adam. Who was he, and where did he get tricked – and why?

And so it was that your Lord said to the angels, "*I'm going to place a caretaker on the earth.*"

But then (the angels) said, "*Are You going to put someone there who's going to cause chaos and disorder and shed blood, while we magnify Your praise and extol Your Holiness?*"

(Allah answered them), saying, "*I know what you don't know.*" [30]

Thereafter, He (brought Adam into being) and taught him the names (and qualities) of everything (in the natural world).

Then He placed (the natural world) before the angels and said, "*Now tell Me the names (and qualities) of all of these things (you see here before you,) if you're so certain (that I made a mistake).*" [31]

"*All glory belongs to You!*" they exclaimed. "*We know nothing about any of this, other than what You've already taught us, for You are the Knowledgeable and the Wise.*" [32]

Then He said to Adam, "*Tell them the names (and qualities of these things).*"

After he had finished doing so, (Allah) said to (the angels):

"*Didn't I tell you that I know what's beyond understanding within the heavens and the earth and that I know what you do openly and what you hide?*" [33]

Why did Shaytan Disobey Allah?

So then We gave an order to the angels, saying "*Bow down (in respect) to Adam.*"

Then they all bowed down; but (a jinn named) Iblis (who was there watching) didn't bow down.

He refused in his **ARROGANT** pride and chose to cover over (his awareness of the truth). [34]

We said to Adam, "*Both you and your mate can live in this garden and eat freely of its bounty to your fill, but don't go near this one tree, for it will lead you into corruption.*" [35]

However, they (were tempted) by Shaytan and banished (from the home) where they had been.

So then We ordered, *"Get down from here, and live in conflict with each other! Inhabit the expanse of the earth, and fend for yourselves for a while!"* [36]

Then Adam learned words of repentance from his Lord, and He turned towards him in forgiveness, for He's the Acceptor of Repentance, the Merciful. [37]

So We (softened Our attitude towards Adam and his wife) and said, *"Get down from here altogether, but if any guidance ever comes to you from Me, whoever follows My guidance will have nothing to fear or regret.*

*"However, those who hide and deny Our proofs, they shall be companions of the **FIRE**, and that's where they're going to stay!"* [38-39]

Remembering Allah's Agreement with the Jews

> **Background Info... v. 40**
>
> After presenting a quick summary of the importance of Adam and Hawwa (Eve), the Qur'an now turns our attention to the important issues raised about the Children of Israel. That is another name for the Jewish people.
>
> They got a lot of favors from Allah and they were asked to be a good example to other nations around them. Allah made an agreement with them about this.
>
> This section begins with Allah talking directly to the Jews and asking them to think about their obligations and their shortcomings in carrying them out. Then we are presented some brief stories from their early history to prove that they have not lived up to their duty to Allah.
>
> This is a good step to take as a way to explain why the Jewish agreement was canceled and replaced first by the mission of Prophet 'Esa (Jesus) and then by the mission of Prophet Muhammad.

Children of Israel! Remember the favor I bestowed upon you. Fulfill your agreement with Me, even as I've fulfilled My agreement with you, and don't be afraid of anyone but Me. [40]

> **Background info... v. 41**
>
> Some Jews of Medina used to write short verses of the Torah on leather scraps and then sell them to the illiterate Arabs to be used as good luck charms. (*Asbab ul-Nuzul*)

Believe in what I'm revealing, which confirms the teachings with you now, and don't be the first to reject it, and don't sell My verses for a little gain.

Be **mindful** of Me! [41]

Don't confuse the truth with falsehood, nor conceal the truth knowingly. [42]

Be constant in prayer, practice regular charity and bow down to Me, along with those (Muslims) who are already bowing down (in worship). [43]

Don't be Hypocrites

Background info... v. 44

A Jewish man in Medina gave permission to his relatives to consider Muhammad to be a prophet, but he himself refused to accept Muhammad's teachings. This verse was revealed in comment. (*Asbab ul-Nuzul*)

Will you ask other people to be righteous, but then forget your own selves? You study the scriptures, so why won't you understand? [44]

Strengthen yourselves through perseverance and prayer, though it isn't easy, save for the truly humble [45] - those who realize that they're going to meet their Lord and that they will return to Him. [46]

Children of Israel! Remember the blessings that I bestowed upon you and how **I favored** you above all others in the world. [47]

So beware of a day when no soul will be able to help another, when no intercession will be accepted, nor any payment (offered) will sway, nor any help come. [48]

23

Allah Saved the Children of Israel

Remember that We saved you from Pharaoh's people, who enslaved you and tormented you, killing your sons while letting your women live. That was an enormous test from your Lord! [49]

Then remember that We parted the sea and rescued you, while drowning Pharaoh's people as you stood there watching! [50]

Yet, also remember that while We met with Musa for forty nights, you took (to worshipping a statue of) a cow and did a terrible crime. [51] Even after that We forgave you so you could learn to be truly **thankful**. [52]

Recall that We gave Musa the (revealed) scripture and the *standard* (to judge between right and wrong), so you could be guided. [53]

Remember when Musa (returned to) his people (carrying that revealed message) and said:

"*My people! You've wronged yourselves by taking this calf (as a god). Say you're sorry to your Lord, and eliminate (within) yourselves (your love for worldly things). That's the best thing you can do in the sight of your Lord.*"

24

So (Allah) turned to you (in forgiveness), for He's the Acceptor of Repentance, the Merciful. [54]

Allah was Patient with Israel

Remember the time when you said, "*Hey, Musa! We're never going to believe in you until we see Allah face to face!*"

For that you were struck down with a thunderous **BOOM**, even as you stood there watching! [55]

Yet, even after that We revived you out of your daze so you could have (another chance) to be grateful. [56]

We caused the clouds to spread shade over you and sent manna and quails down upon you, (saying), "*Eat of the wholesome things that We've provided for you.*"

We were never harmed (when they rebelled); rather, they only harmed themselves. [57]

An Example of Disobedience

Background Info... v. 58-59

The ancient Children of Israel entered a town named Shattim, just east of the Jordan River. They were supposed to be a good example of Allah's people, but they failed and were acting badly in the town. They worshipped idols and did a lot of bad deeds in front of the people. (The Qur'an mentions this story again in 7:161-162.)

Prophet Muhammad said that instead of preaching about the forgiveness of Allah by saying, "*hittatun*", the Israelites said to the locals, "*Hintatun,*" which means, "A grain in a husk." And so, they were mocking Allah's orders. (*Bukhari*)

Remember (the time when you were approaching a new land) and We gave the following command:

"*Enter this town, and eat freely of the abundance you find there, but pass through its gates humbly and preach to people to be sorry (for their sins) and (to seek the) forgiveness (of Allah).*

"*(If you act in a good way,) then We will forgive you your sins and increase the (fortunes) of those who are good.*" [58]

Nonetheless, dishonest people altered the order they received (and behaved poorly towards the inhabitants of the town).

And so We sent down upon the criminals an air-borne plague, for they persisted (in doing wrong). [59]

Trials in the Desert

> **Background Info... v. 60-61**
>
> Allah provided a lot of help to the Children of Israel after they escaped slavery in Egypt. However, the Children of Israel began to grumble against Musa on account of the harsh, nomadic lifestyle that they had to follow as they wandered in the deserts.
>
> In Egypt they lived in houses and had a settled, farming way of life, even though they had harsh labor quotas and other miseries. The price of freedom was also more hardship, but they failed to realize this and perhaps they still suffered from a form of mental slavery to their old lifestyle.

Remember the time when Musa searched for water for his people. We told him, "*Tap the rock with your staff.*"

Right away twelve bubbling springs gushed forth, and every clan found its own place. So eat and drink from the resources that Allah provides, and don't cause bad times in the world. [60]

Yet, also recall the time when you complained, "*Hey, Musa! We're tired of eating the same thing (day after day), so call upon your Lord for us to bring us the harvest of the earth: herbs, cucumbers, garlic, lentils and onions.*"

"*What?*" (Musa) cried out. "*Would you trade what's better for what's worse? Go back to some (place like) Egypt, and then you'll get what you're asking for!*"

(As a punishment for their ungratefulness,) they were stricken with humiliation and misery. They brought the wrath of Allah down upon themselves because they rejected His signs and **KILLED** His messengers for no good reason – and that's because they were a rebellious and defiant (people). [61]

Allah is the Lord of All

> **Background Info... v.62**
>
> This verse was revealed to answer the question of Salman Al Farsi. He was a Persian who was raised as a Zoroastrian (a religion that worships two gods). He had spent a number of years as a Christian, before finally accepting Islam.
>
> He asked the Prophet about the fate of all those righteous Christians with whom he lived and studied before he entered into Islam. The Prophet casually remarked that those people were going to be in Hellfire, (probably thinking that anyone less than a pure monotheist was in trouble with Allah.)
>
> Salman described his inner reaction to the Prophet's words like this: "The entire earth became dark and **gloomy to me.**" But then this verse was revealed from Allah **to correct the Prophet's incorrect** opinion. *(Asbab ul-Nuzul)*

Those who believe (in Islam) and those who are Jewish, Christian or Sabian, anyone who has faith in Allah and the Last Day and who does what's morally right, their reward will be with their Lord, and they'll have nothing to fear or regret. [62]

The People Receive the Law

(Children of Israel), remember when We established a covenant with you at the towering heights of Mount Tūr:

"Hold firmly to what We've given to you, and remember what it contains so you can be mindful (of Allah)." [63]

However, you later turned your backs on it! If it wasn't for Allah's favor and mercy extended towards you, you would've surely been lost. [64]

And so it was that you knew some (of your people) were breaking the Sabbath rules, (yet, you did nothing). So We said to them, *"Be (like) rejected apes!"* [65]

We made an example of them in their own time and for all times to come - a lesson for those who are mindful (of Allah). [66]

The Story of the Spotless Cow

Remember when Musa said to his people, *"Allah has commanded that you sacrifice a cow."*

They replied, *"Surely, you're not serious?"*

(Musa) answered them, saying, *"God forbid (that I would speak) so lightly."* [67]

So they demanded, *"Call upon your Lord for us to specify exactly what kind of cow (He wants)."*

Then Musa replied, *"Neither too old nor too young, He says, but somewhere in between. Now do as you're told."* [68]

"Call upon your Lord on our behalf again," they implored, *"to tell us what color it should be."*

So Musa answered, *"A light brown cow, rich in tone and pleasant (to the eye)."* [69]

"Call upon your Lord on our behalf," they pleaded (once more), *"to point out its variety, for all cows look the same to us. If Allah wills, then we'll be rightly guided."* [70]

"He says an unyoked cow," (Musa replied,) *"neither worn out from plowing nor watering the fields. It should be in good condition without any mark or blemish."*

Then they answered, *"Ah! Now you've given us a complete description,"* but even still they offered the sacrifice only grudgingly. [71]

The Torah on Unresolved Murder

Remember the time when (some of) you murdered a man and then took to accusing each other (individually)? Allah would soon bring to light what you had concealed. [72]

We said, "*Apply some of (the principle of absolution) to (this situation),*" and in this way Allah saves lives from being taken (unjustly) and shows you His signs so you can understand. [73]

Yet, (in spite of this guidance), your hearts only hardened like stone, even harder!

Though indeed among stones are some from which rivers may flow, others which crack under pressure and let water flow, as well as others that fall down for fear of Allah, and Allah is not unaware of what you're doing. [74]

Dealing with Rejection

(Muhammad,) how can you hope to convince (the Jews of Medina) to believe in you?

Some of them, after hearing and understanding the words of Allah, *changed them on purpose!* [75]

When they meet the believers they say, "*We also believe (in Allah)!*"

But when they're alone among themselves they say, "*We shouldn't let them know what Allah revealed to us (in our scriptures), for they'll only have better arguments to use against us by quoting the words of your Lord.*"

Don't you see (their **GAME**)? [76]

Don't they know that Allah is aware of what they hide and of what they bring out in the open? [77]

The Ignorance of the Crowd

Background Info... v. 78

Some Jewish rabbis of Medina had certain religious writings in which their long-awaited prophet was described - *including a description of what he looked like.* When they found that Muhammad resembled this description, it is said that they changed the descriptions in their scrolls to make it seem as if he did not fit the physical profile.

A Jewish rabbi who had converted to Islam, 'Abdullah ibn Salam, confirmed that this took place, and when this action of the Jewish scholars was publicly announced, this verse was revealed in response. (*Asbab ul-Nuzul*)

Ruin to them for what their hands fake, and ruin to them for (the gains) they make! [79]

False Claims of Mercy

Now among (the Children of Israel) there are the uneducated (masses) who know nothing of (their) scripture and who believe only in what they want to believe. They follow nothing more than their own fickle whims! [78]

Background Info... v.79

Before the coming of Islam, some Jews of Medina used to write short verses of the Torah on leather scraps and sell them to the Arabs, claiming they were holy charms that would bring good luck. That is what this verse is referencing. (*Asbab ul-Nuzul*)

So ruin to those who write (holy) scriptures with their own hands (to sell as good luck charms) and say, "*Here, this is from Allah*," to make a grubby little profit from it.

Background Info... v. 80-82

The Jews of Medina had a belief that the world would last no more than 7,000 years, and that any Jewish people who went to Hellfire would be punished for only seven days, with each day equaling a thousand years.

After that, then the punishment would be over. This verse was revealed to answer that idea. (*Asbab ul-Nuzul*)

They say, "*Well, our punishment in the Fire will only be temporary.*" Ask them, "*Did Allah promise you that? If He did, then He won't go back on His word, or are you saying something about Allah that you're not sure of?*" [80]

No way! Whoever earns the wages of sin and is enveloped in evil will be among the companions of the Fire for all time, while those who believe and do what's morally right will be with the companions of the Garden for all time. [81-82]

The Sworn Duties
of the Children of Israel

Remember the time when We took an agreement from the Children of Israel, saying:

"Don't serve anything in place of Allah. Honor your parents and relatives. Be kind to orphans and to the poor. Speak in wholesome language to others, and lastly, establish regular prayer and practice regular charity."

However, later on you turned your backs (on these rules), all of you, save for a few, and you backslide even now! [83]

The Sin of Fighting Each Other

Background Info... v. 84

Before the coming of Islam to Medina, the three Jewish tribes of the city would make alliances with one or both of the local Arab tribes (named the Auws and Khazraj).

When the two tribes would fight, it often happened that Jews would be facing against other Jews in battle, and they would also sometimes kidnap each other for ransom.

When the fighting would be over, the Jewish leaders would sell their fellow Jews to each other's tribes, and they called upon their scripture as a justification. (Asbab ul-Nuzul)

Remember that We took another agreement from you, saying, *"You must not kill or drive each other away."*

You made a **PROMISE** to this and can attest to your oath, and yet you're the ones who still kill and banish each other and take sides against each other shamefully in bitter rivalry.

Yet, when some (of your rivals) are brought to you in chains, you ransom them, though it was forbidden for you to drive them off in the first place!

Do you believe in only one part of (your) scripture and then ignore the rest? What other fate can there be for people who behave like this, save for utter disgrace in this life?

On the Day of Judgment, however, there's going to be an even steeper price to pay, for Allah is not unaware of what you've been doing.

These are the kinds (of people) who buy the life of this world at the cost of the next. Their punishment won't be reduced, nor will they find anyone to help. [84-86]

We gave scripture to Musa and raised up many messengers after him, and We gave clear evidence to 'Esa (Jesus), the son of Maryam, and strengthened him with the Holy Spirit (of Angel Jibra'il).

Now do you (Children of Israel) become arrogant whenever a messenger comes to you with something that you don't want to hear? You called some impostors, and others you killed! [87]

The Children of Israel Reject the Last Prophet

> **Background Info... v. 88-90**
>
> Before the Prophet arrived in Medina, the Jews of Khaybar, a settlement to the north of Medina, had a war with the Arab tribe of Ghatafan. They suffered a defeat in the first battle, but then called upon Allah, **saying, "O God, we beg in the name of the unlettered prophet that You've promised us to grant us victory over them."**
>
> At their next battle, they inflicted a great defeat upon their enemies. After the Prophet Muhammad (p) came to Medina and began preaching, the majority of Arabia's Jews denied him, claiming that they already had all the truth they needed from God. This passage was revealed as a way to remind the Jews of what they had prayed for and now rejected. (*Asbab ul-Nuzul*)

Among the (Jews of Medina) are some who say, "*Our hearts are the*

wrappers (that contain all the knowledge of God)."

No way! Allah's curse is upon them because they rejected Him, and they only have a tiny remnant of faith. [88]

When a book from Allah does happen to come to them, one that confirms what they already have in their possession, and although they've long prayed for success against those who rejected (faith) and although they recognize (the new book's connection with their own), *even still they reject it!*

The very curse of Allah is upon those who cover (the light of faith within their hearts)! [89]

They sold their souls for a miserable price by rejecting - *out of petty jealousy* - what Allah revealed, simply because Allah would bestow His grace (equally) upon His servants, (regardless of race,) as He wills, and so they've earned **ANGER** on TOP of **ANGER**.

There's a humiliating punishment awaiting those who cover over (their awareness of the truth). [90]

When they're told, "*Believe in what Allah has revealed,*" they say, "*We only believe in what He revealed to us (before)."*

So then they're rejecting all other revelation, even if it's the truth and confirms (the prophecies) they already have!

So ask them, *"If you really believe in (God's revelations), then why did you murder the prophets of God in the past? Musa came to you with proof; yet, you worshipped a calf, and even after that you continued to do wrong."* [91-92]

Remember when We took your promise as the towering heights of Mount Tūr loomed over you.

(We had said,) *"Hold strongly to what We've given to you, and listen to it."*

However, (by their actions they showed that) they (might as well have) answered, *"We hear and we disobey."*

Therefore, they were (later) forced to take in (a drink made from the shavings of the melted) calf's (dust), precisely because they buried (their inner yearning for Allah).

Say to them, *"The motivations of your faith are terrible, if you even have any faith!"* [93]

Who are the Real Chosen Ones?

Ask (the Jews), *"If the home of the next life is yours alone, to the exclusion of all others, then wish for death if you're so certain."* [94]

Yet, they will never wish for death on account of the sins that their hands have sent on before them. Allah knows all about every wrongdoer! [95]

In fact, you'll find that they crave life more than any other people - *even more than the idol-worshippers*!

Every one of them wants to live a thousand years. Yet, long-life won't save them from their due punishment, for Allah is watching everything they do. [96]

Don't Deny Allah's Agents

Background Info... v. 97-99

Some Jews visited the Prophet in his masjid in Medina. A rabbi among them **named 'Abdullah ibn Suwriya** asked him the name of the angel who was bringing him his revelations.

When the Prophet answered that it was Jibra-il (Gabriel), the rabbi said, "*Jibra-il?* **He is our enemy. He's acted** against us many times. The worst time was when he sent the news to our prophet that Nebuchadnezzar would destroy Jerusalem. We sent someone to kill Nebuchadnezzar in Babylon; yet, Jibra-il steered him away, saying: '*If your God commanded him to destroy you, then He will not help you overcome him. Since no order (of Allah's help) exists, why would you try to kill him?*' (So, Muhammad,) if you would have said Mika-il, the one who brings rain and mercy, then we would have followed **you."** (*Baydawi*)

At about the same time, 'Umar ibn al Khattab (d. 644) was having a conversation with some Jewish scholars in one of their small schools. During this particular visit, a Jewish scholar named **'Abdullah ibn Suwriya** noticed Muhammad passing by in the street and **told 'Umar that he should** go out to see him.

Before leaving, 'Umar asked the Jews why they didn't follow Muhammad, and they replied that it was because Muhammad was friends with Jibra-il, who was their enemy.

When 'Umar went out to meet Muhammad, the Prophet immediately recited these three new verses to him, before he could tell him about his conversation with the Jews.

'Umar was amazed and said that he was just coming to tell Muhammad about something the Jews had said about the same issue. **In later years, 'Umar said of this incident, "Afterwards, I became rock-solid in my faith."** (*Asbab ul-Nuzul*)

Say to them:

"Whoever is an enemy to Jibra-il, (the angel) who delivers (revelation) to your heart by Allah's will, reaffirming previous revelations, and who is the bearer of guidance and good will to the believers – even more, whoever is an enemy to Allah, His angels, His messengers and to both Jibra-il and Mika-il, then, indeed, Allah is an enemy to those who cover over (the awareness of the truth that exists within their hearts)." [97-98]

And so it is that We're revealing to you self-evident verses that no one can deny save for those who are corrupt. [99]

The Corruption of Babylon

Every time they made a pledge, *some of them pushed it aside*, for without a doubt many of them had no faith. [100]

Even now, when Allah has sent them a messenger confirming their previous revelations, some of those who've received earlier revelation try to hide (their scriptures) behind their backs - *pretending not to know about them!* [101]

They follow the satanic chanting (of their ancestors), even though Sulayman was against it. Sulayman never rejected (Allah), for only the devilish cover over (their awareness of the truth).

Such people teach others how to do magic and other similar practices, like those that were handed down to two Babylonian leaders (named) Harut and Marut.

Yet, they never taught anyone anything without warning them first, "*We're only here to tempt you, (so don't believe in what we teach) nor renounce your faith.*"

So (the spell-casters) learned from them how to create marriage problems between a man and his wife, but they could never succeed except by Allah's leave.

What they learned only harmed themselves and brought them no gain. They knew that those who practiced (magic) had no share in the next life. What they've sold themselves to is terrible. *If they only knew!* [102]

If they only would've believed (in the truth) and been mindful (of Allah), then they would've earned from Him a far greater reward. *If they had only realized that!* [103]

Learn from the Mistakes of the Past

Background Info... v. 104

Some Jews used to go to the Prophet and say, *ra'ina,* which was a word in both Arabic and Hebrew. In Arabic, it meant one thing, namely *pay attention to us* or *look after us,* while in the local slang of the Jews it meant *listen, because you hear nothing.*

The Jews used to say the word to Muhammad (p) and then snicker among themselves. A local companion named Sa'ad ibn 'Ubadah, who knew what they were doing, threatened some Jews one day for disrespecting the Prophet like that. They said in their defense that it was a word also used by the Arabs, even though it had a different meaning.

This verse was revealed to the Prophet in response. And so Muslims are asked not only *not* to use this word, because some of the Jews were using it to disrespect Muhammad, but they're asked to say something more respectful all together. (*Asbab ul-Nuzul*)

O you who believe! Don't address (the Prophet in a demanding way by saying), *"Pay attention to us."* Instead you should say, "*We're ready to listen,*" and then listen (to him), for those who bury (their ability to have faith in Allah) will suffer a painful punishment. [104]

W e don't withdraw any of Our (previously revealed) verses or cancel them out altogether unless We replace it with a similar one or better. Allah has the power to do all things. [106]

The Faithless continue to Doubt

> **Background Info... v. 107-108**
>
> Idol-worshippers and visiting Jews used to ask Muhammad for all kinds of miracles to prove his prophethood. One day a crowd went to the Prophet, and one man asked that Muhammad turn a hill into gold. Another man asked for a holy book to come down from the sky, while yet another man, named 'Abdullah ibn Abi Umayyah, asked for a special revelation addressed to him personally. Some new believers also were beginning to ask such petty questions, as well. This passage was revealed as an answer to that type of questioning. (Asbab ul-Nuzul)

> **Background Info... v. 105**
>
> Whenever Muslims in Medina asked their Jewish friends to believe in Muhammad, the Jews would say that what Muhammad brought was good, but they only wished he brought something better than that. This verse talks about that situation. (Asbab ul-Nuzul)

Those who cover up (their desire for Allah's truth) among the Followers of Earlier Revelation and from among the idol-worshippers never want any good to come to you from your Lord, but Allah is the One Who decides who receives His mercy - *and Allah is the master of endless bounty!* [105]

Allah Reveals What He Wants

> **Background Info... v. 106**
>
> This verse was revealed in response to the charge that some Meccans made that Muhammad would sometimes cancel out a Qur'anic rule as the years progressed.
>
> They said, "Look at Muhammad, how he commands his companions to do something and then forbids it to them and commands the opposite. He says something today and takes it back tomorrow." (Asbab ul-Nuzul)

D on't you know that Allah has control over the heavens and the earth and that no one can save or protect you apart from Him? [107]

Would you (Muslims, who claim to) believe, question (and doubt) your Messenger (Muhammad), even as Musa was (doubted and questioned) by his followers in the past?

Whoever trades their faith for rejection (of faith) only wanders away from the middle path. [108]

Beware the Teasing of the Faithless

Background Info... v. 109

A Jewish leader and poet in Medina, Ka'b ibn al Ashraf, was inventing poetry to make fun of Muhammad (p) and his companions and also to get the Quraysh of Mecca to continue their attacks on the Muslims. The Prophet is told in this verse to be patient and calm in the face of these attacks. (*Asbab ul-Nuzul*)

Many of the Followers of Earlier Revelation will selfishly try to destroy your faith, even after they know the truth. So pardon them, and pay them no mind until Allah fulfills His purpose, for Allah has power over all things. [109]

Establish **regular prayer**, and give in charity, for the good (deeds) that you send ahead (of you for Judgment Day) are waiting with Allah, and Allah is watching everything you do. [110]

Testing Claims of Immunity

Background Info... v. 111-113

A group of Christians from Najran visited Medina to interview the Prophet and learn more about him. Some Jewish rabbis came and debated religion with them in a public place, and their argument became so heated that the rabbis and Christians each accused the other of not understanding religion and having no foundation for their teachings. This passage was revealed as a comment on this event. (*Asbab ul-Nuzul*)

There (are some who) say, "*No one will go to Heaven except Christians and Jews,*" but that's only their wishful thinking. Say to them, "*Prove it, if you're so certain of the truth.*" [111]

No way! Whoever submits his face before Allah and does what's right will be allowed to enter the Garden, and they'll have no reason to fear nor regret. [112]

The Jews say, "*The Christians have no basis (for their teachings),*" and the Christians say, "*The Jews have no basis (for their teachings).*" Yet, both groups claim to study the same Book!

Those who have no knowledge talk like that. Allah will judge between them in their dispute on the Day of Assembly. [113]

Don't Prevent Worship

Background Info... v. 114

This verse refers to the idol-worshippers of the Quraysh tribe, who used to prevent the Muslims from praying near the Ka'bah in Mecca, and who later prevented them from coming for pilgrimage after they fled to Medina. (*Asbab ul-Nuzul*)

Who is more oppressive than the one who forbids the calling of Allah's name in His houses of worship? Those who are eager to ruin them have no right to enter them save in fear (of Allah). They'll have nothing but **disgrace** in this world and a painful punishment in the next. [114]

Allah is Everywhere

Background Info... v. 115

When the Muslims in Medina were asked to turn away from Jerusalem in their prayers in favor of facing the Ka'bah in Mecca, some Jews complained about it. This verse was revealed as an answer.

To Allah belongs the East and the West; wherever you turn - there He is!

He's ever-present and full of knowledge. [115]

Allah has No Children

The (Christians) claim that Allah has (given birth) to a son! All glory to Him! No way! Everything in the heavens and the earth belongs to Him, and everything is compliant to His will. [116]

He originated the heavens and the earth, and when He gives an order, He only has to say, "*Be*," and it is! [117]

Don't Disrespect Allah

Background Info... v. 118

An idol-worshipper named Rafi' ibn Huraymilah asked the Prophet the question that follows in the verse below. (At-Tabari)

Those who have no knowledge ask, *"So why doesn't Allah speak to us or show us proof (of His existence)?"*

That's what those who came before them said, for their hearts are all the same. To those who are firm in their convictions, We've shown Our signs already. [118]

What of the People of the Past?

Background Info... v. 119

The Prophet said out loud one day, "If only I knew what my ancestors have done." This verse was revealed in comment. (Asbab ul-Nuzul)

We sent you, (Muhammad) with the truth so that you could give good news and also so you could warn. You won't be held responsible for the companions of the burning blaze. [119]

They will never Stop Trying to Turn You to their Ways

Background Info... v. 120-121

The Jews of Medina and Christians of Najran were trying to influence the Prophet towards their own positions, thinking that, as Islam was growing, they might be able to influence its course.

These verses were revealed in response, informing the Prophet that he should not follow either side, but rather listen only to Allah and what He reveals. (Asbab ul-Nuzul)

The Jews and the Christians will never be satisfied with you until you adopt their values.

Say to them:

"*The guidance of Allah is the only true guide.*" If you were to give in to them even after His truth has come to you, then you would have no best friend or helper who can save you apart from Allah. [120]

Those to whom We've given scripture (in the past,) and who follow it as it should be followed, believe in it sincerely, but whoever rejects it – they will be the ones who will lose. [121]

Children of Israel! Remember the **Blessings** that I bestowed upon you and how I **favored** you above all other nations. [122]

So then protect yourselves against a day when no soul will be able to help another, when no intercession will be accepted, nor any payment (offered) will sway nor any help come. [123]

Ibraheem Establishes a House of Worship in Mecca

Background Info... v. 124

Prophet Ibraheem (Abraham) is a central figure in Judaism, Christianity and Islam. He lived about four thousand years ago in Mesopotamia, a land that is called Iraq today.

After he chose to surrender himself to Allah, he was rewarded with prophethood. Soon he took his family and followers on a long journey through the western Fertile Crescent as nomads.

He had two main sons, Isma-il (Ishmael) and Is-haq (Isaac). He settled the first son in west-central Arabia while the second son remained with him in southern Syria or Palestine.

Call to mind that Ibraheem was tested by his Lord with certain rules, which he completed, so (Allah revealed) to him, "*I'm going to make you a **leader** among the people (of the world).*"

To which he inquired, "*And of my descendants, too?*"

(Allah) answered, "*(Yes), but My pledge will not include any wrongdoers (among them).*" [124]

38

to think, or who bow down and prostrate themselves (to Allah in prayer). [125]

Remember that Ibraheem said, "*My Lord, make this settlement a tranquil place, and bless its citizens who have faith in Allah and the Last Day with the fruits (of Your bounty)."*

(Allah) answered, "*I will also provide (prosperity) for a while to its citizens who cover over (their awareness of the truth), before I put upon them the punishment of the* **FIRE** - *the worst destination of all!"* [126]

Remember when Ibraheem and Isma-il were raising the foundations of the House, Ibraheem said:

"*Accept this from us, Our Lord, for You are indeed the Hearing and the Knowing. Our Lord!*

"*Help us to submit (to Your will), and also make our descendants a submissive community towards You.*

"*Show us the places where we must perform our rituals, and accept our repentance, for You are indeed the Acceptor of Repentance and the Merciful."* [127-128]

And remember that We established the House to be a peaceful place of gathering (for all) people, so take Ibraheem's place (of worship) as your own.

We did indeed arrange for Ibraheem and (his son) Isma-il to cleanse (and maintain) My House for (the sake of) those who walk around it, who rest by it

"Our Lord! Raise messengers from among our descendants who will convey Your signs.

"Teach them the holy revelation, give them wisdom and purify them, for You are truly the Powerful and the Wise." [129]

Ibraheem's Values and Traditions came before Judaism

> **Background Info... v. 130-134**
>
> This passage was revealed when some Jews went to the Prophet in Medina and told him that when he was dying, Yaqub (Jacob) asked his children to follow religious practices that were equivalent to what they (the Jews of Medina) were practicing in their own times.

W ho would turn away from the way of Ibraheem except for the one who would tarnish his own soul?

As it happened, We specifically chose him in this world, and in the next life he's going to be among the righteous. [130]

When his Lord said, *"Submit,"* he replied, *"I submit myself to You, the Lord of All the Worlds."* [131]

Ibraheem left this legacy to his descendants, as did (his grandson) Yaqub, who said, *"My children, Allah has chosen this way of life for you, so don't leave this (earthly) life unless you're surrendered (to Allah)."* [132]

Did you witness Yaqub's final moments before death? *"What will you serve after I'm gone?"* he asked his children.

"We're going to serve your God," they answered, *"and the God of your fathers, of Ibraheem, Isma-il and Is-haq, the One True God, and to Him we submit."* [133]

That community has long since passed away. They will be paid back for what they did, as you will be for what you do, and you won't be asked about what they did. [134]

True Religion came before Judaism and Christianity

> **Background Info... v. 135-137**
>
> In a public dispute, the leaders of the Jews of Medina and some visiting Christians from Najran tried to convince Muhammad (p) to join their religion.
>
> The Jews said that Musa was the best prophet, and that the Torah was the best book, while the Christians likewise talked about 'Esa (Jesus) and his Injeel (Gospel).
>
> They disagreed with each other and also chose not to accept Muhammad's (p) message. This passage was revealed as a result. (*Asbab ul-Nuzul*)

They say, "*Be a Jew,*" or "*Be a Christian and be saved.*"

Say to them, "*No way! We follow the creed of Ibraheem, the natural monotheist, and he never made partners (with God).*" [135]

Then say to them, "*We believe in God and in what He sent down to us and to Ibraheem, Isma-il, Is-haq, Yaqub and the tribes (of Israel).*

"*(We believe in the message) given to Musa and 'Esa and in (the messages) given to all the other prophets from their Lord. We regard each of them as equally authentic, and we surrender ourselves to God.*" [136]

If they come to believe as you do, then they will have found guidance, but if they turn away, (then know) that they're splitting away (from Allah's religion). Even still, Allah is enough protection against them, for He's the Hearing and the Knowing. [137]

Where is the Proof?

Background Info... v. 138

This verse is a reference to the habit of some Arab Christians who used to add a dye to the water they used for baptism. The idea was that the new color signified their new faith. This verse makes a word-play on that practice.

(Say to the Christians:)

"*We've (baptized) ourselves with the color of **Allah**, and what better color is there? He's the only One whom we serve.*" [138]

Then ask them, "*Why are you arguing with us about (the nature of) Allah, when He's the Lord of us both?*

"*You're responsible for your actions, even as we're responsible for ours, though we're more sincere to Him (than you).* [139]

"*Or are you saying that Ibraheem, Isma-il, Is-haq, Yaqub and the tribes (of Israel) were Jews and Christians?*"

Ask them, "*Do you know **MORE** than Allah?*"

Who is more wrong than the one who hides the evidence from Allah that he has with him? Allah is not unaware of what you're doing. [140] That was a community that has long since **passed away**. They will be paid back for what they did, as you will be for what you do, and you won't be asked about what they did. [141]

A Change of Focus
from Old Religions to Islam

Background Info... v. 142-152

When the Muslims were living in Mecca, and for about a year after that in Medina, they faced towards Jerusalem (far to the north) whenever they prayed. It may have been a way to make a statement to the Meccans that the Ka'bah shrine, filled with idols as it was, was being misused. In any case, the Prophet always expressed his desire to face the Ka'bah in prayer, and he used to pray to Allah about it.

Very early in the year 624, the Prophet received a new commandment from Allah (verse 2:144) that directed him to turn away from Jerusalem and ever after to face towards Mecca in prayer, a change for which the Prophet had been wishing for some time. (Note that verses 142 and 143 were revealed *after* verse 144.)

As the news spread throughout the neighborhoods of Medina and the surrounding countryside over the following days, people generally obeyed the new dictate, but a small amount of confusion ensued among some of the less fervent Muslims.

To the more thoughtful believers, however, this change showed them that the time to purify the shrine in their old hometown would soon be at hand.

Background Info... v. 143

Some people passed away before the change in the prayer direction was ordered. Their relatives went to the Prophet and asked if their deceased relatives were deficient in their record of good deeds and prayers on account of not having ever prayed facing towards Mecca. This verse was revealed to let them know that Allah will not let their past good deeds go to waste.
(Asbab ul-Nuzul)

And so it is that We have made you into a **moderate** community so you can be a witness to all people, even as the Messenger is a witness to you.

We first made you pray in the (unusual) direction of (Jerusalem) to test which of you would truly follow the Messenger and which of you would not.

(The switch towards Mecca) was indeed a tough (change to make), though not for the ones who were guided by Allah.

Allah won't let your (previous prayers that showed your true) faith go to waste, for Allah is kind and merciful to all people. [143]

The foolish among the people now ask, *"Why have the faithful now changed their usual direction of prayer (from Jerusalem in the north to Mecca in the south)?"*

Say to them, *"To Allah belongs the East and the West; He guides whomever He wills to the straight path."* [142]

We've seen you look to the sky for guidance, so now We'll turn you towards a more pleasing direction.

Now you can turn your face towards the Sacred Masjid (in Mecca), so turn your faces towards it wherever you happen to be.

The Followers of Earlier Revelation can see the proper reasoning in this from their Lord, and Allah is not unaware of what they're doing. [144]

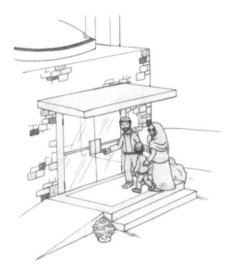

However, even if every convincing proof were presented to them, they still wouldn't join with you in your direction (of prayer), nor you with them.

They can't even agree amongst themselves about a direction. If you were to follow their whims, even after everything that's come to you, then you would clearly be in the wrong. [145]

Those to whom We gave revelation (in the past) know the criteria for this, even as they know their own children; yet, some still cover the truth knowingly! [146]

(Remember that) truth comes from your Lord alone, so don't be in doubt about it. [147]

Everyone has a goal
Towards which he turns.
So make your goal
the doing of good
wherever you are.

Allah will bring you
all together (one day),
for He has final power
over everything. [148]

No matter from where you start out, face towards the Sacred Masjid (in prayer). It's the honest truth from your Lord, and He's not unaware of what you're doing. [149]

So no matter from where you start out, face the Sacred Masjid (in prayer), and wherever you may be turn your faces

willingly to avoid public disagreements. Only wrongdoers will argue further.

Don't be **AFRAID** of them; fear Me instead, and I will shower My grace and guidance down upon you, [150] even as We've already sent one of your own kind as a messenger so he could read Our (revealed) verses to you and purify you, as well as teach you scripture and wisdom and knowledge that you didn't know before. [151]

So remember Me, and I'll remember you. Give thanks, and don't cover over (the faith that dwells within your heart). [152]

You will be Tested

Background Info... v. 153-154

After the Battle of Badr, which was fought between the Meccans and the Muslims of Medina in 624 CE, some people suggested that the people who died left this world and have no more good coming to them. This passage was revealed in response. (*Asbab ul-Nuzul*)

O you who believe! Seek courage with perseverance and prayer, for Allah is with the persevering. [153] Don't say that those who've been killed in the path of Allah are dead. No, they're living (in the next realm), though you might not perceive it. [154]

Be sure that We're going to test you in some things like fear, hunger and loss of wealth and self, and also in the fruits (of your labor), but give good news to those who patiently persevere, [155] who say,

when stricken with adversity, "*To Allah we belong, and to Him we return.*" [156]

The blessings and mercy of their Lord are upon them, and they're the ones who are truly guided. [157]

Walk between the Hills on Hajj

Background Info... v. 158

Now we learn something about the Islamic ritual of the *Hajj*, or Pilgrimage to Mecca. It is a required, once-in-a-lifetime journey for every adult Muslim male and female who can afford it and is physically fit enough to travel.

There are many parts to the week-long event, and the two hills mentioned in this verse are the same small hills that Hagar, the mother of Isma-il, ran between seven times in her desperate search for water before there was a city there.

The people of Medina used to avoid walking between those hills during pre-Islamic days (when they visited Mecca for pilgrimage for their idols), for they thought it was a unique tradition of the Quraysh.

Some of the Meccan converts, as well, stopped performing rituals there because there was some concern about the fact that the idol-worshipping Quraysh had built alters dedicated to two of their idols, *Isaf* and *Na'ilah*, on each hilltop.

The Muslims asked the Prophet about it, and this verse was revealed in response, saying that it was a valid part of the pilgrimage (though when the Muslims gained control over Mecca they removed the idols). (*Ibn Kathir*)

(The two hills) of *Safa* and *Marwah* are symbols of Allah. Whoever makes a pilgrimage to the House, or who visits (at other times), is not guilty if he walks between them. Whoever does good for goodness' sake will always find appreciation with the knowing Allah. [158]

Those who hide the evidence and the guidance that We've sent down - (especially) after it's already been made clear to people in the scripture - are condemned by Allah and those who have the right (to condemn), [159] except for those who repent, reform themselves and proclaim the truth, for in that case they'll be forgiven.

Truly, I am the Acceptor of Repentance and the Merciful. [160]

Those who cover over (their awareness of the truth) and then leave this life while actively trying to cover it over, will have to suffer the disapproval of Allah, the angels and of all people combined. [161]

They will stay that way, and their suffering won't lessen nor will it end. [162]

The Signs of Allah

> Truly, within the creation
> of the heavens and the earth,
> in the alternation of night and day,
> in the sailing of ships through the sea for
> people to profit and trade,
> in the water sent down by Allah
> for the dry land to live,
> in the diversity of creatures,
> in the changing patterns of the clouds
> and winds between the earth and sky:
> in all of these things
> are signs for the wise. [164]

> **Background Info... v. 163-164**
>
> When verse 2:163 was revealed, some pagans (in Medina) marveled at it. One of them remarked, "There's only one God? Then let Him reveal a verse for us if He's so truthful." Then verse 2:164 came to the Prophet, and he recited it."
> (Asbab ul-Nuzul)

Yet, even still there are people who would make others equal with Allah. They love them as much as they should love Him, but the love of the faithful for Allah is far stronger.

If only the wrongdoers could glimpse the penalty that awaits them, then they would finally realize that all power belongs to Allah and that Allah is a stern punisher. [165]

Your god is One God; there is no god but He, the Compassionate, the Source of Mercy. [163]

(On the Day of Judgment), those who were followed will distance themselves from their (hapless) followers.

They'll see the punishment waiting there just for them, and they'll break all bonds with them. [166]

Then their (frightened) followers will cry out (in bewilderment), "*If only we had the chance again, just as they're leaving us now, we would've left them!*"

(However, there's no going back), and so they'll be shown their evil deeds and be filled with utter regret. There will be no escape from the Fire. [167]

Keep Your Food Pure

O people! Eat only what is lawful and wholesome. Don't follow in the footsteps of Shaytan, for he's clearly your enemy. [168]

He'll order you to indulge in evil and shameful behavior and to speak (lies against) Allah that you can't even imagine. [169]

Old Habits are No Justification

> **Background Info... v. 170-171**
>
> The reply quoted here in verse 170 was made by a group of Jews to the Prophet after he had invited them to Islam. (*Asbab ul-Nuzul*)

When they're asked to follow what Allah has revealed, they say, "*No way!*

We'll hold on to the traditions of our ancestors."

What! Even though their ancestors had no sense, nor any guidance? [170]

The example of trying to reach them is like a shepherd shouting (words of wisdom) to sheep. They're deaf, dumb, blind and devoid of sense! [171]

What is Forbidden to Eat?

O you who believe! Eat of the wholesome things that We've provided for you, and give thanks to Allah, that is if you truly serve Him. [172]

He's only forbidden you from eating animals that have died by themselves, blood, pork and (anything) that was dedicated to (idols) instead of Allah.

However, if one of you has no choice but to eat of these things, without wanting to, nor returning to them (after your desperate situation is over), then he's not guilty of sin, for Allah is forgiving and merciful. [173]

Those who hide the revelations of Allah and gain a little something by doing it are eating nothing but fire. Allah won't address them on the Day of Standing (for judgment), nor will He purify them, for a painful punishment will await. [174]

They're the ones who've bought mistakes instead of guidance and punishment instead of pardon. How eagerly do they seek the **FIRE**! [175]

That's because while Allah was revealing the scripture truthfully, they were arguing against the scripture and increasing in their opposition. [176]

What is the Foundation of Faith?

Righteousness isn't turning towards the East or the West. Righteousness is believing in Allah, the Last Day, the angels, the scriptures and the prophets. (Righteousness) is spending of your wealth, for love of Him, on relatives, orphans, the poor, travelers, and on those who ask (for help).

(Righteousness) is freeing slaves, establishing prayer, giving in charity, fulfilling your agreements, and being patient in danger, hardship and adversity. These (people) affirm the truth and are mindful (of their Lord). [177]

What about Revenge?

> ### Background Info... v. 178-179
>
> There was a street fight in Medina between some men of different clans, and the stronger group yelled at the other, saying that they would kill a free man of theirs in revenge if one of their own slaves were killed or that they would kill a man of them if one of their own women were killed.
>
> This was an Arabian custom known as *retaliation* in which any harm done to one member of one's own tribe or clan would be harshly repaid on the family or associates of those who did it.
>
> When news of this public challenge reached the Prophet, these verses were revealed that laid out the idea that only the one guilty of a crime should be punished and that going overboard in demanding excessive revenge was wrong. (*Asbab ul-Nuzul*)

O you who believe! In the event of a murder being committed, fair retribution is in order, (but only the murderer shall be held to account). Whether a free man is guilty of murdering another free man, or a servant of a servant, or even a woman of a woman, (no one except the one who did the crime may be punished).

But if a relative (of the victim) chooses to forgive the guilty (person), then he should be dealt with fairly and should settle a penalty to be paid with gratitude. This is a compromise from your Lord and a mercy.

After this, whoever goes beyond the limit (by taking revenge on the innocent, in spite of this clear directive,) will be punished severely. [178]

(Innocent) lives are protected through the law of fair retribution, so the sensible among you will restrain themselves. [179]

Making a Last Will

It's the duty of every believer who owns property to make a *will* when he (or she) is near death, and he should bequeath fairly to his parents and next of kin. This is binding upon everyone who is mindful (of their duty to Allah). [180]

If anyone changes the will after learning of it, (then know that) they'll be guilty and accountable, and Allah hears and knows all things. [181]

However, if someone feels that the deceased was unfair to him, then he may bring about a (legal) settlement, and he won't earn any guilt, for Allah is forgiving and merciful. [182]

The Month of Ramadan

Background Info... v. 183

The Islamic style of fasting is a dawn to dusk abstention from food, liquids and intimate relations. Lying, cheating or fighting can also ruin a person's fast.

This month-long training teaches Muslims to maintain those good habits of moral behavior and control over their bodily needs for the rest of the year. Previously revealed religions have also contained a fasting component, and the principle is not new.

Learning to control the body and its desires is the path to lifting up the heart and mind, and that is the goal of *taqwa*, or mindfulness of Allah.

O you who believe! Fasting is prescribed for you, even as it was prescribed upon those before you, so you can increase your **mindfulness** (of Allah). [183]

(Observe the fast for) a set number of days, but if someone is ill or on a long journey then he can make up the days he missed later.

Anyone who would have an exceptional hardship from fasting (has the option) to make up for it by feeding the poor instead, and if someone freely gives more than he must, it's that much better for him! Fasting is really good for you, if you only knew. [184]

Ramadan is the month in which the Qur'an (began) to be revealed as a source of guidance for all people, as clear evidence of the truth and as the standard of (right and wrong).

So when you see the new moon (signaling the start of Ramadan), fast the entire month, though the very ill and those traveling should fast (later when it's more convenient to do so), for Allah wishes ease and not hardship.

Complete the fast, and praise Allah for His guidance, so you can learn to be thankful. [185]

Don't be Afraid that Allah won't Notice You

> **Background Info... v. 186**
>
> A visitor from a far village went to the Prophet and asked if Allah was far away, thus requiring people to shout loudly in their supplications to be heard by Him, or if He was near, in which case people could whisper to Him. The Prophet remained silent and did not answer. Then this verse came to him, and he recited them aloud.
> (*Ibn Kathir*)

*W*hen My servants ask you
about Me, I am near,
and I listen to every caller
the moment he calls upon Me.

So let them also listen
to My call and believe in Me
so they can follow the right way. [186]

Allowances after Nightfall

> **Background Info... first half v. 187**
>
> When fasting was first introduced as a personal duty, there was some confusion in the community in Medina about what was allowed for them to do after sunset. When 'Umar ibn al-Khattab complained one day about his confusion, this Qur'anic verse was revealed.
> (*Ibn Kathir*)

*Y*ou (men) *are* allowed to approach your wives during the *nights* of Ramadan. They're like a garment for you, and you're like a garment for them.

Allah knows what you were doing in secret among yourselves, so He turned to you and forgave you. Now you may approach your wives and seek what Allah has allowed.

(You may) eat and drink until the white thread of dawn appears distinct from its black thread. Then fast until the night approaches again, but abstain from your wives (even at night) when you're in retreat in the masjids for deeper worship.

These are the rules set by Allah so keep well within them. He makes His (revealed) verses clear for people so they can (learn to be) mindful (of Him). [187]

Don't bring Ruin upon Each Other

Don't eagerly consume each other's wealth in wasteful pursuits or try to bribe those in authority, hoping to consume unlawfully the property of others. [188]

How can We Use the Moon?

When they ask you what the new moon signifies, tell them, "*You can use it to calculate the date for people and to regulate the pilgrimage rites.*"

There is no Good in Sneaking

(Know that) there's no virtue in going "through the back door." Virtue comes from listening to Allah, so go "through the front door," (and conduct your affairs openly). Be mindful of Allah so you can prosper. [189]

When can You Defend Yourself?

This treaty stipulated that the Muslims had to turn back and would not be allowed to complete their journey to Mecca that year, but the following year they would be allowed to enter the city for three days to perform their pilgrimage rites.

As the following year approached, there was some discussion and concern among the Muslims as to whether or not the pagan Quraysh would continue to uphold their end of the bargain. This passage was revealed about this concern, and it informed the Prophet that if the Meccans went back on the deal and attacked the pilgrims on their journey, they had prior permission to fight back if necessary. (Asbab ul-Nuzul)

Fight in the way of Allah those who fight you, but don't go beyond the limits (of decency and humane conduct), for Allah has no love for those who go beyond the limits. [190]

Fight the (the idol-worshippers) wherever they're found, and drive them out from where they drove you out, for oppression is worse than death, but don't engage them at the Sacred Masjid (in Mecca), unless **they** attack you there first.

If they do, then slay them, for that's the reward of those who cover over (their awareness of the truth and do wrong on account of it). [191]

Though if they stop their aggression, (then remember that) Allah is forgiving and merciful. [192]

If they continue to practice oppression, then fight them until oppression is no more and Allah's way of life prevails.

If they seek peace, then you seek it as well; yet, continue to pursue the (persistent) wrongdoers (among them). [193]

On the Sacred Months

Background Info... v. 194

Arabian custom, purported to trace its roots to Ibraheem (Abraham) and Isma-il (Ishmael), held that four months of the year were sacred, in which all tribal feuds, wars and hostilities were to cease to allow pilgrims to complete their visits to shrines throughout the land.

The Ka'bah in Mecca was the most important of them all. The months of Dhul Qa'dah, Dhul Hijjah and Muharram were reserved for the major pilgrimages to Mecca, which would encompass many days of strict devotion, while the month of Rajab was reserved for minor pilgrimages of a few days.

Now about the sacred months: for the sacred months and all other restricted things, there is the law of fair retribution.

And so, if one of (your enemies) goes out of bounds against you (during those truce months), then you may retaliate likewise against him.

Be mindful of Allah, and know that He's with those who practice self-restraint. [194]

Don't Abandon Allah's Cause

Background Info... v. 195

Some years after the Prophet passed away, a Muslim army was fighting the Byzantines not far from Constantinople. One of the Prophet's companions, a native of Medina, rushed into the enemy lines and broke through.

Some Muslims who were watching from a different area of the battlefield told Abu Ayyoub al-Ansari that that man was throwing himself into destruction.

Abu Ayyoub said, "We understand the meaning of a verse (from the Qur'an) better than you, for it was revealed about us (Helpers)...

'When Islam became strong, we, the Helpers, met together and said, 'Allah has honored us with being the companions of His Prophet and in supporting him until Islam became victorious... We had before neglected the needs of our families, estates and children. Warfare has ceased, so let us go back to our families...'

'So this verse was revealed about us, and the 'destruction' refers to staying with our families and estates and abandoning struggle (in Allah's cause)." (Tirmidhi, Abu Dawud, Nisa'i)

Don't hesitate to use your own resources in the struggle, and don't cause your own destruction from greed. Do what is right, for Allah loves those who do good. [195]

Perform the Pilgrimage to Mecca

Background Info... first half v. 196

Thus we are introduced to the Islamic ritual of pilgrimage, or Hajj. This is the famous journey to Mecca that all able-bodied and financially capable Muslims must make at least once in their life. The official pilgrimage is held in the first part of the month named Hajj, while pilgrimages performed outside of that month are counted as extra merit.

There are a number of religious rites to be performed during the pilgrimage, with the main goals being to gain greater insight into the shortness of this life and also to bring home the reality of our ultimate return to Allah.

Perform the major pilgrimage and the minor pilgrimage in the service of Allah, though if you're prevented, then send an affordable offering instead. (Know that no one should) shave their heads until the offering has reached the appointed place.

Some Exemptions for Special Circumstances

Background Info... 2nd half v. 196

There is an allowance for the person who cannot wait until the end of the week-long Hajj to shave his hair due to a medical emergency. A man named Ka'b

He explained his story in the following words: "This (verse) was revealed about my situation in particular, but it is also for all of you in general. I was carried to Allah's Messenger, and the lice were falling in great numbers on my face.

'The Prophet exclaimed, 'I never thought your struggle (with lice) had become so serious as what I see. Can you afford a sheep?' I answered no, and then the Prophet said, 'Fast for three days or feed six poor people, each with a small measure of food, and now shave your head.'" (Bukhari)

So the man's pain was relieved, and he offered compensation for having to shave his head early.

If one of you is sick or has something wrong with your scalp that makes shaving immediately necessary, then in compensation (for completing this part of the pilgrimage ritual too early), you can either do fasting, feed the poor, or offer something in sacrifice.

However, when more stable circumstances allow you to perform the pilgrimage and lesser-pilgrimage (rituals as they should normally be done), then offer a sacrifice according to your means.

Whoever doesn't have enough money (to purchase an animal for sacrifice) should fast for three days during the pilgrimage and seven days after he returns (home), completing ten.

This is ordained for all those who don't live near the **Sacred Masjid**. Be mindful (of your duty) to Allah, and know that He's severe in retribution. [196]

Take up the Pilgrim's Garb

The months of pilgrimage are well known (to all). Whoever resolves to fulfill his duty within them, then there should be no intimate relations, immorality or arguing. Whatever good you do is well known to Allah.

Provide for the journey, (but remember) that mindfulness (of Allah) is the best provision to take, so all you insightful people, be aware of Me! [197]

Furthermore, there's nothing wrong in seeking the bounty of your Lord (through trade) during the pilgrimage. When you pour down into the plain of 'Arafah all together, remember Allah at the Sacred Monument. Remember Him as He showed you the way, for before this you were (a people) astray. [198]

Then move quickly along with the other people at the proper place, and ask Allah's forgiveness for your sins, for Allah is forgiving and merciful! [199]

53

Remembrance of Allah in All Places

Background Info... first half v. 200

At the conclusion of their own pilgrimage rituals, the pagan Arabs used to hold a kind of rally on the plains of Mina in which each clan used to shout and boast about how great its ancestors were. This verse was revealed to ask the Muslims to turn their exuberant focus towards Allah. *(Ibn Kathir)*

When you've finally completed the holy rituals, commemorate Allah - even as you used to commemorate your ancestors (before you were believers) – yet (do it) with far more passion and enthusiasm!

There are some people who pray, *"Our Lord, give us the best in this world,"* though they'll have no share in the next life. [200]

While there are others who pray, *"Our Lord, give us the best in this world, the best in the next life and protect us from the punishment of the Fire."* [201]

They will receive their share for their efforts, for Allah is quick to settle accounts! [202]

Remember Allah (during your pilgrimage at the plain of Mina) for the (three) appointed days, but if anyone hurries away after two days, it's not a sin, nor if he stays longer, as long as he guards (his conduct). Be mindful (of Allah) and know that you will all be gathered before Him (in the end). [203]

The Temptations of Earthly Life

Background Info... v. 204-206

A Meccan pagan named Akhnas ibn Shariq ath-Thaqafi arrived in Medina one day and heaped praises upon the Prophet and Islam. He swore that his aim was to enter into Islam, and he swore to Allah that he was sincere. The Prophet was pleased with his words, but then ath-Thaqafi left the city without converting.

Next, ath-Thaqafi began destroying a patch of crops and chopping off the legs of some cattle he found grazing nearby. He had only feigned sincerity and allegiance to the Prophet in order to mock him. This passage was revealed in response. *(Asbab ul-Nuzul)*

There's one kind of person who will try to dazzle you about this worldly life with his words, and he'll swear to Allah that he's sincere at heart, *but he's the most determined enemy!* [204]

When he turns his back from you, he looks to make mischief everywhere he can in the world, and he goes around damaging crops and cattle- *and Allah doesn't love disorder!* [205]

When he's told, "*Be mindful of Allah*," his arrogance causes him to go on sinning even harder. Hᴇʟʟꜰɪʀᴇ is punishment enough for him - *what a terrible place to rest!* [206]

Background Info... v. 207

The good man being referenced here is Suhayb ar-Rumi, a convert to Islam who wanted to flee Mecca for the safety of Medina. When he was leaving the city, a group of thugs from the Quraysh followed him and tried to seize him.

He stood his ground and drew his bow saying, "People of Quraysh! You know well that I'm faster and more accurate than any of you with my bow. By Allah, none of you will be able to reach me before I let loose all my arrows, and I will fight the survivors with my sword. Make a choice: either fight here, or let me go, and I will tell you where I hid my money and property in Mecca."

They agreed to let him go in exchange for his wealth, so Suhayb told them and later entered Medina poor and penniless. When the Prophet was informed of this he exclaimed, "The father of Yahiya made a bargain! He made a bargain!" (*At-Tabari*)

However, there's another kind of person who sells his life to earn Allah's pleasure, and Allah is kind to His servants. [207]

Be Firm in Your Resolve

Background Info... v. 208-211

Ibn 'Abbas (d. 687) explained that this passage was revealed with regards to some Jewish converts to Islam who tried to harmonize their practice of Islam with what they used to practice of Jewish customs. And so they still held the Sabbath in esteem and forbade themselves from eating the milk or meat of certain animals that were forbidden in Judaism.

Some other Muslims rebuked them for synthesizing the two faith traditions, but the Jewish converts felt they could do it, and when the matter was brought before the Prophet for resolution, they told him, "The Torah is the Book of God, too, so let us follow it, as well."

This passage was revealed telling them that they had to commit to God's last revelation wholeheartedly to be counted among the true believers. (*Asbab ul-Nuzul*)

Oyou who believe! Surrender yourselves to Allah completely, and avoid the path of Shaytan, for he's your clear enemy.

If you backslide after knowing the truth, (it won't harm Allah in the least), for He's powerful and wise. [208-209]

So what are they waiting for - for Allah to appear in the billowing clouds with a host of angels to settle the matter once and for all? But all matters will go back to Allah in the end. [210]

Ask the Children of Israel how many evident signs We sent them, though if anyone substitutes (something else for) Allah's (rules) after having received them, know that Allah is a **SEVERE PUNISHER**. [211]

This world is alluring to those who cover over (their awareness of the truth), and they scoff at those who believe.

However, those who were mindful (of their duty to Allah) will be held higher on the Day of Assembly, for Allah will provide unlimited resources to whomever He wants. [212]

All people were once a single community, and Allah raised messengers among them to give glad tidings (of Paradise) and also warnings (of Hellfire).

He also sent the scriptures of truth to be a judge between people in their disputes.

However, after the clear evidence came to them, those who received these (earlier) revealed messages, out of factionalism and pride, fell into disagreement.

Yet, by His grace, Allah guided the sincere believers out of their disputes and brought them to the truth, for Allah guides whomever He wants towards a straight path. [213]

Be Prepared for Testing and Trial

Background Info... v. 214

This verse was revealed to console the Muslims who had arrived in Medina, having to leave behind in their hometown all their wealth and property, which were immediately seized by the pagans. Hardship is a way for Allah to help His sincere servants increase in their faith and become worthy of even greater favor and reward later on down the line. (*Asbab ul-Nuzul*)

Did you think you could enter Paradise without experiencing what those before you did?

They were tested through affliction and loss, and (some were) so shaken that even their messenger joined with them in crying, "*When will Allah's help arrive?*" (Remember) that the help of Allah is always near! [214]

What is Good Charity?

Background Info... v. 215

This verse was revealed when a wealthy man named Amr ibn al-Jamooh asked the Prophet, "How much should we give in charity, and upon whom should we give it?" (Asbab ul-Nuzul)

They ask you what they should spend (in charity).

Tell them, "*Anything you can give to help parents, relatives, orphans, travelers and the poor is good, and every good you do is known to Allah.*" [215]

Fight, but Only in the Way of Allah

Background Info... v. 216-218

About two months before the Battle of Badr (624), the Prophet sent a small scouting party of eight men to gather intelligence about the intentions of the Quraysh. He instructed his men to spy on their caravans and attempt to gain news from them. Two days later, the scouts found a small caravan and pretended to be travelers on the road in order to mingle with them.

Some of the scouts suggested to their leader that it would be fortuitous for them to capture the caravan and return it to Medina. Accordingly, they seized two of its four overseers and directed the caravan away from the direction of Mecca. (A third caravan attendant named 'Amr was killed, while a fourth escaped and fled to Mecca.)

After the scouting party returned home with the spoils, Muhammad angrily scolded them, saying, "I did not order you to fight during the sacred month." Indeed, the attack might have occurred on the last day of the sacred month of Rajab. The Quraysh in Mecca complained very publicly that Muhammad broke the sacredness of the month, and they sent a delegation to Medina to confront him about it.

Meanwhile, Muhammad arranged for the two captives to be freed, and he impounded the goods of the caravan, rather than distributing them to the impoverished immigrant Muslims from Mecca. (One of the ransomed captives decided to accept Islam, and he remained in Medina by choice.)

The scouts, for their part, were mortified, and they were shunned and embarrassed. These verses were revealed as a response to the Quraysh delegation, who had asked why the Muslims would fight in the sacred truce months, and they pointed out that they had no right to claim injury when they had previously murdered and tortured so many Muslims for thirteen years in Mecca, adding insult to injury by seizing their wealth when they fled for their lives. After this passage was revealed, the Prophet ordered the booty to be distributed to the Muslims. (Asbab ul-Nuzul) Another report says that he returned the caravan to the Quraysh. (Baydawi)

Fighting (in the cause of Allah) is a duty laid down upon you, even though it might be unpleasant for you.

However, you may hate something that's good for you and love something that's bad for you. **Allah** knows, and you don't (always) know (which is which). [216]

When they ask you about fighting in a sacred month, tell them:

"Fighting in it is indeed wrong, but an even greater wrong in the sight of Allah is to discourage people from His way, to reject Him, and to keep people out of His Sacred Masjid, even driving out those who were already living there!"

Oppression is worse than (enduring) killing, (and the oppressors, who will never tolerate your existence), will always seek to wage war against you until they make you give up your faith, if at all possible.

(Just remember) that those who renounce their faith - *and leave this life in a state of rejecting it* - will have wasted their deeds in this world.

In the next life, they'll be among the companions of the **FIRE**, *and that's where they're going to stay!* [217]

Those who believe, however, and who suffer exile and strive in the cause of Allah can count on the mercy of Allah, for Allah is forgiving and merciful. [218]

Liquor and Gambling have More Harm than Good

> **Background Info... v. 219**
>
> 'Umar ibn al-Khattab (d. 644) and Mu'adh ibn Jabal asked the Prophet to give the community a definite ruling on intoxicants, pointing out that imbibing them caused drunkenness and debauchery. This verse was revealed to the Prophet, causing 'Umar to ask for more clarification.
>
> Later on in Medina, verse 4:43 was revealed forbidding praying while drunk. Some time after that, 'Umar asked for an even more definitive injunction, and verses 5:90-91 were revealed, forbidding all intoxicants categorically. (*Abu Dawud, Tirmidhi*)

When they ask you about liquor and gambling, tell them, *"There's both great harm and benefit in them for people, but the harm is greater than the benefit."*

When they ask you how much they should spend in charity, tell them, "*Whatever you can spare.*"

This is how Allah makes His verses clear so you can better understand [219] how they relate to this life and the next.

Fairness to Orphans

> ### Background Info... v. 220
>
> When verses 4:10 and 6:152 were revealed concerning the importance of not wasting or stealing the property of an orphan, those who had orphans and their property under their care became very strict in keeping their possessions separate from the property of the orphans for whom they cared, so much so that they would even prepare meals for the orphans from separately owned ingredients.
>
> If the orphan children didn't finish their food, the guardians used to set it aside until the orphan either ate it or it spoiled. Many such people went to the Prophet for they disliked the inconvenience and wastage, and this verse was revealed in response, which said that it wasn't wrong to mix foods that were bought from the two different monetary sources. (*Ibn Kathir*)

When they ask you about orphans, tell them, "*The best thing you can do is to help them. If you're their guardian, and you happen to mix your affairs with theirs, (never forget) that they're your brothers, (so keep track of their goods faithfully).*"

Allah knows the troublemaker from the really good person. If Allah had wanted, He could've put you into as weak a

position (as they), for Allah is powerful and wise. [220]

Don't Marry an Idol-worshipper

> ### Background Info... first part v. 221
>
> The Prophet sent a man named Abu Murthid Ghanawi to Mecca in order to bargain with the Quraysh for the freedom of some Muslim converts they had captured.
>
> While he was in Mecca, Abu Murthid saw an old mistress of his from pre-Islamic days named 'Inaq. She wanted to have relations with him, but he refused her advances, explaining that, "Islam has come between you and me."
>
> He did express a willingness to marry her, but wanted to confer with the Prophet first. Then he concluded his business with the Meccans and returned to Medina whereupon he asked the Prophet if he might marry 'Inaq.
>
> The Prophet asked about her, and when he was informed that she was an idolater, the first sentence of this verse was revealed forbidding Muslims from marrying those who make partners with Allah.
> (*Asbab ul-Nuzul*)

(Men), don't marry any women who make partners (with Allah) until they become believers.

Background Info... last part v. 221

As for the remainder of this verse, a man named 'Abdullah ibn Rawaha had an African maidservant whom he slapped in anger one day. He felt remorseful and went to the Prophet for advice. The Prophet asked what her habits were, and 'Abdullah mentioned that she was a very pious Muslim who practiced the faith perfectly.

The Prophet answered saying, "'Abdullah, she is a true believer." Whereupon 'Abdullah swore that he would free her and marry her, and he did. Several people went to the Prophet thereafter and, thinking that 'Abdullah had married a *pagan* maidservant, took it as a sign of the permission to marry pagans.

They then asked the Prophet to let them marry pagan women to whom they were attracted, as well. This second part of this verse prohibiting marriage with pagan servants was revealed in response. (*Asbab ul-Nuzul*)

A maidservant who has faith is **better** than an idol-worshipper, even though you may be strongly attracted to her. (Women), don't marry men who make partners (with Allah) until they believe.

(And for women,) a male servant who has faith is **better** than an idol-worshipper, even though you may be fond of him.

The influence (of idol-worshippers) will lead you to the Fire, while Allah calls you to the Garden and to His Own forgiveness. He makes His verses clear to people so they can be reminded. [221]

An Intimate Prohibition

Background Info... v. 222

The Jews of Medina had a general habit of forcing their women to leave their homes when they were having their monthly times, and neither would they eat nor drink with them.

Some local Arabs also adopted the custom. (Men from Mecca did not subscribe to this practice.)

A mixed group of local and immigrant Muslim men, with this issue in mind, asked the Prophet about what was allowed and proper, and this verse was revealed in response. (*Ibn Kathir*)

They're asking you about monthly times, so tell them, "*This is a time of hurt and impurity for women, so don't be (intimate with them) until they're relieved of it. Then, after they've purified themselves, you may again go to them as allowed by Allah. Indeed, Allah loves the repentant, and He loves the pure."* [222]

Intimate Permissions

Your women are like your fertile fields, so cultivate them as you wish, but always do something beautiful beforehand (so they know that you love them).

Be aware (of your duty to Allah), knowing that you'll have to stand in His presence one day, so convey good news to the faithful. [223]

Fairness during Times of Marital Trouble

Don't take the name of Allah as an excuse if the promise is against doing good, acting rightly or making peace among people, for Allah hears and knows (what you're doing). [224]

Allah won't hold you responsible for (unrealistic) promises (or foolish things said) without forethought, but rather for the intentions in your hearts, for Allah is forgiving and forbearing. [225]

Now, those (men) who swear (in anger) to abstain from (having intimate relations) with their wives (cannot prolong their period of abstinence for more than) four months (and must either begin divorce proceedings to set them free or reconcile with them).

If they do (renounce their oath and reconcile with them), Allah is forgiving and merciful. [226] Though if they're determined to initiate the divorce (proceedings, then remember that) Allah hears and knows (all things, so behave in a proper manner). [227]

On Divorce

Divorced women should wait for three monthly cycles (before seeking remarriage). If they believe in Allah and the Last Day, then they shouldn't conceal (the news) of anything that Allah may have created in their wombs.

It would be best for their husbands to make up with them (in that case), if they were of a mind to (do that). (Remember that women) have rights, just as (men) do in all fairness, though men have been given an edge over them, and Allah is powerful and wise. [228]

A divorce (pronouncement) can only be (revoked) twice. (After that) they must either (make up once and for all) and stay together lovingly, or (they must) end their relationship (in a spirit of) fairness.

Women are Allowed to Start a Divorce

You (men) are not allowed to take back anything you gave to (your wives), unless both sides fear breaking the rules set by Allah. If so, then there will be no sin on either of them if she returns something (of her dowry) to be free (of her husband).

These are the rules set by Allah, so don't go beyond them; whoever (goes beyond) the rules set by Allah, they're truly in the wrong. [229]

Don't Take Marriage and Divorce Lightly

(If a man pronounces) divorce (against his wife the third, irrevocable time), then he cannot remarry her until after she's been married and divorced by another.

If this condition is met, then there is nothing wrong for either of them if they reunite, intending to follow the rules of Allah. These are Allah's rules, clarified for those who understand. [230]

When you (men initiate) divorce (proceedings against) women, and they've fulfilled the end of their waiting period, then either reconcile with them fairly and stay together, or let them go fairly.

Don't take them back in order to be spiteful and cruel, for whoever does that brings corruption upon his own soul.

Don't take Allah's verses lightly. Remember His favors upon you, and (contemplate the meaning of) what He revealed to you of the Book and the wisdom (that came along with it), as both of them are for your instruction.

Be mindful of Allah, and know that Allah is well aware of everything (you do). [231]

Don't Prevent former Wives from Remarriage

Background Info... v. 232

A man named Ma'qil ibn Yasar gave his sister in marriage to a man in the community, but the couple soon divorced. After some time passed, however, both the man and the woman began to miss each other, and they both desired to get married again. (The man had never said 'divorce' three times, so he was still eligible to remarry her again.)

When the man approached Ma'qil and asked to remarry his sister once more, Ma'qil was outraged and said, "You thankless man! I honored you and married her to you, but you divorced her! By Allah! She will never be returned to you!"

This verse was revealed to the Prophet concerning this situation, and when it was recited to Ma'qil, he said, "I

---

hear and obey my Lord!" He then let the man remarry his sister, and he paid the compensation for having to break his vow. (*Bukhari, Abu Dawud, Tirmidhi, Bayhaqi*) So, this verse is a warning for family members who may try to stop a divorced couple from getting back together.

When you've divorced women, and they've completed the waiting period, don't prevent them from marrying their former (husbands), if they've agreed with each other in a fair manner.

This instruction is for all those among you who believe in Allah and the Last Day. That's the most wholesome course of action, and Allah knows (why), even if you don't know. [232]

On Child Care and Maintenance Issues

Mothers should nurse their children for two full years. This (time period) is for the one who can complete this term. (During this time, the father,) the one to whom the child was born, must support (the expenses of the child) according to his means, though no one will be forced to do more than he is able.

Neither the mother nor the father should be treated unfairly on account of their child. This also applies to whoever must assume responsibility (in the event of the father's death).

On Widows and Remarriage

If any of you (husbands) die leaving widows behind, then they must wait for four months and ten days (before they can remarry).

When they've finished that term, then there will be no blame upon you if they honorably do as they please with themselves, and Allah is well-informed of what you do. [234]

If both (parents) discuss and then agree to wean (the child before two years is up), and have consulted upon this, then there is no blame on them for that.

There's also no blame on (any of) you (men) if you propose (to a widow), nor (is there anything wrong if you secretly) desire (to marry one while she's still completing her waiting period). Allah already knows if you're thinking about them.

If you want to hire a nurse-maid for your children, there is no blame on you for that, either, provided that you pay (the wet-nurse) according to the reasonable (amount) that you agree upon.

Just don't make secret commitments unless you can speak to them in respectable terms, and don't finalize the marriage details until the appointed waiting period is over.

Know that Allah is already aware of what's on your minds, so be wary of Him, and know that Allah is forgiving and forbearing. [235]

Dowry Details

Background Info... v. 236-237

The Prophet married a woman named Umaymah bint Sharahil. After the wedding ceremony was finished, she was escorted to where the Prophet was sitting, and he extended his hand to her.

(Above all), be mindful of Allah, and know that Allah is watching whatever you do. [233]

There's no blame on you in divorcing women before the consummation of marriage or the settling of the dowry, as long as (the bride) is compensated with a gift - the rich and poor as they're able. A fair gift is a duty upon those who want to do what's most proper. [236]

However, if you divorce (a woman) before the consummation of marriage and after the settling of the dowry, then half of the dowry must be given to her unless she forgives it, or (the groom) in whose hand is the marriage tie chooses (to give her the full dowry).

Giving the whole to her is closer to piety, so don't fail to be generous to each other, for Allah is watching whatever you do. [237]

Don't Neglect the Prayer even in Times of Fear

Guard the (times of) prayer, especially the middle prayer, and stand before Allah in a compliant fashion. [238]

If you feel threatened (by an enemy force should you pray in the normal way), then pray while standing or riding, but when you're in a secure place once more, then remember Allah in the way He taught you – in the way you didn't know before. [239]

Provide Support for Widows

Those (husbands) who leave widows behind them should provide for them (in their wills at least) a year's expenses and a place to stay.

If (any widow) leaves (her home before that), then you won't be blamed for what they reasonably do with themselves. (Remember that) Allah is powerful and wise. [240]

Divorced women should also be given reasonable maintenance. This is a duty for those who are mindful (of Allah). [241] That's Allah making His verses evident for you so you can understand (them better). [242]

Running from an Enemy won't Save You

Background Info... v. 243

There is a story from the Jews that has been passed along in some of the books of Qur'anic commentary that this verse is referring to a group of Israelites who fled the plague in fear, only to die anyway. They were later restored to life upon the supplication of Prophet Dhul Kifl (Ezekiel).

Have you ever considered those who fled from their homeland in fear, thinking they would be safe? They numbered in the thousands! Therefore, (as a punishment for their cowardice), Allah said to them, *"So die, anyway!"*

Then He restored them to life. Allah grants His favor to people, though most people are thankless. [243] So fight in the cause of Allah (without fear that you might die), and know that Allah hears and knows (all things). [244]

Support Allah's Cause with What He Gave You

Background Info... v. 245

After this verse was revealed, the Jews of the tribe of Banu Qaynuqa began to ridicule Islam, saying that Muhammad's God was stricken with poverty. Verse 3:181 was revealed in response. Also see 5:64 and 36:47.

Who is it that will lend to Allah a beautiful loan, which He will then redouble and increase many times?

Allah is the One Who withholds (resources), and (He is the One Who) grants (bounty to His creatures, so never think you're doing Allah a favor by supporting His cause), for you're (all) going to go back to Him. [245]

The Children of Israel Ask for a King

Background Info... v. 246-251

Musa led the Israelites out of Egyptian bondage. His people disobeyed Allah when they were asked to enter Canaan and take possession of it from idol-worshippers. And so they were forced to wander in the desert for forty years. (See 5:20-26)

When both Musa and that generation of disobedient adults passed away, Joshua became the leader of the people. They successfully entered the Promised Land and established their rule. For the next three centuries, however, the

Israelites were disunited, often fought with one another, and adopted many pagan customs in the process.

From time to time, leaders called Judges arose who imposed their authority over the wider community. Some of these Judges were even prophets. Shamil (Samuel) was the last great one among these authority figures, and he came at a time (approx. 11th century BCE) when the Israelites demanded a strong king to unite them against their many enemies.

Have you ever considered the chiefs of Israel who came after (the time of) Musa? They said to a prophet (named Shamil), "*Set up a king for us, and then we'll fight in the cause of Allah.*"

(Shamil, sensing their trick), replied, "*And maybe when you're commanded to fight, you won't fight at all!*"

They (insisted they would, however), by saying, "*Why wouldn't we fight in the cause of Allah? We've been driven from our homes and families.*"

Nonetheless, when it came time to fight, they turned back, save for a few among them. Allah knows who the wrongdoers are. [246]

When their prophet told them, "*Allah has chosen Talut to be your king,*" they objected, saying, "*How can he be made our king when we're more qualified than he is to rule? He's not even rich enough!*"

"*Allah has selected him over you,*" he answered, "*and endowed him with knowledge and talent. Allah gives the*

right to rule to whomever He wants, and Allah is infinitely more knowledgeable (than you)." [247]

Then their prophet said to them, "*You'll see a sign to prove that leadership is his right in that the Ark of the Covenant will be given back to you.*

"*Within it is tranquility from your Lord, for it contains the relics of the families of Musa and Harun. It will be carried (back to you) by the angels, themselves. This will be your sign if you (really) have faith.*" [248]

When Talut set out with his army (to face the Philistines), he addressed (his men), saying, "*Allah will test you by that stream. Whoever drinks from it won't be allowed to march any farther with me. Only those who abstain from it will go with me, or who at the very least drink only a sip from their hand.*" All of them, save for a few, drank from the stream.

Then after they crossed over (the stream), the (few remaining) faithful (soldiers) lamented, "*We're no match for Jalut and his army today.*"

However, those who were certain they would meet Allah one day said, "*How many were the times when a small force defeated a larger one by Allah's will? Allah is with those who persevere!*" [249]

As they advanced upon Jalut and his forces, they prayed, "*Our Lord, pour determination down upon us, make our stance firm and help us against this nation that rejects (faith).*" [250]

And so by Allah's will they routed them, and Dawud killed Jalut. Allah also gave (Dawud) leadership skills, wisdom and whatever else He wanted to teach him.

If Allah didn't allow one people to deter another, then the world would be filled with turmoil, but Allah is infinitely bountiful to the entire universe. [251]

On Religions of the Past

These are the revelations of Allah that We're reciting to you in all truth, for you, (Muhammad), are one of the messengers. [252]

Of those messengers, We've favored some above others; Allah spoke directly to one (of them), while others were raised to a higher rank. To 'Esa, the son of Maryam, We gave miracles, reinforcing him with the Holy Spirit.

If Allah had wanted to (intervene), the later followers (of all these messengers) would never have fought with each other after receiving the evidence. Yet, they chose to argue; some believed, and some denied.

If Allah had wanted to (intervene), then they would've never fought amongst themselves. Allah does what He wants. [253]

On the Importance of Charity

O you who believe! Spend (in charity) out of what We've supplied to you before the day comes when no bargaining will be accepted, when no friendship will matter nor intercession sway.

(That will be the day) when those who rejected (faith) will finally realize that they were in the wrong. [254]

The Verse of the Throne

Allah! There is no god but He:
the Living, the Everlasting!
He never gets tired,
nor (does He) rest.

Everything in the heavens
and the earth belongs to Him;
who can intercede with Him
without His consent?

He knows what's ahead of (all people)
and what they've left behind,
while they have none of His knowledge
except for what He decides.

His throne extends
over the heavens
and the earth,
and He never tires
in their safekeeping.

He alone is the Most High,
the Lord Sovereign Supreme. [255]

On Religious Freedom

> **Background Info... v. 256**
>
> When the conflict between the Muslims and the Jews of the Banu Nadir was settled, with the requirement that the Jews had to leave the city and move elsewhere, it was found that there were a number of Arab children living among the Jews.
>
> This was not unusual, as some were adopted, while others were being raised as Jews with their (Arab) parents' consent. The reason why some Arab children were raised as Jews is because of a curious local custom. If a woman was considered to be barren, she would vow that if she ever was able to give birth, she would raise the baby as a Jew in compensation for the miracle. This happened from time to time.
>
> The Medinan Muslims did not want these Arab children to leave with the Jews, and they asked the Prophet if they could take custody of them. This verse was revealed in response. The Prophet gave the Arab children the choice of going with the Jews or becoming a part of the wider community in Medina. Some left, and others remained. (*Asbab ul-Nuzul*)

*T*here is no (permission) to force (anyone into following this) way of life. The **TRUTH** stands clear from error. Whoever rejects falsehood and believes in Allah has grasped a firm hand-hold that will never break, for Allah hears and knows (all things). [256]

To those who believe, Allah is a protector Who will lead them out of darkness and into the light. To those who cover over (their awareness of the truth), falsehood is their protector, and it will lead them out of the light and into the darkness.

They'll be the companions of the **FIRE**, *and that's where they're going to stay!* [257]

The Story of Ibraheem and the Arrogant King

Have you pondered (the tale of the arrogant king) who argued with Ibraheem about his Lord and the power which Allah allowed him to use? When Ibraheem announced, *"My Lord is the One Who gives life and death."*

(The king) cried out, *"I'm the one who (decides) who lives and who dies!"*

Ibraheem replied, *"Well, Allah makes the sun rise from the East, so can **you** now make it rise from the West?"*

This is how the one who covered (the knowledge of faith in his heart) was silenced, for Allah gives no guidance to people who are unjust. [258]

Asking Allah for Proof

(Have you learned the lesson) of the one who passed by a ruined town, whose roofs had all tumbled down? *"Can even Allah restore this place after so much decay?"* he mused.

So Allah caused him to die for a hundred years, and after that He raised him back to life and asked, *"How long have you been there?"*

"A day, maybe less," was his answer.

"Not so," declared (Allah), *"you were there for a hundred years after, and while your food and drink are preserved, look at your donkey (for it has died and rotted to bones). I'm going to make your example a sign to others, so look closely (as I raise your donkey back to life). Do you see how We knit the bones together and cover them with flesh?"*

When (the man) began to understand, he declared, *"Truly, Allah has power over all that exists!"* [259]

A Demonstration for Ibraheem

Even Ibraheem had once asked, *"My Lord, show me how You bring the dead to life."* (Allah) replied, *"Don't you believe (that I can do it)?"*

"Of course!" answered Ibraheem. *"I'm only asking for my own satisfaction."*

So (Allah) said, *"Take four birds, and train them to come to you (when you call); then divide them up, placing them on separate hills. Call to them, and they'll come swiftly to you. (In this lesson), know that Allah is powerful and wise."* [260]

Charity Increases Blessings

The example of those who spend their money in the cause of Allah is like that of seed grain. From it seven robust stalks rise, and each stalk contains a hundred grains! Allah gives abundantly to whomever He wants, for Allah is enough of a provider and is full of knowledge. [261]

Charity is Not for the Humiliation of Others

> **Background Info... v. 262**
>
> This verse was revealed in response to the willing and cheerful charity that Uthman ibn Affan gave to support Muhammad's mission.
>
> He went to the Prophet and said, "I have eight thousand silver coins. I am keeping four thousand for myself and my family, while I am lending to Allah the other four thousand." The Prophet answered, "Allah bless what you kept and also what you gave." (*Asbab ul-Nuzul*)

Those who give their money in the cause of Allah, and who neither remind others about what they spent nor humiliate (the poor to whom they give charity), will be rewarded by their Lord. They'll have no reason to fear or regret. [262]

Kind words and forgiveness are much better than charity that hurts. Remember; Allah is self-sufficient and is forbearing. [263] O you who believe! Don't negate your charity by making others feel they owe you or by humiliating (the poor).

This is what the **braggers** do when they give (money in charity) to be seen by other people, for they don't really believe in Allah and the Last Day.

They're like a rock covered only by a little soil that a torrent of rain soon washes away, exposing the hard bare stone underneath.

They can't do anything with what they've earned, for Allah doesn't guide people who cover over (their awareness of the truth). [264]

The example of those who spend their money seeking only to please Allah and to strengthen their own souls is like a high garden where rain is plentiful and the harvests are double. Even if there's no heavy downpour, the dew is enough! Allah is watching everything you do. [265]

Who wants to have an orchard full of date palms and grapevines, with streams flowing underneath and produce of all kinds, but then be stricken with old age while his children are still small, and then have a scorching whirlwind come and destroy it all?

That's how Allah makes His revelations clear so you can think carefully. [266]

What is True Charity?

O you who believe! Spend in charity out of the good things that you've earned and (of the harvest) of the earth that We've allowed to grow for you.

Don't choose to spend (in charity) items of inferior quality - *things that you wouldn't even want to receive yourself!* Know that Allah is self-sufficient and is praiseworthy. [267]

Shaytan scares you with fears of poverty and tempts you to do shameful things, while Allah promises you pardon and grace. Allah is enough of a provider, and He is full of knowledge. [268]

He grants wisdom to whomever He wants, and whoever receives wisdom gains great benefits thereby; yet, only the insightful ever realize this. [269]

Whatever you spend in charity or pledge to give is well-known to Allah. The wrongdoers, (who never give), will have no one to help them, (even as they help none). [270]

So if you donate to charity in public, it isn't wrong, though giving in secret to those in need is much better for you, as this will help to erase some of your sins. Allah is well-informed of everything you do. [271]

Charity is a Sincere Offering to All Who Need It

Background Info... v. 272

Some Muslim converts disliked giving charity to their non-Muslim relatives, and they asked the Prophet about this. This verse was revealed telling them that it was perfectly allowed to give in charity to non-Muslims, as helping another human being is a good act, regardless of the religion of another person. (*Asbab ul-Nuzul*)

It's not required for you to convert the (needy people to your religion before you give to them in charity), for Allah guides whomever He wants.

Whatever you spend (in charity) is done for the good of your own soul, for in so doing you've (shown that you're) seeking Allah's face alone.

Whatever good you spend will come back to you, and you won't be shortchanged. [272]

(Give to) the needy (missionaries) engaged in the cause of Allah who are prevented from going abroad to support themselves in the world - whom the ignorant consider to be well taken care of because of their modesty.

You can recognize them by their faces for they don't ask people persistently. Whatever good you spend, Allah knows about it. [273]

Background Info... v. 274

'Ali ibn Abi Talib, the Prophet's younger cousin, once had four silver coins. He donated one to charity at night, one during the day, one secretly and one in public. The Prophet went to him and said, "This (verse) is for you." Then he recited this new revelation. (*Asbab ul-Nuzul*)

Those who spend their money (in the cause of Allah) through the night and through the day, in secret and in public, will have their reward with their Lord, and they'll have no reason to fear or regret. [274]

The Prohibition of Interest and Other Business Matters

Those who devour interest-money will have no standing except for that of someone who's been knocked down by the touch of Shaytan – *demented*. That's because they say that business and taking interest-money are the same, *but Allah has made business lawful while forbidding interest!*

Whoever listens to this warning that has come from his Lord and desists (from accepting interest may retain the interest already accrued).

73

Then the matter will rest with Allah. Whoever continues (taking interest after this) will (soon) be among the companions of the Fire, *and that's where they're going to stay!* [275]

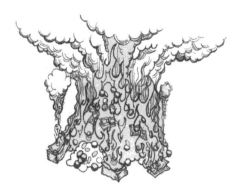

Allah cancels out any profits made through interest but adds to acts of charity, for Allah has no love for thankless sinners. [276]

Truly, those who believe and do what's morally right, who establish regular prayer and give the required charity will have their reward with their Lord, and they'll have no reason to fear or regret. [277]

You can Keep Your Original Money

Background Info... v. 278-281

This passage was revealed after Mecca surrendered and was under Muslim authority. An Arab tribe in the countryside named the Banu 'Amr was owed money by the tribe of Banu al-Mughirah. The loan also had a certain interest rate attached to it. Verses 278-279 were revealed to the Prophet and he warned the Banu 'Amr that unless they gave up collecting interest on the loan owed to them, (for the Banu 'Amr were insistent about it), he would fight them.

The Banu 'Amr agreed to forgo the interest if the principle were repaid immediately, but the Banu al-Mughirah could not afford this stipulation, and the Banu 'Amr would not back down. Verses 280-281 were revealed, and the Banu 'Amr finally agreed to let the debt be repaid slowly.

Also, in his treaty with the Christian community of Najran, the Prophet used this passage to say that they must give up interest-transactions or their treaty of peace would be canceled.

O you who believe! Be mindful of Allah, and forego any interest that's owed to you, that is if you really believe. [278]

If you don't, then beware of war on the part of Allah and His Messenger. Though if you repent, then you may keep your principal investment. You will do no wrong, and neither will you be wronged. [279]

If a person who owes you money is in financial difficulty, give him time until his circumstances improve, but if you forgive his debt altogether, as an act of charity, that's better for you, if you only knew. [280]

Be mindful of the day when you'll be brought before Allah, for then every soul will be repaid for what it's earned, and no one will be treated unfairly. [281]

The Importance of Business Contracts

Background Info... first part v. 282

The Prophet made a deal with a bedouin to buy his horse. After the price was agreed on, the Prophet asked the bedouin to follow him to his house so he could get the money to pay him.

The bedouin followed but at a slower pace, and along the way other people saw the horse and offered to buy it from the bedouin for more money than what he had agreed to with the Prophet.

When the bedouin arrived at the Prophet's house the bedouin said, "If you want to buy this horse, then offer a price for it or I'll sell it to someone else."

The Prophet, rightly thinking that he had already closed the deal with the bedouin, said, "Didn't I already agree to buy the horse from you?"

The bedouin said, "By Allah, I haven't sold it to you." Then people gathered while the two were disputing. Eventually the bedouin backed down, but the point was made that in the absence of a written contract for a one-time deal, witnesses are asked to be present. (Ahmad)

O you who believe! When negotiating transactions involving future obligations and (delivery) schedules, finalize any agreement in writing. Let a legal secretary accurately record the terms between each side.

No legal secretary should refuse to write as Allah taught him, so let him record (the contract accurately). Let the borrower read out the terms (as the secretary writes), and let him fear Allah his Lord, and not leave out any obligation on his part.

If the borrower is mentally handicapped, suffering from some illness or (in health too poor) to dictate (the terms) himself, then let his representative dictate the contract faithfully, and have two of your men to act as witnesses.

If two men are not available, then choose a man and two women of whom you approve to be the witnesses, because if one of the (women is not **skilled** at business) and makes a mistake (in future legal testimony), then the other can remind her. If the witnesses are summoned, then they must not refuse to come.

Never neglect to draw up a contract for future transactions, whether for large or small sums.

That's most fair in the sight of Allah and better for proof and avoiding doubt (concerning your reputations) among yourselves.

If the transaction involves merchandise for only a one-time, face-to-face deal, then there's nothing wrong if you forego a written contract, but have witnesses for commercial contracts.

Ensure that the witnesses and secretaries remain unharmed, for it would be a great sin on your part (if you pressured them unfairly). Be mindful (of Allah), for it's Allah Who is teaching you, and Allah knows about all things. [282]

If you're traveling and a legal secretary is unavailable, then taking a deposit (is good enough to seal the deal). If one of you makes a good-faith deposit with another, then let the trusted one fulfill his duties and fear Allah his Lord.

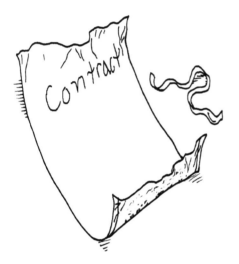

Never hide any evidence, for whoever does that will have his heart tarnished with sin, and Allah knows everything you do. [283]

What should We Believe In?

All things within the heavens and the earth belong to Allah. Whether you reveal what's in your soul or conceal it, Allah will make you answer for it. He'll pardon whom He pleases and punish whom He wills, for Allah has power over all things. [284]

The Messenger believes in what his Lord revealed, as do the faithful. Each of them believes in Allah, His angels, His books and His messengers.

(The believers say), "*We don't consider one of His messengers as being better than another.*"

(They pray), "*We hear, and we obey, (and we seek) Your forgiveness, Our Lord, for we (know that our) final destination is back with You.*" [285]

Background Info... v. 286

When verse 284 was revealed, Abu Bakr, 'Umar, Mu'adh ibn Jabal and others went to the Prophet and knelt down humbly, saying, "Messenger of Allah, we swear by Allah that this is the hardest verse ever revealed for us. All of us speak inwardly of things that we don't like in our hearts, for all of us would love to own the whole world. If we're condemned for what we think to ourselves, then we're doomed."

The Prophet replied, "This is how the verse was revealed." The companions lamented that they couldn't bear such a strict burden, and the Prophet suggested they could either disobey Allah like the people of Musa did or they could obey Allah. They reaffirmed their faith, and a year passed with no further word from Allah on this issue.

Then this verse was revealed that gave them relief, saying that Allah would not burden a soul beyond what it could bear; And so Allah would not hold people to account for what they imagined within their own thoughts. (*Asbab ul-Nuzul*)

Allah will not burden any soul beyond what it can bear. Each will enjoy the good of what it earns, as indeed each will suffer for the wrong. (Pray then these words:)

"Forgive us, our Lord,
if we forget or sin.

Don't test us, our Lord,
as those before us have been.

Don't burden us, our Lord,
with something beyond our capacity.

Forgive us our faults,
and grant us Your mercy.

You alone are our protector;
so help us against
those who reject (faith in You)." [286]

The Family of Amrām

3 Âlī 'Imrān

Medinan Period

👉 Introduction

The main focus of this chapter, which is named after a family of Jewish priests whose line stretches back to the time of Musa and Harun (Aaron), is to introduce the idea that Allah has sent an eternal message to the world in a continuous (and evolving) chain of prophethood. Judaism, Christianity and other religions were founded by true prophets who taught monotheism and righteous living, and there has been no corner of the globe that God has not touched with His message. Each successive revealed religion was more advanced than the last, reflecting the corresponding rise in human civilization and cultural development.

If the people that each prophet left behind, however, lost or distorted his teachings, then a later prophet might be raised to correct their descendants. The stories of Maryam (Mary) and 'Esa (Jesus) are introduced in this regard, as their example was meant to show how Judaism could be reformed. Prophet Muhammad is offered as the last in a long line of messengers from Allah who all taught essentially the same basic message of salvation. The Prophet said of this chapter, "Learn and recite the chapters of the Cow and Amrām for they are the most radiant lights of the Qur'an." *(Ahmad)*

In the Name of Allah,
the Compassionate, the Merciful

*A*lif. Lām. Meem. [1]

Allah: there is no god but He, the Living, the Everlasting. [2]

He revealed this Book to you as a truthful confirmation of previous (revelations), just like He revealed the Torah and the Injeel [3] before this as a guide for all people.

He also revealed to you the (prophetic) standard (of right and wrong).

Those who cover over (their ability to have faith) in these proofs of Allah will suffer the severest punishment, for Allah is powerful and utterly intense in vengeance. [4]

Division Leads to Disintegration

Background Info... v. 5-9

This passage was revealed for a specific reason. An eye-witness told the story in the following words:

"My brother and I were present in a gathering that is more precious to me than even red camels. My brother and I had arrived and found that some of the leaders of the companions were sitting close to one of the Prophet's doors.

"We didn't want to be away from them, so we sat near the room also. Then they mentioned a verse and began arguing over it until they were shouting. The Messenger of Allah was so angry that when he came out to them his face was red. He threw sand on them and said:"

'Listen people! This is how nations before you were destroyed, on account of their arguing with their prophets and contradicting parts of their scriptures with other parts. The Qur'an does not contradict itself, rather it testifies to the truth of itself. Therefore, however much knowledge you have of it then implement it, and whatever you don't know of it, refer the matter to those who have knowledge about it.'" (Ahmad)

There's not a thing on the earth nor in the sky that's hidden from Allah. [5] He's the One Who shapes you in the womb as He wills. There is no god but He, and He's the Powerful, the Wise! [6]

He's the One Who is revealing this scripture to you. Among its verses are some that are plain and clearly understood. They're the foundation of the Book.

There are also other (verses, however), whose meanings are hard to understand (and can be interpreted differently). Those who have hearts bent towards arguments dwell upon (the verses) that can be understood in more than one way.

They try to cause division (among the community) by giving them their own (misleading) interpretations, but only Allah and insightful people know their true meaning.

They're the ones who proclaim, "*We believe in the (whole of the) Book, because it's all from our Lord.*"

Only those who think deeply ever truly understand. [7]

"*Our Lord,*" (they pray), "*don't let our hearts go astray, now that You've shown us the way. Shower us with Your mercy, for truly You are the Generous One.*

"*Our Lord, You're going to gather all people together one day, and there's no doubt about that, for Allah never breaks His word.*" [8-9]

Allah's Plan will Prevail

Say to those who reject (the truth), *"You'll soon be defeated and gathered together in Hellfire - and how terrible a resting place!"* [12]

You've already been given a sign in the two armies that clashed (at the battle of Badr). One (army) was fighting in the cause of Allah, while the other was resisting Him.

With their own eyes (your opponents) saw you to be twice their number, (even though you were outnumbered by them), for Allah reinforces with His help whomever He wants. There's a lesson in this for those who have eyes to see! [13]

About the Worldly Things

A s for those who cover over (their inner desire for faith), neither their money nor their children will save them in the least from Allah – *they'll just be more fuel for the flame!* [10]

They're no better than the people of Pharaoh and all those (faithless people) before them who denied Our signs. Allah seized them for their sins, *and Allah is a strong punisher.* [11]

P eople are infatuated with the (worldly) pleasures they so ardently desire, such as women, children, piles of gold and silver, fancy horses, livestock and productive land. These are the things of this worldly life, but nearness to Allah is the best investment! [14]

Say to them, *"Should I tell you about what's far better than (the pleasures of this life)? In their Lord's presence, those who were mindful (of Allah) will have gardens beneath which rivers flow and pure and holy companions to live with forever.*

" (In Paradise) they'll find Allah's good pleasure, and Allah ever watches over His servants." [15]

"They're the ones who used to say, 'Our Lord, we believe, so forgive us our sins and protect us from the punishment of the Fire.' [16] *They're the patient, sincere, devout and charitable, and they seek forgiveness (for their shortcomings) even at the early light of dawn."* [17]

The Mistakes of the Past

> **Background Info... v. 18**
>
> Two rabbis from Damascus arrived in Medina desiring to meet with the Prophet. When they were in his presence, they asked him his name.
>
> They then requested that he answer one question of theirs that, if he answered it correctly, would convince them that he was, in fact, the foretold prophet of which their scriptures had spoken.
>
> They asked him, **"What is the greatest verse in the Book of Allah?"** This particular verse was revealed to the Prophet, and the rabbis, being filled with wonder, accepted Islam. (*Asbab ul-Nuzul*)

Allah says that there is no god but He, as do the angels and the people of knowledge who are firmly grounded (in true learning). There is no god but He, the Powerful, the Wise! [18]

The (only correct) way of life in the sight of Allah is surrender (to His will). The Followers of Earlier Revelation didn't take to opposing views except out of jealousy of each other after they received this knowledge.

Whoever rejects the proofs of Allah (should remember) that Allah is swift in settling accounts. [19]

If they argue with you, then say to them, "*I've surrendered my whole self to Allah, as have those who follow me.*"

Then ask the Followers of Earlier Revelation and the unschooled (people of Arabia) who've never received (any revelation before), "*Will you now surrender yourselves (to Him)?*"

If they surrender themselves (to Allah), then they will have found guidance. If they turn back, well, your duty was only to convey the message, and Allah is watching His servants. [20]

Those who reject the signs of Allah and who killed the prophets and killed those who called for justice among people, even though it was against all right (to kill them), give them the news of a painful punishment. [21]

Any good they do is wasted both in this life and the next, and they'll have no one to help them. [22]

Allah Decides His Response

> **Background Info... v. 23-25**
>
> This passage was revealed on an occasion when the Jews asked Muhammad's opinion about a legal judgment, and they refused to accept his ruling even though it was congruent with their religion. (*Ibn Kathir*)

Have you ever considered (the case of the Jews of Medina) who received a portion of the scripture in the past?

Now they're being called to the (last) Book of Allah to settle their disagreements; yet, some of them turn away and decline (the offer of help)! [23]

That's because their excuse is to say, "*Our punishment (from Allah) will only last a set number of days,*" but they're deceived in their religion by the very (lies) they themselves have fabricated! [24]

How will it be when We gather them all together on that day of which there is no doubt, when every soul will get what it deserves without any unfairness? [25]

The Call of Allah will Triumph

> **Background Info... v. 26-27**
>
> When the Muslims were busy digging a trench around Medina just before the Battle of the Trench, a large stone was encountered in one of the digging pits. Some companions called the Prophet over to see what could be done about it, and he came to examine it. Then he took up a pick, struck at it, and it shattered sending sparks in several directions.
>
> The Prophet then told his men that in those sparks of light he saw visions of Islam triumphing over Persia, Byzantium and Yemen. The hypocrites and Jews of the city scoffed when they heard about what he said and teased the Muslims about it. This passage was revealed in response. (*Bayhaqi*)

Proclaim (this supplication so they can understand what your beliefs are):

"*Lord of All Dominion! You grant authority to whom You please and bring down whom You will. You empower*

whom You please and weaken whom You will. In Your hand is all good, and You have power over all that is. [26]

"You make the night merge into day and the day merge into night. You bring life from death and death from life, and You grant resources to whomever You want without any limit." [27]

**Know a Person
by the Company They Keep**

The believers should never take as best friends those who cover over (their awareness of the truth), in preference to those who believe, unless it's absolutely necessary in order to protect yourselves from them (by keeping them close).

Whoever does that (without that one, valid excuse) will find no help from Allah. Allah is personally warning you (against disobeying Him), for the final destination (of all things) is back to Allah. [28]

Say to them, "*Whether you hide or reveal your inner-most thoughts, Allah knows them, even as He knows everything*

within the heavens and on the earth, for Allah has power over all things." [29]

A day (will come) when every soul will be confronted with the good that it's done and also with the evil that it's done, and it will wish that its evil were far away! Allah is personally warning you (to beware of His judgment), though He's kind to His servants. [30]

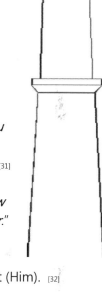

Say to them, "*If you truly love Allah, then follow me, so Allah can love you and forgive you your faults, for Allah is forgiving and merciful."* [31]

Then say, "*Now follow Allah and His Messenger."* If they turn away, (then know that) Allah has no love for those who reject (Him). [32]

The Continuity of Allah's Message

Background Info... v. 33-120

A large number of verses in this chapter (most of those that talk about 'Esa (Jesus), Judaism or Christianity) were revealed to the Prophet during a series of very intense discussions with the Jews of Medina, but also with a visiting delegation of Christians from Najran, an area in Arabia several hundred miles to the south.

The Christians had come (around sixty in number) with their chief priest, 'Abdul Masih, and several high officials who had the favor of the Byzantine Roman Emperor.

They had received a letter from the Prophet asking for their submission to the Islamic state, but they wanted to find out more about this new faith called Islam, and the Prophet graciously received them.

When they arrived the Prophet allowed them to conduct their religious services in the main masjid in Medina. Their officials and even laymen were dressed in such fine clothes that the people of Medina remarked that a delegation of its kind had never been seen before.

When the initial discussions began, the Prophet invited them to join Islam, but the Christians claimed that they were already submitted to God. Then the Prophet challenged them to a public debate the next day.

When morning came, Salman al Farsi seated the Christians on one side of an open field. The Prophet arrived some moments later carrying his baby grandson Husayn, while his other young grandson Hassan held his finger.

His daughter Fatimah and her **husband 'Ali also sat behind the Prophet.** When the discussions began, the Prophet brought up a number of points, including the Christian teachings of the trinity and salvation by 'Esa (Jesus) dying, along with some lesser issues like the eating of pork, the drinking of alcohol and the use of the cross as a symbol.

Relevant verses from this chapter were revealed sometimes within the meetings and other times during rest breaks. (Verses 33-34 were perhaps the first revelations recited to the crowd.) Surviving accounts indicate that the Prophet got the better in these debates and that some of the visitors even accepted Islam.

The remainder, who chose to continue in their religion, concluded a fair treaty with the Prophet and returned home with a healthy respect for the new faith.

Truly, Allah chose Adam, Nuh and the families of Ibraheem and Imrān above all others in the world. [33] They were all descended from one line, and Allah hears and knows all (about such) things. [34]

The Story of Maryam

A woman of the family of Imrān prayed, "*My Lord, I dedicate my unborn child to Your service. So accept this from me, for You're the Hearing and the Knowing.*" [35]

After she gave birth, she cried, "*Oh my Lord, I've delivered a girl!*" Allah knew better (the value of that child) she bore.

"*A male is not the same as a female,*" she said, "*and so I will call her Maryam, and I commend her and her children to Your protection against Shaytan, the Outcast.*" [36]

Her Lord accepted (the child) graciously, and she grew up healthy and well under the sponsorship of Zachariah to whom she was assigned (as a dependent). Whenever he would enter her room, he would find her provided with food.

"*Maryam,*" he would ask, *"where did all this (food) come from?"* "*It's from Allah,*" she would reply, *"and Allah provides to whomever He wants without any limit.*" [37]

Then Zachariah, (seeing the virtue of Maryam), called to his Lord, saying, "*My Lord, give me a pure and virtuous descendant of my own, for You hear all requests.*" [38]

Then the angels (appeared before him), even as he was standing there in his room.

They said to him, "*Allah sends you the good news of (a son) named Yahiya. He's going to announce the truth of a word from Allah, and he'll be a disciplined prophet in the tradition of the morally righteous.*" [39]

(Zachariah, being astonished,) asked, "*How can I have a son, my Lord, when I'm old and my wife is barren?*"

"*So it will be,*" (the angel) replied. "*Allah does whatever He wills.*" [40]

"*But my Lord!*" (Zachariah) pleaded. "*Give me a sign.*"

"*Your sign,*" he replied, "*will be that for three days you will be unable to speak to anyone, except through gestures. Remember your Lord frequently (during this time), and glorify Him in the evening and in the morning.*" [41]

The Birth of the Messiah

The angels (appeared) to Maryam and said, "*Maryam! Allah has chosen you and purified you. He's chosen you above the women of all nations,* [42] *so be compliant to your Lord, prostrate yourself, and bow down with those who bow (before Allah).*" [43]

(This story) that We're revealing to you, (Muhammad), was previously unknown (to you), for you weren't there when the (male relatives) chose reeds randomly to decide who among them must provide (financial support) for Maryam, and you certainly weren't there when they argued (over the outcome). [44]

When the angels (again returned to Maryam after some time had passed), they said, "*Mary! Allah gives you the good news of a word from Him. He's going to be called the Messiah, 'Esa, the*

85

son of Maryam. He'll be honored in this world, as well as in the next, where he'll be among those nearest (to Allah)." [45]

"He will speak to people in childhood and also when he's grown, and he's going to be one of the morally righteous." [46]

"*But my Lord!*" she cried out. "*How can I have a son when no man has touched me?*"

"*And so it is that Allah creates whatever He wants,*" the angels replied. "*When He decides something, He only has to say, 'Be' and it is.*" [47]

"He will teach him scripture and fill him with wisdom (by teaching him) the Torah and the Injeel. [48] (Thereafter He's going to appoint) him as a messenger to the Children of Israel."

What will 'Esa (Jesus) Teach?

"(And 'Esa) will also tell (his people), *'I've come to you with a sign from your Lord. I'm going to breathe life into a lifeless clay bird that I'll create by Allah's command, and I'll heal the blind and the lepers and bring the dead to life, all by Allah's command.*

'I'll tell you what you consume (and waste of the world), as well as what you

store away (of good deeds for Judgment Day). (Know that) in all of these things is a great sign if you really have faith.* [49]

'I've also come to verify the truth of the Torah that was revealed before me and to make lawful some things that were forbidden to you before.

'I'm coming to you with proof from your Lord, so be mindful of Allah and obey me. [50] To be sure, Allah is my Lord and your Lord, so serve Him. That's a straight way (of life)." [51]

When 'Esa (began his mission and) noticed the disbelief (of his people), he (looked for helpers), saying, "*Who will help me (call the people) to Allah?*"

(Then a group of) disciples (began to follow him, and), they said, "*We'll help (you call people) to Allah, for we believe in Allah, and you can be our witness that we're truly surrendered (to His will).* [52]

"*Our Lord, We believe in what You've revealed, and we follow this messenger, so record us among those who bear witness.*" [53]

However, it wasn't long before (the faithless) contrived a plot, though Allah did the same - *and Allah is the best planner of all!* [54]

(After his people rejected him,) Allah said, "*'Esa, I'm going to take you completely and lift you up to Myself. I will purify (your reputation which has been tarnished) by those who reject (the truth).*

"I will make those who follow you superior to those who cover over (their awareness of the truth), even until the Day of Resurrection. Then all of you will come back to Me, and I'll judge between you in those matters in which you differed." [55]

"As for those who reject (the truth), I'm going to punish them with a harsh penalty in this world, as well as in the next, and they'll have no one to help them. [56]

"As for those who believe and do what's morally right, they'll be paid their reward. (Know that) Allah has no love for those who do wrong." [57]

Don't Take 'Esa (Jesus) as a God

> **Background Info... v. 58-60**
>
> One of the Christian priests in the delegation from Najran asked the Prophet, "Why are you belittling our lord ('Esa/ Jesus)?"
>
> The Prophet replied, "What am I saying (to which you're objecting?)"
>
> They answered, "You're saying he's just an (ordinary) servant."
>
> The Prophet said, "Yes, he is a servant, but of God, and he is His Messenger, and His word that He bestowed upon the virgin Maryam (Mary)."
>
> The Christians became angry and asked, "Have you ever heard of a human being without a father? If you have then point out to us someone like him!" Then this passage came equating 'Esa with Adam as merely another creation of God.
> (Asbab ul-Nuzul)

These are the verses that We're reciting to you, (Muhammad), and they're a wise reminder. [58]

The example of 'Esa in the sight of Allah is like that of Adam. He created him from dust, saying, *"Be,"* and he was. [59] The truth is from your Lord, so don't be assailed by doubt. [60]

> **Background Info... v. 61**
>
> After verses 58-60 were recited, then the Prophet recited verse 61. The Prophet adjourned the day's dialogue with the Christians and actually asked that his entire household, including his daughter Fatimah, be called to witness the interfaith dialogue the following morning.
>
> The leader of the delegation decided against further participation, especially the idea of invoking God's wrath against those who lied, and signed a peace treaty with Muhammad before returning home with his party. He also asked the Prophet to send a liaison along to be their judge in financial disputes, as they were impressed with Islam's emphasis on absolute fairness at all costs. The Prophet chose a trusted companion named Abu Ubaydah to go with them.
> (Ibn Kathir)

If anyone argues further with you, now that the truth has come to you, (then challenge them,) saying, *"Come, let's meet together: our children and your children, our women and your women, ourselves and yourselves. Then we'll invoke (Allah) and ask Allah to condemn those who lie."* [61]

87

Say to them:

"*Followers of Earlier Revelation! Let's agree on what we hold in common: that we serve no one other than Allah, that we don't assign divinity to anyone besides Him, and that we don't exalt one of our own kind to be lord in place of Allah.*"

If they turn away, then say to them, "*Bear witness that we've surrendered ourselves (to Allah's will).*" [64]

Ibraheem Was not a Jew or a Christian

> **Background Info... v. 65-69**
>
> This passage was revealed when a Jewish rabbi in the interfaith gathering said, "Muhammad! You know that we have the best claim to Ibraheem's religion – more than you or anyone else - *and he was Jewish*. You're just jealous of God." (*Asbab ul-Nuzul*)

However, the only true resolution to the debate is affirming that there is no god besides (the One True) God, for He is, without a doubt, the Powerful and the Wise. [62]

If they turn aside, (remember that) Allah knows best who the disobedient are. [63]

> **Background Info... v. 64**
>
> The Christian delegation meeting with Muhammad disagreed amongst themselves concerning the nature of 'Esa (Jesus), much as modern Christian denominations dispute with each other on basic doctrinal issues.
>
> Some in the delegation believed 'Esa was only the son of God, while others held him to be a co-god in a trinity. A third faction said he was God in the flesh. The Prophet exploited this disunity among them to his advantage, and this verse was revealed as a suggested common statement to which all could agree. (*Ibn Kathir*)

Followers of Earlier Revelation! Why do you drag Ibraheem into your disputes? The Torah and Injeel weren't revealed until long after him. Don't you have any sense? [65]

Aren't you the ones who argue over things you already know? So why argue over things that you know nothing about? Clearly, Allah is the One Who has accurate information, whereas you lack it. [66]

Ibraheem was neither a Jew nor a Christian. Rather, he was a natural monotheist, submissive (to Allah's will), and he certainly wasn't an idol-worshipper. [67]

The first among the people (of this world) who resemble Ibraheem the most are those who follow (his example), like *this* prophet (Muhammad) and his followers. Allah is the protector of all who believe (in I lim)! [68]

There are some from among the Followers of Earlier Revelation who desperately wish to mislead you, but they wind up only misleading themselves without realizing it. [69]

The Jealousy of the Followers of Earlier Revelation

Followers of Earlier Revelation! Why do you try to hide the signs of Allah, even after witnessing them yourselves? [70]

Followers of Earlier Revelation! Why do you wrap the truth with falsehood and hide the truth on purpose when you know better? [71]

Among the Followers of Earlier Revelation are some who say to each other, "(*Tell the Muslims*) you have faith in what the believers received in the early morning, but then denounce it at the end of the day.

"You might be able to cause the weak (in knowledge among them) to return (to their old religions). [72] *Don't believe anyone (of another religion) unless he believes in yours."*

Say to them, "*True guidance is Allah's guidance. (Are you afraid that) someone else might get something similar to what your (ancestors) got in the past or that they might argue with you in the sight of your Lord (with that knowledge?)"*

Then say to them, "*All favors are in Allah's hand, and He grants them to whomever He wants, for Allah is caring and knowing.* [73] *He decides who receives His mercy, and Allah is the master of tremendous favor."* [74]

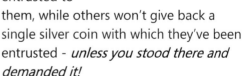

(There are, of course, honest people) among the Followers of Earlier Revelation. They will return a fortune in gold entrusted to them, while others won't give back a single silver coin with which they've been entrusted - *unless you stood there and demanded it!*

That's because they say, "*We're not obligated by our faith (to be fair with those of another religion)."* Yet, how terrible do they lie against Allah, and well they know it! [75]

No way! Whoever maintains his bond (with Allah) and remains aware (of his duty to Him should know that) Allah loves those who are mindful (of Him). [76]

A Little Gain Now at the Cost of Forever

Background Info... v. 77

A man named Al-Ashath disputed with a Jewish man over their joint ownership of a strip of land with a well on it. Al-Ashath claimed he was a part owner but that the Jewish man denied him his right, while the Jewish man said Al-Ashath never owned any of it.

When asked by the Prophet, Al-Ashath admitted that he had no evidence to back his claim. Then the Prophet asked the Jew to swear to Allah that the land was all his, and the matter would be settled in his favor. On hearing that, Al-Ashath protested, saying that the Jew would swear falsely, and thus he would lose his fair share of the property.

This verse was revealed, and the Prophet, allowing the Jew to keep the land by himself after he swore it was all his, said, "Whoever makes a false oath to deprive a Muslim of his property will meet Allah when He is angry with him." (Bukhari, Muslim) The Prophet also said, "An oath will be accepted from a defendant (when there is no physical proof against him)." (Bukhari)

Those who barter away their bond with Allah, along with their faith, making a little profit along the way, will have no share in the next life. Allah will neither address them nor notice them on the Day of Assembly, nor will He cleanse them (of their sins), for they will have a terrible punishment! [77]

Falsifying the Message of Scripture

There are some from among (the Followers of Earlier Revelation) who distort the meaning of their scriptures when they read them aloud, so much so that even though it sounds like scripture, in fact, it's not!

Yet they claim, "*This is from Allah's Own presence,*" but it's not from Allah's Own presence! *They knowingly lie against Allah!* [78]

Background Info... v. 79-80

During the ongoing interfaith meeting that is the subject of many verses in this chapter, a rabbi from Medina, along with the chief priest of the Najrani Christians, asked Muhammad, "Do you want us to worship you and take you as our Lord?"

Muhammad replied, "I ask Allah's protection if anyone else besides Him is worshipped or if I were to order you to worship anyone else besides Him. He didn't send me to (ask you to worship me), nor did He order that from me." This passage was then revealed, and he recited it to them. (Asbab ul-Nuzul)

It's not the place of a mere mortal who's been given scripture by Allah, along with sound wisdom and the gift of prophecy, to tell people, "*Worship me instead of Allah.*"

Rather, he should say, "*Become people of the Lord as you've learned in the scriptures and as you've studied.*" [79]

Neither will a (true prophet) of Allah order you to take angels or prophets as lords (in place of Him). Would he order (the truth to be diluted) after already getting you to surrender (to Allah)? [80]

Allah's Message is Clearly Shown into History

Allah took a covenant with the (ancient) prophets (and their followers), saying, "*I've given you the scripture and the (source of) wisdom. If another messenger ever comes to you (after your time), who confirms the truth of what you now possess, then (your descendants) must believe in him and help him.*"

(Then Allah) said, *"Do you agree to this pledge?"*

To which they answered, "*Yes, we agree.*" Then (Allah) said, "*So witness (your promise), even as I'm witnessing it along with you.* [81] *Whoever breaks (this pledge) after this will be openly rebellious.*" [82]

Are they looking for a way of life other than the Way of Allah? Is this what they do even though all things within the heavens and the earth surrender willingly or unwillingly to Him, and even though all things must return to Him? [83]

Say to them, "*We believe in Allah and in what was revealed to us, as well as in what was revealed to Ibraheem, Isma-il, Is-haq, Yaqub and the tribes (of Israel), and (we believe) in what was given to Musa and 'Esa and to all other prophets from their Lord.*

"We don't claim that one of them was better than another, and to Him we surrender." [84]

Now if anyone looks for a way of life other than submission (to Allah), it will never be accepted of him, and in the next life he'll be among the losers. [85]

On Weak Faith

How can Allah guide a people who've resolved to cover over (the light of faith within their hearts), even after once having believed and witnessed to the truth of their messenger, and even after proof had come to them?

Allah won't guide such corrupted people. [86]

Their reward is the condemnation of Allah, the angels and all of humanity, [87] and that will be their condition for all time.

Their punishment will neither lighten nor will they get a break. [88] Exempted are those (among them) who repent and reform themselves, for Allah is forgiving and merciful. [89]

As for those who reject (the truth) after once having believed, and who grow even more stubborn in their rejection, their repentance will never be accepted for they've gone so far astray. [90]

Those who cover over (their ability to see the truth) and who die in that state will never be able to ransom themselves - *no, not for all the gold in the world!*

A painful punishment awaits them, and they'll have no one to help them. [91]

Defining Righteousness

You'll never achieve virtue until you've (learned) to give to others (in charity) from even your most prized possessions, and whatever you spend in charity is known to Allah. [92]

Reconnecting
with Ibraheem's Way of Life

The Children of Israel were allowed to eat any type of food before the Torah was revealed, except for what Israel made unlawful for itself.

So challenge them, (when they reject the lifting of some dietary restrictions), "*Come forward and read from the Torah concerning this if you're so honest!*" [93]

Then, whoever invents a lie after this and attributes it to Allah, they're wrongdoers. [94]

Be True to Ibraheem's Tradition

Say to them, "*Allah speaks the truth, so follow the creed of Ibraheem, the natural monotheist, for he didn't make partners (with Allah).*" [95]

The first house (of worship) for people was built in Becca, a blessed place from which emanates clear guidance for all. [96]

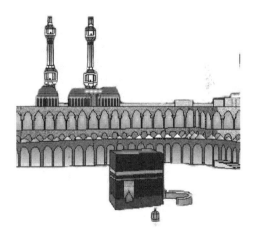

There are clear signs (of its sanctity) there, such as the place in which Ibraheem once stood.

(It's a sanctuary) in which anyone can find safety. And so it's a duty laid upon all people from Allah that all who are able should find a way and make a pilgrimage to the House.

Whoever still rejects (the truth), there's nothing that Allah needs from anyone in the entire universe. [97]

Remain True to Your Faith

Say to them, *"Followers of Earlier Revelation! Why do you refuse to accept (the truth) of Allah's (revealed) verses, especially since Allah witnesses everything you do?"* [98]

Then ask them:

"Followers of Earlier Revelation! Why do you try to prevent those who believe from following the path of Allah, attempting to make it seem crooked, while witnessing (that Allah is the truth)? Allah is not unmindful of what you're doing." [99]

Don't be Tricked into Disunity

Background Info... v. 100-109

Before Islam came to Medina, the two large, local Arab tribes of Auws and Khazraj were prone to making war upon each other. In times of peace, the two sides would compose poetry belittling the other side and praising their own bravery and courage.

After Islam came, both tribes made peace with each other and began to merge into a unified Muslim identity. One day a Jewish man named Shas (Shammas) ibn Qays happened to pass by a gathering of men from both tribes, and he became incensed that these old enemies should be so friendly with each other.

He told a young friend of his to join them and start reciting poetry from their old days of conflict, particularly about the day when the Auws nearly wiped out the Khazraj.

The young Jew started doing this, and within a short time the men of each tribe

---

began taunting each other like they used to do before Islam. Passions rose so high that men began unsheathing their swords and challenging each other to fight.

When the Prophet was informed about what was going on, he rushed to the street where the men were gathered and physically stood between the two mobs, calling for calm, and reciting this newly revealed passage loudly and trying his best to bring the anger of both sides down.

The men relented after some time and then felt ashamed and began weeping, reaffirming their ties of religious brotherhood.

One of the men later recalled, "On that day we hated no one more than the Messenger (for trying to make us forget our past feuds). Then, he waved his hand to us, we stopped, and Allah brought us together again.

Afterwards, we never loved anyone more than we loved the Messenger. I have never seen a day that had such an evil and sad beginning, only to have a **good end, like that day had."** (*Asbab ul-Nuzul, Ibn Is-haq*)

O you who believe!

If you listen to some of the Followers of Earlier Revelation, they might (confuse) you into renouncing your faith after you had believed! [100]

How could you reject (your faith) while Allah's verses are being directed towards you and while His Prophet is by your side?

Whoever holds firmly to Allah will be guided towards a straight path. [101]

O you who believe! Be mindful (of Allah) as much as you should be mindful (of Him), and don't let death come upon you without being surrendered (to His will). [102]

Hold firmly all together to the rope of Allah, and don't be divided. Remember His favors you received, for when you were enemies, He brought your hearts together in love and made you brothers as a favor from Him.

You were on the brink of a fiery pit, but He saved you from it. This is how Allah makes His verses clear so you can be guided. [103]

So let there arise from among you a community that will invite (people) to the good and command (others to follow) what is known (to be right) while forbidding (them from) what is unfamiliar

(to Allah's way of life), for it is these who will be the successful ones. [104]

Don't be like those who divided themselves and took to conflicting views, even after receiving clear evidence of the truth. Tremendous punishment awaits them [105] on the day when some faces will be beaming brightly, while others will be overcast in darkness.

Those whose faces will be overcast (from their shame) will be asked, "*Did you cover over the truth (of Allah in your heart) after having once believed in it? So now experience for yourselves the punishment for your rejection!*" [106]

On the other hand, those whose faces will be bright and beaming (with joy) will remain within the mercy of Allah forever. [107]

These are the (revealed) verses of Allah that We're conveying to you so that the truth can be established. Allah doesn't want any oppression (to exist) anywhere in the universe. [108] To Him belongs all things within the heavens and the earth, and all issues will go back to Him (for their resolution). [109]

You are the best community brought out from humanity. You encourage what is recognized (as right), and you forbid what is unfamiliar (to Allah's good way), and you believe in Allah.

Now if the Followers of Earlier Revelation only had (this kind of sincere) faith, it would have been much better for them.

Some of them (truly) believe (and practice their religion sincerely), but most of them are disobedient and wicked. [110]

Background Info... v. 111:

A Jewish rabbi, 'Abdullah ibn Salam, converted to Islam along with his family and some associates. The six most powerful leaders of the three Jewish tribes went to him and beat up him and his family. This verse was revealed in response to their injuries in order to console them. (*Asbab ul-Nuzul*)

However, they can do you no real harm, save for some small injuries, and if they ever fought against you, they would most likely turn and flee with no one to save them. [111]

Disgrace overshadows them wherever they're found, except when they cling to Allah or cling to another people, for they've earned the burden of Allah's wrath and utter misery is spread over them.

That's because of their rejecting the signs of Allah and killing the prophets against all right. They did that because they had rebelled and overstepped all bounds. [112]

Jews and Christians are not All the Same

Background Info... v. 113-115

Jewish converts to Islam such as Asad ibn 'Ubayd, Tha'labah ibn Sa'yah and 'Abdullah ibn Salam are the immediate reference here. (*Asbab ul-Nuzul*) So this verse is referring to converts to Islam mainly from Judaism.

They're not all the same, for among the Followers of Earlier Revelation is a group that stands throughout the night reciting the revelations of Allah, and they bow themselves (before Him). [113]

They believe in Allah and the Last Day while encouraging what's known (to be good) and forbidding what's unfamiliar (to Allah's good way of life), and they hurry to do acts of righteousness.

They're among the morally upright. [114] Nothing will be rejected of the good they did, for Allah knows about those who are mindful (of Him). [115]

As for those who cover over (the knowledge of the truth in their hearts), neither their money nor their children will save them in the least from Allah.

They'll be companions of the **FIRE**, *and that's where they're going to stay!* [116]

The example of what they spend in the life of this world is like a chill wind that brings bitter **frost**. It strikes down the fruit of the harvest of those who've done wrong to their own souls.

Allah is not doing any injustice to them; rather, they're bringing it upon their own selves. [117]

Don't Make Friends with those who would Destroy You

> **Background Info... v. 118**
>
> This verse was revealed after the Jews of Medina shed any pretenses of neutrality or goodwill and became openly hostile to the Muslims and their religion.
>
> Some Muslims, who had close working relationships with the Jews before Islam, still tried to maintain those close friendships afterwards, even though many of their old friends were now working against the faith. This verse is admonishing them for this.
> (Ibn Kathir)

O you who believe! Don't take those from outside your own ranks to be your intimate companions, for they'll try anything to corrupt you, as they only want to ruin you.

Bitter hatred issues from their mouths, and what their hearts are hiding is far worse. We're making these verses clear for you, *if you would (only use) your sense!* [118]

Really now! You're ready to love them while they have no love for you - even though you believe in all of (Allah's) scriptures.

Whenever they meet you, they spare no effort to say, "*We believe (in Allah), too!*"

Yet, when they're away from your presence, they gnaw at their fingertips in rage against you.

Say to them, "*Perish in your hatred! Allah knows all the secrets of the heart.*" [119]

If you're doing well, it aggravates them, but if some misfortune befalls you, they're delighted.

If you would just remain patient (in adversity) and be ever mindful (of Allah), then their scheming won't harm you in the least, for Allah encompasses everything they attempt. [120]

On the Battle of Uhud

Background Info... v. 121-127

The famous Battle of Uhud took place in the year 625 near a small cluster of low mountains just outside of Medina. The Meccan idol-worshippers, who wanted to avenge their loss at Badr the year before, organized an army of about 3,000 foot soldiers and cavalry and marched towards the city of their foes.

The Prophet (and 'Abdullah ibn Ubayy) wanted to defend from the city, but many of the younger companions were eager to go out and fight, assuming Allah would help them as He had at Badr the year before. Eventually, the Prophet gave in to their desire, and although some companions changed their minds, the Prophet explained that once a **Prophet suits up for battle, he doesn't** remove his armor until Allah has made a resolution. (*Bukhari*) So the Muslims met the idol-worshippers in battle with 700 men (and a few women).

Originally the Muslims had set out with 1,000 men, but 300 men, following **the hypocrite, 'Abdullah ibn Ubayy, left** the battlefield and returned to Medina. (Ibn Ubayy claimed he was angry at the Prophet for not heeding his advice to **remain behind the city's walls for** defense. Later he changed his excuse to **saying that he didn't think a real battle would happen, and that's why he** returned home.) The dispirited Muslims **were roused to courage by the Prophet's** words, and the battle began in earnest.

The greatly outnumbered but more disciplined Muslims were winning the fight at first, and the Meccans began to flee. However, some archers that the Prophet placed on a hill to guard a rear pass left their posts against orders to collect booty from the battlefield.

This enabled a surprise rear attack by the Meccan cavalry led by Khalid ibn Waleed, who was not yet a Muslim.

After some confusion, the beleaguered Muslims were forced to retreat backwards up the small mountain of Uhud, but then they eventually held their ground, though many Muslims (about 70) had been slain. The Meccan army returned to their camp claiming victory, even though the battle was actually more of a draw, for just as many Meccans lay dead as Muslims. Muhammad brought a contingent of his followers back out for battle again the next day, but the Meccans decided to withdraw in the night, holding on to their narrowly won bragging rights. (*Ibn Hisham*)

Remember that morning, (Muhammad), when you left your family to assign the believers to their battle stations (at the Mountain of Uhud). Allah was listening, and He knew (all about it). [121]

Remember when two of your regiments almost lost the will to fight. Yet, Allah was their guardian, *and the believers should trust in Allah!* [122]

As it happened, Allah had already helped you once before at the (Battle of) Badr when you were only a small force, so be mindful of Allah so you can show your gratitude. [123]

Remember that you (had to rally) the believers, saying, "*Isn't it enough (to know) that your Lord will help you with three thousand angels?* [124]

"*Really now, if you hold firm (in the face of hardship) and are mindful (of Allah), then even in the face of an onslaught, your Lord will send five thousand angels rushing in a massive blitz!*" [125]

Allah didn't convey this good news for any other reason than to assure your hearts, for there is no help save from Allah, the Powerful and Wise. [126]

(Through your efforts, He intended) to vanquish a section of the faithless or steep them in notoriety, so they would have to turn back in unfulfilled frustration. [127]

> ### Background Info... v. 128-129
>
> Once after a dawn prayer, the Prophet prefaced his usual supplications by asking Allah to curse certain of the most hated Meccan idol-worshippers. He stopped in mid-sentence when this passage was revealed, for it told him it was not his place to call curses down upon anyone.
> (Ibn Kathir)

Now it's not your place to pardon them or punish them, for they're certainly oppressors. Everything within the heavens and the earth belongs to Allah. [128] He forgives whomever He wants and punishes whomever He wants, and Allah is forgiving and merciful. [129]

Patient Perseverance

O you who believe! Don't consume interest-money, doubled and redoubled! Be mindful of Allah so you can be (truly) successful. [130]

Beware of the **FIRE** that's been prepared for those who cover over (their awareness of the truth). [131] Obey Allah and His Messenger so you can receive mercy. [132]

Race together towards your Lord's forgiveness and to a Garden as wide as the heavens and the earth - *reserved only for those who were mindful (of Allah).* [133]

They spent (in the cause of Allah) in good times and bad, restrained their temper and overlooked the faults of others. Allah loves those who are good. [134]

Seek the Forgiveness of Allah

Background Info... v. 135-136

A man named Nabhan saw a beautiful woman in Medina. He wooed her, bought her some food and embraced her. He felt ashamed later and told the Prophet about what happened. This passage was then revealed in comment on the incident. (Asbab ul-Nuzul)

They were the ones who, when they committed some indiscretion or wrong act against their souls, remembered Allah and sought His forgiveness. Who can pardon except Allah?

Furthermore, they don't consciously recommit those (sins after having repented of them). [135]

Their reward will be forgiveness from their Lord and gardens beneath which rivers flow in which they'll live forever - *what an excellent reward for those who labored (in the world for Allah)!* [136]

Many ways of life have passed away before your time. So travel all over the world, and see how those (former civilizations) that denied (the truth) came to an end. [137]

This is a clear lesson for people and also a source of guidance and admonition for those who are mindful (of Allah). [138]

Explaining the Loss at Uhud

Background Info... v. 139-141

The Muslims were winning at the battle of Uhud until fifty archers the Prophet had set to watch a rear weakness abandoned their posts to collect the goods the fleeing Meccans had left behind. Many Muslims died in the resulting counterattack of the Meccans. When the Prophet returned to Medina with his dispirited forces after the disaster, the women of the city came out beating their faces with their hands in sorrow over their dead husbands and sons.

The Prophet cried to Allah, **"Is this what became of your Messenger?"** Then this passage was revealed to console him, and he recited it to the people. The resolve of the believers was restored, even if only slowly, and thus many were purged of lingering doubt and weakness of faith. (Asbab ul-Nuzul)

Don't lose hope or get despondent, for you must triumph, *that is if you really believe.* [139]

For sure, if you're injured, know that others have been injured likewise. We alternate days (of triumph and defeat) among (nations) so that Allah can make known those who believe and also so that He can take for Himself martyrs from among you.

Allah has no love for oppressors, (and He may use other nations to keep them in check). [140]

Even more than that, Allah (uses such setbacks) as a way to purge the believers (of any impurities) and to erase the gains of those who cover over (their awareness of the truth). [141]

Did you think that you could enter Paradise without first being tested by Allah so He could make known who among you strives hard (in His cause) and (who among you) perseveres (under pressure)? [142]

And so you (said that) you wanted to give your life (in His cause) before you met death, (though that was before you actually saw it), *and now you see (death) right in front of you!* [143]

No One will Live Forever

Background Info... v. 144-148

During the confusion of the Meccan counterattack at Uhud, some Muslims thought Muhammad had been struck down and killed. (Ibn Qami'a, a fierce pagan warrior, even boasted of killing the Prophet to his fellow pagans, though he had succeeded in killing only the Prophet's standard-bearer, Mus'ab ibn Umayr, and he mistook him for the Prophet.)

The Muslims then raised their voices in lamentation, and this caused many Muslims to further lose heart and flee. One man called out that he wished 'Abdullah ibn Ubayy would come and cut a deal with Abu Sufyan, while another cried out that the Muslims should

abandon Islam and return to the idols, for if Muhammad were a true Prophet, he would not have been killed.

Muhammad had only been hit and wounded on his face; he didn't remain down. Instead, he stood and cried out loudly, "Come to me, servants of Allah!" So thirty companions, such as 'Ali, Abu Bakr and a woman named Nusaybah bint K'ab, among others, formed a protective cordon so the Prophet could be whisked away to the slope of Uhud in an expeditious way.

Another companion, named Anas ibn an-Nadr, who didn't see the Prophet in the confusion, called to the fleeing Muslims near him, saying, "People! If Muhammad has been killed, surely his Lord is alive and will never die. What would you want to do with your lives after he was no longer here? Fight for what he fought for! O Allah! I ask for Your forgiveness for what they've said, and I have nothing to do with it!" Then he fought on until he was killed. This passage was revealed about that desperate episode and also about men such as Anas who stood firm against all odds. (*Baydawi*)

Muhammad is no more than a messenger. There were many messengers who passed away before him. If he dies or is killed, would you then turn and run away?

Anyone who runs away does no harm to Allah in the least, and Allah will quickly reward (those who serve Him) in gratitude. [144]

No one can die without Allah's permission, (for every soul has) an appointed time written (for it). So if anyone desires the rewards of this world,

We'll give them to him, and if anyone desires the rewards of the next life, We'll give them to him, and We'll swiftly reward those who are thankful. [145]

How many were the prophets who fought alongside men of the Lord? They never lost heart, even after all that befell them in the cause of Allah, nor did they weaken or surrender.

Allah loves those
who patiently persevere! [146]

Their words (of strength) were nothing more than this: "*Our Lord!*" they prayed, "*Forgive us our sins, make our stand firm, and help us against the people who cover over (their awareness of You)!*" [147]

Allah gave them a reward in this world, and (they'll receive) an excellent reward in the next life, for Allah **LOVES** those who do good. [148]

A Hard Lesson at Uhud

O you who believe! If you follow (the suggestions of) those who cover over (their faith in Allah), they might make you turn away (from faith, yourselves); then your retreat (from faith) would be to your own loss. [149]

By no means!
Allah is your protector
and the best helper of all! [150]

We're soon going to put panic into the hearts of those who rejected (true faith) in return for their holding others as equals

with Allah – (a position for which) He sent no authority!

Their home is in the Fire, *and how terrible a place for the wrongdoers!* [151]

Background Info... v. 152

The Prophet had left 'Abdullah ibn Jubayr (d. 625) in charge of 50 archers, and he told them not to move from their place, even if they saw the rest of the army being defeated. When the Meccans began to flee, the archers saw the Meccan women running away over the hills, pulling up their dresses as they ran, exposing their anklets.

A cry went up among the archers, "The war booty! The war booty!" Ibn Jubayr ordered the men to stay in position. However, they argued with him, and most abandoned their posts, thinking they could safely start collecting war booty. That disobedience cost the Muslims dearly, as the Meccan cavalry launched a counterattack that caused the deaths of some 70 Muslims. *(Ibn Hisham)*

Later on, in Medina, some of Muhammad's followers began complaining, asking how they could have lost the battle when they were assured that they would win. This verse was revealed in response, telling them that Allah was holding up His end of the bargain, while some from among them (the archers) failed to do their part by running after material gains. *(Asbab ul-Nuzul)*

Allah was certainly fulfilling His promise when, by His leave, you were about to vanquish your foes (at the Battle of Uhud), but then you flinched and argued over your orders (to guard the mountain pass).

You disobeyed (the Prophet's orders) after (Allah) showed you (the war-booty) that you coveted.

Some among you desired the things of this world, while others desired the next life. He allowed you to be distracted from your enemy so He could test you (in order to discipline you, and even though you failed in your duty), He's forgiven you, for Allah is limitless in His favor towards those who believe. [152]

When you were scrambling up the slopes (of Mount Uhud in full retreat), not even noticing those around you, the Messenger was behind you, calling you to come back (and face the enemy, but you ignored him).

So Allah brought the disappointment (of shame) upon you, even as you disappointed (the Prophet by running away from him.

This added shame) befell you so that you wouldn't feel bad only for the (captured goods) you missed, but also for what you suffered, as well, and Allah is well-informed of all that you do. [153]

Then, after this time of distress, He allowed a feeling of peace and confidence to descend upon a group of you.

Even still, another faction (of your people) took to venting their frustrations and spoke out against Allah, thinking thoughts of pagan ignorance, saying, "*Don't we have any say in the matter?*"

Say to them, "*Surely every command belongs to Allah.*" They try to hide their lack of conviction from you by lamenting, "*If only we were in charge, there would've been far fewer casualties (from the battle).*"

Say to them, "*Even if you had remained in your homes (within the city of Medina, like you had wanted from the beginning), those whose time it was to die would still have gone forth to their place of death.*"

This was merely (a test) so Allah could show your true feelings and purge (any impurities) in your hearts, for He knows the secrets of the mind. [154]

Those who deserted (their posts on the battlefield) on the day the two armies clashed (at Uhud) were made to fail by Shaytan, (who had some influence over them) because of some (sins) they had earned before. However, Allah forgave them, for Allah is forgiving and forbearing. [155]

Affirmation in the Ultimate End

O you who believe! Don't be like those who cover (their awareness of the truth), and who despair over their brothers (who've died) while traveling the land or in battle, crying (loudly):

" *If only they would've stayed here with us (safe at home), then they wouldn't have died or been killed.* "

Allah brings this regret upon their hearts, for only Allah has the power to preserve life or take it away, and Allah sees everything that you do. [156]

Know that if you're killed or if you happen to die in the cause of Allah, forgiveness and mercy from Allah are far better than (all the worldly possessions) they can collect. [157]

(Know that) if you happen to die or are killed that you're going to be gathered back to Allah (in the end anyway). [158]

It's only due to Allah's mercy that you're gentle with the (believers in their time of stress), for if you were ever to be harsh with them they would scattered away from you.

So overlook their shortcomings, pray for their forgiveness and seek their counsel on relevant issues. When you have come to a mutual decision, then put your trust in Allah, for He loves those who trust in Him. [159]

If Allah is helping you,
who can defeat you?

If He forsakes you,
who can help you after that?

So the believers should put
their trust in Allah. [160]

Trust in the Prophet

> **Background Info... v. 161-164**
>
> This passage was revealed in response to an incident in which some hypocrites started a rumor that the Prophet had withheld a blanket from the distribution of the captured Badr war booty. This verse reminds the Muslims that unfairly taking anything from the booty is a sin and that it is foolish to accuse the Prophet, who is the least interested in material goods among them all, of withholding something.
> (Ibn Kathir)

No prophet should ever withhold anything, for whoever withholds something will be made to give restitution for what he withheld on the Day of Standing (for judgment).

Then every soul will be paid back for what it's earned, and no one will be wronged. [161]

Can someone who follows Allah be equal to someone who has Allah's wrath drawn over him, and whose home is in Hellfire? *How terrible a destination!* [162]

These two types (of people) are on entirely different levels in the sight of Allah, and Allah is watching everything they do. [163]

And so it was that the believers were favored by Allah when He raised up a messenger from among them who recited the verses of Allah to them, purified them, and who taught them scripture and wisdom; they were lost in error before. [164]

There is a Lesson in Failure

What! After a single setback in which you inflicted twice (the damage) that you suffered, (you begin to question Allah), saying, "*How could the (disaster at Uhud) have happened?*"

Say to them, "*You were the cause of your own (defeat through your own disobedience), for Allah has power over all things.*" [165]

What you experienced on the day when the two armies met (at Uhud) was by Allah's permission so that He could **TEST** the believers [166] - *and the hypocrites, too.*

When they were told, "*Come and fight in the cause of Allah, or at the very least defend yourselves,*" (they offered) excuses, saying, "*If we knew a fight was (really)* going to happen, then we would've surely followed you (in the battle)."

They were much closer to disbelief than belief that day. They said with their lips the opposite of what was in their hearts, and Allah knows what they were hiding. [167]

Now they're lamenting, after they've been sitting (in safety all along), "*If only (our slain friends) would've listened to us (and not fought in the Battle of Uhud), then they wouldn't have been killed.*"

(Then challenge the hypocrites by) saying, "*So save yourselves from death, if you have that power!*" [168]

The Reward for Ultimate Sacrifice

Background Info... v. 169-171

A man named Jabir was silently lamenting the loss of his father at the Battle of Uhud. The Prophet saw him and asked, "Why are you looking so glum?" Jabir answered, "My father was killed, and he left behind debts and children."

The Prophet replied, "Let me tell you, Allah doesn't speak to anyone except

from behind a veil, and He talked to your father (in Paradise) for he had fought (and died). He said to him, 'My servant, ask Me whatever you wish, and I shall grant it.' Your father said, 'Send me back to the world to be killed again fighting in Your cause.' Allah answered, 'I have already given the order that no one can go back to it.' So he answered, 'Lord, then tell those who will come after me (about the reward).'"

Then the Prophet announced to his grieving companions that Allah had taken the souls of the martyrs who perished at Uhud and placed them within the bodies of green birds and set them free in Paradise. They get all that they need from the fruit trees and streams of Paradise, and they spend time every day perched beneath the throne of Allah on special branches shaped like candelabras.

When they first noticed the endless luxury of Paradise, they asked out loud, "Can someone inform (our relatives and friends in the world) about how well we live here, so they can stop mourning over us and continue to strive like we did?" Allah told them that He would do that, and thus He revealed this passage to Muhammad so all his followers would know. (*Abu Dawud, Asbab ul-Nuzul*)

Don't think that those who are killed in the cause of Allah are dead. No way! They're alive and getting their needs met in the presence of their Lord. [169]

They're rejoicing in His bounty, and also because (they know that through their sacrifice) the ones they left behind are (better) protected from fear and distress. [170]

They're rejoicing in the good pleasure of Allah and in His bounty! Truly, Allah

106

doesn't let the reward of the faithful ever become lost. [171]

The Resolute and the Brave

Those who responded to the call of Allah and the Messenger (to march to Badr once again, one year after Uhud), even while some of them were still wounded (from Uhud), (should know that) there's a valuable reward for those who do good and remain mindful (of Allah). [172]

Even after people told them, "*A great force (of men) is massed against you, so fear them,*" (instead of wavering), it only increased their conviction and they said, "*Allah is enough for us, and He's the most favorable (One upon Whom) to rely.*" [173]

And so they returned with the grace and bounty of Allah, and no harm overcame them (for the Meccans had failed to appear). They were following the pleasure of Allah, and Allah is the master of tremendous bounty. [174]

It's only Shaytan who instills the fear of his minions in you, so don't fear them. Rather, fear Me if you (really) do believe. [175]

Don't worry over those who rush to reject (Allah), because they don't do any harm to Allah at all. Allah wants to exclude them from any share in the next life - *except for suffering a terrible punishment!* [176]

Those who buy rejection (of the truth) at the cost of faith don't do the least bit of harm to Allah. They're going to receive a painful punishment indeed! [177]

Those who cover over (their awareness of the truth) shouldn't think that their (apparent) free reign (and their illusion of power) is to their advantage.

We're only giving them more time to increase in their sinfulness, and then a humiliating punishment will await them! [178]

Why does Allah Test Us?

Allah won't leave the believers in the (weak) position that they're now in until He separates what is filthy from what is wholesome, nor will Allah give you insight into what is beyond human perception. Instead,

He chooses from among His messengers as He wills (and assigns each his own level of success).

So believe in Allah and His Messenger, for if you believe and remain mindful (of your duty to Allah), then this will secure for you a valuable reward. [179]

Those who greedily hoard what Allah has provided them from out of His bounty shouldn't think that it will be to their advantage.

On the contrary, it's to their detriment, for soon what their greed held back will be tied around their necks on the Day of Assembly.

To Allah belongs the inheritance of the heavens and the earth, and Allah is well-informed of everything you do. [180]

No One should Belittle Allah

Background Info... v. 181-182

After verse 2:245 was revealed to the Muslims, Abu Bakr paid a visit to a rabbinical school in a Jewish neighborhood in Medina. He found one of their scholars, Finhas ibn Azoura', surrounded by students.

Abu Bakr spoke to him, saying, "Fear Allah and accept Islam, for I swear to Allah that you know Muhammad is the Messenger of Allah who has brought Allah's truth to you. It is written in your Torah, so believe and accept it. Lend a goodly loan to Allah so He will double your reward and admit you into Paradise."

Finhas replied, "Abu Bakr, you're suggesting that Allah borrows money

Allah heard (the boast) of those who said, "*Allah is poor while we are rich!*" We're going to record their statement, along with their unjust murdering of the prophets of old against all right.

We're going to say to them:

"*Taste the punishment of the burning agony!* [181] *This is for what you did with your own hands.*"

However, (in the Next Life) Allah will never bring harm to those who (sincerely) served Him. [182]

Yet, they also said, "*Allah made us promise to reject every messenger unless he comes with a sacrifice of burnt offerings.*"

Say to them, "*Many messengers came to you before me with clear evidence and even with that for which you're asking. So why did you kill them if you're being so honest?*" [183]

Then if they deny you, (Muhammad), so, too, were other messengers denied before who came with clear evidence, sober prophecies and enlightened scripture. [184]

It will be a Hard Road

Every soul will have to experience death, and on the Day of Assembly each of you will receive your full payback.

The one who is saved from the Fire and who is admitted into the Garden will have achieved the **ultimate** goal.

The life of this world is nothing more than material gains and illusions. [185]

You're certainly going to be tested through your wealth and your own selves, and you're going to hear much that will distress you from those who received scripture before you, and from those who make partners (with Allah).

Yet, if you persevere and remain mindful (of your duty to Allah), then this will determine many results. [186]

Recall that Allah took an agreement from those who received previous revelation.

They were (supposed to make the message of Allah) clearly evident to people and not to hide it, but they threw it away behind their backs and made a little profit off of it. What a despicable bargain they made! [187]

Don't think that those who are smug (in their deceit) and who love to be praised for what they *didn't* do – don't think that they'll escape retribution, for a painful punishment awaits them. [188]

To Allah belongs the control of the heavens and earth, and Allah has power over all things. [189]

The Call of Faith in Allah

110

me, and I also love it when you worship your Lord.'

"Then he used a water skin to perform ablution, without wasting any water, and he stood up in prayer and cried until his beard became wet. Then he prostrated and cried until the floor was wet. Then he laid down on his side and cried.

"When Bilal came to alert the Prophet about the coming of the dawn prayer, (he saw the Prophet's eyes red from weeping), and he said, 'Messenger of Allah! Why are you crying when Allah has already forgiven your future and past sins?'

"He answered, 'Bilal, what's keeping you from crying, when this night these verses were revealed to me? Whoever recites them, but then doesn't think deeply upon them, will be ruined.'"
(Ibn Kathir)

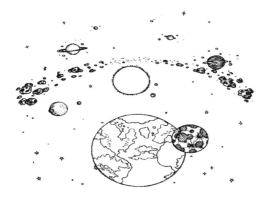

Truly, in the creation of the heavens and the earth and in the alternation of night and day are signs for people who think deeply. [190]

They remember Allah while standing, sitting or lying down on their sides, and they contemplate the creation of the heavens and earth, (saying):

"Our Lord! You didn't create all of this for nothing!

Glory be to You! Save us from the punishment of the Fire. [191]

Our Lord, whomever You send into Hellfire is indeed covered in shame, and the wrongdoers will never find anyone to help them." [192]

"Our Lord, we've heard the call of one who calls us to faith. 'Believe in the Lord,' (he said), and we do have faith.

Our Lord, forgive us our sins, pardon our shortcomings and take our souls back to You in the company of the righteous. [193]

Our Lord, grant us what You've promised us through Your messengers, and save us from humiliation on the Day of Assembly, for You never break Your word." [194]

Equality in Righteousness before Allah

Background Info... v. 195

Umm Salamah was the first woman to migrate from Mecca to Medina during the exodus of Muslims from pagan persecution. She once asked the Prophet why Allah **didn't mention women** specifically when He praised those who migrated for His sake. This verse was revealed to answer her question. (Bukhari)

Their Lord has accepted them (and will comfort them by) saying:

"I'll never let the efforts of any of you who made an effort (in My cause) become lost, be he male or female, for you're equally from each other.

"Those who left their homes, or who were driven away, or who suffered in My cause, or who fought or were killed, I will pardon their shortcomings and admit them to gardens beneath which rivers flow - and a reward from Allah's Own presence is the best reward of all!" [195]

Don't be fooled by those who bury (their capacity to believe in Allah) and who seem to do (whatever they want in the land without getting punished). [196]

It's only a brief time of pleasure for them - *a time that will be followed by Hellfire* – and oh, how terrible a destination! [197]

However, those who are mindful (of their duty) to their Lord will soon find themselves among gardens beneath which rivers flow, *and there they'll live forever!*

(That's) a privilege from Allah, and what's with Allah is best for the righteous. [198]

The Sincerity of True Jews and Christians

> **Background Info... v. 199**
>
> This verse was revealed when the king of Abyssinia died. He was the Christian king who accepted a number of Muslim refugees who had fled persecution in Mecca, and who refused to hand them over to a visiting delegation of Meccan idol-worshippers who wanted to imprison them.
>
> The Prophet asked his community to pray for him, and he beseeched Allah to accept him and forgive him.
>
> When the hypocrites of Medina heard about this, they began taunting the Muslims for praying for someone who was not of their religion. This verse was revealed in response. (*Asbab ul-Nuzul*) Some commentators say the king accepted Islam before he died.

Among the Followers of Earlier Revelation are some who believe in Allah and in the revelation sent to both you and to them.

They are amazed by (the power of) Allah and don't sell the verses of Allah for a small profit. They'll certainly have their reward waiting with their Lord, for Allah is quick in settling accounts. [199]

O you who believe! Be patient (in adversity, strive together) in perseverance, and labor on. Be mindful (of your duty) to Allah so you can be truly successful. [200]

The Women

4 An-Nisā'
Medinan Period

☞ Introduction

The greater part of the various verses of this chapter was revealed during the fourth year after the arrival of the Prophet in Medina at a time when many social issues were being addressed. There were long-standing Arab customs about which the community asked the Prophet with regard to marital life, gender equality and the family. Although traditional Arabian culture held little regard for the rights or status of women, the basic premise taken by the Qur'an was that women were the equals of men before Allah. This was quite a revolutionary concept in a society that devalued women to the point of practicing infanticide against unwanted female newborns.

The Qur'an altered or abolished many such ignorant Arab customs and offered a new compact in the family structure. While men were still given the symbolic leadership role in the family, the rights of women were vastly expanded and documented in scripture. The most noble husband, in the words of Muhammad, is the one who is most kind and dutiful to his family. This chapter also talks about the dangers that hypocrites pose to a morally ordered society. Interfaith issues are also addressed with regard to some of the theological differences among Islam, Judaism and Christianity.

In the Name of Allah,
the Compassionate, the Merciful

O people! Be mindful of your Lord Who created you from a single soul and from it (He) created its mate.

From these two were raised all the multitudes of men and women (all over the world).

Be mindful of Allah, the One in Whose name you demand your mutual (rights), and (have respect for women from whose) wombs (you are all born), for Allah is certainly watching you. [1]

The Strong must not Oppress the Weak

Return to the orphans (who are under your care) their rightful property (when they're of mature legal age), and don't substitute your inferior goods for their superior ones. Don't swallow up their possessions by losing track of them in yours, for that's an enormous crime. [2]

Don't Marry Orphan Women to Oppress Them

If any of you (men) fear that you might not be able to treat orphaned (women) with justice, (by being tempted to marry them for their money while they have no guardian to look after their interests), then marry (other) women of your choice, up to two, three, or four.

If you're afraid that you might not be able to treat (more wives) equally, then marry only one (woman) or (marry a maid-servant) who is under your authority. This will help keep you from committing injustice. [3]

Give women their rightful dowries in the spirit of an honest gift. However, if they return a portion of it to you of their own free will, then accept it and enjoy it as an wholesome pleasure. [4]

When should an Orphan's Inheritance be Given?

Don't entrust those who are immature with the property that Allah provided for you as a support. Instead, feed and clothe them (from your resources) and speak to them kindly. [5]

Test (the level of maturity) of orphans when they reach a marriageable age.

When you determine that they're able to handle the responsibility (of managing their affairs alone), then release their property to them.

Don't be wasteful with their wealth nor
spend it rapidly before they reach
maturity. If the guardian is rich, then let
him claim no compensation.

If he's poor, then he can claim a
reasonable portion. When you're
prepared to release their goods to them,
take witnesses in their presence, though
no one can do a better accounting than
Allah. [6]

General Inheritance Rules

Both men and women have a share in
(the estates) that their parents and nearest
relatives leave behind, and whether it's a
little or a lot, there's a calculated share. [7]

If other (more distant) relatives or
orphans or the poor are present at the
time of the distribution, then give

116

something (of the estate) to them and console them with words of kindness. [8]

Those who are charged (with the distribution of the property) should keep in mind the anxiety of having to leave a helpless family behind. Let them be mindful (of Allah) and speak words of comfort. [9]

Those who unjustly consume the property of orphans only fill their bellies with fire, and for (their callousness they'll soon be made) to roast in a raging blaze! [10]

Who Gets What?

> ### Background Info... v. 11
>
> There are two reports about why this verse was revealed. A report in Bukhari says that it was revealed when a dying man asked the Prophet about how he should apportion his estate. A different report in Ahmad, Abu Dawud and Tirmidhi gives the following reason:
>
> A widow went to the Prophet with her **two daughters and said,** "Messenger of Allah, these are the two daughters of **Sa'd ibn ar-Rabi'** (another version says Thabit ibn Qays) who was killed when he was with you on the Day of Uhud.
>
> Their uncle took their property and **inheritance and hasn't left anything for** them. What is your judgment, Messenger of Allah, for I swear by Allah **that they'll** never be able to marry unless they have substance." The Prophet replied that he would wait for Allah to decide the matter, which was a way of saying he would wait for a revelation from Allah.
>
> A little while later, this verse was revealed. The uncle was summoned to the Prophet and was told to give two-thirds of the estate to the daughters and

one-eighth of it to the mother and that he could keep whatever was left.

Either event could have been the cause for this revelation, though the second event seems more likely given the well-developed background information.

Allah Himself gives you the following directions about your children's (inheritance): the male shall receive a portion equal to what's given to two females.

If there are only females, two or more, then their share is two-thirds of the estate; if only one, her share is half. For parents, a sixth share of the inheritance to each, if the deceased left children.

If the deceased left no children and his parents are the only heirs, then the mother gets a third, unless the deceased left brothers, for in that case the mother will get a sixth. (These distributions will be apportioned only) after the payment of any obligations and debts.

You don't know whether your parents or your children are more deserving (of their share), so (accept) these as the settled amounts that are ordained by Allah, for Allah is knowing and wise. [11]

(Men), in what your wives leave, your share is half if they left no children. If they left children, then you'll receive a fourth, after the payment of any loans and debts.

In what you leave, the share (of your widows) is a fourth, if you left no children, but if you left children, then your widows will get an eighth, after the payment of any obligations and debts.

If the person whose inheritance is in question has left neither parents nor children, but has left a single brother or sister, then that sibling will get a sixth of the estate; but if there are more siblings, then they will split a third (of the estate among themselves), after the payment of any obligations and debts, so that no loss is caused to any.

This is Allah's decision, and Allah is knowing and forbearing. [12]

These are the rules set by Allah. Whoever obeys Allah and His Messenger will be admitted to gardens beneath which rivers flow, and there they shall remain – *and that's the greatest success!* [13]

Whoever disobeys Allah and His Messenger and goes beyond His rules, then they'll be admitted into Hellfire, and there they shall remain - *a humiliating punishment!* [14]

On Shameful Behavior

If any of your women are guilty of *shameful behavior*, (then you must) have the evidence of four (honest) witnesses from among you (who will testify) against them.

If they testify (in court against them), then confine them to their homes for life, or at least until Allah provides for them some other way (to reform their behavior). [15]

If two men among you are guilty of *shameful behavior*, punish them both, as well.

If they repent and reform, then leave them alone, for Allah is accepting of repentance and merciful. [16]

Allah accepts the repentance of those who engage in immorality in ignorance and who then repent soon afterwards, for Allah will turn to them in mercy, and Allah is knowing and wise. [17]

The repentance of habitual wrongdoers, however, is in vain, even until (the time of) death when one of them says, "*Now I'm ready to repent.*"

(Allah also will not accept the repentance) of those who die in a state of rejection (of Allah's truth). They're the ones for whom We've prepared a dreadful punishment! [18]

Don't be Mean to Women

O you who believe! You're not allowed to inherit women against their will, neither should you leave them to languish in the hopes of (forcing them to divorce you) and thus getting back part of the marriage gift that you gave them - except in cases where they're guilty of *shameful behavior.*

Therefore, you should live with them in kindness and goodwill.

If you become dissatisfied with them, it may be that you are disliking something through which Allah will bring much good (for you). [19]

However, if you decide to take one wife in place of another, even if you've given the first one a huge pile of gold as a marriage gift, don't take the least bit of it back. Would you try to take it by slander and obvious sinfulness? [20]

How could you take it that way when you both have gone in to each other, and after they've made a solemn agreement with you? [21]

Who are We Forbidden to Marry?

Don't marry those women whom your fathers have married - except for whatever happened in the past, (before this rule was revealed), for it was shameful and despicable and a deplorable custom. [22]

You're also forbidden to marry your mothers, daughters, sisters, paternal and maternal aunts, nieces from your brothers or sisters, foster-mothers who nursed you, foster-sisters (who nursed from the same wet-nurse as you), your step-mothers, your step-daughters in your care, born of a conjugal wife - though there is no sin for you in this if (you divorced the step-daughter's mother) without consummating the marriage, your biological son's wives and also two sisters in wedlock at the same time, except for whatever happened in the past (before this rule was revealed, and vice-versa for women), for Allah is forgiving and merciful. [23]

Conversion to Islam and the Status of Pagan Marriage

> **Background Info... v. 24**
>
> This verse was revealed in answer to a question raised by some of Muhammad's (p) companions, who captured a number of women during the Campaign of Hunayn, in which a bitter and aggressive foe (the tribes of the city of Ta'if) declared war on the Muslims of Medina.
>
> The people of Ta'if foolishly brought out their entire population and wealth to the battlefield under the odd belief that it would make their warriors fight harder. It didn't work, and the warriors of Ta'if fled away, leaving their families behind to be captured.
>
> Soon, some of the companions asked if it was lawful to marry some of those captive women (assuming they would also convert from paganism), but the companions were concerned that some of them were already married to idol-worshippers, whom they knew.

> The men of Ta'if eventually accepted Islam (after some weeks) and sent representatives to Medina to petition the Prophet to get their goods and families back.
>
> He gave them the choice of their families or their captured wealth. They chose their families, and the Prophet asked that all the captured women and children be released.

All women who are already married are forbidden for you (to marry), except for those (pagan women) who come under your control (as maid-servants, and who convert to Islam freely, nullifying their pagan marriage tie).

Allah has ordained (these limits) for you, and except for these (limits) all other (women) are lawful (to marry), provided you court them with gifts from your property, *desiring purity and not just desire.*

Since you gain benefits from them, give them their (marriage gifts) as you're required. However, if after the required (marriage gift) is settled you mutually agree (to modify it), there is no blame upon you, for Allah is knowing and wise. [24]

If any (man) among you doesn't have the means to marry respectable believing women, then he should marry believing women from among those who are under your control, and Allah is fully aware (of the quality) of your faith.

You (people) are all from each other (so don't judge a potential spouse by his or her lower-class status).

Marry (maidservants) with the permission of their retainers, and give them their marriage gifts according to what is fair.

Take them as respectable (wives) and not merely as objects of lust or as secret mistresses.

If they fall into *shameful behavior* after having been taken in marriage then their punishment is half that of higher-class women.

This (allowance for a reduced penalty) is for those among you who fear giving in (to your urges with those who are less able to resist you, and who then should not be held to the same level of accountability as you), though it's better for you that you resist (your immoral urges), and Allah is forgiving and merciful. [25]

Allah wants to make (everything) clear for you so He can guide you towards the (same wholesome) example of those (believing people) who came before you, and (He wants) to turn towards you (in mercy with easy-to-follow regulations), for Allah is knowing and wise. [26]

Allah wants to turn towards you, but those who follow their own whims want to turn you far away (from Allah)! [27] Allah wants to lighten (your burden), for human beings have been created weak (to temptation). [28]

Allah's Mercy is Vast

O you who believe! Don't **eat up** each other's possessions recklessly (in wasteful pursuits).

Rather, let there be business and trade based upon mutual good will.

Neither should you kill yourselves, for Allah is a source of mercy towards you. [29]

As for the one who does that with malicious intent and a desire to do wrong, We'll soon throw him in a fire, and that's easy for Allah to do. [30]

If you avoid the major sins that you were forbidden to do, then We'll erase your minor faults and admit you through a noble gate (leading into Paradise). [31]

Allah Favors each Differently

Don't be jealous of (the material) things, (such as money or fame,) that Allah has blessed some of you with more than others.

For men there is a share of what they earn, and for women there is a share of what they earn.

Ask Allah for His bounty, for Allah knows about all things. [32]

Appoint People in Charge to Distribute the Estate

For (the benefit) of all, We've appointed executors (to distribute the estates) left behind by parents and relatives and those with whom you swore bonds (of brotherhood, and whom you wanted to share in your estate), so give them what is due to them (at the time of distribution), for Allah is a witness to all things. [33]

Dealing with Domestic Disharmony

mean either separation, going away, giving an example or hitting someone, among many other things). However, the next morning around 70 women **complained to the Prophet's wives that** their husbands had physically abused them. The Prophet became upset when he heard about the complaints, and he declared that any man who beats his wife **"is not the best of you,"** which in prophetic terms means **"they're the worst of you."** He also said that any man who beats a woman is not a good man. In other words, the men had misinterpreted or misapplied what the Prophet meant by *daraba*. (*Abu Dawud, Nisa'i*, also see 2:231.)

The historian, Ibn Sa'd, includes a quote from the Prophet about this incident in which he addressed his male followers, saying, **"I cannot bear the** thought of a man with the veins of his neck swollen in anger against his wife **while he's fighting against her."** (As quoted in *Women of Medina*, trans. by Aisha Bewley.) Then the Prophet awaited a ruling from Allah, and this verse was revealed. How is *daraba* to be understood here? The Prophet gave the example when he followed this three step procedure when he was having trouble with some of his own wives. First he talked to them for a few weeks, then he left the house for some weeks; finally he offered them a divorce, so *daraba* is to be understood by the Prophet's example to mean *separate* or offer them a divorce. (See 33:28-29)

Men are responsible for the welfare of women since Allah has given some (of you) more wherewithal than others, and because they must spend of their wealth (to maintain the family).

So mindful and devout women safeguard the private matters that Allah would have them safeguard.

As for those (women) from whom you fear aggressive defiance, caution them (to piety).

(If they remain unmoved by your words), then leave them alone in their beds, and finally, (if they continue in their aggressive defiance), then set them out (by offering them a divorce.)

However, if they give in to you (by abandoning their aggressive and defiant behavior), then you have no (legitimate) grounds to act against them (any further), and Allah is full of knowledge and greatness. [34]

If any of you notice (that a husband and wife) are about to split up, then appoint a mediator from among his family and a mediator from among her family.

If they desire to be reconciled, then Allah will bring about harmony between them, for Allah is full of knowledge and is well-informed. [35]

Spend and Allah will Spend on You

Serve Allah and don't associate any partners with Him. Be good to your parents and relatives, and (be good) to orphans, the needy and your neighbors, whether they're near or far, and also to your companions around you and to travelers and to those (servants) over whom you have control.

Allah has no love for conceited snobs or for the tightfisted or those who get other people to be tightfisted or who hide the bounty that Allah has given them. We've prepared a degrading punishment for all those who cover over (their awareness of the truth)! [36-37]

(Allah also has no love) for those who spend their money only so that other people will notice, and who have no faith in Allah and the Last Day.

Whoever takes Shaytan for a confidant – *oh, what an awful confidant is he!* [38]

What hardship would it be for them to believe in Allah and the Last Day and to spend out of what Allah has supplied to them? Allah knows all about them! [39]

Allah is never unfair, even by as much as a speck. If there's any good thing (that's done), He multiplies it and gives a great reward from His Own Self. [40]

So how about it then? What if We brought from every community a witness and We brought you, (Muhammad), as a witness against these (people)? [41]

On that day, whoever rejected (faith) and disobeyed the Messenger will wish he were made one with the earth, *but they'll never be able to hide any report from Allah!* [42]

Preparing for Worship

Oyou who believe! Don't come anywhere near (to performing) your prayers while intoxicated until you're able to understand what you're saying.

Background Info... last part v. 43

A'ishah, the Prophet's wife, told the story of why this part of verse 43 was revealed. She said, "We were traveling with the Messenger of Allah. When we were camped at Al Baida', a necklace of mine broke off, and the Messenger tarried there to look for it.

"A number of other people also remained with him, and we were far from any source of water. Some people went to (my father), Abu Bakr, and said, 'Do you see what A'ishah has done? She made the Messenger stay with people who have no water.'

"He came to me while the Messenger was sleeping with his head on my leg and said, 'You made the Messenger stay with people, and there is no source of water.' Then he put his hand on my waist preventing me from moving and said, 'Allah will say whatever He wills.' I remained there all night with the Messenger sleeping while resting his head on my leg. In the morning there was no water (for ablution), and Allah revealed this verse of cleansing with the earth.

Don't (pray) in a state of ritual impurity, unless you're on the road traveling, until you've washed your whole body.

If you're sick or on a journey or one of you has come from using the bathroom or had intimate relations and you can find no water (for your ablutions), then you can take clean sand and wipe your faces and hands with it.

Truly, Allah forgives(sins) and overlooks (shortcomings). [43]

The Opposition of the Jews of Medina

Haven't you noticed the case of those who already received some portions of scripture (in the past)? They bargain with mistakes and want to sidetrack you away from the path (of Allah). [44]

Allah knows all about your enemies! Allah is enough of a protector, and Allah is enough of a helper! [45]

Background Info... v. 46

The following example of rude discourse directed towards the Prophet is similar to another episode of disrespectful speech that was discussed in verse 2:104.

By this time in the Medinan Period, many tribal leaders among the Jews were openly hostile towards Islam and Muhammad, and they made no effort to hide their disdain and ridicule of him with insolent public statements and word-plays to make fun of him. This verse was revealed about such disrespectful comments.

Among the Jews are some who will switch words from their right places and say, "*We hear, and we disobey,*" and, "*Listen, may you not hear,*" and, "*Lead us to the fields,*" – all with a twist of their tongue and a disrespect for faith.

If only they would've said instead, "*We hear, and we obey,*" or "*Hear us,*" or "*Have consideration for us*," it would've been far better for them and more respectful besides.

Yet, Allah has cursed them for their disbelief, and even now only a few of them have any (true) faith. [46]

All you (Jews) who received scripture (in the past)! Believe in what We're sending down (to Muhammad), which confirms (the message of the scripture) that's with you now.

(Believe), before We rework the faces of some (of you) beyond all recognition or curse them as We cursed the Sabbath-breakers. Allah's orders will be carried out! [47]

Allah doesn't forgive the assigning of any partner to Him, but He forgives anything else for whomever He wants.

If anyone makes another (being) equal with Allah, then he's inventing an enormous sin. [48]

No Racial Group can Claim Allah as their Own

Background Info... v. 49-50

Some Jewish men went to the Prophet and brought their children with them. They said, "Muhammad, do our children here have any guilt upon them?"

The Prophet answered, "No, they don't."

The Jews then said, "We swear by the One Whom we swear by that we are just like you: every sin we commit during the day is forgiven during the night, and

every sin committed at night is forgiven **during the day." This passage was** revealed in response. (*Asbab ul-Nuzul*)

Haven't you noticed the situation of those (Jews of Medina) who claim they're especially pure?

No way! Only Allah purifies whomever He wants, and no one will ever be wronged by as much as the string of a date seed. [49]

So look at how they've invented lies against Allah, and that's an obvious crime! [50]

Hypocrisy in Alliance with Treason

Background Info... v. 51-52

One of the most important Jewish leaders of Medina was K'ab ibn al-Ashraf. He traveled with seventy of his men to pay a visit to the idol-worshippers of Mecca, who were still celebrating their victory over the Muslims at Uhud.

He wanted to break his treaty with the Muslims by forging an alliance with the Meccans instead, sensing that the Muslims were in a weakened position.

K'ab stayed in the house of Abu Sufyan, the Meccan leader, and a grand meeting was soon held between the men of both sides. At first, the Meccans were wary of K'ab's offer of alliance, citing as proof that they (the Jews) had a religious scripture and that Muhammad had one, as well.

So the Meccans insisted that the Muslims had more in common with the Jews and that they must have had more

126

affinity with one another. (The Meccans had no religious books or scriptures, other than long-standing cultural traditions.)

In order to prove their good will, the Meccans asked the Jewish leaders to bow to two of their idols, which they did, hence the charge that they *believe* in idols.

K'ab proposed that thirty men each from the Jews and the idol-worshippers should touch the Ka'bah and swear a pact against the Muslims in the name of the Lord of that House.

After it was done, Abu Sufyan asked Ka'b if he thought they, the idol-worshippers, were better guided in their religion than Muhammad.

Ka'b asked Abu Sufyan to summarize Muhammad's beliefs, and Abu Sufyan explained how Islam believes in One God.

Then Ka'b listened while Abu Sufyan explained what his own pagan beliefs were, which consisted of a mix of devotion to the idols, maintenance of the Ka'bah and providing guest services to travelers and ransom for captured relatives.

Abu Sufyan closed his speech by criticizing Muhammad for abandoning the ways of his ancestors, cutting himself off from his relatives and making up his own religion.

Afterwards, K'ab replied to the Meccans, "I swear by Allah that you are better guided than he." When word of these events reached Medina, this passage was revealed in response. (*Asbab ul-Nuzul, Ma'ariful Qur'an*)

They told the faithless (idolaters of Mecca) that they (the idolaters) were better guided on the way (of truth) than the believers! [51]

They're the ones whom Allah has cursed, and whomever Allah curses - *there shall be no one to help them.* [52]

Do they think they own a share in (Allah's) kingdom? They're (a people who) won't even give a date crumb's (worth of assistance) to their fellows (who are in need). [53]

Are they jealous of (other) people because of what Allah gave to them from His bounty?

But We had already given these descendants of Ibraheem the scripture and the (path of) wisdom and granted them a mighty kingdom (in ancient times). [54]

Some of them believed, while some of them turned their faces from Him. Well, Hellfire is enough of a roasting flame (to punish those who reject Allah)! [55]

We're going to throw all those who rejected Our signs into a fire, and just as their skins are burnt to a crisp, We'll trade (their old skins) for new skins so they can

Haven't you noticed the case of those (Jews of Medina) who received a portion of the scripture? Yet, they put their faith in idols and superstition!

127

feel the punishment (over and over) again. Truly, Allah is powerful and wise. [56]

We're soon going to admit those who believed and did what was morally right into gardens beneath which rivers flow – *and there they shall remain forever*!

They'll be joined by pure and holy companions. (Even more than that,) We'll enter them into cool shade that stretches forth far and wide! [57]

Don't Take the Right of Another

Background Info... v. 58

Before the Muslims had migrated to Medina, the pagan Quraysh allowed the Ka'bah door to be opened for visitors on only two days a week (Mondays and Thursdays). The Prophet had asked to go in on one of those days, but the keeper of the door key, Uthman ibn Talhah, rudely tried to keep the Prophet and his friends out.

The Prophet said to him, "Uthman, a day will come when you might see the key to the House of Allah in my hand, and then I'll have the power to give it to whomever I wish."

Uthman ibn Talhah replied, "If that happens, then the Quraysh would have been dishonored and scattered!"

The Prophet then said, "No, they will be established in honor." Then the Prophet entered the Ka'bah. As he later explained it, Uthman Ibn Talhah mused that perhaps what Muhammad (p) said might come to pass. He soon decided to convert to Islam, but his angry family forced him to go back to idol-worship.

In the year 630, the Muslims of Medina forced the peaceful surrender of Mecca and occupied the city on a day that saw three large lines of Muslim soldiers,

ten thousand strong, entering in an orderly and impressive procession.

The curious Meccans watched as Muhammad (p) and his close companions walked up to the door of the Ka'bah.

As they approached the building, Uthman ibn Talhah shut the door tight and climbed up on the roof. When the Prophet asked for the key to open the door, his men told him that it was with Uthman up on the roof.

The Prophet looked up and asked for it, but Uthman called down, "If I knew you were the Messenger of Allah, I would not deny you the key."

The Prophet's cousin, 'Ali ibn Abi Talib, climbed up and forcibly snatched the key from his hand and opened the door. The Prophet then went inside and performed a brief prayer. When he came out he saw Uthman ibn Talhah standing there.

'Abbas, the Prophet's faithful uncle, asked if his family could be entrusted with the key and the great responsibility that went along with it. This verse was immediately revealed, so the Prophet asked 'Ali to return the key to Uthman ibn Talhah and to apologize for his rough handling.

A surprised Ibn Talhah said, "'Ali, first you strong-armed me, and now you're being gentle with me?"

'Ali replied, "Allah, the Most High, has revealed a verse about you."

After he repeated it to Ibn Talhah, the amazed idol-worshipper walked off happily.

Suddenly, the Prophet called out to him, asking him to remember the conversation they had had so many years before.

Uthman ibn Talhah remembered, and he instantly declared his faith in Islam.

The Prophet then announced to the crowds that the right to be custodian of the Ka'bah's key would remain with Uthman ibn Talhah's family forever and that only an unjust man would deprive them of their right. *(Asbab ul-Nuzul, Ma'ariful Qur'an)*

Allah orders you to return the things you've been trusted with to those who are owed.

When you judge between people, always judge with fairness.

Truly, the values that Allah teaches you are quite excellent! Indeed, Allah listens and observes. [58]

only obedience (to a leader) in **righteousness."** *(Bukhari, Muslim, Ahmad)*

O you who believe! Obey Allah, the Messenger and those who are in authority among you.

If you have any kind of disagreement among yourselves, refer it to Allah and His Messenger, that is if you (really) believe in Allah and the Last Day. That's the most beneficial way for achieving a settlement. [59]

The Dangers From Within

Nadir tribe, to solve the problem, but the Jew wanted to go to Muhammad for judgment. The Jew forced Bishr to accompany him to see the Prophet.

After both sides stated their case, the Prophet ruled in favor of the Jew. Bishr was outraged, and he left to look for 'Umar ibn al-Khattab (d. 644). When he found out where he was, he then dragged the Jewish man along with him to get a 'second opinion.' When they approached 'Umar, Bishr complained to him, saying that Muhammad had found in favor of the Jew against him, and then he challenged 'Umar to give a better ruling.

'Umar replied, "*Is that so?*" and he told the men to wait outside for a moment. 'Umar went into his house and belted a sword around his waist. He emerged and drew his sword in front of the startled men. He began to whack Bishr with the flat side of his weapon until he agreed to back down. 'Umar said, "This is the way I will judge for the one who doesn't agree with the judgment of Allah and His Messenger."

Some reports say that 'Umar actually killed Bishr and that the heirs of Bishr brought their case before the Prophet.

In either case, 'Umar was absolved for his actions by the revelation of these verses, which all but declared that the hypocrites are *de facto* enemies of Allah.

Afterwards people gave 'Umar the nickname of *al-Farooq,* which means that he judged rightly. (*Asbab ul-Nuzul, Ma'ariful Qur'an*)

Haven't you seen the case of the (hypocrites) who declared that they believe (in the revelations) sent down to you and in those sent down to those before you?

(They only make these claims because) they would rather get verdicts (for their disputes) from the flawed (leaders among the Followers of Earlier Revelation), even though they were ordered to reject falsehood.

And so Shaytan's desire is to lead them farther astray into misguidance. [60]

When they're told:

"*Come to what Allah has revealed, and come to the Messenger,*" you can see how the hypocrites turn their faces away from you in disgust. [61]

How will it be then when they're trapped with misfortune on account of what their hands have prepared? Then they'll come to you, swearing to Allah, saying, "*We only meant the best and to (help people) reconcile.*" [62]

Allah knows what's in the hearts of those who are like that, so steer clear of

130

them. Yet, still speak words that will touch their souls. [63]

Messengers are to be Obeyed

Background Info... v. 64-65

Two Muslims in Medina had a dispute over irrigation rights. The first man (Tha'laba) was a native of the city, while the second man (az-Zubayr) was a cousin of the Prophet who had immigrated from Mecca. The Prophet listened to both men and found in favor of Az-Zubayr.

(The settlement essentially was a compromise that said that the men must take turns irrigating their fields.)

Tha'laba became angry and accused the Prophet of merely siding with his cousin. That remark upset the Prophet, and he became saddened. This passage was revealed in response. (*Asbab ul-Nuzul*)

We only sent messengers so they could be obeyed according to the will of Allah.

Now if they would've just come to you, (Muhammad), when they were being wrong to their own souls and asked for Allah's forgiveness - *and the Messenger had asked for their forgiveness*, they would've found that Allah accepts repentance and is merciful. [64]

But no, by your Lord, they have no faith unless and until they make you, (Muhammad), the judge between them in all their disagreements.

They must not allow any resistance towards your decisions to appear in their souls, but rather they should accept (your decisions) with the greatest conviction. [65]

Background Info... v. 66-68

After the event involving Bishr and the Jew was made public knowledge (see 4:60-63), the Jews of Medina started taunting the Muslims, saying that they claim to have a prophet, but then they fail to obey his commands.

Then the Jews boasted that when their prophet (Musa) told them they had to kill other Jews to get Allah's forgiveness (after the golden calf incident), their forefathers did so. Then the Jews asked the Muslims that if they had received a command like that, would they have obeyed it? This passage was revealed in response. (*Ma'ariful Qur'an*)

If We had ordered them to sacrifice their lives or to leave their homes (and migrate to a new land), very few of them would've done it.

If they just would've done (the little) that they were asked to do, it would've been better for them, and their resolve would've been strengthened. [66]

Then We would've given them a great reward from Our presence and guided them towards a straight path. [67-68]

Background Info... v. 69-70

A man named Thawban, who was very much attached to the Prophet and loved him dearly, once went to him with a particular concern.

He explained that he loved him (the Prophet) so much that he hated to be parted from his company – even for an instant. Then he said that he was afraid

131

that he might not see him in Paradise, given that Muhammad would be in the ranks of the prophets up there and would thus be in a higher place than he and also given the fact that he (Thawban) might not even make it into heaven.

This passage was revealed to console this concern, pointing out that in Paradise, even the different grades and levels will have occasion to meet and mingle. (*Asbab ul-Nuzul, Ibn Kathir, Tabarani*)

On another occasion, addressing the same issue, the Prophet said that on the Day of Judgment, everyone will be with the one they love, i.e., those who loved the Prophet would be with him. (*Bukhari*)

He also once said that other categories of people who will be in this beautiful fellowship include honest businessmen, those who are faithful in their worship and those who do a lot of extra praying. (*Ma'ariful Qur'an*)

Whoever obeys Allah and the Messenger will be with those who have the favor of Allah upon them, (among whom are) the prophets, the true (in faith), the witnesses (who sacrificed their lives in Allah's cause) and the righteous. What a beautiful fellowship! [69]

This is the bounty of Allah, and it's enough that Allah knows (about all things). [70]

When in Dangerous Territory

Background Info... v. 71-73

Due to the constant raiding and attacks of the pagans in the countryside, the Muslims were discouraged from moving about in the land alone.

When the Prophet organized patrols or sent out skirmishers to clear an area of raiders, some men of Medina would go absent without leave or otherwise conveniently get "lost" to avoid any potentially dangerous situations.

If the patrols were successful and drove off pagan raiders, capturing booty in the process, these laggards would lament their loss of material gains. That is the subject matter of this passage.

O you who believe! Be cautious and only venture out (into dangerous places) either in groups or all together. [71]

For sure, there are some among you who try to lag behind (when you're on the road). If misfortune befalls you, they say, "*Allah was gracious to us by not keeping us among them to witness (their misfortune)."* [72]

However, if some good fortune befalls you from Allah, he'll say, as if he didn't know you closely, *"Oh, how I wish I could've been there with them because I would've had a great time!"* [73]

What is a Legal War?

Background Info... v. 74-75

Even though the Muslims had migrated to the safe haven of Medina, Muslims were not allowed yet to defend themselves from the Meccans, who harassed, tortured and killed Muslims with impunity both within Mecca and in the countryside. This quoted supplication in verse 75 was what the Muslims were asking of Allah.

This passage was then revealed, giving Muslims permission to defend themselves. *(Ma'ariful Qur'an)*

Let them fight in the cause of Allah, those who sell the life of this world for the life of the Hereafter.

To the one who fights in the cause of Allah, whether he's killed or achieves victory, We're soon going to give him a great reward. [74]

And why *shouldn't* you fight in the cause of Allah and in the cause of those who, being weak, are mistreated: the men, women and children whose only cry is:

"Our Lord! Save us from this land whose people are oppressors. Send us someone from You who will protect us, and send us someone from You who will help!" [75]

Those who have faith (in Allah) fight in the cause of Allah, while those who cover over (their ability to have faith) fight in the cause of falsehood, so fight against the allies of Shaytan, for truly Shaytan's plan is weak. [76]

Don't be Cowardly

Background Info... v. 77-79

This passage was revealed with **regards to several of Muhammad's** followers who were severely persecuted in the early days of the Meccan period.

At that time they were begging Muhammad to let them fight back against the idol-worshippers who would daily assault them in the streets and vandalize their property. Muhammad always refused their request and counseled them to be patient and engage in more religious activity.

After the Migration to Medina, the order finally came to fight the Meccans, and many of these same men became reluctant to go to war. The Prophet said, "Allah has guaranteed the struggler in His cause that He will either bring him death and admit him to Paradise, or He will help him return home safely with whatever rewards and war booty he has gained." *(Bukhari)*

133

Haven't you seen the people who were told to restrain their hands (from fighting) and who were counseled instead (to concentrate on) establishing prayer and giving in charity?

When the order finally came for them to fight, a bunch of them became more scared of people than they were scared of Allah!

"Our Lord!" they cried out. *"Why have You ordered us to fight? Won't you postpone it for us, at least for a while longer?"*

Say to them, *"The enjoyment of this world is indeed short. The next life is better for the one who is mindful (of Allah). You won't be wronged by as much as the string of a date seed!* [77] *Wherever you are, death will find you, even if you lodge yourselves in mighty towers!"*

Whenever good fortune befalls them, they say, *"This is from Allah,"* but if they're ever hit with a setback they say, *"This is all your fault, (Muhammad)."*

Say to them, *"Every (outcome) is from Allah."*

So what is it with these people that they don't understand a single phrase? [78]

Any good that comes your way is from Allah, while any misfortune that befalls you is your own fault. We sent a messenger to people, and Allah is enough of a witness for that! [79]

Whoever obeys the Messenger obeys Allah, while whoever turns away (from you, Muhammad,) well, We didn't send you to be their caretaker. [80]

They say, *"We obey,"* but when they leave you a bunch of them talk badly through the night on the opposite of what you've taught them, though Allah is keeping a record of their nightly meetings, so steer clear of them.

Place your trust in Allah, for Allah is enough to take care of things. [81]

Haven't they considered the Qur'an with care? If it were from any other (source) besides Allah, then they would've found many matters of disagreement within it. [82]

Whenever the (hypocrites hear) rumors about safety or impending danger, they announce it publicly (without checking on it first).

If they would only refer the matter to the Messenger or to the proper authorities among them, then investigators could check on the incidents with them.

If it wasn't for Allah's grace and mercy towards you, all save for a few of you would've followed Shaytan. [83]

Fight in the Cause of Allah

> **Background Info... v. 84-85**
>
> This passage was revealed about the appointment to fight once again at Badr, an appointment that the elated Meccans made with the Prophet after they prevailed at Uhud. (See 3:172 and footnotes.)
>
> Some Muslims hesitated to follow the Prophet when he began making preparations for this march.
>
> So this verse is saying, in other words, if no one else follows the Prophet in opposing evil, it won't be his fault. The Meccans wound up not appearing at all.

(Muhammad,) fight in the cause of Allah, though you're only responsible for your own self.

Rally the believers. Perhaps Allah will restrain the hostility of the faithless, for Allah is the strongest power and the strongest punisher. [84]

Whoever makes a recommendation in a good cause becomes a part of it. Whoever makes a recommendation in an evil cause shares responsibility in it. Allah has the power to direct all things. [85]

Spread Goodwill for the Sake of Allah

When someone gives you a greeting, return it with a nicer greeting than that or one about the same, for Allah is keeping track of all things. [86]

Allah! There is no god but He. He's going to gather you all together on the Day of Assembly, and there's no doubt about that! Now whose word can be more honest than Allah's? [87]

Don't Let the Hypocrites Make You Go Bad

Background Info... v. 88

A constant cause of concern for the authentic Muslims in Medina was the issue of the hypocrites. They were a large faction of people who pretended to enter Islam, but who conspired against it. They were the proverbial *fifth column*.

Just before the Battle of Uhud was to begin, the one thousand-strong Muslim force was reduced by three hundred men when a contingent of hypocrites suddenly withdrew back to Medina.

When the battle was over, the beleaguered, though not destroyed, Muslim veterans were disputing over what to do about them.

Some wanted them punished, while others wanted them left alone in the hope that they would reform themselves. Another group of hypocrites were Meccans who had migrated to Medina, but who then later reneged on their faith and returned to Mecca.

And so the true believers were divided into *two opinions* about these kinds of people. This verse was revealed pointing out that there was little hope of salvaging those whom Allah has abandoned. (*Ma'ariful Qur'an*)

Background Info... v. 89-90

Suraqah ibn Malik visited Medina after the battles of Badr and Uhud had passed. He asked the Prophet for a peace treaty between the Muslims and his tribe, the Banu Mudlaj. The Prophet sent Khalid ibn Waleed, who had become a Muslim by that time, to return with Suraqah to seal the peace treaty. The main points of the treaty were these:

1) The Banu Mudlaj would not support the Quraysh of Mecca any more.

2) Anyone who allies with the Banu Mudlaj becomes a party to this treaty's terms;

3) If the Quraysh ever come to accept Islam, the Banu Mudlaj would do the same thing also.

This passage was then revealed about their case. (*Asbab ul-Nuzul*)

The (hypocrites) only want you to cover over (the truth of Allah in your hearts) like they've covered it over (in their hearts), for then you'll be on the same level.

So what's wrong with you that you've split into two groups (of opinion) about the hypocrites?

Allah has thrown them by the wayside because of what they've earned.

Do you want to try and guide one whom Allah has left astray? Whomever Allah leaves astray will never discover a way (out of darkness)! [88]

So, don't take best friends from among them until they migrate, for Allah's sake, (to Medina).

136

If they become rebels (and make war against you), then capture them or kill them (in battle) wherever you find them.

Don't take close allies or helpers from among them, unless it's with those who join a group with which you have a treaty (of peace), or those who come to you with hearts that hold them back from fighting you - and fighting their own people!

If Allah had wanted, He could've given them an advantage over you, and they would've fought you.

If they stay back and don't try to fight you and instead send you (offers) of peace, then Allah hasn't given you any legitimate reason (to fight against them). [89-90]

You'll find other (hypocrites) who want to gain your confidence and the confidence of their own people. However, every time they're tempted (by their twisted desires), they fall into them.

If they neither leave you (to openly join your enemy) nor give you any peace (while remaining among you), other than merely not (attacking you at the moment), then you may capture them and kill them wherever you encounter them. In their case, We've given you clear permission (to fight) against them. [91]

The Penalties for Murder

His mother and brothers yelled at him and beat him, ordering him to give up Islam. They left him tied up under the blazing sun, and Harith ibn Zayd succeeded in making Ayyash, under torture, renounce his faith in Islam.

After they let him free, Ayyash began to feel angry at having been abused and forced to give up his faith. He swore to Harith ibn Zayd that if he ever found him alone he would kill him. Some time later, Ayyash again escaped to Medina and renewed his commitment to Islam. After the Conquest of Mecca, Ayyash found Harith walking in the street and set upon him and killed him.

The people around him began shouting that Harith had become a Muslim. Ayyash, who didn't know he had recently converted, was filled with remorse.

He immediately went to the Prophet and said, "Messenger of Allah! You know about my situation with Harith, and I didn't know he had entered into Islam when I killed him." This passage was revealed in response. (Ibn Kathir)

A believer should never kill another believer, though if it happens by mistake, (then a penalty must still be paid). If someone kills a believer (accidentally), then he must free a believing servant and pay monetary-damages to the family of the deceased, unless they decline it freely.

If the deceased belonged to a community that is hostile to you and he was a believer, the freeing of a believing servant (is enough).

If he belonged to a community with which you have a treaty, then again monetary-damages must be paid to his family, and a believing servant must be freed.

If someone cannot get (a servant to free, out of a financial hardship or some other reason), then a fast of two consecutive months must be observed by him, and this is a concession from Allah, for Allah has all knowledge and wisdom. [92]

If someone kills a believer on purpose, then his reward is in Hellfire, *and that's where he's going to stay!* The wrath and curse of Allah will be upon him, and a harsh punishment will be prepared for him. [93]

It is not for You to Judge Another Person's Sincerity

Background Info... v. 94

The Prophet had sent out a patrol into the countryside to guard against Meccan or bedouin raiders. The patrol came upon a lone bedouin named 'Amr who gave the Islamic greeting of peace.

The Muslims didn't take any action against him, but one man from among them named Muhallam, who had previous quarrels with 'Amr in the days before Islam, killed him and took his camel.

When the patrol returned to Mecca, the Prophet scolded Muhallam harshly.

In another incident, the Prophet sent out a patrol under the command of a man named Miqdad, and he came upon a district where some enemy pagan bedouins were. They all fled, except for one wealthy man who declared his faith in Islam. Miqdad decided not to believe him, and he struck him down.

Another member of the patrol was horrified and said, "You killed a man after he said there was no god other than Allah! By Allah, I'm going to tell what you did to the Prophet."

When the patrol returned and the Prophet was informed, he ordered Miqdad to be summoned and said, "Miqdad! Did you kill a man who declared there is no god other than Allah? What will you do tomorrow when you face (someone else) who says the same thing?"

Miqdad explained to the Prophet his reasons for doing what he did, and he further postulated that the man was only saying what he did to spare his life and keep his valuables.

The Prophet became livid and said, "Were you able to look into his heart to see if he was truthful or not?" The man said he was sure, but the Prophet remarked, "What will happen to you if he complains against you on Judgment Day? Did you kill a man who said there was no god but Allah? You're ruined because you don't know what he was really saying."

Then verse 94 was revealed, and the Prophet said, "He was a believer who hid his faith among his disbelieving people. He declared his faith to you, but you killed him, even though you used to hide your faith before in Mecca." (Bazzar)

Miqdad passed away some years after that, but when he was buried in the earth his body was found exhumed the next day. He was reburied and found exhumed two more times. Finally, the body was thrown into a wooded area after the Prophet remarked that the earth was not accepting his body because it was tainted with sin. This verse was revealed about this affair. (Asbab ul-Nuzul)

O you who believe! When you go abroad (to fight) in the cause of Allah, check carefully (before taking action against those whom you meet on the battlefield, and about whose intentions you're uncertain).

Don't say to an (enemy soldier) who (seems to pause) to offer you the greetings of peace, "*You aren't a believer,*" (wanting to kill him) in your greed for the temporary riches of this life.

There's plenty of profits and prizes with Allah. You used to (kill for profit) like that before (accepting Islam), until Allah placed His favor upon you. So check carefully (whom it is you're confronting), for Allah is aware of everything you do. [94]

Some Earn More than Others in Allah's Cause

Background Info… v. 95-96

After these two verses were revealed, the Prophet's main secretary, Zayd ibn Thabit, said that he was sitting with the Prophet in a gathering when the old blind man, Ibn Umm Maktoum came to them.

Zayd asked about his case, since he was handicapped by his blindness and unable to join the Prophet when he called the men to fight the idol-worshippers, even though he wished he could help. Zayd remarked that the Prophet leaned over on his (Zayd's) thigh and that the weight of the Prophet's leaning became amazingly heavy.

139

> The Prophet was sweating as the revelation was coming to him, and the crushing weight on Zayd's leg only eased when the revelation was finished.
>
> Then verse 95 was amended by revelation to say that a valid excuse absolved a person from having to serve. The Prophet asked Zayd to write down what he was reciting on a parchment. (*Bukhari*)

Him with a valuable reward above those who remain (at home). [95]

That's a special designation given especially by Him, along with His forgiveness and mercy, for Allah is forgiving and merciful. [96]

Migrating away from an Evil Land

The believers who sit (at home) without a valid excuse and who never get hurt are not equal to those who struggle in the cause of Allah with their money and their persons.

Allah has granted a higher grade to those who struggle and use their money and their persons over those who sit (at home).

> **Background Info... v. 97**
>
> This verse was revealed concerning the case of some secret converts to Islam who chose to remain in Mecca among the idol-worshippers, even though they could have easily escaped to Medina and lived by their convictions openly. They were trying to play both sides of the game, as it were, and their situation was known to the Muslims in Medina.
>
> Some of these lukewarm converts marched alongside of their fellow Meccans to the Battle of Badr and lost their lives in the battle as they fought against the Muslims of Medina. The Prophet also said of them that when the angels were taking their souls, they were berating them harshly for their poor choices and asking them the questions presented here in this passage. (*Bukhari*)

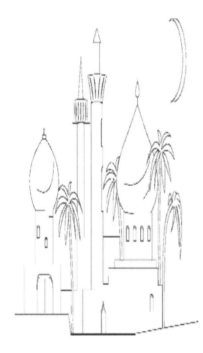

When the angels take the souls of those who died while in a state of injustice against their own selves (through their constant mingling with the hostile among the faithless), they're going to ask (the sinful souls), "*What was your situation in the world?*"

Allah has promised good to both, but those who struggle are distinguished by

They'll answer by saying, "*We were weak and oppressed in the land, (and that's why we never left the enemy's territory.)*"

140

The (angels will answer them,) saying, "*Wasn't Allah's earth big enough for you to move yourselves away (to some place safer)?*"

They're the ones who will find their resting place in Hellfire, and oh what an evil destination it is! [97]

Background Info... v. 98-100

When word of verse 97 reached the secret converts who remained in Mecca after the Battle of Badr, one old man named Habib al-Laythi told his sons, **"Carry me (to Medina), for I'm a weak old man, and I don't know the way."** His children began the two-week journey northward, carrying him on a stretcher.

Eventually, they had to stop just shy of their goal, as their father was near death. He clasped his hands together, **and his last words were, "O Allah, this is for You, and this is for Your Messenger. I choose You even as the Messenger of Allah chose You with his own hand."**

When news of his death reached Medina, the Prophet said that had he reached the city, his reward would have been more complete.

This passage was revealed in response, saying that Allah will give a full reward, even to refugees who die on their journey towards the sanctuary of faith. (*Asbab ul-Nuzul*)

However, those who were (truly) weak and oppressed, the men, women and children who had neither the means nor the ability (to flee) nor (who found a leader) to direct their way (are not to blame), for they can (still cling to the) hope that Allah will forgive them, for Allah pardons and forgives. [98-99]

Whoever leaves his home in the cause of Allah can find in the world many safe hideouts, for it's a wide and spacious place.

If he dies as a refugee far away from home for (the sake) of Allah and His Messenger, his reward is due with Allah, and Allah is forgiving and merciful. [100]

Prayer in Dangerous Places

Background Info... v. 101-104

The Prophet led a group of Muslims on patrol near a place named Asafan. The time for the early afternoon prayer arrived, and the Muslims were praying in congregation when a party of Meccan raiders (led by Khalid ibn Waleed) appeared in the distance.

One of the pagans counseled that this was the best time to attack the Muslims, while another suggested that there was a second prayer (the late afternoon) in which the Muslims took even more interest, and the man suggested that that would be a better time to strike.

While the idol-worshippers were debating when to strike, the Prophet concluded the group prayer and recited this newly revealed passage, explaining what the idol-worshippers were plotting.

When the next prayer time came, the Prophet ordered his men to pray while

141

holding their weapons, and the two rows of men alternated standing and bowing, so there would always be one line able to respond to the enemy if need be.
(Abu Dawud)

When you travel through the open countryside, it isn't wrong if you shorten your prayers out of the fear that the faithless might ambush you, for those who cover over (their ability to have faith) are clearly your enemies. [101]

When you're with (other Muslims on a journey, Muhammad), and you stand up to lead them in prayer, assign one group of the (believers) to stand (for prayer) with you, taking their weapons with them, (while the others stand guard).

When they finish their prostrations, let them set up (their guard-positions) in the rear, and let the other group which didn't pray yet come forward and pray with you - taking all precautions and holding their weapons.

The faithless would eagerly attack you in a single rush, if they (saw that) you were without your weapons or away from your gear.

It isn't wrong, however, if you pack your weapons away when it's raining or if you're too ill to carry them, but even still take every precaution for yourselves.

Truly, Allah has prepared a humiliating punishment for those who cover over (their awareness of the truth). [102]

When you've concluded the prayer, remember Allah while standing, sitting or lying down on your sides, and when you're free from danger, perform the prayer-ritual (in the normal way), for prayers are a duty upon the faithful at set times. [103]

Don't hesitate in pursuing the enemy. If you're suffering from hardship, (know that) they're suffering similar hardships, too.

(Remember that) you have hope in Allah, while they have hope in nothing. Allah is full of knowledge and wisdom. [104]

Hypocrites may Try to Use You

Background Info... v. 105-113

This entire passage was revealed in response to a situation that occurred due to a theft. A suspected hypocrite named Ta'ma ibn Ubayrak (aka Bashir) had a neighbor named Rifa'ah.

Ta'ma came to know that Rifa'a had a bag of flour in his house, and at that time early in the Medinan Period, many Muslims were suffering from deprivation, so Ta'ma broke into Rifa'a's house, took the big bag of flour and proceeded to walk home with it, not realizing that the bag had a small hole in it and was leaking a trail of flour after him.

When he reached his home and understood what had happened, he became frightened, ran to the house of a Jewish neighbor named Zayd, and gave him the bag to hold, not telling him that it was stolen property.

The owner of the flour, following the trail to Ta'ma's house, demanded his property. Then Ta'ma swore to the crowd of his relatives (that was quickly gathering) that he didn't take it and that he knew nothing about it. Rifa'a swore that he knew Ta'ma took the bag, and he pointed to the trail of flour that led to his door.

Then Ta'ma pointed out that the flour trail led away from there to the house of a Jew, and Ta'ma promptly swore that the Jew stole the flour.

(Another version of the story has Rifa'a being told that a cooking fire was seen in Ta'ma's house, causing him to go there to investigate, with Ta'ma claiming he got the bag from a companion named Labid, with the charge eventually being craftily shifted by Ta'ma's family to the the Jew in question.)

The crowd proceeded to the home of the Jew, and he produced the bag, claiming that Ta'ma asked him to hold it and that he didn't know it was stolen.

Other Jews also corroborated his story. The identity of the thief was uncertain then, with both Ta'ma and the Jew accusing each other (and an indignant Labid fuming in their midst).

Ta'ma's relatives came up with the idea that they should ask the Prophet to come and argue for their side, and they went to him and tried to convince him that Ta'ma was innocent.

Rifa'a and his family, on the other hand, were convinced that Ta'ma was the real culprit and that he was trying to mask his crime by framing an innocent person.

The relatives of Ta'ma, however, were so persuasive and passionate in their defense, that the Prophet was nearly convinced of their position, even to the point of suggesting that Rifa'a and his family were falsely accusing a Muslim family of theft.

The Prophet decided to wait for a resolution from Allah. After only a few days at most, this passage was revealed to the Prophet.

And so the Jew was declared innocent of the crime. Ta'ma then fled the city and renounced Islam in favor of idolatry.

He found no peace in Mecca among the pagans, however, for when the woman he had taken up lodging with in Mecca found out about his criminal past, she threw him out of the house.

Penniless and hungry, he eventually broke into a house in Mecca by tunneling through a wall. The wall collapsed on him, however, and killed him. (Asbab ul-Nuzul, Ma'ariful Qur'an)

We sent the Book down to you in all truth, so you can judge between people as directed by Allah. Therefore, don't let yourself be (used) as an advocate by traitors. [105]

Rather, seek the forgiveness of Allah, for Allah is forgiving and merciful. [106]

Offer no defense on behalf of those who've betrayed their own souls, for truly Allah has no love for underhanded sinners. [107]

They may hide (their intentions) from other people, but they can't hide (them) from Allah, for He's in their midst when they plot in the night - using the kinds (of vile) words that He detests! *Allah surrounds them in everything they do!* [108]

They're the kind of people on whose behalf you may offer a defense in this world, but who is going to defend them against Allah on the Day of Assembly, and who will take care of things for them then? [109]

If anyone commits an offense or otherwise wrongs his own soul, but then later seeks Allah's forgiveness, he will find Allah to be forgiving and merciful. [110]

If anyone earns a sin, he earns it against his own soul. Allah is full of knowledge and wisdom. [111]

If anyone earns a fault or a sin and then blames it on someone else who is

innocent, he will carry (upon himself both) the lie and an obvious sin. [112]

If it wasn't for Allah's favor and mercy towards you, a group of (the hypocrites) would've certainly schemed to lead you astray, but they've only succeeded in leading their own souls astray.

They're not able to cause you any real harm, for Allah has sent down the Book to you and (the standard of prophetic) wisdom, and (He taught you) what you didn't know (before). Allah's favor is powerfully inclined towards you. [113]

In most of their secret talks there's nothing good (being said or planned).

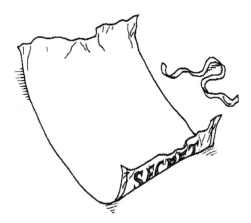

However, if someone is encouraging a charitable deed, (planning) an exemplary (act that will help many) or (devising ways to) make peace between people, (then being secretive is allowed).

Whoever engages (in secret discussions) for these (ends), while looking only for the pleasure of Allah, soon shall We give him a valuable reward. [114]

Enemies of Allah will be Defeated

If anyone works against the Messenger, even after guidance has been clearly brought to him, and follows a path other than that of a believer, well then We'll leave him on the path that he's chosen and then lead him straight into Hellfire – *and what a terrible place to go*! [115]

What Kind of a Friend is Shaytan?

Allah doesn't forgive (the sin of) making others equal with Him, but He forgives any other sins besides this for whomever He wants.

Whoever makes others equal with Allah has made a huge mistake and gone far off into error. [116]

(The idol-worshippers) call upon goddesses (for favors) in place of Him, but they're really calling upon a relentless devil! [117]

Allah had cursed Shaytan, but he (was defiant and challenged Allah), saying, "*I will trap a certain number of Your servants.* [118]

"*I'll trick them and urge them (to do bad deeds). I'll order them to slit the ears of cattle (for the sake of mindless superstition) and to disfigure what Allah created.*"

145

Whoever takes Shaytan for a protector in place of Allah is clearly lost in bewilderment! [119]

Shaytan makes them promises and urges them (to commit sins), but Shaytan's promises are nothing more than tricks. [120]

(His followers) will have their home in Hellfire, and they'll find no way out. [121]

However, We're soon going to admit those who believed and did what was morally right into gardens beneath which rivers flow – *and there they shall remain forever*! Allah's promise is true, and whose word can be more honest than Allah's? [122]

What is the Best Way?

> **Background Info... v. 123-124**
>
> A group of Jews told their Muslim listeners, "We're better guided than you. Our prophet came before your prophet. Our book came before your book, and we're more worthy of Allah than you."
>
> The Muslims offered that their prophet came last and was thus the best of all due to his superseding all others. *(Ibn Kathir, Asbab ul-Nuzul)*

Neither your desires nor the desires of the Followers of Earlier Revelation (can prevail).

Whoever does wrong will be repaid accordingly, and he'll find neither a best friend nor helper besides Allah. [123]

Whether they're male or female, whoever does what's morally right and has faith will enter the Garden, and not the least bit of injustice will be done to them. [124]

Whose way of life can be better than the one who submits himself to Allah, does what's morally right and follows the way of Ibraheem, the natural monotheist? Indeed, Allah even took Ibraheem as a friend. [125]

Everything in the heavens and on the earth belongs to Allah, and He embraces all things. [126]

Don't Oppress
Widows and Orphans

They're asking you for instructions (on how to treat) women, so tell them:

"Allah (Himself) gives you (men) instructions on (how to treat) them. (Follow) what's been recited to you in (this) book concerning women who have orphaned children, and from whom you're withholding their rightful property - and yet you seek to marry them (to get at their wealth or you avoid marrying them without letting them marry others in order to keep control of their property)!

"And also (follow the rules that you have been given concerning) the helpless children (in your midst). Your (duty) is to do justice to orphans, (so you must be fair and give widowed women and their orphaned children their inheritance)! There's not any good deed that you can do, without Allah knowing all about it." [127]

Treat Women with Fairness

Background Info... first part v. 128

Here is the background story for the revelation of the 'abandon' part of this passage. A man named Ibn Abi as-Sa'ib wanted to divorce his wife because she had grown old and he was disenchanted with her. The woman didn't want a divorce, and so she suggested an alternative.

She said, "Don't divorce me. Let me look after my children and set aside a few nights each month for me." The man accepted this arrangement. *(Asbab ul-Nuzul)*

If a wife fears aggressively defiant behavior (or abuse) from her husband, or she is afraid he will abandon her (without warning or support), it isn't wrong for them if they arrange a fair settlement between themselves (to mutually change the stipulations of the marriage contract or for her to initiate a divorce).

A (fair) settlement is best, even though people's souls are swayed by greed. If you do good and guard yourselves (against committing injustice, remember that) Allah is well-informed of whatever you do. [128]

You'll never be able to achieve fairness between women, (if you happen to have more than one wife), no matter how hard you try, though don't turn away (from one wife) altogether, as if you were leaving her to languish.

If you come to a friendly understanding and remain aware (of your duty to Allah, know that) He's forgiving and merciful. [129]

However, if (a married couple) has irreconcilable differences (and must separate), Allah will provide for all concerned from His abundance, for Allah is the One Who cares for all things and is wise. [130]

Allah is in Control

All that is within the heavens and on the earth belongs to Allah.

And so it was that We directed those who received revelation before you that they should be mindful of Allah, just as We've also directed you (Muslims) to do likewise.

If you reject (Him, just remember) that all things within the heavens and on the earth belong to Allah and that Allah is free of all needs and (is the only One) worthy of being praised. [131]

Again, everything in the heavens and on the earth belongs to Allah, and Allah is enough to take care of all affairs! [132]

If He ever wanted to, He could destroy all you people and create another species, because Allah has the power to do that.

If anyone desires a reward in this life, (remember) that in Allah's (hands) are the rewards both of this life and of the next, and Allah hears and watches (over all things). [133-134]

Stand up For Justice

O you who believe! Stand up firmly for justice as witnesses before Allah, and (be fair witnesses even if it's) against your own selves, your parents or your relatives, as well.

(Also, be fair), whether it's (against) the rich or the poor, for Allah can best protect (the legitimate interests) of both sides.

Don't follow your own desires, for only then can you (judge) with fairness. If you distort (the truth) or fail to do justice, then know that Allah is well-informed of whatever you do. [135]

Don't be Unreliable in Your Faith

O you who believe! Believe in Allah and His Messenger and in the Book that He sent down to His Messenger, and believe in the books that He sent down to those who came before (your time, as well.)

Whoever rejects Allah, His angels, His books, His messengers or the Last Day has made a huge mistake and gone far off into error. [136]

Those who believe, but who then cover over (their faith), then believe again, and then *again* cover over (their faith) - *and go on increasing in their rejection*, Allah won't forgive them nor will He guide them on the path (of truth). [137]

Tell the hypocrites that there's (nothing) for them to look forward to (in the next life other than) painful punishment. [138]

So those who take as their best friends (people) who've rejected (Allah) in preference to the believers - *are they looking for high status among them?* Yet, all high status belongs to Allah! [139]

He's already sent down to you (the instructions) in the Book that when you hear the (revealed) verses of Allah being mocked and ridiculed, you're not allowed to sit with (such people) until they turn to a different topic.

If you did (stay there, while insults were being hurled against Allah's revelations), then you would be no better than they.

(Know that) Allah will collect the hypocrites and all those who covered over (their faith, and He will throw them) all together into Hellfire. [140]

They're the ones who bide their time and watch you, (looking for any signs of weakness).

If you gain a victory from Allah, they say, "*Weren't we on your side all along?*" but if the faithless gain (the upper hand), they say (to their allies), "*Aren't we more valuable to you now, because we protected you from the believers?*"

Allah will judge among all of you on the Day of Assembly, and Allah will never give those who covered over (their faith) a way (to succeed completely) over the believers. [141]

The hypocrites think that they're outsmarting Allah, *but He's the One outsmarting them!*

When they stand up to pray, they stand sluggishly, only wanting to have people see them. They don't remember Allah very much at all! [142]

(They're) distracted all throughout (their prayer), not being (completely loyal) to one side or the other. You'll never find the way for someone whom Allah leaves astray. [143]

O you who believe! Don't take those who cover over (their faith) as best friends in preference to other believers. Do you want to give Allah the very evidence to use against you? [144]

The hypocrites will be in the lowest depths of the Fire, and you'll find no one to help them. [145]

(They're all doomed) except for those who repent and reform themselves and who then hold firmly to Allah and purify their way of life in Allah's sight.

If they do all of that, then they'll be (counted) among the believers, and Allah will soon grant a valuable reward to the believers. [146]

(All you people,) what would it do for Allah to punish you if you're thankful and you believe?

(Know that) Allah is appreciative (of the good you do) and that He knows (about all things). [147]

Don't be Quick to Spread Bad News

> ### Background Info... v. 148-149
>
> An angry dinner guest was complaining in public that his hosts did not feed him well.
>
> When the Prophet learned of this, he received this revelation in response that tells believers not to complain in public about anything they don't like unless it is concerning some injustice. (Asbab ul-Nuzul)
>
> The Prophet said, "Allah, the Exalted, has forgiven my community for what they talk about to themselves, as long as they don't talk about it in public or implement it." (Bukhari)

Allah doesn't like for bad news to be announced in public, except where injustice has been done, for Allah hears and knows (all things). [148]

Whether you tell others about a good deed or hide it, or forgive (someone) for doing something bad (to you), know that Allah has the power to forgive (all sins). [149]

Allah and the Israelites

Those who seek to cover over (the true knowledge of) Allah and His messengers and who want to separate Allah from His messengers by saying, "*We believe in some but reject the rest,*" and those who try to take a (compromising) middle course - they're all equally covering over (the light of faith within their hearts).

We've prepared a humiliating **PUNISHMENT** for those who cover over (their faith)! [150-151]

To those who believe in Allah and His messengers and who make no distinction between any of the messengers, We will soon give them their reward, for Allah is forgiving and merciful. [152]

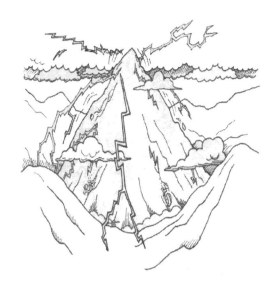

The (Jewish leaders among) the Followers of Earlier Revelation (in Medina) are asking you to bring down a (holy) book from the sky for them (to see, before they will accept you as a true prophet).

(Their forefathers) asked Musa for an even greater (miracle than that) when they demanded of him, "*Show us Allah in the flesh!*"

They were seized by thunder (and rendered unconscious) for their unjust presumption! Yet, they worshipped the calf even after all the clear proofs that had come to them!

Even still We forgave them, and We also gave Musa a clear mandate (to lead them). [153]

For their covenant We (brought them) to the raised heights of the mountain, (and afterwards, while they were traveling,) We had commanded them, "*Enter this (city's) gate with humility.*" We also commanded them, "*Don't violate the Sabbath*," and We took from them a solemn promise. [154]

True Knowledge is not Inborn

However, they broke their promise, rejected the signs of Allah, killed the prophets against all right, and now they're saying:

"*Our hearts are the covers (within which are written Allah's truth, so we don't need any other revelations).*"

But no! Allah has set a seal upon (their hearts) on account of their rejection, and they have only a little faith. [155]

(Even more, they're in that kind of situation because) they covered up (Allah's truth), made false charges against Maryam, and said:

"*We killed 'Esa, the Messiah, the son of Maryam.*"

However, they didn't kill him, nor did they crucify him, but it was made to appear to them that they did.

Those who argue about it are full of doubts and have no (concrete) information.

Instead, they only follow their own made-up ideas, for they certainly didn't kill him. [156-157]

Certainly not! Allah raised ('Esa) up to Himself, for Allah is powerful and wise. [158]

Each of the Followers of Earlier Revelation must believe in ('Esa) before they die, for on the Day of Standing (for judgment), ('Esa) will be a witness against them. [159]

For the misbehavior of the Jews, We made certain (foods) forbidden to them

that were (otherwise) good and wholesome - (food) that was allowed to them (before), but they had hindered too many people from Allah's path, (and were thus given these harsh dietary guidelines as a punishment). [160]

They took interest money, even though they were forbidden to, and they used up people's wealth foolishly.

We've prepared a terrible punishment for those among them who reject (the truth). [161]

However, those (Jews) who are firmly educated and who have (true) faith - they believe in what's been revealed to you, as do those who pray and give in charity to the poor and who believe in Allah and the Last Day.

Soon We will grant them a **valuable** reward. [162]

All Prophets Taught the Same Message

We've sent revelation to you, (Muhammad), in the **same way** that

We sent revelation to Nuh and to the messengers who came after him. We sent revelations to Ibraheem, Isma-il, Is-haq, Yaqub and the tribes (of Israel), as well as to 'Esa, Ayyoub, Yunus, Harun and Sulayman, and We gave the Zabur to Dawud. [163]

We've already told you the story of some of the messengers, but of others We haven't. *Allah even spoke directly to Musa.* [164]

The messengers gave good news, as well as warnings, so that people (who lived generations) after (the time) of each messenger would have no plea (of ignorance) against Allah, for Allah is powerful and wise. [165]

This Message is from Allah

Background Info... v. 166-167

Some prominent Meccans visited Muhammad in Medina and said, "We asked the Jews about you, and they said they didn't know anything about you

(and your authenticity as a prophet). So show us who is corroborating your claim that Allah **sent you as a messenger."** This passage was revealed in response. (*Asbab ul-Nuzul*)

Allah testifies that what He sent down to you was sent from His Own knowledge, and the angels testify, as well, though Allah is enough of a witness, Himself! [166]

Those who cover (the light of faith within their hearts) and keep others away from the path of Allah have strayed far away in error. [167]

Allah won't forgive those who cover over (their ability to have faith in Him) and who do wrong, neither will He guide them towards any pathway, *save for the pathway to **HELLFIRE***, and there they shall remain forever, and that's easy for Allah (to make happen). [168-169]

O people! The Messenger has come to you in all truth from Allah, so believe! It's in your best interest to do so.

However, if you reject (the truth, know that) everything in the heavens and on the earth belongs to Allah, and Allah is full of knowledge and wisdom. [170]

153

A Call to Christians to Abandon False Teachings

Followers of Earlier Revelation! Don't go to extremes in your religious (doctrines), and don't make statements about Allah that aren't true.

'Esa, the son of Maryam, was a messenger from Allah and His (creative) word bestowed upon (the virgin) Maryam and a spirit sent from Him. So believe in Allah and His messengers (who were mortal men).

Don't say, "*Trinity.*" Don't do it, as that would be best for you. Truly, God is just one God, *glory be to Him!* He's (far above) having a child!

He owns everything in the heavens and on the earth, and Allah is quite enough to take care of matters (for Himself)! [171]

The Messiah never refused to be God's servant, nor have the angels, nor the nearest (people devoted to Him). Whoever arrogantly refuses to serve Him will be gathered back to Him (for judgment). [172]

Those who believed and did what was morally right will be given their due reward by Him, *and even more out of His bounty!*

But those who were hesitant and arrogant will be punished by Him with a painful punishment, *and they'll find no*

one to help them or protect them besides Allah! [173]

O people! Absolute proof has now come to you from your Lord in that We've sent you a clear light. [174]

So those who believe in Allah and hold firmly to Him will soon be admitted to (a state of) mercy and grace from Him, and He will guide them to Himself along a straight path. [175]

More on Inheritance Law

Background Info... v. 176

A man named Jabir ibn 'Abdullah was on his deathbed, and he asked to see the Prophet. He had no parents or children to whom he could give his estate, but he did have seven sisters.

He was unsure about how much inheritance he should leave for them to split amongst themselves, whether a half or two-thirds. He was vexed greatly for he didn't want to give the wrong amount and be accountable to Allah. The Prophet told him to ease his mind, and this verse was revealed in answer. So the sisters received two-thirds of the estate to divide amongst themselves. (*Asbab ul-Nuzul*)

Now they're asking you for (an additional) legal decision (concerning inheritance in cases in which there are no descendants or ascendants).

Say to them, "*Allah gives you the following instructions for people who leave neither descendants nor ascendants as heirs. If it's a man who dies and he leaves a sister, but no children, she will get half the estate he leaves. If (the deceased was) a woman who left no children, her brother gets her estate.*

"*If there are (only) two sisters (left as heirs), they will get two-thirds of the estate (to share between them). If there are brothers and sisters, males and females, (then they will share the entire inheritance, with) the male receiving twice the share of the female.*"

And so Allah makes things clear to you so you won't do anything wrong, (and remember that) Allah knows about all things. [176]

The Banquet Table

5 Al Mā'idah
Late Medinan Period

☞ Introduction

This chapter was revealed over many months in Medina near the later days of the Prophet's mission. So it addresses a wide variety of issues, many of them reflecting the intense interfaith dialogues going on within the city. The memorable lines contained in the middle of verse three, which speak of the completing of Islam as a way of life, were revealed during the Prophet's last pilgrimage in the year 632.

Some believe that that passage may have been the last Qur'anic revelation the Prophet received. It was this passage that led many of Muhammad's closest followers to conclude that the ministry of their beloved guide was coming to a close. The Prophet reportedly said of this chapter: "The chapter of the Banquet Table has been revealed as the last stage in the revelation of the Qur'an. Therefore, take what has been pronounced as lawful within it as lawful forever, and take what has been pronounced unlawful in it as unlawful forever." *(Ma'ariful Qur'an)*

In the Name of Allah,
the Compassionate, the Merciful

O you who believe! Fulfill your obligations!

You're allowed (to eat) all domestic livestock, except for (the animals) that have been forbidden to you by mention (of their names or categories).

You're also forbidden to hunt (wild animals) while you're under (pilgrimage) restrictions, and Allah certainly makes rules that He wants. [1]

O you who believe! Don't violate (the holiness) of the symbols of Allah, nor violate the holy month (of *Hajj*) nor (the animals) brought for sacrifice nor the decorations that identify them nor the safety (of those who visit) the Sacred House looking for the bounty and approval of their Lord.

However, when you're freed from the restrictions of the holy places and pilgrim's clothes, you may go hunting (animals for food) once more.

Don't let (your) hatred for some people, who once kept you out of the Sacred Masjid, lead you into being spitefully wrong in return.

Help each other in righteousness and mindfulness (of Allah), but don't help each other in sinfulness or aggression.

Be mindful of Allah, for Allah is strict in the final outcome. [2]

Some Dietary Guidelines

You're forbidden to (eat the following things):

➤ Meat from animals that died by themselves
➤ Blood
➤ Pork
➤ Anything that was dedicated to any other name besides Allah's name
➤ Anything that was killed by strangling, a blunt strike, falling or by being slashed to death
➤ Anything that's been (partly) eaten by a wild animal - unless you're able to slaughter it (properly)
➤ And anything that was sacrificed on stone (altars).

You're also (forbidden) to divide (up meat portions among people) by drawing marked (arrowheads) to make random selections, for that method is immoral.

This day, those who cover over (the truth of Allah) have given up all hope of (destroying) your way of life.

So don't be afraid of them; rather, fear only Me. This day, I have perfected your way of life for you, completed My favor upon you and have chosen for you Islam as your way of life.

If anyone is forced by desperate hunger (to eat the forbidden things that were mentioned before), with no desire to do wrong, (then they may eat the forbidden foods for survival purposes only), for Allah is forgiving and merciful. [3]

Now they're asking you what else is allowed for them (to eat), so tell them, "*You're allowed to (eat) anything that's healthy and pure and also what you've taught your trained hunting animals (to catch), as you were already directed by Allah.*

"*(You may) eat what they capture for you, but be sure to declare the name of Allah over it. Be mindful of Allah, for Allah is quick in taking account.*" [4]

This day, everything healthy and pure has been made lawful for you.

The (ritually slaughtered) food of those who received scripture in the past is also lawful for you, and your food is lawful for them.

(With regards to marriage, you're allowed to marry) good, believing women, and (you may also marry) good women from among those who received scripture before your time, but only if you give them their required marriage gifts and only if you desire decency and not lustful behavior or secret affairs.

If someone rejects (faith in Allah), then his deeds will be rendered useless, and in the next life he'll be among the losers. [5]

Preparing for Prayer

O you who believe! When you prepare yourselves for prayer, wash your faces and your hands up to the elbows.

Wipe the top of your heads (with water), and (wash) your feet to the ankles. If you're in a state of greater impurity, then bathe your whole body.

However, if you're sick, on a journey, answered the call of nature or were intimate with (your spouses) and you can't find any water (to wash yourselves), then you can take either clean sand or soil and use it to wipe your faces and hands.

Allah doesn't want to put you into any hardship; rather, (He wants to) purify you and complete His favor towards you, so you can be thankful. [6]

Remember the Favors of Allah

Remember the favors of Allah that have been bestowed upon you, and remember His covenant that He concluded with you when you said, "*We hear, and we obey.*"

Be mindful (of Allah) for Allah knows what you're thinking. [7]

O you who believe! Stand forth firmly for Allah as witnesses to fair dealing.

Don't let the hatred of others towards you make you swerve towards injustice or towards being unfair (to them in return). Be fair, for that's the closest to being mindful (of Allah).

So be mindful then, for Allah is well-informed of everything you do. [8]

Allah made a promise to those who believed and who did what was morally right that they'll receive forgiveness and a great reward. [9]

Whoever rejects (their natural faith in Allah) and denies Our (revealed) verses will be among the companions of the burning blaze. [10]

Allah Protected the Prophet from Harm

Background Info... v. 11

A man named Ghawrath met with the leaders of the hostile tribes of the desert, namely the Muhareb and Ghatafan tribes, and asked if they wanted him to kill Muhammad. They agreed and asked him how he could possibly accomplish that. He replied that he would take Muhammad by surprise. Ghawrath bided his time and kept an eye out for an opportunity to approach his prey.

One day, he saw Muhammad sitting alone under the shade of a tree with his sword on his lap. He approached him and casually asked if he could have a look at the blade. The Prophet handed it to him, and Ghawrath drew it and immediately pointed it at the Prophet menacingly, though he couldn't bring himself to thrust it in for the kill.

Finally, he asked him, "Muhammad, aren't you afraid?" Muhammad replied that he was not. Then Ghawrath said two or three times, "Who will protect you from me now?" Muhammad answered, "Allah will."

Ghawrath hesitated and then suddenly dropped the sword. Muhammad picked it up and called to his nearby companions. While the assailant was still sitting there, Muhammad narrated the incident and then Ghawrath was allowed to go free.

Some time later, Muhammad was visiting the Jewish neighborhood of the Banu Nadir, seeking their assistance in settling a blood-money suit brought by a desert tribe against one of the companions who had killed two of their men.

Ka'b ibn Ashraf, the Jewish leader, invited the Prophet into his courtyard and bade him and his companions to sit under the shade of a wall while he ostensibly went to order food to be made. Ka'b then retreated into another room and told a man named 'Amr ibn Jahsh ibn Ka'b to drop a heavy stone from the roof down upon Muhammad to kill him.

Just before the man could do the deed, however, Angel **Jibra'il** came and warned the Prophet, who promptly got up and left. This verse was revealed soon afterwards, referencing both incidents, and was meant to emphasize that Allah would protect this prophet until the end of his mission. (*Asbab ul-Nuzul, Ibn Kathir*)

O you who believe! Remember the favor of Allah that He bestowed upon you when certain people made plans to move their hands against you, but He restrained their hands from ever reaching you.

So then be mindful of Allah, and the believers should trust in Allah! [11]

An Appeal to Jews and Christians

And so it was that Allah made a covenant with the Children of Israel.

We appointed twelve scouts from among them (to go into the land of Canaan to gather intelligence in preparation for their entry).

Allah had already told (the Children of Israel), "*I'll be with you as long as you establish regular prayer, give in charity, believe in My messengers, respect them, and loan to Allah a beautiful loan.*

"*For sure, I'll erase your shortcomings and admit you into gardens beneath which rivers flow. If any of you cover over (your ability to have faith) after this, then he's truly wandered far from the even path.*" [12]

However, because (the Children of Israel) broke their agreement, We cursed them and allowed their hearts to grow hard.

(They changed the words of revelation) by rearranging them from their (proper) places, and they forgot a good part of the message that was sent to them.

Even still you'll find many of them engaged in new trickery, *but forgive them and try to overlook (their shortcomings), for Allah loves those who are good.* [13]

We also took a covenant from those who call themselves Christians, but they forgot most of the message that was sent to them.

That's why We've let them become disunited in mutual envy and hatred of each other, even until the Day of Assembly.

Allah will soon inform them (of the true meaning) of that in which they were engaged. [14]

Followers of Earlier Revelation! Our Messenger has come to you revealing many things that you used to hide in (your religious) scriptures and passing over many (practices of the past that are now unnecessary). A (new) **LIGHT** and a clear scripture have come to you from Allah. [15]

With these Allah will guide any who seek His good pleasure towards the pathways of peace and safety.

Furthermore, He'll lead them out of darkness and into a light, by His will, and lead them to a straight path. [16]

On Judeo-Christian Claims

Those who say that God is 'Esa, the Messiah, the son of Maryam, are covering over (the real truth).

Say to them, "*Who has the power to hold back Allah if He wanted to destroy the Messiah, the son of Maryam, his mother and everyone else on earth?*

"*To Allah belongs the control of the heavens and the earth and everything in between. He creates whatever He wants, for Allah has power over all things.*" [17]

The Jews and the Christians say, "*We're the sons of God, and He loves us (above all others).*"

Then ask them, "*So, why will He punish you for your sins (if you don't repent of them)? No way! You're only mortals from among the (many peoples) that He's created. He forgives whomever He wants, and He punishes whomever He wants.*

"*The control of the heavens and the earth and all that's in between them belongs to Allah, and back to Him is the final destination.*" [18]

Followers of Earlier Revelation! Now Our Messenger has come to you making (things) clear for you after a pause in (the chain of) Our messengers. That way you won't be able to say, "*No bearer (of good news) or warner ever came to us!*"

Now a bearer (of good news) and a warner has come to you, and Allah has power over all things. [19]

The Children of Israel and the Promised Land

Recall when Musa said to his people, "*My people! Remember Allah's favor towards you when He placed prophets within your midst, and when He placed you in charge (of your own destiny after you were enslaved in Egypt) and how He gave you what He hadn't given to any other nation. [20]

"My people! Enter the holy land, which Allah has assigned to you, and don't turn back, for then you'll be among the losers." [21]

"But Musa!" they cried. "There's a powerful nation already here in this land, and We'll never be able to enter it unless they leave. If they go away, then, and only then, can we go in!" [22]

However, two God-fearing men - upon whom Allah had granted His favor - came forward and (boldly) suggested, "Enter (their main stronghold) through a certain entrance (that we discovered on our scouting mission).

"When you're inside (the walls of the city), victory will be yours, so trust in Allah if you really have faith." [23]

(Yet, many of the people persisted in their cowardice) and said, "Musa! As long as they're present we'll never be able to enter this land - even until the end of time! You and your Lord can go and fight while we sit here (and watch)." [24]

(Musa) called out, "My Lord! I only have power over myself and my brother, so separate us from these rebellious people!" [25]

(Allah) answered, "So indeed it shall be. This land will be forbidden for them for forty years. Until then, they'll wander aimlessly in the wilderness, but don't feel depressed on account of these rebellious people." [26]

The Story of Habeel and Qabeel

Background Info... v. 27-31

According to early Jewish scholars, Adam apparently had to allow his children to marry each other, given that there were no other people around for that purpose (a logical conclusion).

One of Adam's daughters, however, was very beautiful and desirable, thus setting up a potentially tense competition between his two eldest sons. (Jubilees 4:1-12 and Enoch 85:1-10.)

Many early Muslim commentators have also adopted this view and repeated this explanation in their commentaries, including Ibn Kathir. According to the story, Qabeel (Cain) and Habeel (Abel) both desired to be married to her, and they quarreled about it.

To settle the dispute, both men had to offer something to Allah in sacrifice. Habeel's sacrifice was accepted, while Qabeel's was not, (as evidenced by it not catching fire,) and that's the reason why Qabeel was so driven by anger that he would take the life of his brother. It was, then, the first recorded crime of passion.

R elate to them the story of the two sons of Adam in all accuracy. They both presented an offering (to Allah), but it was accepted from one, though not from the other. (In a jealous rage, Qabeel) said to his brother, "*I'm going to kill you*!"

"*Allah (only) accepts offerings,*" (Habeel) replied, *"from those who are mindful (and sincere to Him)*." [27]

(Then he tried to reason with his angry brother), saying, "*If you raise your hand against me to kill me, I won't raise my hand against you to kill you, for I fear Allah, the Lord of All the Worlds*. [28]

"*As for me, I want you take my sins upon yourself to add them with yours, for then you'll become a companion of the Fire, and that's the payback of all those who do wrong*." [29]

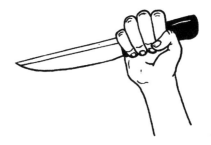

(Qabeel's jealous) soul incited him to murder his brother, and so he killed him and became hopelessly lost. [30] Then Allah sent a raven, scratching on the ground, to show him a way to hide the body of his brother.

"*I'm doomed!*" he cried out. "*Couldn't I (at least have been) like that raven over there and buried my brother's body?*" Then sorrowful regret began to rise up within him. [31]

It was for the sake (of that crime) that We made it a principle for the Children of Israel that if anyone took a life, unless it be (to punish) a murder or to prevent the spread of chaos in the land, that it would be as if he had murdered the whole of humanity.

On the other hand, if anyone saved a life, it would be as if he had saved the life of the whole of humanity.

However, even though Our messengers came to them with clear evidence (of the truth) - even after that many of them continued to commit abuses in the land. [32]

The Most Severe Punishment

The punishment for those who wage war against Allah and His Messenger, and who strive hard to cause chaos and murder throughout the land, is execution or crucifixion or the cutting off of their hands and feet from opposite sides or (at the very least) exile from the land.

That's the humiliation that they'll receive in this world, but an even more painful punishment awaits them in the next, except for those who repent before they fall into your power, for in that case know that Allah is forgiving and merciful. [33-34]

The Best Goal to Seek

O you who believe! Be mindful of Allah. Aspire to get closer to Him, and exert your utmost in His cause so you can be successful. [35]

As for those who cover over (their inner knowledge of the truth), even if they had everything in the whole wide world, *and even double that*, and offered it as a ransom on the Day of Assembly, no offers to avoid punishment will be accepted - and their punishment will be painful! [36]

Their only wish will be to get out of the Fire, but they'll never be able to escape from it, for their punishment will endure. [37]

The Punishment for Stealing

As for the thief, male or female, cut off the hand of both by way of payback, for this is a fitting (example of poetic justice) from Allah as a consequence for (the sin) they earned, and Allah is powerful and wise. [38]

Though, if (the thief) repents after his crime and reforms himself, then Allah will turn to him (in forgiveness), for Allah is forgiving and merciful. [39]

Don't you know that the control of the heavens and the earth belongs to Allah? He punishes whomever He wants, and He forgives whomever He wants, for Allah has power over all things. [40]

Facing Down the Hypocrites of Medina

Background Info... v. 41

Muhammad (p) could not read or write Arabic, and he certainly did not know how to read or understand Hebrew. When the rabbis of Medina would quote from the Torah in their discussions with Muhammad, some of them would purposely leave out some lines as they translated from Hebrew into Arabic in order to keep some information secret. Jewish converts to Islam would often point this out to the Prophet. (See 2:100-103.) A Jewish man of Khaybar committed adultery, and based upon his high status his fellow Jews were reluctant to apply any harsh punishment to him.

They resolved to send him to Muhammad (p) for judgment on the pretence that if he ruled in favor of the flogging that the Qur'an called for [24:2], then he would be a secular leader in their eyes, and they could follow him. However, if he ruled in favor of stoning, as the Torah prescribed, then he was an actual force to be reckoned with, and the Jews must be on their guard against him.

They then went to the Prophet who was sitting with some companions in the masjid and asked what they should do about this adulterer. Muhammad remained silent and either called for some rabbinical students to be brought to him or he himself accompanied them to one of their small yeshivas, or religious schools (the reports do not specify).

The Prophet said to the Jewish scholars, "I appeal to you by God who revealed the Torah to Musa. What punishment does the Torah prescribe for an adulterer?" One of the rabbis answered, "They are rubbed with ash, defamed and whipped, and the defamation comes by placing both guilty parties back to back on a donkey that is led around the streets."

The others present affirmed their agreement, but the Prophet noticed that one man among them was keeping silent. The Prophet was told that his name was Ibn Surya, and then he appealed to him for his answer to the question, making him swear an oath to God to be truthful.

When Ibn Surya replied that the actual punishment was death, the Prophet further questioned him, saying, "When is the first time in which you disobeyed the order of Almighty God?" Ibn Surya replied, "One of our ancient king's relatives committed adultery, and the stoning was put off.

Then a lesser noble also was found to have been adulterous, and the king wanted him stoned. However, his family objected, saying that they wouldn't let their relative be stoned unless the king's relative was stoned first. It was then that they compromised on the punishment among themselves (and lessened it)."

The Prophet then asked a rabbi to read from the Torah about adultery, and the man began to read the appropriate section from a scroll, but he kept his finger over the verse calling for stoning and read the verses before and after it. The Jewish convert to Islam, 'Abdullah ibn Salam, (also a former rabbi) informed the Prophet that the first rabbi had skipped a line, and he asked the man to remove his finger and read the verse. When he did, the Prophet then answered, "I judge by what is in the Torah."

Then he ruled that the adulterers were to be stoned. The adulterous couple was then taken out and stoned, but the Prophet did not take part in it. This verse was revealed concerning this and other similar affairs in which the Jews asked for Muhammad's rulings on various issues. (Asbab ul-Nuzul)

Messenger! Don't lose yourself in grief over those who race each other into rejection, (whether it be from) among those (Arab hypocrites) who say, 'We believe' with their lips, but whose hearts are devoid of faith, or it be among the Jews (of Medina), who will listen to any lie and accept (any slander) told to them by people who never even met you!

They switch words from their proper sequence, and they say, "If (Muhammad) gives you (what you like to hear,) then take it, but if not, then beware."

If Allah wants to put someone into utter turmoil, you can do nothing for them against Allah (and His plan). (The ones to whom He does that) are those whose hearts Allah has no desire to purify. They'll have nothing but disgrace in this world, and in the next life they'll have a severe penalty to pay. [41]

The (Jews of Medina) listen to lies and eat up anything that's been prohibited to them. If they do happen to come to you and ask you to solve their internal disputes, you can either render a verdict or decline to hear the case altogether.

If you decline (to get involved), they can't do any harm to you at all (in their spite). If you choose to decide cases for them, then judge fairly between them, for Allah loves fair judges. [42]

However, why are they coming to you for decisions at all when they have their own Torah right there with them?

It already contains Allah's commandments. Yet, they turn away from it even still, for they're not really all that faithful. [43]

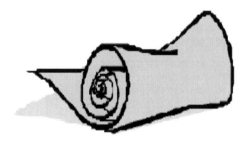

We revealed the Torah, and it contained both guidance and enlightenment (within its pages). The prophets (of old), who surrendered (themselves to Allah's command), used it to judge among the Jews, and the rabbis and legal scholars (also used it to render their judgments, as well).

(They were given the job of protecting and living by) the portion of Allah's Book that was entrusted to them, and they witnessed to their duty.

Therefore, (you Jews of Medina), don't be afraid of (disappointing mere) people. Rather, be afraid of (disappointing) *Me*, and don't sell My (revealed) verses for a petty price. If anyone judges by any other standard than what Allah has revealed, then they're truly covering over (the truth). [44]

We decreed for them in (the Torah): "*A life for a life, an eye for an eye, a nose for a nose, an ear for an ear, a tooth for a tooth, and a wound in exchange for a wound.*"

Now (this principle has been amended,) so if anyone chooses to refrain from retaliating, for (the sake of) charity, then it's an act of atonement for himself. If anyone judges by any standard other than what Allah has revealed, then they're truly wrongdoers. [45]

We sent 'Esa, the son of Maryam, following in their footsteps, to affirm the (truth of the) Torah that had come before him, and We gave him the Injeel, in which there was both guidance and enlightenment, as an affirmation of the Torah that had come before him.

(The Injeel) was a source of guidance and also admonition for those who were mindful (of Allah). [46]

Therefore, let the people of the Injeel judge by what Allah revealed in it. If anyone judges by any standard other than what Allah has revealed, then they're truly rebellious. [47]

Revelations are the Tools for Making Good Judgment

Background Info... v. 48

Four leading Jewish men of Medina, including K'ab ibn Asad and Shas ibn Qays, wanted to see if they could corrupt the Prophet away from being sincere in his religion. They went to him and told him that they were the leaders of the Jews, and if they converted then all the Jews would follow them. Their only requirement was that he render a biased judgment in favor of them in a dispute they had with some men of their community. This verse was revealed concerning this incident. (*Asbab ul-Nuzul*)

Now We've sent the Book to you, (Muhammad), in all truthfulness, affirming the scriptures that came before you and safeguarding within it (the truth of the previous revelations), so judge between (the Jews and Christians) according to what Allah has revealed (to you).

Don't follow their petty whims and thus swerve away from the truth that's come to you.

We've given to each one of you (differing religious groups) a legal tradition and a clear method (for dealing with legal issues).

If Allah had wanted, He could've made you all into one community, but He tests you in what He's given you, so forge ahead as if you were racing towards everything virtuous.

Your ultimate return is back to Allah, and He's going to show you (the truth) of those things about which you argued. [48]

Therefore, judge between them according to what Allah has revealed, and don't follow their petty whims.

Be wary of them so they won't seduce you away from what Allah has sent down to you.

If they turn away (and ignore your rulings), then know that Allah wants to punish them for some of their sins. As it is, most people are disobedient! [49]

Are they looking for a (flawed) ruling (that's similar to how people used to judge) in the ignorant (days before Islam?)

For those who are convinced (of the truth in their hearts), who can be a better judge than Allah? [50]

Don't Look to Enemies for Alliance

Background Info... v. 51-53

In his first days in Medina, the Prophet had concluded treaties of mutual security with the three Jewish tribes of the city. After some months it was learned that the Banu Qurayzah Jews were playing both sides of the fence, so to speak.

While publicly appearing to be friendly with the Muslims, they had also invited a delegation of Meccan leaders to a secret summit in their fortress just outside Medina proper.

A group of Muslim riders was sent out to turn the Meccan delegation back, while the senior companions debated what to do about this obvious betrayal. The Muslim patrol was unable to intercept the Meccans, and thus they got through.

This particular passage concerns the case of two men who were present among the Muslims as they debated what to do, and it concerns their alliances with the Jews of Medina.

The first man, 'Ubadah ibn as-Samat, said, "Messenger of Allah, I have many Jewish allies. They appear to be ascendant, but I will turn to Allah and His Messenger and abandon the protection of the Jews. I will look for refuge in Allah and in His Messenger."

Then the hypocrite, 'Abdullah ibn Ubayy, told Muhammad, "I'm a man who's afraid that changing times might

168

O you who believe! Don't take Jews and Christians as your closest allies, for they're only the close allies of each other.

Whoever among you turns to them (for alliances, in place of a believer,) is one of them, for Allah doesn't guide corrupt people. [51]

Do you see those who have a sickness in their hearts? They run eagerly to them after exclaiming, "*We're afraid that changing times might bring disaster down upon us!*"

It may be that Allah will grant a victory or a decision, as He wills, and then they'll be sorry for what they've been hiding within themselves. [52]

Then the believers will be the ones to say, "*Are these (hypocrites) the same ones who swore their strongest oaths by Allah that they were on your side?*"

Whatever they do is of no use, and they're going to be the ones who will lose. [53]

O you who believe! Whoever among you falls away (from following) his (Islamic) way of life should know that Allah will soon produce a people whom He will love - *and who will love Him back*!

They'll be easygoing with other believers, yet stern against the faithless, striving in Allah's way and paying no mind to all the blame that accusers may heap upon them.

That's Allah's favor, which He grants to whomsoever He wills, and Allah embraces all things and is full of knowledge. [54]

Who is Your True Friend?

Your (true) closest allies are Allah, His Messenger and those who believe.

They're the ones who establish prayer, give in charity and who bow down (in sincere worship). [55]

The Fellowship of Allah

> **Background Info... v. 56**
>
> After talking to 'Abdullah ibn Salam, as mentioned in the previous background note, the Prophet walked out of the masjid while people were still inside praying and kneeling. He saw a beggar who appeared to be happy. "Has anyone given you anything?" he asked him. The beggar replied in the affirmative and showed the Prophet a gold ring.
>
> When the Prophet asked who gave it to him, the beggar pointed to the Prophet's cousin, 'Ali ibn Abi Talib. "How did he give it to you?" The Prophet asked. The beggar replied that 'Ali had shoved it in his hand while the former was in the process of bowing down in prayer. The Prophet said, "Allah is the greatest," and then this verse was revealed to him. (*Asbab ul-Nuzul*)

Whoever turns towards Allah, His Messenger and the believers – *that's the fellowship of Allah* - and they shall be victorious! [56]

Don't Ally with those Who Disrespect You

O you who believe! Don't take those who mock and belittle your way of life as best friends, whether from among those who received a scripture before you or from among those who reject (the truth). Be mindful of Allah if you're true believers. [57]

> **Background Info... v. 58-59**
>
> For a time, whenever the Muslim call to prayer was announced in Medina, some Jews made it a point to tease the Muslims on their way to the masjid by mocking the prayer positions and laughing. This passage was revealed in response. (*Asbab ul-Nuzul*)

When you announce your call to prayer, they mock and belittle it, for they're a people who have no understanding. [58]

Say to them, "*You Followers of Earlier Revelation, are you making fun of us for no other reason than that we believe in Allah and in the revelation that came down to us, as well as in the revelations that came before us? (It may just be) that most of you are rebellious (against Allah)*." [59]

> ### Background Info... v. 60
>
> A number of Jews went to Muhammad and asked him in which prophets he believed. He began his reply by reciting verse 2:285, which mentions that Muslims must accept all true prophets from Allah
>
> When Muhammad then mentioned that he believed in 'Esa (Jesus), the Jews rejected his answer saying, "We swear to Allah that we've never heard of a more unfortunate religion both in this life and in the afterlife than yours, and we don't know any religion more evil than yours." This verse was revealed in response. (*Asbab ul-Nuzul*)

Say to them, "*Should I tell you about something worse than those (people, whose religion that you're ridiculing), and for which Allah took (your ancestors) to task?*

"*Those who had Allah's curse and wrath drawn over them, some of whom were like apes and pigs, and they were the servants of falsehood. They're much worse in status and that much farther astray from the even path!*" [60]

When they come to you, they say, "*We believe (in Allah), too*," but they're really coming with rejection (of your teachings) on their mind, and when they leave you,

they go out with the same (sentiment), and Allah knows all about what they're hiding. [61]

You see most of them rushing into sin and misbehavior and eating whatever they've been prohibited to eat. *What they're doing is pure evil!* [62]

Why aren't their rabbis and legal scholars admonishing them against using sinful language and eating what they've been prohibited to eat? *(The lies) they're promoting are pure evil!* [63]

Don't Think that Allah as Miserly

> ### Background Info... v. 64
>
> A Jewish man of Medina named Nabbash was ridiculing the Prophet for asking for donations to support his cause. Another Jew named Finhas often chided Muslims by saying, "God's hands are tied up," in effect, suggesting that Allah was a miser Who didn't spend of His bounty for the benefit of humanity. This verse is a reply to that statement. (*Asbab ul-Nuzul*)

The Jews (of Medina) have said, "*Allah's hand is tied up*." Well, let *their* hands be tied up, and let them be cursed for what they've said.

No way! Both of His hands are stretched out wide, and He expends as He wills. The revelation that's coming to you from your Lord causes belligerency and rejection to grow in most of them!

As it is, We've instilled antagonism and hatred among them that will last even

171

until the Day of Assembly. Every time they stoke the fires of war, Allah extinguishes them, though they persist in trying to cause chaos in the land. Allah has no love for those who cause chaos. [64]

If only the Followers of Earlier Revelation would've believed and been mindful (of their duty to Allah), then We would've glossed over their shortcomings and admitted them into gardens of delight. [65]

If only they would've held firmly to the Torah, the Injeel and all the revelation that was sent to them from their Lord, then they would've enjoyed themselves from every side.

Although there are men from among them who are on the right track, most of them participate in sinful conduct. [66]

A Call to the Jews and Christians

> **Background Info... first part v. 67**
>
> The Prophet explained why the first half of this verse came to him, saying, "When Allah, the Exalted, sent me with my message, I was overwhelmed with it, and I knew that many people were against me."
>
> This call to action reminded him about the importance of fulfilling the duty that Allah had laid upon him. A'ishah said that anyone who says that Muhammad ever hid anything from the revelation was a liar and that if he ever were to hide a verse, it would have been this one. (Bukhari, Muslim)

Messenger! Proclaim what's been revealed to you from your Lord, for if you don't, then you will have failed to deliver the message.

> **Background Info... second part v. 67**
>
> The second half of this verse was revealed to alleviate the Prophet's fear of being murdered by assassins in his sleep. He was with his wife A'ishah one night, but he remained awake and uneasy.
>
> When she asked him why he wasn't sleeping, he said, "I wish there was a good man to watch over us tonight." A'ishah then narrated that while they were talking, they heard a noise outside their door that sounded like weapons being clanked together. The Prophet called to the unknown people outside of his door, and two trusted men, Sa'ad and Hudhayfah, answered that they were coming to stand guard over his house.
>
> The Prophet then slept for a time but then woke up and recited this new verse, "Allah will defend you..." He then called out to his volunteer guardians and asked them to go home, for Allah would look after him. (Tirmidhi)

Allah will defend you from the people (who seek to harm you), for Allah doesn't guide those who reject (His message.) [67]

Say to them, "*Followers of Earlier Revelation! You have no (legitimacy) unless you hold firmly by the Torah, the Injeel and all the revelation that has come to you from your Lord.*"

(Sadly), it's the very revelation itself that you've been receiving from your Lord that's making most of them increase in belligerency and rejection, but don't be worried over people who reject (Allah). [68]

Those (Muslims) who believe, along with the Jews, the Sabians and the Christians, anyone who believes in Allah and the Last Day and who does what's morally right, they'll have no cause for sorrow or regret. [69]

And so it was that We made a covenant with the Children of Israel and sent them messengers. However, every time a messenger came to them with what they didn't want (to follow) - *they called some of them imposters, and others they killed!* [70]

They didn't think there would be any dangerous repercussions from it, so they became blind and deaf (to faith).

Yet, even then, Allah kept turning towards them (to give them more chances), though many of them remained blind and deaf (to faith). Allah was watching what they were doing. [71]

On the Trinity

Those who say that Allah is the Messiah, the son of Maryam – they're covering over (the truth)!

The Messiah, himself, said, "*Children of Israel! Serve Allah, the One Who is my Lord and your Lord.*"

Whoever makes partners with Allah, well, Allah will forbid him entry into the Garden, and instead the Fire will be his home – and the corrupt will have no one to help them. [72]

Those who say that Allah is one of three (in a trinity) are covering over (the truth, as well), for there is no god but the *One* God.

If they don't stop what they're saying, then a painful punishment will overtake those among them who cover over (their awareness of the truth). [73]

So why don't they turn to Allah and ask for His forgiveness? Allah is forgiving and merciful! [74]

The Messiah, the son of Maryam, was no more than a messenger, and *many messengers passed away before him*. His mother was an honest woman - *they both had to eat food (like any other mortal human being).*

Do you see how Allah is making His proofs clear for them? Yet, look how they're deceived away (from the truth)! [75]

Ask them, "*Are you going to serve something besides Allah - something that has no power to bring you any harm or benefit? (Well, then remember that) Allah is the Hearing and the Knowing.*" [76]

Then say to them, "*Followers of Earlier Revelation! Don't go beyond the boundaries in your way of life without any justification, nor should you follow the fickle whims of the nations who went astray before you, for they've misled many from the even way.*" [77]

Jews must not Ally with those Opposed to Allah

Background Info... v. 78-81

The Jews of Medina were used to making tribal alliances with the pagan Arabs around them. The Old Testament, however, is very clear and forbids Jews from having such alliances, let alone friends, from the ranks of idolaters.

Yet, the Jews of Medina, particularly the Banu Nadir and the Banu Qaynuqa, forged these alliances of mutual protection and friendship with the pagan

tribes and with the Quraysh of Mecca, culminating in the grand alliance of Jews and pagans that resulted in the Siege of Medina. Islam barely survived, and this desperate time provides the context for the serious tone in this passage.
(Ibn Kathir)

Those who covered up (Allah's truth) from among the Children of Israel were cursed by Dawud's own tongue and also by 'Esa, the son of Maryam, for their disobedience and constant violation (of Allah's law). [78]

They rarely discouraged each other from the immorality in which they themselves used to indulge, and their actions were quite evil! [79]

Now you see many of (the Jews of Medina) turning towards the faithless (idol-worshippers for alliances), and the deeds that they're sending ahead for themselves are quite evil, indeed!

Allah's anger is upon them, and they will linger in eternal damnation. [80]

If only they would've put their faith in Allah and in the Prophet and in what was revealed to him, then they would've never taken (idol-worshippers) for allies. However, most of them are disobedient. [81]

How do True Christians View Islam?

(Muhammad,) you're going to find that out of all the people who hate the believers, the Jews (of Medina) and the idol-worshippers (of Mecca) are the strongest (in their hostility).

However, those whom you'll find to be nearest to the believers in love are those who say, "*We are Christians*," for among them are priests devoted to learning and monks who have given up the world, and they're not arrogant. [82]

When they hear what was revealed to the Messenger, you see their eyes overflow with tears for they recognize the truth of it.

Then they pray, "*Our Lord! We believe! Record us among the witnesses.* [83]

"*What can hold us back from believing in Allah and in the truth that has come to us, since we've always been yearning for our Lord to admit us to the company of the righteous?*" [84]

Allah will reward them for what they've said with gardens beneath which rivers flow – *and there they shall remain* - and that's how Allah rewards (those who do) good. [85]

However, those who reject (the truth) and call Our (revealed) verses nothing more than lies will be companions of the raging blaze. [86]

All Things in Moderation

O you who believe! Don't forbid the good things that Allah has allowed for you. Just don't overindulge (in lawful things), for Allah has no love for the overindulgent. [87]

How to Pay for a Broken Promise

Background Info... v. 88

During one of his speeches, Muhammad reminded people about the seriousness of the Day of Judgment, and many left the gathering in tears. Ten men gathered in a home. Among them were **Abu Bakr, 'Ali ibn Abi Talib, 'Abdullah ibn Mas'ud and Salman al-**Farsi, and they swore that they would fast every day, pray all night, never sleep in a bed, never eat meat, and dedicate their swords to Allah's cause.

When the Prophet heard about this, he called them together and said, "Do you think it's right that you made the oath that you did?" They replied that they did it for the sake of righteousness.

The Prophet then said, "I didn't command you to do like that. Your bodies have rights upon you, so fast but then eat, pray but then sleep, and also eat meat. Whoever objects to my way is

175

not of me." Then the Prophet went out and delivered a speech in which he said:

"What's wrong with some people? They forbid sex, food, perfume, sleep and the pleasures of this world. I have not ordered you to be priests or monks, for it is foreign to my faith to give up meat and sex, as it is also foreign to renounce the world and live like a hermit.

The trial for my people is fasting, and the renunciation of the world for them is *jihad* (struggling in Allah's cause), so serve Allah and never make any partners with Him, for the people who came before you were ruined by extremism.

"They were hard on themselves, and so Allah became hard on them, You see the ruins of their monasteries and hermit caves."

This verse was revealed to reinforce that legitimate needs must not be curtailed in extreme ways. (*Asbab ul-Nuzul*)

Background Info... v. 89

In a direct continuation of the events surrounding the previous background note, the ten men who made such an extreme oath to worship non-stop then asked the Prophet what they should do about their previously made pledge, and this verse was revealed giving them a way to rid themselves of it, though with a penalty to pay. (*Asbab ul-Nuzul*)

Allah won't hold you to any impossible things that you (foolishly) swear (to do), but He will hold you to account for your serious pledges (that you make and then fail to fulfill).

So to make up for breaking (an impossible) promise, you must feed ten poor people with what you would normally feed your family, or you may clothe them, instead, or free a bonded servant.

If all of these options are too difficult for you, then fast for three days.

That will make up for the (foolish) promises (you cannot keep) - but safeguard (all) your (serious) promises!

This is how Allah explains His verses clearly for you so you can be thankful. [89]

Eat from the resources that have been provided for you by Allah, and be mindful of Allah - *the One in Whom you believe*. [88]

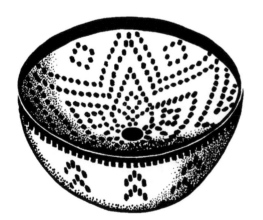

Liquor and Gambling are Now Forbidden

their wine jugs in the streets of Medina, causing it to collect in great puddles.
(Ibn Kathir)

Background Info... v. 90-92

Very early in the Medinan period, 'Umar ibn al-Khattab had asked the Prophet for a definitive ruling on alcohol, and verses 2:219-220 were revealed, which called it more harmful than good. On another occasion, Umar asked again, and 4:43 came in response, which forbade people to offer prayers while drunk. The final prohibition in this verse came about due to a drunken rampage of the Prophet's uncle Hamza.

'Ali' ibn Abi Talib was making preparations for his marriage to the Prophet's daughter Fatimah. He went out to saddle his two camels and was intending to go to some Jewish goldsmiths to buy some jewelry to present to his bride-to-be at the wedding banquet, but when he came upon his camels, he found they were hacked to death.

He cried out in anguish and asked those near the stable who had done such a thing. He was told that Hamza was at a drinking party with some friends of his from Medina and that a singer with them had sang, "Hamza, there are some old camels tied up out in the yard. Go and drive your sword in their flesh." Hamza staggered out and hacked the camels up and took some meat back to the party.

In distress, 'Ali ran straight to the Prophet to tell him what had happened. When he was informed, the Prophet went immediately to the house where the party was taking place. He began to berate Hamza for his violent act, but Hamza, who had swollen eyes from his binge drinking, told the Prophet, "You're nothing but the slave of my father."

The Prophet knew he was drunk and left. This passage was revealed making liquor forbidden, and it is said that when the people heard it, they were dumping

Oyou who believe! Truly, liquor and gambling, stone altars (dedicated to idols) and (making random choices to decide distributions of goods by blindly picking marked) arrowheads (from a bag) are all the disgraceful works of Shaytan, so forsake them so you can be successful! [90]

Shaytan wants to stir up hostility and hatred among you with liquor and gambling, so as to hinder you from remembering Allah and (also to hinder you) from prayer. Won't you give up (your bad habits)? [91]

Obey Allah and obey the Messenger, and be cautious (of what will do you harm).

If you turn back, then know that Our Messenger must only proclaim (the message) clearly. [92]

Your Past Sins are Forgiven

Those who believe and who do what's morally right won't be held responsible for (the alcohol or gambling proceeds) they've consumed (in the past), just so long as they're mindful (of Allah) and believe, *while doing what's morally right.*

Again, so long as they're mindful (of Allah) *while holding to faith.* And again, so long as they're mindful (of Allah), *and then do what's good,* for Allah loves those who are good. [93]

Hunting Restrictions in Mecca

O you who believe! Allah is going to test you with the hunting prey that comes within reach of your hands and spears, so

He can distinguish who (among you) fears Him sight unseen.

Whoever breaks (the following prohibition) after this will have a painful punishment. [94]

O you who believe! Don't kill any hunted prey while under (pilgrimage) restrictions.

If anyone does that on purpose, then to make up for it a domestic animal equal in value to the one he killed must be brought in offering to the Ka'bah, overseen by two fair people among you.

(He can also make up for it) by feeding poor people or fasting according to the calculated equivalent (of that many meals), so in this way he can feel the seriousness of his action.

Allah forgives what happened in the past, but whoever does it again will find that Allah will exact a penalty from him, for Allah is powerful and a master of payback. [95]

178

However, you are allowed to hunt any prey that lives in or on the sea and to use it for food, as a benefit for yourselves and for those who are traveling.

But again, you're forbidden to hunt game animals on land so long as you're consecrated under (pilgrimage) restrictions.

Be mindful of Allah for He's the One to Whom you'll be gathered back. [96]

Allah made the Ka'bah, the Sacred House, to be a stable refuge for people. (He also sanctified) the sacred (truce) months, the offered animals, and the decorations that identify them, so you can know (by seeing them) that Allah has knowledge of whatever is in the heavens and on the earth and that Allah knows all about everything. [97]

Know that Allah is strict in punishment but also that Allah is forgiving and merciful. [98]

There is no other duty laid upon the Messenger than to proclaim (the message), and Allah knows what you show and what you hide. [99]

> **Background Info... v. 100**
>
> The Prophet was giving a speech in which he said that Allah has cursed those who drink liquor, make it, serve it, sell it or buy it. A bedouin stood up and asked, "Messenger of Allah, I was a merchant in this trade, and I made a lot of money from selling liquor, so will it be to my benefit if I spend those profits in obedience to Allah?"
>
> The Prophet replied, "Even if you spend it during a pilgrimage, in *jihad* or through charity, it won't make any difference to Allah, for Allah accepts nothing but what is wholesome." Then this verse was revealed. (Asbab ul-Nuzul)

Say to them, "*Evil is not equal to what's wholesome, even though evil is so widespread that it seems normal and good to you. Be mindful of Allah, you people of understanding, so you can be successful.*" [100]

Learning to Trust in Allah's Wisdom

> **Background Info... v. 101-102**
>
> One day, the Prophet gave such a stirring sermon in the masjid that the people in general were weeping. In the midst of this outpouring of emotion, a man came forward and asked, "Who is my father?"
>
> Obviously, the man's question was totally inappropriate to the mood of the venue! The Prophet told the man his father's name, and then this passage was revealed. (Bukhari)

O you who believe! Don't ask questions about (trivial) things that would be difficult for you if they were explained to you in detail.

However, if you ask (about religious stipulations) when the Qur'an is being revealed, then they'll be clarified for you.

Allah forgives that (kind of honest questioning), for Allah is forgiving and forbearing. [101]

Now some people before you questioned (their messengers) constantly like that, and eventually they fell into rejection (of Allah). [102]

Allah didn't set up (such superstitions as slitting the ears of she-camels) to mark them (and their milk) as reserved (only for idols), sending (animals) to roam in pastures (as especially blessed by idols), dedicating male-camels if they had a certain number of matings, or reserving she-camels (because they give birth only to female calves).

It's only those who reject (the truth) that have invented such lies against Allah, and most of them have no reasoning ability. [103]

> **Background Info... v. 104**
>
> If a person converted to Islam, the Meccans tried to shame him (or her) by accusing him of turning his back on his ancestors and insulting their longstanding family traditions and memory. This verse was revealed in response. (*Ma'ariful Qur'an*)

When they're told, "*Come to what Allah has revealed, and come to the Messenger,*" they say:

"*The customs of our ancestors are good enough for us.*" However, their (ancestors) had **NO SENSE**, nor did they have any guidance! [104]

O you who believe! Look after your own souls, for no harm can come to you from the wayward people if you cling to guidance.

You're all going to return to Allah, and then He'll explain to you (the true meaning) of all that you did. [105]

Choosing Witnesses for a Will

Background Info... v. 106-108

Two Christian men named Tameem and Adiyy used to make frequent trips between Medina and Mecca. On one journey, a new Muslim from the Quraysh named Budayl went with them, but he became very ill along the way in a place that had no Muslims. Before he died he secretly wrote a will and put it in his bag.

Then he called his two Christian companions and put all of his property into their custody and made them agree to distribute it to his family upon their reaching Medina. When the two men returned to Medina, they gave all the **property to the man's relatives, but they** concealed a prized silver drinking bowl decorated with gold. When the man's family found the written will (that mentioned the bowl in the luggage,) they asked the two men about it, but they swore they never saw it.

They were brought to the Prophet who asked them to swear to Allah that **they didn't have it, and they swore that** they did not, and a ruling was given in their favor. Some time later, the expensive bowl turned up in Mecca with a goldsmith, and the man who had it said he had bought it from Tameem and Adiyy.

Some friends of the deceased took the bowl to Medina and swore by Allah that it had belonged to their dead friend and was a part of his estate; they also claimed that their witness was more reliable than that of the other two men. When summoned once more, the two Christians said that Budayl had sold it to them before his death, that there were no witnesses to the transaction, and that **was why they didn't mention it in the** previous hearing.

The Prophet ruled in favor of Budayl's relatives, and the Christians had to pay for the value of the bowl. This passage was then revealed to give guidance for people who find themselves in similar circumstances. (*Asbab ul-Nuzul*)

O you who believe! Appoint witnesses among yourselves whenever death comes near to one of you (in order to witness the recording of) your will. (Choose) two just people from among you, either from among your own (family) or from outside of it.

If you're traveling through the land and death is about to overtake you, and if you have doubts about (the emergency witnesses you must choose), then stop them after the ritual prayer has ended and ask them to swear an oath to Allah, saying:

"*We don't want any worldly gain in this affair, even if one of our close (relatives stands to gain), nor will we hide any testimony before Allah. If we did that, then we would be acting sinfully.*" [106]

If it becomes known that those two committed the sin (of perjury), then let two others stand up in their place who are (close relatives of the deceased) and thus have a more rightful claim.

Let them swear to Allah, saying, "*We swear that our testimony is more accurate than these other two and that we haven't stretched (the truth), for if we did so then we would be acting wrongfully.*" [107]

That's the most appropriate (thing to say) so they can (be influenced) to give their testimony in the way it was supposed to be done, or (at the very least) so they might fear that the testimony of others might contradict their own testimony.

Be mindful of Allah and listen, for Allah doesn't guide the disobedient. [108]

What will 'Esa Say on Judgment Day?

One day, Allah will gather the messengers together and ask them: "*How (did people) respond (to your preaching)?*"

They will answer, "*We don't have any information about that, for You're the One Who knows what's beyond perception.*" [109]

Allah will then say, "*'Esa, son of Maryam! Recall My favors upon you and your mother. I supported you with the Holy Spirit. (I allowed) you to speak to people in infancy, as well as when you were fully grown.*

"*I taught you the scripture and gave you wisdom, along with the Torah and the*

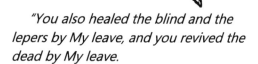

Injeel. You made a bird out of clay by My leave that you breathed to life, and it became a (real) bird by My leave."

"*You also healed the blind and the lepers by My leave, and you revived the dead by My leave.*

"*I prevented the Children of Israel (from harming) you while you were showing them the clear evidence, though the faithless among them said, 'This is nothing more than some kind of magic.'*" [110]

"*I also inspired the disciples to believe in Me and in My messenger, and they said (to you), 'We believe, and you be (our) witness that we're surrendered (to Allah's will).'*" [111]

The Doubting Disciples

Once the disciples said, (in a moment of doubt), "*'Esa, son of Maryam! Can your Lord send down upon us a banquet table from heaven?*"

"*Be mindful of Allah,*" 'Esa answered, "*if you're really (true) believers.*" [112]

They replied, "*We only want to eat from it to satisfy (the doubts) in our hearts, so we can know (for certain) that you're truthful and also to witness a miracle for ourselves.*" [113]

'Esa, the son of Maryam, prayed, "*O Allah, our Lord! Send down upon us a banquet table from the sky so there will be a joyous occasion for the first and the last of us, and also as a sign from You. Provide for us, because You're the best provider.*" [114]

"*I will send it down to you,*" Allah said, "*but if any of you cover over (your ability to have faith) after this, then I'll punish him like I haven't punished anyone else in all the worlds!*" [115]

Esa's Testimony Continues

Allah will say (on Judgment Day): "*'Esa, son of Maryam! Did you tell people, 'Worship me and my mother as gods in place of (the One True) God?*"

"*Glory be to you!*" he'll reply. "*I could never have said what I had no right (to say), and if I ever said something like that, then You would've known about it.*

"*You know what's in my heart, while I don't know what's in Yours, and You know all hidden mysteries.*" [116]

"*I never said anything to them except what You commanded me to say: 'Worship Allah, my Lord and your Lord.' I was their witness while I lived among them. When You took me up (to Heaven), You became their Watcher, and You're a witness over all things.*" [117]

"*If You choose to punish them, well, they're Your servants (to treat as You please), though if You choose to forgive them, (then of course You can because) You're the Powerful and the Wise.*" [118]

Allah will declare, "*This is a day in which the truthful will benefit from their honesty, for they shall (be rewarded with) gardens beneath which rivers flow - and there they shall remain forever!*"

Allah will be pleased with them and they with Him – and that's the greatest success! [119]

To Allah belongs the control of the heavens and the earth and whatever is within them, and He has power over all things. [120]

The Livestock

6 Al An'ām
Late Meccan Period

☞ Introduction

This chapter gets its name from the large number of verses discussing the strange beliefs that the idol-worshippers had about their farm animals. The Qur'an mentions quite a few of them and answers them one at a time. Because most of these verses were revealed in the final years of the worst of the Meccan attacks against the Muslims, we can also see a large number of strong statements, with the words of the idol-worshippers recorded along with the answers Allah is telling the Prophet to give in response.

In the Name of Allah,
the Compassionate, the Merciful

Praise be to Allah, the One Who created the heavens and the earth and (Who) made both the darkness and the light.

Even still, those who cover over (their faith) continue to hold others as equals with their Lord! [1]

He's the One Who created you from clay and then decided the length (of your lives). There's yet another deadline with Him, as well, though you're in doubt about it. [2]

He's (the only) God within the heavens and on the earth. He knows what you hide and what you show, and He knows what you're earning (on your record of deeds). [3]

Yet, no sign from their Lord ever reaches them without their turning away

from it, and now they're denying the truth when it comes to them (this time, as well).

Soon they'll be given more prophecies about what they've been talking against! [4-5]

Don't they see how many generations We destroyed before them, (peoples) whom We had established in the land

184

more firmly than you (people of Mecca are established today)?

We sent abundant rain down upon them from the sky and provided them with streams of flowing water beneath them. Yet, We destroyed them for their sins and let new generations arise after them. [6]

In Answer to the Faithless

Background Info... v. 7

A Meccan idol-worshipper named 'Abdullah ibn Umayyah told the Prophet that he wouldn't believe in him unless he (Muhammad) climbed up to heaven and brought him back a book that mentioned him ('Abdullah) by name and that commanded him to believe in Muhammad as a messenger.

Then 'Abdullah further said that even if this happened, he still wouldn't believe. This verse was revealed in response. (*Asbab ul-Nuzul*)

If We sent a written page down to you that they could touch with their very own hands, those who cover over (their ability to have faith) would be sure to say, "*This is clearly no more than magic!*" [7]

Background Info... v. 8-16

'Abdullah ibn Umayyah, accompanied by an-Nadr ibn al-Harith and Nawfal ibn Khalid, approached the Prophet some time after the revelation of verse 6:7, and the group said once again that they wouldn't believe unless Muhammad brought a book from the sky for them, but this time they added that it should be carried by four angels who would swear that they were from Allah.

This passage was revealed in response. Later on, 'Abdullah did accept Islam, and he was martyred in the Battle of Ta'if. (*Ma'ariful Qur'an*)

They also say, "*So why isn't an angel being sent down to him?*" Though if We *did* send an angel, then the issue would be settled at once, and they would have no more time to delay! [8]

And if We *were* to send down an angel, We would send him (in the form) of a man, and that would cause them to be confused about something they're already confused by! [9]

And so it was (Muhammad) that many messengers before you were ridiculed by their critics, but they were (eventually) surrounded by the very thing at which they laughed. [10]

Say to them, "*Travel throughout the world, and see how those who denied (the truth) were brought to an end.*" [11]

Then ask them, "*Who owns everything in the heavens and the earth?*"

Tell them, *"(It all belongs) to Allah. He wrote down (the rule) of mercy for Himself, and He's going to gather all of you together for the Day of Assembly. There's no doubt about that!*

"Those who don't believe will lose their own souls, for any (and all creatures) that rest within the night or the day belong to Him, and He's the Hearing and the Knowing." [12-13]

Ask them, *"Should I take someone other than Allah for my protector, when He's the Originator of the heavens and the earth? He feeds others, but He is never (in need of being) fed!"*

Say to them, *"I've been ordered to be among the first of those who surrender (to Him), so don't you be among those who make partners (with Allah)."* [14]

Tell them, *"If I were ever to disobey my Lord, then I would be in utter fear of the punishment of a momentous day. On that day, whoever has (the punishment) turned away from him, it will be due only to His mercy, and that will be the clearest success of all."* [15-16]

If Allah touches you with some setback (in your life), there's no one who can remove it but He, and if He touches you with something positive, (know that) He has power over all things!

He is the Irresistible One Who towers over His servants, and He's the Wise and Well-informed. [17-18]

You Know this Message is True

Background Info... v. 19-20

The Meccan leaders went to the Prophet one day and said, "We don't see anyone (important) believing in your message. We asked the Jews and Christians about you, and they said they have no mention or descriptions of you (in their scriptures), so tell us who is testifying to the idea that you're a messenger, as you claim." This passage was revealed in response. (*Asbab ul-Nuzul*)

Ask them, *"So what's the most convincing proof?"*

Then say to them, *"Allah is the witness between you and me that this Qur'an has been revealed to me by inspiration, so I can warn you and all who come into contact with it (of Allah's coming judgment). So can you really declare that there are other gods equal with Allah?"*

Say to them, *"No! I don't testify that (there are many gods besides Him)!"* Then say, *"Truly, He's only One God, and I disown whatever you join with Him."* [19]

Those to Whom We've given holy books (in the past) also recognize (the truth of) this (teaching about only One God), even as they know their own children, but those who've lost their own souls refuse to believe. [20]

The Punishment for only Pretending to Listen

Background Info... v. 25

The most important Meccan leaders stopped to listen to what the Prophet was saying one day. Among them was a widely traveled man named an-Nadr ibn al-Harith, who often told the Quraysh stories from the lands in which he had sojourned. After a few minutes they asked an-Nadr, "What is Muhammad talking about?"

An-Nadr answered, "By the One Who made the Ka'bah, I don't know what he's saying, but I see him moving his lips and talking about nothing more than tales of past peoples, just like the ones I used to tell you about." This verse was revealed in response. (*Asbab ul-Nuzul*)

The Evil Fate of Idolaters

Who's more wrong than the one who invents a lie against Allah or who denies His (revealed) verses? The unjust will definitely never succeed! [21]

One day, We're going to gather them all together and say to those who made partners (with Allah), "*Where are all the partners you claimed (in place of Allah)?*" [22]

There won't be any commotion they can use (as a distraction) other than to say, *"We swear to Allah, our Lord, we never made partners (with Allah)!"* [23]

See how they're going to lie against their own souls! However, (the excuses) they made up will only put them further into trouble! [24]

Among them are some who pretend to listen to you; (therefore, as a punishment) We've cast a veil over their hearts to prevent them from understanding, as well as put a deafening silence in their ears.

Even if they saw every one of the proofs (of Allah), they would never believe in them, even to the point that they come to you and debate.

As it is, those who cover over (their ability to have faith) are already saying, "*These (verses) are nothing more than ancient tales!*" [25]

Background Info... v. 26

This verse concerns the Prophet's pagan uncle, Abu Talib, who offered his nephew protection but refused to accept Islam no matter how much the Prophet

Others just keep themselves away from (hearing the Qur'an) and are thus kept away, but they're only destroying their own souls without their even realizing it! [26]

If you could just see it, when they're placed before the Fire! They're going to cry out, *"If only we could be sent back (for another chance), then we would never deny the proofs of our Lord! We would indeed be on the side of the faithful!"* [27]

But no! What they used to hide will become crystal clear for them, and even if they were returned (to life), they would still fall into forbidden things, for they're truly a bunch of liars! [28]

Then they say, *"There's nothing beyond our lives here on earth, nor will we ever be raised to life again."* [29]

Oh, if you could just see it when they're brought before their Lord! He's going to tell them, *"Isn't this real enough now?"* They'll answer, *"Of course it is, by our Lord!"* Then He'll say, *"So now taste the punishment for rejecting (Me)!"* [30]

Those who deny their meeting with Allah are truly lost, even until the Hour (of Judgment) comes upon them suddenly.

That's when they'll cry out, *"Oh no! We never thought this (would happen)!"*

They will have to bear their own burdens on their backs, and evil are the burdens they're going to bear! [31]

So just what is the life of this world save for entertainment and distraction? The best home (of all) is the home of the next life, (which has been reserved) for those who were mindful (of their ultimate fate), so won't you think deeply on it? [32]

Words of Strength to a Prophet Under Attack

We know all about the stress that their words are causing you, (Muhammad,) but it's not *you* that they're rejecting. It's the (revealed) verses of

Allah that the wrongdoers are condemning. [33]

Even so, other messengers were rejected before you, and they were patient against the criticism they faced, even until Our help finally reached them. No one can change the (commanding) words of Allah.

(That's why) some of the stories of previous messengers have come to you (to give you strength and inspiration). [34]

If their dislike of you is stressful, (you must realize) that even if you (opened) a tunnel in the ground or raised a ladder to the sky and brought them a miraculous miracle, (they would still never believe in you).

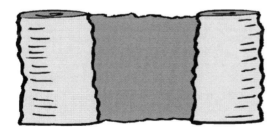

If Allah had wanted, He could've brought them all together into guidance, so don't be affected by (their) ignorance. [35]

The ones who listen will readily accept (your message), but as for the dead (at heart), well, Allah is going to resurrect them and bring them all back to Him anyway. [36]

They ask, "*So why isn't a miracle being sent down to him from his Lord?*"

Answer them by saying, "*Allah is able to send down (miracles if He so chooses),*" but most of them don't understand. [37]

There isn't a creature on the earth nor anything that flies on wings without its being organized into communities just like you.

We haven't left anything out of the Book! All (those creatures) are going to be brought back to their Lord (in the end). [38]

Those who deny Our proofs are deaf and dumb in (self-inflicted) darkness. Whomever Allah leaves to wander (will remain lost), while whomever He wants (to guide) will be placed on a straight path. [39]

Say to them, "*Think about it. If Allah's wrath suddenly overtook you or the Hour (of Judgment) came, would you call upon any other besides Allah? Answer me if you're so honest.*" [40]

"*No way! You would definitely call upon Him! Then, if He so desired, He could take away (the situation) that made you call upon Him in the first place! In that case, you would utterly forget (the idols) that you so often join with Him!*" [41]

The Nations that Turned Away

And so it was that We sent other (prophets) before you to the nations (of the world), and We inflicted (upon those nations) suffering and hardship so they could learn to be humble. [42]

So why didn't they learn to be humble, when the suffering that We sent came upon them? On the contrary, their hearts became harder, and Shaytan made their deeds seem proper and good to them. [43]

When they finally forgot the reminder they had received, We opened the doors to them of every (material blessing), and while they were in the middle of boasting about all (of Our gifts) they were given, *We suddenly seized them*, leaving them (in utter ruin) and despair! [44]

And so the corrupted people were cut off at the root! So praise be to Allah, the Lord of All the Worlds! [45]

Allah's Proofs are Self-Evident

Background Info... v. 46-51

This passage was an answer to the pagans of Mecca who insisted that if Muhammad (p) were a true prophet of Allah, then Allah would have made him rich and given him magical powers. The logic used to answer this charge is simply that Allah has all the power and treasure and that it's not necessary to give those things to a prophet just to prove his claim. (*Ma'ariful Qur'an*)

Now ask them, "*Do you think that if Allah took away your hearing and your sight and sealed up your hearts that any other god besides Allah could restore them to you?*"

Do you see how We explain the proofs in differing ways? Yet, still they turn away! [46]

So then say to them, "*Do you think that if Allah's punishment came upon you suddenly or with fair warning, that anyone else would be destroyed except the unjust?*" [47]

We don't send messengers with any other purpose than to give good news and to warn so that the believers can improve themselves, and, indeed, they'll have nothing to fear nor regret (on the Day of Judgment). [48]

190

However, those who deny Our proofs will have punishment descend upon them because they never prevented themselves from doing wrong. [49]

Say to them, "*I'm not telling you that I have Allah's treasures with me, nor do I know what's being kept hidden, and I'm not telling you that I'm an angel, either. I'm only following what's been revealed to me.*"

Then ask them, "*Are the blind and the seeing the same? Won't you think it over?*" [50]

Warn those who have the worry within themselves of being brought back before their Lord that they won't have anyone to help them nor speak up for them except Him, and for that reason they should be mindful (of Him). [51]

A Society of Equals

> ### Background Info... v. 52-53
>
> One day some chiefs of the Quraysh approached the Prophet's uncle, Abu Talib, and explained that they couldn't be seen in Muhammad's gatherings, as low class people and former slaves were always in attendance.
>
> When Abu Talib told the Prophet, 'Umar ibn al-Khattab, who was present, suggested that perhaps if the Meccan nobles came to attend, the rest of the people would move aside.
>
> Some time later, the Prophet was sitting in a gathering of his followers, and a group of Meccan nobles including 'Utbah, Harith ibn Nawfal and others walked by. They saw Bilal the African, Suhayb the freed Byzantine slave, Salman

> the freed Persian slave and various other men of mixed races and social classes.
>
> The Meccan nobles didn't want to listen to Muhammad in the company of those whom they thought of as commoners, slaves and unworthy poor people, so they asked the Prophet to send them away so they could meet with him alone.
>
> Verse 52 was revealed immediately, telling Muhammad not to turn the commoners and others away just to please the rich and arrogant nobles of his city. (*Asbab ul-Nuzul*)
>
> After this verse was revealed, 'Umar feared he had erred and begged forgiveness from the Prophet. Verse 53 was revealed to comfort 'Umar and explain that this was Allah's way of testing and thus reforming people. (*Ma'ariful Qur'an*)

Don't send away (the common people) who call upon their Lord in the morning and evening, seeking His approving gaze.

You're not responsible for anything they (think or do), nor are they responsible for you. (Therefore, there's no reason for) you to turn (the common people) away, (just because the pretentious people want you to,) for if you did that, then you would become a tyrant yourself! [52]

This is how We test some of them by letting them compare (their social status) with others, so they might say, "*Are these (commoners) the ones whom Allah has favored among us?*"

191

distressed, and he walked alone in a field pensively.

He looked up and saw Angel **Jibra'il** in a cloud, and the angel asked him if he wanted him to make two mountains fall upon Mecca to destroy the people. The Prophet replied that he didn't, and his only desire was for the Meccans to have children who would serve none but Allah. This passage was revealed in response to their mocking and daring. (*Muslim*)

Doesn't Allah know best who the thankful are? [53]

When the (people) who believe in Our (revealed) verses come to you, say to them, "*Peace be upon you.*"

Your Lord has written it upon His (Own nature) to be merciful, so if any of you did sinful deeds in ignorance but then repented and improved (his conduct), then He is forgiving and merciful. [54]

That's Our explanation of the verses (of this Qur'an) so the (self-destructive) path of the bad people can be exposed. [55]

Believe in the One True God

Background Info... v. 56-58

The Meccans used to taunt the Prophet, saying, "So bring down upon us the suffering that you're promising us." It was a way to mock him and show that he was powerless to do it. However, as the Qur'an points out in many places, Allah can punish, but He gives people time for a while so they can come to repent. After a particularly tense exchange with some Meccans who mocked him greatly, the Prophet was

Say to them, "*I'm forbidden to serve those whom you call upon besides Allah.*"

Then say to them, "*I'm not going to follow your foolish whims, for if I did, then I would be going far off the path, and I wouldn't be among the guided.*" [56]

Then say, "*I'm following the clear evidence of my Lord, but you're denying Him. (The punishment that) you (dare) to be hurried on isn't in my power to bring. The command belongs to Allah alone. He speaks the truth and is the best of all Deciders.*" [57]

Finally, say to them, "*If (the punishment) that you (dare) to bring on sooner were in my power to bring, then the issue would be solved right away between me and all of you, for Allah knows who the wrongdoers are.*" [58]

The keys to what is beyond (human) perception, the treasures of which are known to no one save Him, are His alone. He knows what's in the earth and in the sea.

Then (those souls) are brought back to Allah, their true protector. It's in His power to judge, and He's swift in reviewing (their records). [62]

Ask them, "*Who's the One Who can save you from the dark (dangers) of both land and sea, when you're (forced to) call upon Him trembling and in fear, saying, 'If only He would save us, then we would ever be grateful'?"* [63]

Not even a leaf falls without Him knowing it, nor a single grain is lodged in the darkness of the earth, nor is there anything fresh or withered without it already being recorded in a clear ledger. [59]

He's the One Who (temporarily) takes hold of your souls (while you sleep) in the night, and He knows all about what you do in the day.

At dawn He causes you to rise up (from your sleep), so a set number (of days consisting of your life span) can be marked off. In the end, you're going to go back to Him, and then He's going to show you the meaning of all that you did. [60]

He's the Irresistible, towering high over His servants! He's appointed guardians to watch over you even until the time when death comes upon one of you.

Our messenger (angels) take each individual soul, and they never fail in their task. [61]

Then say to them, "*Allah is the One Who can save you from these and from all other miseries – and yet you're still making others equal (with Him)!"* [64]

And then tell them, "*He has the power to send disasters upon you from above you and from under your feet, and (He has the power) to confuse you (and divide you into opposing) factions so you can experience violence from each other.*" Do you see how We explain the verses in different ways so they can understand? [65]

Yet, your people are denying this (message) even though it's the truth. Say to them, "*I'm not responsible for taking care of your affairs.*" [66]

Every message has a set time limit, and soon you will know (the truth)! [67]

Don't Sit with those who Disrespect the Qur'an

Whenever you see people wading into (pointless arguments) about our (revealed) verses, you must turn away from them until they change to a new topic. If Shaytan ever makes you forget this, you can leave the gathering of the wrongdoers the moment you remember. [68]

> **Background Info... v. 69-70**
>
> Some companions approached the Prophet and asked him about verse 68, for they were afraid that since people always end up disagreeing or arguing about something, the mere act of getting together might become a source of sinfulness since argumentative people are always present and eventually start disrespecting Allah or His way of life.
>
> Verses 69-70 were then revealed, explaining that people can go to gatherings and not be held accountable for the vain arguments and useless quibbling of others that may suddenly come out, as long as they have no intention of joining in except to stand up for truth and goodness. If the foolish keep on going, then leave their company. (*Ma'ariful Qur'an*)

Those who are mindful (of Allah) will have no account in this regard, for their only duty is to remind them so that perhaps they can (gain an) awareness (of Allah's truth). [69]

However, you must go away from (the company of) those who treat their way of life as a joke or a game, and who are fooled about the truth of this world's life.

Remind them that every soul destroys itself by its own course of action and that it won't find any best friend nor advocate besides Allah. Though it may offer every kind of bribe (to avoid the penalty it will have to pay), none will be accepted.

That's the fate of those who destroy themselves through their own actions. They'll have nothing to drink but scalding water, and a terrible punishment (awaits them) on account of their (attempt at) covering over (the truth). [70]

Calling to Allah's Guidance

Say to them, "*Should we call upon others besides Allah when they can't do us any good or harm? If we did that then we would be turning back on our heels after having been guided by Allah!*

194

"(We would be) like the one who's been made into a fool by devils: wandering around in the world aimlessly - all the while his companions try to guide him back, saying, 'Look over here!'"

Then say to them, "*The only true guidance is Allah's guidance, and we've been commanded to surrender ourselves to the Lord of All the Worlds and to establish prayers, being mindful (of Him), for He's the One to Whom we're going to be gathered back.*" [71-72]

He's the One Who created the heavens and the earth for a true purpose. The day when He says, "*Be*" is (the day) something is.

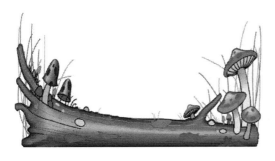

His word is the truth, and all dominion is His on the day when the trumpet will be blown. He knows what's beyond human perception, as well as what's plainly evident, for He's the Wise and Well-informed. [73]

Ibraheem and His Noble Legacy

Background Info... v. 74-83

Ibraheem lived in Mesopotamia nearly four thousand years ago. His people were idol-worshippers, and his own father was an ardent idolater and possibly a maker of idols.

There is a great amount of Jewish legend concerning Ibraheem's father Azar, whom they know as Terah. (Some Muslim scholars of antiquity such as Razi have held that Azar is just a title, with the true name of Ibraheem's father being Tarakh.)

If it is true that Ibraheem's father was a carver of idols, as this lore suggests, then this would have given the young man insight into the futility of idols. One old Jewish story states that Ibraheem's father used to make his son carry small idols in the streets to sell. One day, Ibraheem was tired and sat by a river to rest.

On a whim, he threw one of the idols into the water to see what would happen. He instantly became terrified at the thought of being struck down by lightning or suffering some other horrible fate, but then nothing happened to him. He mused that the idol couldn't even save itself from drowning or punish someone who had disrespected it, and thus he disbelieved in the idols that were made by men's hands.

It happened once that Ibraheem said to his father Azar, "*Are you taking idols for gods? It seems to me that you're a people making an obvious mistake.*" [74]

That's the result (of Our demonstration) to Ibraheem, when We showed him that We have all dominion over the heavens and the earth, and thus he was convinced (that the idols were false). [75]

When the night had overshadowed him, he looked up and saw a (bright) star. "*This is my Lord,*" he had exclaimed, but when (the star) set (below the horizon), he said, "*I don't like things that disappear.*" [76]

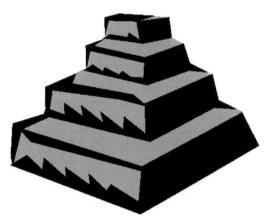

Then he saw the moon rising, and he exclaimed, "*That's my Lord!*"

However, when the moon also vanished (below the horizon), he said, "*Unless my Lord gives me guidance, then I'll be mistaken like the rest of the people.*" [77]

Then he saw the sun rising (in all its glory), and he exclaimed, "*Now that's my Lord! That's the greatest!*"

However, when the sun also vanished (below the horizon), he (realized that Allah was not a mere object that could be seen or felt.

And so when he returned to his city) he proclaimed, "*My people! Now I'm truly free of your making partners (with Allah)! I've set my face upon the One Who initiated the heavens and the earth, and I'll never make partners (with Him).*" [78-79]

His people began to argue with him, so he told them, "*Are you arguing with me about Allah, after He's guided me? I'm not afraid of the partners you've made*

with Him, for nothing happens without My Lord's permission.

"*My Lord encompasses everything within His knowledge, so won't you take a reminder?*" [80]

"*How can I be afraid of those partners you've made in place of Him, when you're not even afraid to make partners with Allah without any authority whatsoever?*

"*So which of our two factions should feel safer then? (Tell me if you think) you know!*" [81]

Background Info... v. 82

When they heard this verse, the companions were afraid and asked the Prophet how anyone can possibly go to heaven, since all have done wrong against their souls (i.e., sinned), even sometimes after having become believers. The Prophet explained that the word *zulm* here, which usually means oppression, darkness or wrongdoing, is to be equated with the sin of *shirk*, or idolatry. (*Ma'ariful Qur'an*) Also see verse 31:13 for the background and result of this verse's message.

"It's only those who believe and who don't confuse their faith with something wrong that are secure, for they're the ones who've been guided." [82]

That was the kind of logic concerning Us that We gave to Ibraheem to use against his people. We raise up whomever We want **STEP-BY-STEP**, for your Lord is full of wisdom and knowledge. [83]

(In time,) We granted him (a son named) Is-haq and (a grandson named) Yaqub, and We guided each of them. Even before them we had guided Nuh, and among (Nuh's) descendants were Dawud, Sulayman, Ayyoub, Yusuf, Musa and Harun. That's how We reward those who do good. [84]

(Also among his descendants were) Zachariah, Yahiya, 'Esa and Ilyas. They were all among the righteous, as were Isma-il, Al Yasa', Yunus and Lut.

We favored each of them above (anyone else in) all the worlds, along with their parents, children and brethren. We chose them and guided them to a straight path. [85-87]

This is Allah's guidance, and He uses it to guide whomever He wants among His servants. If any of them make partners with Him (after knowing the truth), then all their efforts will go to waste. [88]

They were the ones to whom We gave the scriptures, sound judgment and the gift of prophecy. If any (of their descendants) disbelieve in these things, then We'll transfer their obligation to another people who won't reject them. [89]

They were the ones who received Allah's guidance (in the past), so emulate them in guidance. Then say to (the skeptical Meccans), *"I'm not asking you for any reward for all of this. This is no less than a reminder to all the worlds!"* [90]

The Reality before Allah

> **Background Info... v. 91**
>
> Muhammad was speaking with a visiting Jewish rabbi named Malik ibn as-Sayf, and the rabbi became angry when the Prophet pointed out that Allah did

197

They're not thinking highly enough about Allah when they say, "*Allah never sends anything down to mortal men.*"

Then ask them, "*So who sent down the scripture that Musa brought? It was a light and a guidepost for people, but you've turned it into an odd collection of pages for show, while still holding back much of it. Were you taught things that neither you nor your ancestors knew?*"

Say to them, "*Allah (knows the truth);*" then leave them alone to guess and speculate. [91]

This (Qur'an) is the Book that We've sent down to bring blessings and also to confirm whatever came before it, so you can warn (Mecca,) the mother of all cities and all those around it (of Allah's coming judgment).

Those who believe in the next life will believe in this, and they'll guard their prayers strictly. [92]

Who's more wrong than the one who invents a lie against Allah and who says, "*I've been inspired,*" when he hasn't been, or who says, "*I can reveal something just like Allah reveals*"?

If you could only see how the corrupt will be during the confusion of their death throes.

The angels will reach out with their hands (and say), "*Away with your souls. This day you'll get your payment – a humiliating punishment on account of your saying things about Allah against all right and because you arrogantly (rejected) His signs!*" [93]

And so you'll come back to Us - bare and alone – just as We created you the first time.

You'll leave behind everything We ever granted you, and We won't see any of the intercessors accompanying you that you thought were your partners. All relations between you and them will be severed, and all your delusions will have merely led you astray. [94]

What are the Signs of Allah in Nature?

Allah causes grains and seeds to split and sprout, for He brings life from death and death from life. That's how Allah is to you, so how is it that you're so deceived (about His nature)?" [95]

He splits the dawn (from the night) and made the night for rejuvenation and rest, while the sun and the moon are for counting the passage of time.

That's how He's arranged (for your world to work, for He's) the Powerful and the Knowing. [96]

He's the One Who made the stars (as reference points) to guide you on your way through the unknown regions of land and sea, and this is how We explain Our signs for people who know. [97]

He's the One Who produced you all from a single soul. (So understand that this world that you inhabit) is a place to linger, and it's also a point of departure. This is how We explain Our verses for people who understand. [98]

He's the One Who sends down water from the sky and uses it to produce plants of every kind. From them, We grow lush green vegetation bringing forth grain piled high.

From date palms, clusters of dates hang within easy reach, and there are vineyards of grapes and olives and pomegranates, as well!

(They're all) similar (in form) but different (in variety), and when they start to bear fruit - just look at their fruit when they ripen! In all these things are signs for people who believe. [99]

Allah is above All Definitions

Yet, they're turning the jinns into (Allah's) partners, even though *He* created *them*, and they're assigning sons and daughters to Him without any knowledge!

All glory be to Him in the highest! (He's high) above what they make Him out to be! [100]

The original start of the heavens and the earth is due to Him, so how can He have a son when He has no female consort? He created everything, and He knows about all things. [101]

That's Allah for you, your Lord; there is no god but He, the Creator of everything, so serve Him (alone), for He has power over every affair. [102]

No vision can comprehend Him; yet, His comprehension is over all vision, for He's the Subtle and Well-informed. [103]

Proof has now come to you from your Lord. If anyone will allow their good sense to see it, then it will be to his own (benefit). If anyone chooses to remain blind to it, (then it will be to his own harm, so tell them,) "*I'm not your guardian.*" [104]

That's how We explain the verses in various ways so they can say, "*You've learned it well,*" and so We can clarify things for those who know (how to recognize the truth). [105]

On Tolerance

(Muhammad), follow what's being revealed to you from your Lord, for there is no god but He, and turn away from those who make partners (with Allah). [106]

If it would've been Allah's will, then none of them would've ever (taken idols) as partners (with Allah).

However, We didn't send you to be their guardian, nor are you the one who has to arrange their affairs. [107]

> **Background Info... v. 108**
>
> The revelation of this verse came about when the Prophet was attending to his uncle, Abu Talib, who was very ill. A delegation of Meccan chiefs came to make a last ditch effort to persuade Muhammad to compromise before the influential, yet elderly, Abu Talib passed on.
>
> When Abu Talib asked Muhammad what he wanted of the Meccans, he explained that he would only accept the truth of the One God from them. Then he made the famous statement that "even if they put the sun in my right hand and the moon in my left, neither will I desist nor compromise in this message."
>
> The pagans, oddly enough, felt their religion was being insulted, and they warned Muhammad that they would begin insulting his God if he didn't desist from his stubbornness.
>
> This verse then came cautioning the Prophet to be more sensitive to the unbelievers when engaging in dialogue.

Don't insult those (idols) that they call upon besides Allah, for they might insult Allah in their ignorance, out of spite.

We've made each community's actions seem appropriate and good to itself, but in the end they're all going to go back to their Lord.

Then We're going to tell them the meaning of everything they ever did. [108]

The False Promises of the Faithless

> **Background Info... v. 109-111**
>
> One of the Meccan leaders said to the Prophet, "Muhammad, you're telling us that Musa tapped a rock with a stick and that twelve springs gushed out, that 'Esa raised the dead to life, and that the Thamud had a miracle camel. Well, then bring us some of those miracles, and then we'll believe in you."
>
> The Prophet asked them what kind of a miracle they wanted, and they said, "Turn that hill named Safa into gold." The Prophet answered, "If I did that, would you believe in me?" The gathered crowd answered in the affirmative.
>
> Then the Prophet walked away and invoked Angel Jibra'il, who came to him invisibly and said, "If you want, I will transform that hill into gold, but (Allah) doesn't make such a miracle unless He would follow it up with punishment, so do you want to leave them alone until they repent?"
>
> The Prophet said, "Leave them alone then until they repent." Then this passage was revealed, and the Prophet recited it to the crowd. (*Asbab ul-Nuzul*)

They swear to Allah with their strongest oaths that if only a miracle came to them, then they would believe for its sake.

Say to them, "*Miracles are in Allah's presence (and they come only by His command),*" but how can you be made to understand that even if (such miracles) came, they would still not believe? [109]

We're going to steer their hearts and eyes away, even as they refused to believe in the first instance, and We're going to leave them in their disobedience to wander blindly. [110]

Even if We *did* send angels to them or caused the dead to speak to them or gathered every (other kind of proof) before their very eyes, they still wouldn't believe, save for Allah's will, as most of them are ignorant. [111]

Every Prophet had Enemies

And so it is that We've made a diabolical enemy to oppose every prophet, drawn from among both jinns and men, who would inspire each other with dazzling words of deception.

If your Lord had wanted, then they would've never been able to do it, so leave them and what they're inventing alone. [112]

Let those who don't believe in the next life indulge in (their lies) to their heart's content, let them feel pleased about it and let them get whatever they can out of it. [113]

Say to them, "*Should I look for a judge other than Allah, when He's the One Who sent you a fully explained scripture?*"

Those who've been given a scripture (before you) know that it's been sent down by your Lord in all truth, so don't be among those who doubt. [114]

The orders of your Lord are fulfilled with truth and justice, and no one can change His orders, for He's the Hearing and the Knowing. [115]

If you were to follow what most (people say) here on earth, then they would lead you away from the path of Allah, for they do nothing but guess, and they do nothing but make guesses. [116]

Your Lord knows better who is straying from His path, and He knows better who is being guided. [117]

A Reminder
of the Forbidden Foods

You can eat whatever (meat) that's had Allah's name pronounced over it (at the time of slaughter), if you believe in His (revealed) verses. [118]

And why shouldn't you eat of those things that have had Allah's name pronounced over them? He's already explained for you in detail what's forbidden, unless you're forced to eat it (out of desperation).

However, (when it comes to issues of food,) many (thoughtless people) mislead others for their own selfish reasons and without any knowledge. Your Lord knows best who's going beyond the boundaries. [119]

Background Info... v. 121

Some idol-worshippers were objecting to the Prophet's teaching that animals found dead by themselves should not be eaten. One of them said, "Muhammad, tell us about a sheep. If it died by itself, then who killed it?"

The Prophet said, "Allah caused it to die." Then the pagan, thinking he was being clever, said, "So, you're claiming that what you and your followers kill is lawful and what the dog and the hawk kill is lawful, while what Allah kills is unlawful?" This verse was revealed in response. (*Asbab ul-Nuzul*)

Leave off all sinning, whether done in the open or in secret, for those who indulge in sin will be repaid with the consequences of whatever they did. [120]

So don't eat of (any meat) that hasn't had Allah's name pronounced over it (at the time of slaughter), for that would be an act of disobedience.

Truly, devils try to inspire their associates (among people) to argue with you, and if you obeyed them, then you would be no better than an idol-worshipper. [121]

Background Info... v. 122-123

This passage is a reference to the conversion of the Prophet's uncle, Hamza ibn 'Abdel-Muttalib.

The Prophet was walking one day, and his cruel indirect paternal relative, Abu Jahl, threw dung on him. The Prophet saw Hamza coming into town, returning from a hunt while he was carrying a bow in his hand.

He complained to him of what Abu Jahl had done, and Hamza became angry and confronted Abu Jahl with his bow raised high.

Abu Jahl began to tremble, but he defended himself saying, "Father of Ya'la, don't you see what he's brought? He's brought confusion to our minds, insulted our gods and left the ways of our forefathers."

Hamza replied, "And who's more ridiculous than you? You worship stones instead of Allah, so I testify that there's no god but the One God, that He has no partners, and that Muhammad is His servant and Messenger." This passage was revealed in response. (*Asbab ul-Nuzul*)

Can someone who was **DEAD** (to faith), and then whom We brought back to **life** with the light (of truth) that guides his steps among people, be equal to someone who is lost in darkness from which he can never come out?

As it is, those who cover over (their awareness of the truth) are pleased with what they're doing, (even though it's wrong). [122]

And so We've placed wicked leaders in every town, drawn from among its most influential citizens, so they can weave their schemes, but in the end they're only scheming against their own souls, even though they don't realize it! [123]

When a verse (is revealed from Allah) and then presented to them, they say, "*We won't believe (in it) until we see (a miracle) like Allah's (other) messengers got.*"

Allah knows best how to send down His message! Those wicked ones will soon be humiliated in Allah's presence, and they will be severely punished on account of their scheming! [124]

If Allah wants to guide someone, He opens his heart up to Islam, and if Allah wants to leave someone astray, He tightens his chest until it's so constricted that *he feels as if he's climbing high up into the sky!*

That's how Allah penalizes those who won't believe. [125]

This is the way of your Lord, and it leads straight (to the truth). We've explained the verses (of this Book) for people who accept reminders. [126]

For them is the realm of peace in the presence of their Lord, and He will be their protector on account of what they did. [127]

Both Humans and Jinn will be Questioned

One day, He will gather everyone together (and say), "*You gathered assembly of jinns! You were very hard on those human beings.*"

Their human associates will answer, "*Our Lord! We benefited from each other (immensely), but now we've reached our deadline, the one that You decided for us.*"

(Allah) will then say, "*Your home will be in the Fire, and you're going to remain there, except as Allah wills, for your Lord is full of knowledge and wisdom.*" [128]

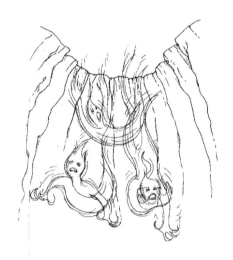

Therefore, We let the wrongdoers (turn towards each other) for close support, (and because of their unholy alliances We will cast them all into Hellfire, regardless of rank, race or status), on account of what they've earned. [129]

(Allah will then say to them all,) "*You gathered assembly of jinns and human beings! Didn't any messengers from among you ever come to you and relate My (revealed) verses to you and warn you of the meeting of this day of yours?*"

(The crowds will sadly answer,) saying, "*We testify against our own selves.*"

The life of the world deceived them, and that's why they'll be made to testify against their own selves, (admitting) that they had rejected (faith). [130]

(For sure, messengers were sent to them for) that (very purpose), because their Lord would never destroy any civilization for its bad conduct while its people were unaware (that they should turn towards Allah). [131]

Everyone is ranked according to what they do, and your Lord is not unaware of what (each of you) is doing. Your Lord is Self-sufficient, and He's a master of mercy.

If it were ever His desire, He could destroy you all and put in your place whomever else He wanted to succeed you, even as He let you arise from the descendants (of previous civilizations) of old. [132-133]

Everything that you've been promised will come to pass, and there's no way you can steer it away. [134]

Say to them, "*My people! Do whatever you can, for I'm going to do likewise.*

Soon you're going to know who will have the (best) outcome in the afterlife, and the wrongdoers will never be successful." [135]

Addressing the Superstitions of the Pagans

The (idol-worshippers) assign to Allah a share of the harvest and the livestock that He (has caused to be) produced. They say on their own (whim), "*This much is for Allah, and this much is for our idols.*"

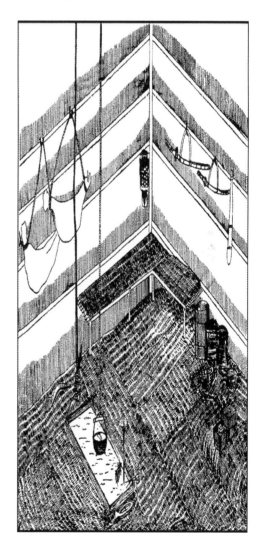

However, the *share* of their idols never gets back to Allah, while the *share* of Allah just goes to support their idolatry! That's an appalling distribution! [136]

Even further, their 'partners' have made the practice of killing their own children seem appropriate and good to most of the idol-worshippers, so much so that it leads to their own destruction and causes confusion in their way of life.

If Allah had wanted to prevent this, then they would've never done that, but leave them alone with what they've invented. [137]

Then they say on their own that certain livestock (animals) and crops are taboo and that no one should eat of them except whomever We (supposedly) allowed to do so.

(They also say) that some livestock (animals) are not meant to be harnessed for labor or that some are not to have Allah's name pronounced over them (when they're slaughtered).

These are all inventions made in Allah's name! He's soon going to pay them back for their invented (superstitions). [138]

Superstition is not Equal to Divine Principles

> **Background Info... v. 139**
>
> This practice mentioned below was a peculiar pagan custom in which calves born to cows marked for sacrifice were specially reserved as food only for the priests of certain idols.
>
> Women were forbidden to eat of these calves, unless they were stillborn calves found within the animals after slaughter. This verse pokes fun at this practice and calls it a mindless superstition to be discarded. *(Ibn Kathir)*

They also say, "*What's in the wombs of certain livestock (animals) will be reserved for our men (to eat) and forbidden for our women, but if it's a stillborn (calf) then everyone can share in it.*"

Well, He's going to repay them soon enough for their (generous) interpretation (of the so-called rules).

He's full of wisdom and knowledge (and would never have invented such things). [139]

Those who foolishly and ignorantly kill their own children are lost!

(They're lost even further because) they've made restrictions on the food that Allah has provided for them by inventing (superstitions) against Allah. They've gone astray and have no guidance. [140]

He's the One Who brought about gardens of plants that grow on climbing vines and plants that don't grow high, orchards of date palms, cultivated fields with vegetables of every kind, and olives and pomegranates, (which are) similar (in form) but different (in variety).

So eat their fruits when they're in season, but give what is due upon them (to the poor) on the day of harvest. Don't let any of it go to waste, for Allah has no love for those who waste. [141]

Some types of livestock were made for labor, while others were made for providing meat. So eat from what Allah provided for you, and don't follow in Shaytan's footsteps, for he's your obvious enemy. [142]

Take (a look) at these eight livestock (animals) that come in pairs: (first examine) a pair of (male and female) sheep, and then a pair of (male and female) goats.

Then ask them, "*Has (Allah) forbidden the two males or the two females or what's in the two females' wombs? Give me a convincing answer if you're so honest!*" [143]

(Now consider the status of) a pair of camels and a pair of oxen.

Ask (the idol-worshippers), "*Has (Allah) forbidden (you to eat of) the two males or the two females or what's in the two females' wombs? Were you there when Allah commanded you about that?*

"*Who's more wrong than the one who invents a lie against Allah in order to lead unknowing people astray? Truly, Allah doesn't guide wrongdoers.*" [144]

Say to them, "*I haven't found anything in what's been revealed to me that would restrict a person from eating something if they wanted to eat it, unless it's a dead carcass or flowing blood or pork – and that's an abomination – or what's impure because it was dedicated to other names besides Allah.*

"*Although if someone is forced by desperation (to eat forbidden foods) and is not trying to be disobedient or seeking to go beyond the bounds, (know that) your Lord is forgiving and merciful.*" [145]

On the Difficult Food Restrictions of the Jews

We made it forbidden for the followers of Judaism (to eat) everything with an undivided hoof, and We also forbade them to eat the fat of oxen and sheep, except for the fat on their backs, entrails and bones.

These (restrictions) were on account of their brazen disobedience, and We're certainly correct (in what We say). [146]

If they accuse you of lying, then say to them, "*Your Lord is the master of mercy and embraces all things, though His wrath will never be turned away from wicked people.*" [147]

Can You Blame Allah for Your Foolish Customs?

Those who make partners (with Allah) say, "*If Allah had wanted to (prevent us from worshipping idols), then neither ourselves nor our ancestors would've ever made partners with Him, nor would we have had any taboos.*"

Now those are the same types of fraudulent arguments that their own ancestors used to employ - *until they felt Our wrath!*

Say to them, "*Do you have some kind of knowledge (to back that claim)? If you do, then show us! You're just guessing, and you're just speculating.*" [148]

Then say, "*Allah has the most convincing arguments, and if He really had wanted, He could've guided you all.*" [149]

Say to them, "*Produce your witnesses to prove that Allah made such restrictions (on food, as you're claiming).*"

If they bring some witnesses (who will falsely testify), then don't remain in such a gathering, nor should you follow the fickle whims of those who treat our (revealed) verses as lies and who don't believe in the next life, given that they make others as equals with their Lord. [150]

The Ten Commandments of Islam

Say to them, "*Come here, and I'll announce the (most important) rules of Allah. They are as follows:*

- Do not take any other as His equal;

- Be kind to your parents;

- Do not kill your children for fear of poverty, as We provide resources for you and for them;

- Do not go near to shameful deeds, whether in public or in secret;

- Do not take a life, which Allah has made sacred, except for a just cause (under the law), and that's His command so you can reflect; [151]

- Do not touch an orphan's property, unless you're going to improve it, until he attains his full maturity;

- Measure (properly);

- Balance justly, and We don't burden any soul beyond what it can bear;

- When you speak, stand up for justice, even if it concerns a close relative;

- And fulfill the covenant of Allah (by struggling in His Cause).

This is what He's commanded of you, so you can take heed. This is My straight path, so follow it. Don't follow other paths, for they'll only divert you away from His path.

This is what He's commanded of you, so you can be mindful (of your duty to Him). [152-153]

This is the Book of Guidance

We then gave the Book to Musa, completed it and explained it thoroughly for those who would be good, so it could be a source of guidance and mercy and so they could believe in the meeting with their Lord. [154]

This (Qur'an) is (a new) scripture that We've revealed as a source of blessing, so follow it and be mindful (of what it says) so you can be worthy of mercy. [155]

(You've been given this new scripture) so that you'll never be able to say, "*Scripture was given to two groups before us, but what they learned from was never introduced to us!*" [156]

Likewise, you'll never be able to say, "*Oh, if only a book had been sent down to us, then we would've followed its guidance better than they.*"

Now clear evidence has come to you from your Lord, and a source of guidance and mercy. Who is more wrong than the one who rejects Allah's signs and turns away from them?

Soon We're going to repay those who turned away from Our signs with a terrible punishment on account of their avoidance. [157]

Are they waiting to see the angels coming for them, or your Lord, or the unmistakable signs of your Lord's (coming)?

On the day when the signs of your Lord do arrive, it won't do any good for a soul to believe in them, if it hadn't already believed in them or made a good account (of its sincerity) through (acts of) true faith.

Say to them, "*Wait, because we'll be waiting, too.*" [158]

Remain Firm on the Truth

Those who break up their way of life into sects and competing factions – *you must have nothing to do with them!*

Their affair lies with Allah, and in the end He's going to tell them the meaning of everything they ever did. [159]

Whoever does something good will be given ten times as much to his credit, while whoever does an evil thing will be credited with one bad deed, and no one will ever be treated unfairly. [160]

Say to them, "*My Lord has truly guided me to a straight way, the established way of life, the creed of Ibraheem, the natural (monotheist), and he was never an idol-worshipper.*" [161]

Then say, "*Truly, my prayers and my sacrifice, my life and my death, are all for Allah, the Lord of All the Worlds. He has no partners, and this is my order, that I must be the first to submit (to His will).*" [162-163]

Ask them, "*Should I look for another lord besides Allah, when He's the Lord of all things? Every soul brings its own results upon none other than itself, and no bearer of burdens can bear the burden of another.*

"*In the end your return is with Allah, and He's going to tell you the meaning of all those things about which you argued.*" [164]

He's the One Who made you successors in the earth, and He's placed some of you in higher positions than others so He can test you with (the varying gifts) that He's given you.

Your Lord is quick to punish, though He's also (quick to show) forgiveness and mercy. [165]

The Heights

7 Al A'rāf
Late Meccan Period

☞ Introduction

This chapter was revealed in the very last days of the Prophet's stay in Mecca. It talks about new events such as start of religious discussions with Jews from the faraway city of Yathrib, who came to Mecca to see who the new prophet was. The Meccan leaders used to ask the Jews questions regarding the status of Muhammad (p) and what the Jewish religion might have to say about him.

So this chapter addresses both the idol-worshippers and the Jews, even as it lays out new religious concepts for the Muslim believers. One such new concept was the place between Heaven and Hell known as the Heights, reserved for those whose records are so finely balanced between good and evil that they don't deserve Heaven or Hell. Eventually, they will all be admitted into Paradise.

In the Name of Allah,
the Compassionate, the Merciful

*A*lif. *Lām. Meem. Sâwd.* [1]

(This is) a book that's being revealed to you (from Allah), so don't let your heart be troubled any more over (how people may respond to it), for with (this Book) you can give warnings and reminders to the believers. [2]

(All you people!) Follow what's been revealed to you from your Lord. Don't follow (the whims) of others or take others besides Him as protectors. How few are the warnings that you take! [3]

Just how many settlements have We destroyed? Our punishment came upon them suddenly by night or while they were taking their afternoon rest. [4]

Regardless, when Our punishment finally came upon them, they cried out, saying no more than, "*We were so wrong!*" [5]

We're going to question those who had Our message sent to them, even as We're going to question the bearers (of all those messages). [6] We'll narrate their complete story to them with full accuracy, for We were never absent (from their midst). [7]

The weighing (of all the evidence) on that day will be fair and just. Those whose scales are heavy (with good) will be successful. [8]

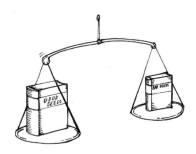

Meanwhile, those whose scales are scarce (of good) will find that they've lost their own souls because they treated Our signs wrongly. [9]

The Fall of Iblis

And so it was that We settled you on the earth, and We provided for you the resources that you need to survive; *yet, how little thanks you give!* [10]

And so it was that We created you and gave you your shape. We then ordered the angels to bow down to (your original ancestor) Adam, and they all bowed down, except for (a jinn named) Iblis, who didn't bow at all! [11]

Allah said to him, "*What's preventing you from bowing down, when I've commanded it?*"

"*I'm better than he is,*" (Iblis) replied, "*for You made me from fire, while You made him from clay.*" [12]

"*Get down and away from here!*" (Allah) ordered. "*This is no place for you to be arrogant. Get out of here, for you're the least (of all creatures).*" [13]

"*Give me time!*" (Iblis) cried out. "(*Give me time) until the day when they're all resurrected.*" [14]

"*You shall have your time,*" (Allah) answered. [15]

Then Iblis said, "*And since it was You Who made me slip up, I'll lie in wait for them on Your 'straight path.'* [16]

"*I'll assail them from their front and their back and from their right and their left, and in the end You'll see that most of them are thankless (towards You).*" [17]

"*Get out of here!*" (Allah) ordered, "*You're banished! If any of them follow you, then I'll fill Hellfire with you all!*" [18]

In the Garden of Eden

"*Adam,*" (Allah said), "*You may live in the garden with your mate and eat whatever you like, but don't go near this one tree, for it will lead you into corruption.*" [19]

Then Shaytan began to whisper suggestions to them, so he could make them see their nakedness, which had been hidden (from their consciousness).

"The only reason your Lord has forbidden this tree to you," (he) told them, *"is because (He's afraid that) you might transform into angels or some other immortal being."* [20]

Then he swore to them both that he was giving them good advice. [21]

In this way, he orchestrated their fall through deception. When they tasted (the fruit) of the tree, then their nakedness became clearly evident to them, and they began to sew leaves together from the garden to cover their bodies.

Then their Lord called out to them, *"Didn't I forbid you from that tree, and didn't I tell you that Shaytan was your clear enemy?"* [22]

"Our Lord!" they cried. *"We've done wrong against our own souls! If You don't forgive us and show us mercy, then we'll be utterly lost!"* [23]

"Go down away from here," (Allah) said, *"and live in the world, (struggling) in competition with each other. It'll be your home and your place of livelihood for a while."* [24]

Then He added, *"You shall dwell in (the earth), and there you shall die, and from it you will be taken out again (for judgment)."* [25]

To the Children of Adam

Children of Adam! We've bestowed upon you clothing to hide the shame (of your nakedness), as well as to adorn you. (Remember, however, that) the robe of *mindfulness* is the best (with which to clothe yourself).

These are some of the verses of Allah (that are being revealed to you, Muhammad,) so they can be reminded. [26]

Children of Adam! Don't let Shaytan deceive you like he did when he got your ancestors expelled from the Garden (of Eden), stripping them of their facade (of innocence) to expose their shame.

Both he and his band (of devils) see you from a place where you can't see them, and We've made devils the allies of those who cover over (their ability to see the truth). [27]

Answering those Who Blame Allah

> **Background Info... v. 28-31**
>
> The pagans of Mecca would often walk around the Ka'bah during religious devotions while completely naked, claiming that it was a longstanding tradition and that it contributed to their purity.
>
> This is what the 'shameful thing' in this verse refers to. (The only people who could perform this ritual fully clothed were Qurayshi tribesmen or people who borrowed clothes from them.)
>
> When the Prophet spoke out against this custom, the pagans offered the excuse quoted in verse 28. This passage was revealed in response. (Ibn Kathir)

When (the faithless) do shameful things, they say, "*These are the customs that we received from our ancestors*," or they say, "*Allah told us to do it.*"

Say to them, "*Allah never commanded shameful things. Are you saying something about Allah without knowing (any better)?*" [28]

Say to them, "*My Lord commands justice and that you dedicate your whole self (to Him) in every act of worship and that you call upon Him with complete sincerity, for all religion belongs to Him. Even as He started you in the beginning, so shall you return.*" [29]

A section of them are guided by Him, while another section has rightfully gone astray because they took devils for their protectors instead of Allah, all the while thinking they were being guided! [30]

Therefore, Children of Adam! Wear your good clothes at every place of prayer, and eat and drink (as you like). However, don't overindulge, for Allah has no love for those who overindulge. [31]

Don't Renounce the World

Now ask them, "*Who has forbidden the exquisite (gifts) of Allah, which He has made available to His servants, and (who has forbidden) the wholesome (things He has) provided?*"

Say to them, "*In the life of this world, (the natural gifts of the earth) belong to the believers, and they will be the only ones on the Day of Assembly who will have them.*"

This is how We clearly explain the verses (of this Book) for people who understand. [32]

Then say to them, "*My Lord has forbidden all shameful deeds, whether done in the open or in secret, (and He's forbidden) sinfulness, flagrant injustice, joining partners with Allah for which He's sent down no authority, and saying things about Allah of which you know nothing.*" [33]

Each Nation is Given One Chance

Every community has been given its own (predetermined) time limit, and when their deadline is due, they can't prolong it even for an hour, nor can they delay it. [34]

Therefore, Children of Adam! Whenever a messenger comes to you from your own kind conveying My verses to you, whoever is mindful (of that message) and reforms himself will have no cause for fear or sorrow. [35]

Those who cover over (their ability to recognize the truth of) Our (revealed) verses and (even worse) treat them in a haughty manner will be companions of the Fire, *and that's where they're going to stay!* [36]

The Fate of Those Who Deny Allah

Who's more wrong than the one who invents a lie against Allah or who denies His (revealed) verses?

They're the ones whose due punishment must come back to them from the book (of deeds), even up to the point when our (angelic) messengers arrive and take their souls, saying, "*Where are all those (false gods) that you used to call upon besides Allah?*"

(The doomed souls will answer), "*They've left us to languish!*" And so they will testify against their own souls that they had indeed buried (their ability to recognize the truth of Allah). [37]

(Allah will say to them), *"Enter into the companionship of all those jinns and humans who have passed away before you - (all of whom) are in the Fire!"*

Every time a new community will enter into (Hell), it will curse its sister-communities that preceded it, so much so that after they've all followed each other into it, the last one will say of the first, *"Our Lord! They're the ones who misled us, so double their punishment in the Fire."*

Then He'll say, *"The punishment is doubled for all!"* They just don't understand! [38]

Finally, the first (community that entered Hellfire) will say to the last (one that entered it), *"So, you're no better than we are after all! Now suffer the punishment for your deeds, (just as we have to)!"* [39]

Those who cover over (their ability to recognize the truth of) Our (revealed) verses and (even worse) treat them in a haughty manner will find no opening (for Allah's forgiveness) in the gates of the sky, nor will they ever enter Paradise – *no, not until a twisted rope can pass through the eye of a needle!*

That's Our way of paying back the bad people! [40] Their resting place will be under layers and layers of Hellfire, and that's how We pay back wrongdoers! [41]

A Conversation between Heaven and Hell

Those who believe and do what's morally right - *and We don't place upon any soul a burden greater than it can bear* – they'll be the companions of the Garden, *and in it they shall remain!* [42]

We're going to erase from their hearts any hidden sense of unease, even as rivers will flow beneath them!

"*Praise be to Allah,*" they'll say, "*Who guided us to this, for we never could have guided ourselves, save for the guidance of Allah. And so it was that messengers from our Lord came to us with the truth!*"

(When they finish their joyous exclamations,) they'll hear the call (of welcome): *"The Garden is right there before you! You've inherited it on account of all that you did!"* [43]

(Now before each group is entered into its set place), the companions of the Garden will call over to the companions of the Fire, saying, "*We've found our Lord's promise to be true. Have you found your Lord's promise to be true, as well?*"

"*Yes,*" they'll answer, but then an announcer (will interrupt them), saying, *"Allah's curse be upon the wrongdoers!* [44] *They're the ones who turned others away from the path of Allah, trying to make it seem crooked, and they were the ones who rejected the next life."* [45]

There will be a screen erected between them, and on high places (in between the two groups) there will be men whose (scales of deeds had balanced perfectly in between good and evil).

They'll clearly recognize (both the people of Paradise and Hell) by their features.

216

(The people in the high places) will call out to the companions of the Garden, "*Peace be upon you,*" and even though they haven't entered into it yet, they'll feel confident of doing so. [46]

When they turn and gaze upon the companions of the Fire, they'll cry out, "*Our Lord! Don't send us among the wrongdoers!*" [47]

The companions of the Heights will recognize familiar men (down in Hellfire) by their features and will ask them, "*What has all your hoarding and arrogance done for you now?* [48]

"*Aren't those (people over there, heading into Paradise,) the same ones that you swore would never receive Allah's mercy? (On the contrary, they're the ones who are now being told), 'Enter the Garden – never more shall you fear nor shall you regret.'*" [49]

The companions of the Fire will call over to the companions of the Garden, saying, "*Pour down some water upon us or anything else with which Allah has provided you!*"

(The companions of the Garden) will answer, "*Allah has truly forbidden those things to those who rejected (Him) - those who took their way of life as a joke and a game, and who were deceived by the life of the world.*"

That day We're going to ᕈᓍᖇᘜᘿᖶ them, even as they forgot their meeting of this day of theirs. *Oh, how eagerly they snubbed Our (revealed) verses!* [50-51]

And so it was that We had sent a book to them filled with knowledge and explained in every detail, as a guide and mercy to people who believe. [52]

So are they just going to wait for (its predictions) to be fulfilled?

On the day, when (its predictions) are fulfilled, those who ignored it before will cry:

"*Our Lord's messengers really did come with the truth! Isn't there anyone now who can intercede for us? Can we be sent back (to earth for another chance), for then we would act differently than how we used to act?*"

They're going to lose their own souls, and all the lies they invented will leave them to suffer. [53]

It is Allah's Right to Command

Truly, your Lord is Allah, the One Who created the heavens and the earth in six stages. Then He established Himself upon the throne (of power). He draws the night like a veil over the day, and each chases the other swiftly.

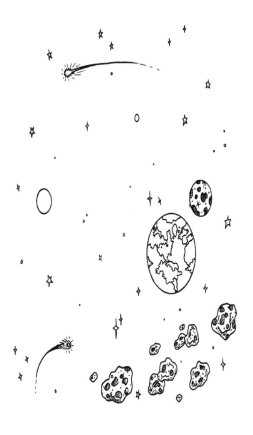

He created the sun, the moon and the stars, and they're all governed (by laws) under His command.

Isn't it His right to create and command? Blessed be Allah, the Lord of All the Worlds! [54]

How You Should Call upon Your Lord

Background Info... v. 55

Some people, based upon customs from pre-Islamic times, used to shout and beseech to Allah in loud and noisy voices. This passage was revealed to counsel people to behave maturely when they call upon Allah. (*Asbab ul-Nuzul*)

Call upon your Lord (in public) with heartfelt pleading, and (also call upon Him) when you're alone, (but in both cases do it in a dignified manner,) for Allah has no love for those who are unruly (in their supplications). [55]

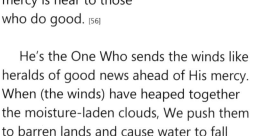

Don't create disorder in the land after it's been made right. Call upon Him with fear and longing, for Allah's mercy is near to those who do good. [56]

He's the One Who sends the winds like heralds of good news ahead of His mercy. When (the winds) have heaped together the moisture-laden clouds, We push them to barren lands and cause water to fall upon it.

Then We use it to grow every kind of lush vegetation. Now that's also how We're going to raise you from the dead, so perhaps you might remember it. [57]

From good, clean earth, plants spring up in their Lord's presence. However, from polluted soil, nothing grows save for meager (weeds), and this is how We explain the verses in so many ways, so you can learn to be thankful. [58]

The People of Nuh Reject Him

We sent Nuh to his people, and he said, "*My people! Serve Allah! You have no other god than Him. I fear for you the punishment of an awful day!*" [59]

The leading men among his people answered him, saying, "*We see that you're clearly mistaken.*" [60]

"*My people!*" he replied. "*I'm not mistaken. Rather, I'm a messenger from the Lord of All the Worlds! I'm only expressing the message of my Lord and advising you, for I know things from Allah that you don't.*" [61-62]

"*Is it so strange for you that a message has come to you from your Lord, carried by a man from among your own people as a warning? (This is how it is) so you can be mindful (of Allah) and have His mercy (sent down upon you).*" [63]

Yet, they denied him, and so We saved him and those who were with him in the boat. We overwhelmed all those who rejected Our signs in the great flood. They were a people who were blind (to the truth)! [64]

The People of 'Ad Reject their Prophet

Background Info... v. 65-72

The people of 'Ad were an ancient civilization that existed over four thousand years ago in present-day Oman and the surrounding area. Their ruined city of Iram was rediscovered by archeologists in 1992. The Qur'an described it as a city of tall towers. When the city was unearthed, it was found to have quite a few tall towers around its outer walls as giant watch posts.

Although the Arabs knew nothing of the 'Ad and their lost city of Iram but faint legends, (it was known as Ubar to the Greeks and Sishur to other civilizations), archeologists excavating the ancient city of Elba in Syria came upon a hidden, four-thousand-year-old library in which the names of all the cities with which it conducted trade were listed. Iram was one of the names recorded.

We sent to the people of 'Ad their brother Hūd, and he said:

"*My people! Serve Allah! You have no other god than Him, so won't you be mindful?*" [65]

The leaders of the faithless among his people answered him, saying, "*We see that you're naïve,*" and, "*We think you're a liar.*" [66]

219

"*My people!*" he said. "*I'm not naïve; rather, I'm a messenger from the Lord of All the Worlds!*" [67]

"*I'm only expressing the message of my Lord, and I'm a trustworthy advisor.* [68] *Is it so strange for you that a message has come to you from your Lord, carried by a man from among your own people as a warning?*

"*Recall that He made you inherit (this land) after the people of Nuh and gave you a high reputation in the eyes of other nations. Recall (all the blessings) that you've received from Allah, so you can be truly successful.*" [69]

"*Have you come to us,*" they asked, "*to have us worship only one God and to give up what our ancestors worshipped? So bring down upon us (all those punishments from your God) with which you've been threatening us, if you're being so honest!*" [70]

"*You've had affliction and wrath from your Lord come upon you already,*" (Hūd) replied, "*(because of your arrogant rejection of the truth).*

"*Are you going to argue with me about the names that you've made up (for your idols), both you and your ancestors, without any permission from Allah? So wait and see, for I'll be waiting with you.*" [71]

Then We saved him and those who were with him through (an act of) mercy from Our Own self, and We cut out the roots of those who denied Our signs and who didn't believe. [72]

The People of Thamud Reject their Prophet

> **F.Y.I**
>
> The Thamud were a tribal group that existed in an area known as Al-Hijr, today located in southern Jordan and Northern Arabia. They were known to the Babylonians, Assyrians and the Greeks, the latter of whom referred to them as the *Thamudaei*. The ruins of their towns and cities were scattered all throughout the area, and the Arabs were well aware of their existence.
>
> Although the area was not well-suited for a large population, income from trade allowed their civilization to thrive from about 2400 BCE to around the fifth century of the common era when their power failed. In their later years, their descendants became known as the Nabateans. The Thamud were also mentioned in the annals of Sargon the Great (d. 2279 BCE).

We sent to the people of Thamud their brother Salih, and he said, "*My people! Serve Allah! You have no other god than Him. Clear evidence has come to you from your Lord!*

220

"This camel (that's been especially sanctified by Allah) is your sign, so leave her to graze on Allah's earth. Do her no harm, or you'll be seized with terrible punishment." [73]

"Remember that He let you inherit (the earth) after the people of 'Ad and gave you homes within the earth out of which you build palaces and fortresses for yourselves, both in the plains and in the mountains, where you carve them (from the mountainsides).

"Remember (all the blessings) that you've received from Allah, and cause no harm or chaos in the earth." [74]

The leaders of the arrogant faction among his people said to the ones whom they thought were weak and powerless, and who had come to believe (in the teachings of Salih), *"Are you really certain that Salih is a genuine messenger from his Lord?"*

Then they answered them, saying, *"Indeed, we do believe in what was sent to him."* [75]

The arrogant ones then said, *"Well, we reject what you believe in!"* [76] Then they (cut the legs of the camel,) crippling her, and brazenly defied the order of their Lord.

They (boasted about it) and said, *"Salih! Bring on your threats, if you're really a messenger (of Allah)!"* [77]

Then the mighty quake took them by surprise, and by morning they were laid flat in their homes. [78]

Salih (saw the damage and then) left them, saying, *"My people! I conveyed to you the message that was sent to me from my Lord. I gave you good advice, but you had no love for advisors."* [79]

The People of Lut Reject Him

Background Info... v. 80-84

Lut was Ibraheem's nephew, and he had followed his uncle out of Mesopotamia many years before. While Ibraheem continued a bedouin kind of lifestyle, Lut (Lot) took his family and servants to the ancient city of Sodom. While he was there, he tried to spread Allah's word among the people of that city, but they were given over to worldly pleasures.

Lut said to his people, *"Are you engaging in the shameful and perverted act, a practice unlike anything (any other people) ever did in the entire world? You're using other men instead of women for your passions? No way! You're a people who've gone out of control!"* [80-81]

His people offered no other response than to say, "*Drive them out of your city, these people who want to be so moral and pure!*" [82]

Then We saved him and his family, except for his wife, for she was one of those who remained behind. [83]

Thereafter, We rained down upon (the city) a shower (of blasted stone), and you can see how those wicked people were ended! [84]

The People of Madyan Reject their Prophet

Background Info... v. 85

Shu'ayb was a prophet sent to the people of Madyan, (*aka* the People of the Thicket), a land in northern Arabia near the city of Tabuk. The original land of Madyan is an old land stretching in an arc across northern Arabia towards the Sinai, and it has been settled with various peoples who have come and gone.

To (the people of) Madyan We sent their brother Shu'ayb, who said, "*My people! Serve Allah! You have no other god than Him. Clear evidence has come to you from your Lord!*

"*So measure and balance honestly (in your trading activities), and don't withhold from people what they're owed.*

"*Don't cause trouble in the world after it's been made right. That will be to your good if you really have any faith.*" [85]

"*Don't stake out every road and intimidate the people who believe in Him away from the path of Allah, trying to imply that there's something wrong with it.*

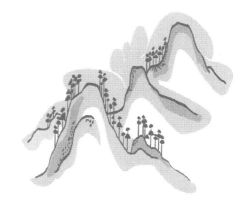

"*Remember how you were so few in number and then He multiplied you, so keep in mind how the disobedient are ultimately (vanquished).*" [86]

"*If there's a section among you who believes in that with which I've been sent and a section that doesn't believe, then just be patient until Allah decides the matter between us, for He's the best One to judge.*" [87]

The leaders of the arrogant faction among his people said, "*Shu'ayb! We're going to drive you out of our settlement, both you and those who believe with you, unless all of you return to our traditions.*"

(Shu'ayb) answered them, saying, "*What! Even though we would hate it!* [88] *We would be lying against Allah if we returned to your traditions, especially since Allah has saved us from them.*

There's no way we would ever return to them unless our Lord Allah allowed (or planned) for it.

"Our Lord comprehends everything in His knowledge, and we trust in Allah. Our Lord! Decide between us and our people in all truth, for You're the best of all who open (matters for decision)." [89]

The faithless leaders among his people said, *"If any of you follow Shu'ayb, then you'll all be losers!"* [90]

And then the earthquake took them without warning, and they were laid flat in their homes by morning. [91]

Those who denied Shu'ayb were reduced (in power), as much as if they never even had a vibrant civilization! It was those who denied Shu'ayb who were the losers! [92]

Shu'ayb (saw the devastation and then) left them, saying, *"My people! I conveyed to you the message that was sent to me from my Lord, and I gave you good advice. So how can I mourn over a people who refused to believe?"* [93]

Arrogant Nations always Respond the Same Way

We never sent any prophet to any settlement without plunging its people into hardship and extreme adversity so they could learn to be humble. [94]

Then We would transform their hardship into prosperity until they advanced and multiplied, so much so that they (inevitably) began to say, *"Our ancestors were also affected by cycles of hardship and prosperity."*

Then We would suddenly seize them when they least expected it! [95]

If the people of those settlements had only believed and been mindful (of Allah in good times and bad), then We would've opened for them blessings from both the sky and the earth.

However, they denied (Allah), so We took hold of them on account of what they earned. [96]

Did the people of those settlements feel so safe from Our wrath, even though it might have come (upon them) in the night while they slept? [97]

Did they feel so safe against its coming in broad daylight while they frolicked about? [98]

223

Did they feel so safe against Allah's plan? No one can feel safe against Allah's plan except people who lose! [99]

Isn't it clear enough to those who eventually inherit the land (after previous nations collapse) that if We wanted, We could punish them for their sins and seal up their hearts so they can no longer hear, as well? [100]

Those were the settlements whose stories We're telling you. Messengers went to them with clear evidence (of Allah's truth), but they were not the ones who would believe in what they had already rejected before.

That's how Allah seals up the hearts of those who (willfully) cover over (their obligation to believe in Him). [101]

We didn't find most of them (living up) to their promise, and We found most of them rebellious and disobedient. [102]

The Meeting of Musa and Pharaoh

Then after (their time) We sent Musa with Our signs to Pharaoh and his nobles, but they treated them wrongfully. Just see how the disobedient scoundrels were defeated! [103]

Musa said, *"Pharaoh! I'm a messenger from the Lord of All the Worlds, and I'm bound to say only what's truthful about Allah. Now I've come to you with clear evidence from your Lord, so let the Children of Israel depart with me."* [104-105]

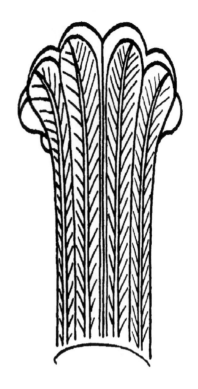

"If you've really come with a (miraculous) sign," (Pharaoh) replied, *"then show it (to me), if you're really being so honest!"* [106]

Then Musa threw his staff (down on the floor), and suddenly it became a serpent in plain sight! [107]

Next, he drew his hand sharply (from his side), and suddenly it was glowing white for all who saw it! [108]

Musa and the Sorcerers

"This is some kind of skilled sorcerer," Pharaoh's nobles began saying (to each other), *"but he just wants to drive you from your land. So now what do you advise?"* [109-110]

224

The (other nobles) said, *"Keep him and his brother occupied and waiting. Meanwhile, send word to all the cities to gather the most skilled sorcerers (we have) back here to you."* [111-112]

When Pharaoh's sorcerers arrived, they first said (to their master), *"Of course, we'll be amply rewarded if we win?"* [113]

(Pharaoh) replied, *"Yes, (you'll be rewarded), for you'll be brought near (to my circle of power)."* [114]

(Then Pharaoh's sorcerers confronted Musa,) saying, *"Musa, will you cast first, or should we go first?"* [115]

"You cast first," Musa answered, and when they threw (their ropes and sticks to the floor and chanted their spells,) they bewitched the eyes of the people and terrified them, for they employed powerful magic. [116]

Then We inspired Musa, saying, *"Now throw down your staff,"* and just like that - it **SWALLOWED** up all the lies they faked! [117]

That's how the truth was proven and their actions were shown to be false. [118]

What did the Sorcerers Say?

And in this way (the sorcerers of Pharaoh) were defeated - and right there (in public)! They were made to look so feeble! [119]

Then, the sorcerers fell flat on the floor and prostrated, saying, *"We believe in the Lord of All the Worlds, the Lord of Musa and Harun!"* [120-122]

Pharaoh (eyed them angrily) and said, *"Are you believing in Him without my permission? This is all just a hoax that you devised back in the city to drive out its (ruling class)! You're going to know soon (who's really in charge)!* [123]

"For sure, I'm going to cut off your hands and your feet from opposite sides and stake you all on wooden posts (until you die)!" [124]

"As for us," (the sorcerers) said, *"we'll be sent back to our Lord.* [125] *You're just taking your revenge out on us because we believed in the signs of our Lord when they came to us."*

(Then they prayed,) *"Our Lord! Pour patience down upon us, and take our souls back to You as ones who have submitted!"* [126]

225

Pharaoh's nobles (looked on in shock) and said, "*Are you going to leave Musa and his people to cause unrest in the land, while they leave you and forsake your gods?*"

(Pharaoh became furious) and said, "*We'll kill their male children and leave their females alive, for we have total power over them!*" [127]

(After Musa left and returned to his people,) he said to them, "*Pray to Allah for help and wait patiently, for the earth belongs to Allah, and He gives it as an inheritance to whichever of His servants that He wills. The final result will be for those who were mindful (of Him).*" [128]

(As they suffered under the yoke of Pharaoh, however, his people began to complain,) saying, "*We've had nothing but trouble both before and after you came to us.*"

(Musa scolded them,) saying, "*Perhaps your Lord will destroy your enemy and make you the inheritors of the earth in order to test you in your actions.*" [129]

How did the Egyptians Respond to the Plagues?

And so it was that We took hold of Pharaoh and his people (and punished them) with years (of drought) and poor harvests so they could perhaps be reminded. [130]

Whenever things got better, however, they said, "*This is due to our own (diligent) efforts,*" though when stricken with hardship they said it was because of the evil omens of Musa and those who were with him.

Their 'evil omens' were nothing more than their (own inventions), as far as Allah's view (was concerned,) but most of them didn't understand. [131]

They said, "*It doesn't matter what miracles you bring out in order to work your magic on us, (Musa,) for we're never going to believe in you!*" [132]

So We sent upon them a disastrous (flood), locusts, lice, frogs and a red-

226

stained thing: signs that were self-explanatory, but they were arrogant, and they were a wicked people. [133]

Every time a disaster would befall them, they would cry, "*Musa! Call upon your Lord for us, invoking His promise to you. If you relieve us of this torment, then we'll truly believe in you and send the Children of Israel away with you.*" [134]

Yet, every time We relieved them of the torment, after it's due course was completed, they broke their word! [135]

So We got them back by drowning them in the sea, for they had (willfully) denied Our signs and were unconcerned about them. [136]

We made a people who were thought of as weak inherit lands in both the two Easts and the two Wests, and they were the lands that We had blessed.

The fine saying of your Lord was fulfilled for the Children of Israel, because they had been patient.

We (eventually) brought down to ruin all the great works and structures that Pharaoh and his people built. [137]

The Children of Israel Start to Waver

We led the Children of Israel across the sea, and soon they came upon a people who were devoted to some idols they had with them. (The Israelites) said,

"*Musa! Make a god for us like the gods they have.*"

(Musa) answered, "*You're an ignorant people!*" [138]

"*As for these (people you've encountered), their (superstitions) are doomed to extinction, and what they're doing is foolish.*" [139]

Then he said, "*Should I look for a god other than Allah, when Allah is the One Who's given you more favors than any other people in all the universe?*" [140]

So remember, (all you Children of Israel), that We saved you from Pharaoh's people, the ones who afflicted you with the worst punishments and who killed your male children while letting your females live. That was an enormous test from your Lord. [141]

Musa Receives the Tablets

We ordered that Musa (should spend) thirty nights plus ten more (upon Mount Tūr), and so the full term of forty nights was completed with his Lord.

Musa left his brother Harun in charge (of the encampment) and had said to him, "*Be my representative with my people. Do what's morally right, and don't follow the way of the morally depraved.*" [142]

When Musa arrived at the place that We decided for him, his Lord addressed him.

Musa replied by saying, "*My Lord! Show Yourself to me, so that I may look upon You.*"

(Allah) replied, "*No, you cannot see Me, but look upon the side of that peak (over there). If it remains in place, then you will have seen Me.*"

When his Lord materialized His glory upon the mountainside, it crumbled into dust, and Musa fell down and fainted.

When he came back to his senses, he said, "*All glory be to You! I turn to You in repentance, and I'm the first to believe!*" [143]

"*Musa!*" (Allah) said. "*I've chosen you above other people with the message (I've sent to you) and the words (I've spoken to you). Take (the revelation) that I'm giving you, and be thankful.*" [144]

We recorded for him on the Tablets everything having to do with instructions, along with their explanations.

"*Take hold of these (laws) firmly, and order your people to take hold of the best within them, for soon will I show you the (ruined) homes of the rebellious (nations that came before you, so you can learn from their examples).* [145]

"*And I shall steer away from My signs those who act arrogantly in the earth against all right. Even if they see the signs, they're not going to believe in them, and even if they see the path of common sense, they're not going to adopt the way.*

"*Rather, if they see any way to go astray, that's the path they'll choose. That's because they denied Our signs (when they first heard of them) and were unconcerned about them.*" [146]

"*Those who deny Our (revealed) verses and the meeting of the next life – their life's work is for nothing. How can they* expect to be rewarded by anything other than what they've done?" [147]

The Children of Israel and the Golden Calf

The people of Musa took a golden calf (for an idol). (They made) it with their own jewelry after he had left them.

(The statue even) seemed as if it were making a sound, but didn't they see that it couldn't speak to them nor guide them on a path?

They took it (as an object of worship), and they were in the wrong. [148]

When they later regretted what they had done and saw that they had made a mistake, they said, "*If our Lord doesn't have mercy on us and doesn't forgive us, then we'll truly be lost.*" [149]

When Musa returned to his people, he was angry and upset. "*You've done evil in my stead while I was gone!*" (he cried.) "*Are you so eager to bring Allah's command down upon you so quickly!*"

Then he put down the Tablets, grabbed his brother by his head and dragged him down.

(Harun) cried out, "*Son of my mother! The people thought nothing of me, and they almost killed me! Don't make (our) enemies celebrate over my predicament, and don't include me among the corrupt!*" [150]

(Then Musa) prayed, "*My Lord! Forgive me and my brother! Admit us to Your mercy, for You're the most merciful of the merciful.*" [151]

Those who took the calf (as an idol) will be engulfed with wrath from their Lord and also with humiliation in this life. That's how We repay those who craft (nothing but lies). [152]

However, those who do wrong, but then repent of it and believe, (should know) that your Lord is forgiving and merciful. [153]

When Musa's anger subsided, he picked up the Tablets, for there was guidance and mercy inscribed upon them for those who revere their Lord. [154]

Then Musa chose seventy of his people (to come) to Our meeting place (to beg for forgiveness.)

When they were caught up in a violent earth tremor (on the mountain), Musa cried out, "*My Lord! If You had wanted, You could've destroyed both them and me long before! Would You destroy all of us for the actions of the foolish among* us? This (whole affair) is no more than a test from You."

"You use (Your tests as a means) to send astray whomever You want and guide whomever You want! You are our protector, so forgive us and be merciful to us, for You're the best of all forgivers! [155] Specify for us what's best in this life, as well as in the next life, for we've turned to You (for guidance)."

Then (Allah) replied, "I bring My punishment to bear upon whomever I want, but My mercy extends over all things. I prescribe it for those who are mindful (of Me), who give in charity and who believe in Our signs." [156]

To Whom will Allah Show Mercy?

(Who are the ones to whom My mercy will extend? It is for) those (Jews and Christians) who follow the Messenger, the unschooled prophet, whom they will find mentioned in their own (scriptures) - in the Torah and the Injeel – for he will command them to do what's recognized (as right) and forbid them from doing what's unfamiliar (to Allah's good way of life).

(The Messenger of Allah) will allow them (to partake of) what is pure and forbid them from what is unclean.

He will release them from the heavy burdens (of their religious law) and from the shackles (of burdensome religious injunctions) that were upon their (necks).

So it shall be that those who believe in (the Messenger of Allah), hold him in the highest regard, help him and follow the light that will be sent down with him, they are the ones who will be successful. [157]

(Muhammad, now) say to them, "O people! I'm the Messenger of Allah who's been sent to you all. He's the One to Whom the control of the heavens and the earth belongs. There is no god besides Him.

"He brings life, and He brings death, so believe in Allah and in His Messenger, the unschooled prophet, who himself believes in Allah and in His words. Follow Him so you can be guided." [158]

The Disobedient Eventually Lose

Among the people of Musa there is a community who guides truthfully and does justice. [159] (In the past), We had divided (the Children of Israel) into twelve tribes.

When his people asked him for water, We inspired (Musa), saying, "*Hit the rock with your staff*." Twelve springs gushed out of it, and every group knew its own place to drink.

We shaded them with clouds and sent down manna and quails, saying, "*Eat of the good things that We've provided for you*." They never did Us any harm (when they disobeyed); rather, they only harmed themselves. [160]

Recall how they were told, "*Reside within this town and eat whatever you want, but speak of humbleness when you enter its gates and walk in humility, for then We'll forgive you your sins and increase (the fortunes) of those who are good*." [161]

Then unscrupulous people among them altered the order they had received (and they behaved poorly towards the inhabitants of the town). So then We sent upon them a plague from the sky, for they persisted in doing wrong. [162]

Who were the Sabbath-Breakers?

> ### Background Info... v. 163
>
> It is said that on the Sabbath day the fish would come close to the shore and nearly bob their heads out of the water, daring the Jews to catch them. The men gave in to these temptations and willfully disobeyed the laws of Musa that had come down to them. (*Tabari*)
>
> (All work, including fishing, is forbidden on Saturdays under Mosaic Law.) The name of the town mentioned in this verse is said to have been Aylah, and it was supposed to have been situated on the Red Sea.

Question them about (the fate of the people of) the seaside town.

They broke (the rules) of the Sabbath, for whenever it was their Sabbath day, the fish (of the sea) would come to them clearly ready to be caught.

However, on days other than the Sabbath, they were nowhere to be found! This is how We tested them, for they were prone to disobedience. [163]

Then a group of (the disobedient people) protested (to the preachers among them), saying, "*Why are you *preaching to (us), when Allah will eventually destroy us anyway or bring a terrible punishment down upon (us for our disobedience)?"*

The (preachers) replied, *"We're doing our duty to your Lord, for you just might become mindful (of Him) yet."* [164]

When they forgot the reminders that had been given to them, We saved those who had spoken out against evil and severely punished the corrupt for their disobedience. [165]

When they boldly went beyond what they were allowed, We said to them, *"Be like rejected apes!"* [166]

Allah's Punishment came upon Them

Your Lord declared that He would send (other nations) against (the Children of Israel,) who would afflict them with humiliating tyranny, even until the Day of Assembly, for your Lord is swift in bringing conclusions; yet, He's also forgiving and merciful. [167]

And so We scattered them throughout the world in a Diaspora. Among them are some who are righteous and also others who are far less (virtuous) than that. We've tested them both in prosperity and hardship so they might return (to the path of Allah). [168]

Later generations came after them, and the scriptures became their responsibility, but they chose the worldly possessions of this life, justifying their choice by saying, *"We're going to be forgiven anyway."*

If similar material possessions ever came their way, they would take hold of them yet again.

Wasn't the scriptural covenant taken from them, (in which they agreed) that they wouldn't say anything about Allah but the truth?

Yet, they're the ones who are studying what's in (the scripture and then misapplying it)! The realm of the next life is better for those who are mindful (of Allah), so won't you understand? [169]

Those who hold firmly to the scripture and who establish prayer – We'll never let the reward of the righteous be lost! [170]

When We brought the towering heights of the mountain above them - like it was a raised CANOPY, so much so that they thought it might fall over on top of them, (We said), *"Hold firmly to what We've given you, and remember what it says so you can be mindful (of your duty to Allah)."* [171]

Humans are Duty Bound to Accept Faith in Allah

When your Lord brings offspring from out of the loins of the children of Adam, He makes them (first) bear witness about themselves by asking them, *"Am I not your Lord?"*

They say, *"Of course, and we are a witness to that!"*

(We do that) so you won't be able to say on the Day of Assembly, *"We had no clue about any of this,"* [172] and also so you won't be able to say, *"Our ancestors took other gods besides Allah in the past, but we're only their descendants, (and it's not our fault that we've followed them without knowing any better). Are You then going to destroy us for the inventions of people who were dishonest?"* [173]

That's how We explain the verses in detail so they might return (to Allah's path). [174]

About the People who Deny Allah

Recite for them the story of the man to whom We sent Our (revealed) verses, but then he slipped right by them (without even a care), enabling Shaytan to follow him. And so he went far off the (moral) way. [175]

If We had wanted, We could've elevated him with the (revelations), but he (stubbornly) clung to the earth and followed his own fickle whims. His example is that of a dog.

If you make a move against him, he just rolls out his tongue, and if you leave him alone, he still just rolls out his tongue! That's the example of those people who deny Our (revealed) verses, so repeat this story so they might be mindful (of its message). [176]

Disgraceful is the example of those who deny Our signs and who do harm to their own souls! [177]

Whoever is guided by Allah, he's truly guided. Whomever He leaves astray, they're in a state of loss! [178] And so it is that We've made many jinns and human beings for Hellfire.

They have hearts, but they don't understand with them. They have eyes, but they don't see with them. They have ears, but they don't hear with them.

They're like cattle – *No! They're even more mistaken than that!* They're completely unconcerned (about Allah's warnings)! [179]

233

Don't Sit with those who Take Allah's Name in Vain

The most beautiful names belong to Allah, so call upon Him using them, but shun the company of those who use His names improperly, for they're soon going to be paid back for what they've done. [180]

They must Pay Attention before Disaster Strikes

Among those whom We've created is a community that guides (others) to the truth and that does justice by it. [181]

However, We're gradually going to bring Our punishment to bear against those who deny Our signs – *(and we will bring that punishment upon them) in ways they can't even detect!* [182]

I'm going to give them some time, for My plan is unchangeable. [183]

Don't (the Meccans) ever consider that their companion, (Muhammad,) just might *not* be possessed by a jinn and that he just might *indeed* be a clear warner? [184]

Don't they see **ANYTHING** in the functioning of the heavens and the earth and in all that Allah has created that might give them an inkling that their time might just be drawing to a close? So what message will they believe in after this? [185]

Whomever Allah leaves astray, there can be no one to guide him, for He will leave them wandering aimlessly in their overconfidence. [186]

When will the Hour Come to Pass?

Background Info... v. 187

Some Jews who were visiting Mecca approached the Prophet and said, "Muhammad, inform us when the Hour (of Judgment) will take place, if you're truly a prophet, for we know when it will be." This verse was revealed in response. (*Asbab ul-Nuzul*)

Now they're asking you about the Hour (of Judgment) – *"When will it come to pass?"*

Say to them, *"Its knowledge is in the presence of my Lord, and no one can predict when it will occur save Him. It weighs heavily upon the heavens and the earth, and it will come upon you out of nowhere."*

Really now, they're asking you as if you were somehow eagerly in search of it! So tell them, *"Its knowledge is in the presence of Allah,"* though most people don't know (anything about it). [187]

234

On Petty Fortune-telling

Background Info... v. 188

Some Meccans asked the Prophet if Allah ever revealed to him what future market prices would be, because they wanted to know when they should buy and when they should sell in order to make money. Others asked him if Allah ever told him which pastures would be fertile and which would be barren. This verse was revealed in response. (*Asbab ul-Nuzul*)

Say to them, *"I have no power to bring either benefit or harm upon myself, except for what Allah allows.*

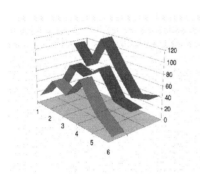

"If I had knowledge of what's beyond perception, then I would've had tremendous good fortune, and no misfortune would have ever come upon me. I'm only a warner and an announcer of good news to those who believe." [188]

How do People Ignore Allah's Blessings?

He's the One Who created you from a single soul, and He made from it her mate, so she could dwell with her (husband as a family).

After they've gone into each other, she soon comes to bear a light burden and carries it around, though when she grows heavy, they both pray to Allah, their Lord, saying:

"If You grant us a perfect and healthy child, we promise that we'll be thankful." [189]

However, when He grants them a perfect and healthy child, they let other (gods) share in the gift that they received, *even though Allah is so high above the partners they make with Him!* [190]

So are they taking (inanimate objects) to be partners with Him, (things that) cannot create anything and that are just created things themselves? [191]

(Those inanimate objects) can't help them, nor can they even help themselves! [192]

(But alas,) even if you show (those idol-worshippers true) guidance, they won't follow you, for it's all the same to them whether you call to them or keep quiet! [193]

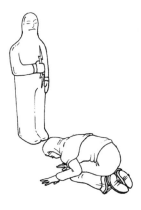

Those upon whom you call besides Allah are merely (created) servants like yourselves.

So go ahead and call upon them, and see if they listen to your prayers, that is, if you're really being so honest! [194]

Do they have feet with which to walk, or hands with which to hold, or eyes with which to see, or ears with which to hear?

Say to those (who believe in idols), *"Call your 'partners,' and plan (your worst) against me, and don't give me any break!* [195]

"My protector is Allah, the One Who revealed the Book, and He protects those who are moral and upright. [196]

"All those whom you call upon besides Him can't help you, nor can they help themselves! [197]

"If you call them to guidance, they won't hear you, and even though you may see their eyes staring at you, they don't see anything." [198]

Background Info... v. 199

When this verse was revealed, the Prophet asked Angel **Jibra'il** (Gabriel) about it. The Prophet later said of this discussion that he was commanded to forgive those who did wrong to him, to be generous to the one who gives him nothing, and to keep relations alive with those who break them with him. (*at-Tabari*)

Many scholars also say it counsels the Prophet to accept what his followers sincerely offer and not to be critical or overly harsh if they fail to measure up due to weakness. (*Ma'ariful Qur'an*)

Commit yourself to forgiving (others by overlooking their shortcomings and actions against you), order good conduct, and turn away from the ignorant. [199]

If any suggestion from Shaytan comes upon you, then seek Allah's protection, for He hears and knows (all things). [200]

Those who bring (Allah) to mind when an evil thought from Shaytan comes upon them are reminded (of their allegiance to Allah), and suddenly they can see clearly again! [201]

236

However, their (evil) 'brothers' will always seek to plunge them into error, and they never let up. [202]

Allah Reveals in His Own Time

> **Background Info... v. 203**
>
> Sometimes the Prophet would receive a whole chapter of the Qur'an at once. Other times he would get only a verse or two. More often than not, he would get a small passage, then affix it to existing passages and thus have a full chapter whose various parts might have been revealed over weeks, months or years.
>
> It happened sometimes, however, that the Prophet wouldn't receive any revealed verses at all, and at such times, the idol-worshippers taunted Muhammad, (p) assuming that he was the author of the revelations and that he was merely unprepared with his material.
>
> This verse instructs Muhammad (p) to tell those people that Allah gives verses when He wants to, and not when people demand them from the Prophet. (Ma'ariful Qur'an)

Whenever you don't bring them a (new) verse (when they expect to hear one), they say, "*Why don't you have your (material) ready yet?*"

Say to them, "*I only follow what's been revealed to me from my Lord, and it's no less than insight from your Lord and a source of guidance and mercy for all who believe.*" [203]

How should We Recite the Qur'an?

> **Background Info... v. 204-206**
>
> While in Mecca, the Prophet would lead clandestine group prayers with his followers – **sometimes in peoples' homes** and other times out in the countryside.
>
> Some of the worshippers would repeat whatever the Prophet said in prayer, which annoyed him, while others would sometimes talk among themselves when they were supposed to be praising Allah.
>
> This passage was revealed to let the believers know they were to keep silent in prayers and maintain a spiritual focus meditating upon Allah. (Ma'ariful Qur'an)

When the Qur'an is being read, listen to it attentively and keep quiet, so you can receive mercy. [204]

Remember your Lord inwardly with humility and awe. Don't speak loudly (when you repeat His praises) in the morning and evening. Don't be careless (about Allah)! [205]

Those (angels) who are the nearest to your Lord aren't too proud to serve Him. So glorify Him, and bow yourselves down before Him. [206]

237

The Spoils of War

8 Al Anfāl
Early Medinan Period

☞ Introduction

This chapter was revealed shortly after the Battle of Badr and deals with a number of issues related to war and **what happens after it's over.** The title of the chapter comes from the discussion over the division of captured goods. One fifth of all captured things (booty) goes to the Prophet so he can pay for the needs of the Islamic movement. (He usually gave everything he received away, so much so that there was often never even any food in his apartment!)

The believers are told not to be afraid if they are called upon to fight an enemy. A key phrase is contained in verse 38, **which sums up the Qur'anic attitude towards those who make** war upon **Allah's community: if you stop your attacks and repent, Allah will forgive you your past actions. If you don't,** then you will be defeated.

In the Name of Allah,
the Compassionate, the Merciful

Background Info... v. 1

After the Battle of Badr, a lot of goods were collected from the battlefield. The fleeing Meccans left weapons, horses, tents and other things. In the evening after the battle, some factions of the Muslims began arguing over how to divide the war booty.

The group that collected it thought it should be theirs (finders keepers), while the groups that either guarded the Prophet after the battle or who kept on pursuing the enemy felt they should have the most for their extra efforts. This verse told the believers to let the Prophet decide what to do with the war booty, and he distributed it evenly. (*Ibn Kathir*)

mindful of Allah and maintain good relations among you. Obey Allah and His Messenger if you're (really true) believers." [1]

Indeed, believers are those who, when they're reminded of Allah, feel a **tremor** in their hearts, and when they hear His verses being recited, their faith is increased. They let their Lord take care of their affairs. [2]

(They're the ones) who establish prayer and spend out of the resources that We've provided for them. [3]

They're asking you about the captured goods (collected after a battle).

Say to them, "*The captured goods belong to Allah and His Messenger, so be*

238

The Battle of Badr

These are the true believers, and they have varying degrees of status, (depending upon their efforts), in their Lord's sight, as well as forgiveness and a generous share of resources (awaiting them in the next life). [4]

(These different grades in status in Allah's sight) are evidenced by the fact that when your Lord had ordered you to leave your home, (Muhammad, to make a stand at the wells of Badr) for a true purpose, a segment of the believers didn't like it, and they argued with you (about it), even after the reality (of the situation) was made evidently clear.

(Indeed, they made it seem as if) they were being marched off to their own deaths right before their own eyes! [5-6]

Allah had promised that one of the two (enemy) groups would fall to you. Although you were hoping that it would be the unprotected (caravan returning to Mecca from Syria), Allah wanted to have the truth of His words demonstrated.

He also wanted to cut off the root of those who covered over (the light of faith within their hearts) so He could demonstrate that the truth is true and falsehood is a lie, no matter how much the bad people hate it. [7-8]

Allah Helped the Faithful at the Battle of Badr

(Remember) how you had fervently asked for the help of your Lord (at the Battle of Badr), and He answered you, saying, "*I will help you with a regiment of a thousand angels.*" [9]

This announcement wasn't made for any other purpose than to assure your hearts, for there is no help except from Allah's presence, and Allah is powerful and wise. [10]

(Remember) how He covered you in a state of rest (just before the eve of battle) to calm your anxiety (as a gift) from Himself, and He made water fall from the sky to cleanse you, to remove the stain of Shaytan, to strengthen your hearts and to make your stance firm. [11]

(Muhammad,) remember also that your Lord inspired the angels (to bring a message of hope to your heart that said), "*I'm with you, so steady the believers. I'm going to put fear into the hearts of the faithless, so raise (your weapons) at their necks and raise (them again to strike) off their fingertips (as they brandish their swords against you)!"* [12]

That's (what they deserve) because they (dared) to oppose Allah and His Messenger. Whoever opposes Allah and His Messenger (should know that) Allah is severe in administering punishment. [13]

"This (defeat at Badr) is for you, (all you enemies of Allah), so taste it!"

Indeed, all those who cover over (their natural faith in Allah) will be punished in the Fire! [14]

O you who believe! When you go forth and engage the faithless in battle, never turn your backs to them. [15]

If anyone turns his back (and runs away) – unless it's part of a strategy (to defeat the enemy through a trick) or to rejoin a battalion – then he's going to bring Allah's wrath down upon him, and his home will be in Hellfire – *the worst destination!* [16]

It wasn't you who struck them down (at the Battle of Badr); it was Allah. When you threw (a symbolic handful of pebbles at the idol-worshippers as the battle

commenced, Muhammad), it wasn't something you did, but Allah Who did it, so He could test the believers with a fine test from Himself, for Allah hears and knows (all things). [17]

That's (why the battle took place). Truly, Allah thwarts the plans of those who cover over (the light of faith within their hearts). [18]

(All you faithless Meccans!) If you had ever looked for a definitive resolution (in your struggles with the believers), then there you have it! The resolution has come to you, so if you would just stop (opposing Allah), it would be better for you.

If you ever return (to fight against the believers,) then We'll bring about the same (result). The forces under your command are of no use to you, no matter how numerous they become, for Allah is with the believers, (and He helps them to achieve victory). [19]

Obey the Messenger of Allah

O you who believe! Obey Allah and His Messenger. Don't turn away from him when you hear (him speaking), nor be like those who say, "*We hear,*" but then they don't listen. [20-21]

Truly, the worst creatures in Allah's sight are those who (intentionally refuse) to hear (when they really can hear) and who (refuse to) respond (when they really can respond, for they don't use) their reason! [22]

If Allah would've known of any good (qualities) within them, He would've made them listen.

However, even if He did make them listen, (owing to their current state), they would've merely turned away and refused (to believe)! [23]

O you who believe! Respond to Allah and His Messenger when He calls you to what will give you life.

Know that Allah can come between a person and his heart and that you'll all be gathered back to Him. [24]

Be mindful of the chaos and trials that affect more than just the sinners among you, and know that Allah is severe in punishment. [25]

Remember how you (Muslims) used to be such a small group (in the early days of the Prophet's mission).

Everyone in the land thought you were so weak; you were constantly afraid of people robbing or kidnapping you, but He found a place of refuge for you (in Medina) and gave you strength with His help.

He also provided wholesome resources for you, as well, so you could be thankful. [26]

Don't Allow Material Concerns to Destroy Loyalty

Background Info... v. 27-28

When the Banu Qurayzah were on the verge of surrendering to the Muslims after the Meccan siege of Medina was lifted, they asked to see an old friend of theirs named Abu Lubaba to get his opinion about what they should do.

They had demanded that the Prophet merely exile them for their betrayal of the Muslims, but the Prophet would only accept their unconditional surrender. The leaders of the Banu Qurayzah knew they had no choice but to do so, but they sent the counter demand that they wanted to pick the one who would judge them. They were inclined to pick the chief of the Auws tribe, Sa'd ibn Mu'adh, as he had been friendly with them before Islam. So they asked Abu Lubaba his opinion about what might befall them if they surrendered.

Abu Lubaba, who was swayed by the fact that some of his family and property were located in the district of the Banu Qurayzah, put his finger over his throat and made a cutting motion, implying that they shouldn't accept any deal because any judgment they would receive would be severe.

Abu Lubaba immediately felt ashamed, for he knew he had betrayed the Prophet by attempting to taint the negotiations.

When he left the fortress of the Banu Qurayzah, he immediately went to the masjid and tied himself to a pillar, vowing not to eat or drink anything until Allah forgave him, even if it meant his death.

After several days he passed out in delirium, but then he was revived and told that Allah accepted his repentance. He then said he would not leave the pillar unless the Prophet came and untied him with his own hands. The Prophet came and did so.

Abu Lubaba offered to give all his money and property away to compensate for his mistake, but the Prophet told him to give away only one third and that would be sufficient. This passage was revealed about this situation. (*Asbab ul-Nuzul*)

Know that your property and your children are no more than a source of testing for you and that with Allah lies your most substantial reward. [28]

Appreciate All that Allah did for You

O you who believe! If you're mindful of Allah, then He'll give you a standard (to judge between right and wrong).

He'll erase your shortcomings from (your record) and forgive you, as well, for Allah is the master of tremendous favor. [29]

Recall how the faithless (idol-worshippers of Mecca) plotted against you, (Muhammad,) either to imprison you, murder you or drive you out (of the city). They were making plans, and Allah was making plans, and Allah is the best planner of all! [30]

When Our (revealed) verses were recited to them, they said, "*We heard this kind of stuff before. If we ever wanted to, we could say things just like this, for these*

O you who believe! Don't betray the trust of Allah and the Messenger, and don't knowingly take things that don't belong to you. [27]

242

(verses) are nothing more than old legends." [31]

Allah will Punish Evil in His Own Time

> **Background Info... v. 32-33**
>
> An-Nadr ibn al-Harith, a vile poet of the Quraysh, had said the things mentioned in this verse to the Prophet in the days when the Prophet was still living in Mecca. In effect, an-Nadr denied revelation and even dared Allah to punish him. This was originally commented upon by the Qur'an (in a Meccan revelation) in verses 70:1-3, and now the punishment he asked for befell him, as an-Nadr was one of those captured and later killed after Badr. (Some reports say he was killed in the battle itself.) (*Nisa'i, Ma'ariful Qur'an*)

Their prayers at the House (of Allah) are no more than **whistling** and the **clapping** of hands. (The only answer such foolish prayers can receive is,) *"Suffer the punishment for your rejection (of Allah's truth)!"* [35]

> **Background Info... v. 36-37**
>
> After the Battle of Badr was over, the pagan Meccans were distraught with grief over their losses of both men and honor. Abu Sufyan, who had safely guided the precious Meccan caravan in from Syria, was called upon by his people to donate money from the trading enterprise to raise a new army to fight the Muslims once more. He made a public call for the other investors to do likewise. When news of this reached Medina, this passage was revealed in response. (*Asbab ul-Nuzul*)

Also remember how they said, *"O Allah, if all of this is really the truth from You, then (we dare You) to send a shower of stones down upon us from the sky. Punish us as hard (as You can)!"* [32]

However, Allah wasn't going to punish them as long as you were still living there among them, nor was He going to do it while they still had time to repent. [33]

So what reason is there for Allah not to punish them now, since they're keeping people away from the Sacred Masjid, even though they're not its (legitimate) guardians?

No one but the mindful can be its guardians, but most of them don't understand. [34]

Those who cover over (the truth of Allah in their hearts) only spend their money to hold people back from the path of Allah, and that's how they're going to keep on spending it.

In the end, they'll have nothing more than regrets, and they'll be overwhelmed (in despair).

Then the faithless will be gathered together at (the edge of) Hellfire so Allah can separate the tainted from the pure and also so He can pile the tainted (sinners) in a heap and throw them all into Hellfire. They're the ones who will be utterly lost! [36-37]

Making Peace With Your Enemies

Tell all those who cover over (their ability to believe) that if they stop (their opposition to Allah's cause), then their past (sins) will be forgiven for them, but if they persist, then the example of the ancients is there (for all to see as a warning). [38]

Go on fighting them until chaos and disorder have ceased and until Allah's way of life prevails, but if (the faithless) end (their attacks upon you, then know that) Allah sees everything that they're doing. [39]

If they refuse (to make peace), then know that Allah is your close comrade, and He's the protector of all and the best source of aid! [40]

How Allah Helps the Believers in Wartime

Know that out of all the captured goods you gain, a fifth of it is reserved for Allah and for the Messenger *and* for close relatives (who are in need), as well as for orphans and (stranded) travelers.

(So, all you believers, don't be upset when that amount is deducted from the total distribution of goods,) if you really have faith in Allah and in (the victory) We sent down to Our servant on a Decisive Day, the day when the two forces met (at battle at Badr), for Allah has power over all things. [41]

(Remember) how you were on one edge of the valley and (the enemy) was on the other, and (remember) how the caravan was located on lower ground than you.

Even if you had made an appointment in advance, you couldn't have timed it so well.

However, it was a foregone conclusion in Allah's (plan) so that those who lived and died (that day) could do so knowing full well (that Allah had arranged this). Allah is indeed the Hearing and the Knowing! [42]

(Remember) that in your dream Allah made it seem to you that they were few in number.

If He had shown you how large a force they really were, you would've been discouraged, and you would've certainly second-guessed yourself, but Allah **PRESERVED** you in your decision, for He knows (how your) hearts (work). [43]

(Remember) that when you met (the enemy in battle), He made them seem to you like a much smaller force than they actually were, and He made you seem fewer in number, likewise.

That was so Allah could bring to a conclusion something that was already determined, for all issues go back to Allah. [44]

O you who believe! When you meet an (enemy) force, be firm and remember Allah often so you can be successful. [45]

Obey Allah and His Messenger, and don't argue with each other, for you might lose your resolve and diminish your strength.

Be patient and carry on, for Allah is with those who are patient and carry on. [46]

Don't be like those (pagans of Mecca) who started from their homes puffed up with pride only so other people would see them.

(Their goal) was to delay others from joining the path of Allah, but Allah surrounds whatever they do! [47]

How a 'Shaytan' was Defeated

> **Background Info... v. 48**
>
> The 'satan' referred to here in this verse was a powerful desert chieftain named Suraqah ibn Malik through whom Shaytan made false promises to the Meccans.
>
> When the army of the Quraysh was mustering and preparing to leave Mecca, the Meccans were more than a little apprehensive about marching out and leaving their city undefended. (The Quraysh had a rivalry with a bedouin tribe called the Banu Bakr, who might take the opportunity to raid Mecca.)
>
> Suraqah, who lived in the vicinity of the Banu Bakr, came riding into Mecca, flanked by strong warriors of his own, and promised the Meccans that he would restrain the ill-will of the Banu Bakr. Then he told the Meccans that no people would ever beat them that day, as long as he was on their side. (As recorded in this verse.)
>
> During the battle, however, when it looked like the Meccans were about to be routed, Suraqah said what the ending of this verse quotes him as saying, and then he fled from the battlefield, much to the astonishment of the Quraysh. (*Ma'ariful Qur'an*)

(Remember) how *Shaytan* made their actions seem good to them and how he told them, "*No people can ever beat you today as long as I'm near you.*"

However, when the two forces came in full view of each other, (Shaytan) turned on his heels and said, "*I'm free of you! I see what you don't see. I'm afraid of Allah, and Allah is harsh in punishment!*" [48]

The Worst of All Creatures

The hypocrites and the sick at heart say, "*These people are being fooled by their religion!*"

However, if someone trusts in Allah, (that's the best thing to do), for Allah is powerful and wise! [49]

If you could just see it - when the angels take the souls of those who rejected (faith) - how they're going to raise up (their hands) towards their faces and their backs (to punish them).

(And then when they enter Hellfire, they'll be told,) "*Suffer the punishment of the raging flame!* [50] *That's (the punishment you deserve) because of what your own hands have sent ahead - and Allah is never unfair to His servants!*" [51]

(Their deeds) are like those of Pharaoh's people and those who went before them. They rejected the signs of their Lord, so Allah seized them for their sins, and Allah is strong and harsh in punishment. [52]

That's because Allah will never (suddenly withdraw) the favors that He's granted to a people unless they change their souls (for the worst), and Allah listens and knows. [53]

As for Pharaoh's people and those who went before them, they denied the signs of their Lord, so We destroyed them for their sins. We even drowned Pharaoh's (army), for they were indeed corrupt. [54]

Who is the Most Despicable?

> **Background Info... v. 55-56**
>
> These verses were revealed about the Banu Qurayzah tribe of Medina that was obligated by treaty to help the Muslims repel the Meccans' grand alliance that came to attack Medina during the Battle of the Trench. Instead, when representatives from the previously expelled Banu Nadir secretly approached the Banu Qurayzah to defect, the chief of the Banu Qurayzah tribe caved in under pressure and agreed to betray the Muslims.

Truly, the worst creatures in the sight of Allah are those who cover over (their awareness of His truth) and who have no faith. [55]

They're the ones with whom you may make a treaty, but who then break their treaties every time. They literally have no concern for Allah! [56]

Therefore, if you ever gain the upper hand over them on the battlefield, scatter them completely, so that those who come after them will have a lesson to consider. [57]

If you fear a *DOUBLE-CROSS* from any group, then throw back (their treaty at them) so you'll at least be on an even level with them, for Allah has no love for the treacherous. [58]

Prefer Peace
but be Prepared for War

Don't let those who cover over (their inner awareness of the truth) think that they can make progress (against Allah), for they can't escape (the punishment they deserve). [59]

Keep yourselves prepared against them to the best of your ability, especially with a strong mobile force that can strike fear into Allah's enemies and your enemies and also other (potential enemies) about whom you know nothing, but about whom **Allah knows**.

Whatever you spend in the cause of Allah will be repaid to you, and you won't be treated unfairly. [60]

(Remember) that if the enemy leans towards peace, then you also must pursue the path of peace.

Trust in Allah, for He's the Hearing and the Knowing. [61]

Be Aware of False Intentions

If (you find) that they're really trying to trick you (through false peace talks,) then Allah is enough for you (against them).

He's the One Who strengthened your hand by His help and (with the aid) of the (faithful) believers. [62]

He united the hearts of the believers (in brotherhood, even though they came from so many diverse backgrounds).

Even if you spent everything on earth, you never could've produced that kind of heartfelt (unity by your own efforts), but Allah brought them together, for He is powerful and wise. [63]

You can Win against
Twice Your Number

O Prophet! Allah is enough for you and for those who follow you among the believers. [64]

O Prophet! **Rally** the believers to battle. If there are twenty among you who persevere, they can beat two hundred; if a hundred, they can beat a thousand of the faithless, for those who cover over (their ability to have faith) are devoid of reason. [65]

For the moment, Allah has eased (your burden), because He knows you're at a disadvantage (in men and material).

As it is now, if there are a hundred persevering people among you, they can beat two hundred. If a thousand, they can beat two thousand by Allah's leave, for Allah is with the persevering. [66]

Prisoners of War

It's not right for a prophet to start taking prisoners of war (wholesale in order to collect their ransoms) when he hasn't even subdued the land.

You (believers) want the temporary goods of this lower world, while Allah wants (to give you the rewards) of the next life, and Allah is powerful and wise. [67]

Background Info... v. 68-69

Before the Battle of Badr, the Prophet told his men that some people from his own tribe of Banu Hashim were in the pagan army and that they had no desire to fight the Muslims, but they had been compelled to join the Meccan force.

He, therefore, asked the Muslims that if they recognized any men from his own clan to spare them in the battle. (*Ibn Is-haq*) They could then ransom them later.

If it wasn't for prior permission granted by Allah, you would've been punished severely for (the ransoms) you took, but go ahead and lawfully enjoy (the profits) you previously made from the war (through prisoner release payments), but be mindful of Allah, for Allah is forgiving and merciful. [68-69]

The Case of 'Abbas, One Captive of Badr

Background Info... v. 70-71

The Prophet's uncle 'Abbas was one of those Meccans taken prisoner. He had in his possession twenty ounces of gold, as he was one of the quartermasters of the Meccan army who was charged with buying food for the men.

When the Prophet came to see him, 'Abbas said he had been a secret Muslim in Mecca. Then he asked if he could be freed and if that gold could be used to pay for his ransom.

The Prophet declined, saying that only Allah knew if he was a true Muslim, for he had marched against the Muslims.

This verse was revealed to the Prophet in answer to Abbas' question. Then the Prophet said that the gold in question was part of the funds used to fight against the Muslims and was thus forfeit.

The Prophet then made 'Abbas responsible for ransoming his nephew 'Aqeel, as well. 'Abbas began to plead poverty, but then the Prophet asked him about the gold he had left with his wife for her and her sons' upkeep should anything happen to him at Badr.

'Abbas was astonished and asked how the Prophet knew about his secret savings and its purpose. The Prophet replied, "Allah told me about it." 'Abbas declared that no one knew what he had done except himself and Allah, and then he declared himself a true and sincere Muslim.

Later on, when the Prophet was distributing the spoils of Badr in Medina, 'Abbas came and asked for some, too.

The Prophet said he could take some, and 'Abbas stuffed his robe full of whatever he could fit in its folds.

He asked for help to carry everything, but the Prophet refused to help him. So 'Abbas dropped several things and hobbled away clutching as much treasure as he could manage, leaving an astonished Prophet puzzling over his uncle's greediness.

In later years, after his fortunes had risen twenty-fold, 'Abbas used to say that Allah repaid him that twenty ounces of gold he lost by increasing his wealth twenty times – a prophecy in this verse for him that came true! (*Ma'ariful Qur'an*)

O Prophet! Say to the captives that you're holding, "*If Allah finds any good in your hearts, then He'll give you something better than what's been taken from you, and He'll forgive you, for Allah is forgiving and merciful.*" [70]

If any of them intend to betray you, then (know that) they've already betrayed Allah.

That's why He gave you power over them, for Allah is full of knowledge and wisdom. [71]

Walking on the Path to Allah

Those who believe and migrate and who struggle with their wealth and their lives in the cause of Allah, as well as those who give them refuge and help – they're the close comrades of each other.

As for those who believe but who don't migrate (from a hostile land), you're not obligated to protect them until they migrate (to an Islamic territory).

Though if they seek your help in religious matters, then it's your duty to help them, unless it would be against a people with whom you've made a treaty. Remember that Allah is watching everything you do. [72]

Those who cover over (their ability to believe) are the best friends of each other. Unless you (trust each other) likewise, then there will be turmoil throughout the earth and great corruption besides. [73]

Those who believe, who migrate and who strive in the cause of Allah, along with those who give them refuge and help them – they're the real believers!

249

They'll have forgiveness and a generous share of resources (in Paradise). [74]

Those who believe later on, who migrate and strive hard alongside of you, are one with you, as well, but ties of family have precedence (in legal matters) in the Book of Allah, and Allah knows about all things. [75]

Repentance

9 At-Tawbah

aka Al-Barā'ah

Late Medinan Period

☞ Introduction

This is the only chapter of the Qur'an that does not begin with an invocation of Allah's mercy. There have been various explanations as to why the traditional phrase of "In the Name of Allah" was left off. Many early Muslims were under the impression that it might be something of a continuation of the last chapter, (and this was the opinion of Caliph Uthman,) while the complimentary view in modern times is that this chapter is unlike all other chapters both in initial tone and content, in that it seems from the outset to be stern and full of warnings to both the remaining pagans of Arabia and the hypocrites.

'Ali ibn Abi Talib explained it exactly in this way by saying that to begin in Allah's name is to have the assurance of His protection, but in this chapter, the opening lines are a revocation of Allah's protection, and thus the introductory invocation of Allah is left off. (*Ma'ariful Qur'an*)

The hidden subtext in this chapter is that Islam was now unstoppable and was clearly on track to ultimate victory. If that weren't a good enough sign for the remaining pagans of Arabia (some of whom had violated their previously signed treaties with the Prophet) and the hypocrites (who still foolishly thought they could stop the progress of Islam), then they truly were as twisted as the Qur'an made them out to be and were, by extension, unworthy of fellowship or entry into Mecca – Allah's holy sanctuary.

So verses 1-37 were revealed soon after the conquest of Mecca with a clear purpose: to cancel all treaties made between the treacherous pagans and the Muslim state - only guarantying the peace for the remainder of the traditional truce months. The Muslims were commanded, however, to continue to honor the treaties they had with those pagan tribes that adhered faithfully to their end of the bargain until the treaty durations expired, even as they were reminded of the looming Byzantine threat to the north.

Here is the background for the remaining verses in this chapter. Verses 38-72 were revealed in the middle part of the year 629, and they concern the Prophet's efforts to organize an army for the journey to Tabuk, a border town that was located at the northernmost reaches of Arabia. Here are the events that led up to the Prophet's call to arms. Local client rulers of the Byzantines (the Ghassanids) had murdered some of the Prophet's envoys. So the Prophet felt obligated to organize a military response.

Late in the year 629, he sent a force of three thousand men (under the command of his adopted son, Zayd ibn Harith) to Syria, to show that such brutality would not go unanswered. After receiving a call for help from Suhrabil ibn Amr, the king of Basra, the Byzantine Emperor Heraclius sent an army of his own, commanded by his brother Theophanous (Theodore), which, drawing upon many local allied Arab tribes, swelled the defenders to anywhere from 10,000 to 100,000 men. (The reports differ and are sometimes greatly exaggerated.) The two armies met in Syria at the famous Battle of Mu'tah.

Regardless of the true number of enemy troops, the odds against the Muslims were bad, and by all rights the Muslims should have been vanquished handily. On the eve of battle, one companion named 'Abdullah ibn Ruwahah said to the uneasy Muslims: "Men, what you're disliking is the same thing that you've come out in search of, in other words, martyrdom. We're not fighting the enemy with numbers or the strength of multitudes, but we're confronting them with this religion that Allah has honored us with. So come on! Both prospects are fine: victory or martyrdom." Then the men said, "By Allah, Ibn Ruwahah is right."

251

When the battle commenced, the Byzantine's massive numbers threatened to drown out the Muslims. However, the Muslims used stunningly unorthodox cavalry tactics and were able to avoid being swallowed up by the endless sea of Byzantines. Zayd eventually fell in the battle, however, and his lieutenant, Ja'far ibn Abi Talib, took command.

When he, too, fell, the third man to take control of the Muslim force, 'Abdullah ibn Ruwahah, said aloud to those around him, "O my soul! If you're not killed, you're bound to die anyway. This is the fate of death overtaking you. What you wished for, you've been granted. If you do what they (Zayd and Ja'far) have done, then you're guided aright!" He fell in the battle shortly thereafter. (Meanwhile, back in Medina, the Prophet sorrowfully informed the people about the death of those prominent companions, before news had ever reached the city. When Ja'far's family was informed of what the Prophet had foreseen, they began to weep uncontrollably, and the Prophet asked them not to weep, for Ja'far was, he explained, now in Paradise.)

After fierce and desperate fighting, Khalid ibn Walid was given command and led a fighting retreat complete with a clever ruse to make it seem as if he were receiving fresh troops. The Byzantines, being stunned by the fierce bravado of the Muslims, also withdrew, but not before claiming victory. When Khalid led the beleaguered survivors back to Medina, some people actually started berating the men as cowards who should have died on the battlefield (citing verses 8:15-16). However, the Prophet came out and stopped the people from saying this, telling them, "No, they're strugglers in Allah's cause who will fight again another day." (Verses 8:65-66 were revealed allowing Muslims to retreat if the odds were more than two to one against them.)

The bold move of the Muslims did impress many southern Syrian and southern Iraqi tribes, and thousands of people from these semi-independent tribes (who were previously allied to either the Byzantines or Persians) accepted Islam. According to the historian Nicephorus, Heraclius was aware of this problem and traveled to Antioch to plan his next move.

His strategy would involve, not surprisingly, brute force. The Byzantines sought to crush the progress of Islam by harassing and oppressing any tribes that converted. (Eventually they began to position troops for a proposed assault on Medina, itself!) After the Byzantines began executing some tribal chieftains who had accepted Islam, and with scattered reports that the Byzantines were organizing Syrian Arabs for an invasion of the south, the Prophet had no choice but to organize an army to meet this northern threat.

So in September of the year 630, the Prophet himself marched an army of 30,000 people (including many women volunteers) northward to Tabuk in response to the threat of the Byzantines. (Many hypocrites sought exemptions from service, however, and feared leaving Medina due to the fact that the Muslims were so poorly equipped. There was also a heat wave afflicting the region, dampening the enthusiasm of the weak at heart.) The Byzantines, however, still smarting from their experience at Mu'tah, wound up withdrawing all their forces from northern Arabia, and no actual fighting took place.

The Prophet used his time in the region (about twenty days) to cement further alliances and also to extract promises of tribute from those tribes that had previously helped the Byzantines, particularly the Ghassanid tribe. (Some local chieftains, impressed with the Muslims, began to convert, as well.)

This successful expedition by the Prophet resulted in offers of allegiance from rulers and chiefs all over the Arabian Peninsula, southern Syria and southern Iraq. And so, the Prophet returned to Medina at the head of a successful mission. Then, verses 73-129 were revealed after the Prophet returned home, and they address a variety of issues related mostly to this campaign and also to the hypocrites.

(This is) an announcement from Allah and His Messenger to all the people gathered on the day of the Great Pilgrimage (in Mecca) that Allah and His Messenger are dissolving all (treaty) obligations with the idol-worshippers.

If you (treacherous idol-worshippers) would only repent, it would be best for you, but if you turn away, then know that you can't frustrate Allah, so give the news of a painful punishment to those who cover over (their faith). [3]

(T his is a declaration) of exemption from Allah and His Messenger to those pagan tribes with whom you've made treaties, (and who've been unfaithful to them). [1]

You (idol-worshippers) may travel (safely) anywhere you wish throughout the land during the (next) four months, but know that your (treacherous) deeds will never frustrate Allah, for Allah is certainly going to bring humiliation down upon those who reject (the truth). [2]

(However, those treaties) that you've made with those idol-worshippers who *have been* faithful to the terms, and who *didn't* give aid to any of your enemies, are not cancelled, so fulfill your obligations with them to the end of (each treaty's) term. Truly, Allah loves those who are mindful (of their obligations). [4]

Now when the truce months have passed, fight the (double-crossing) idol-worshippers wherever you find them. Capture them, surround their (settlements) and ambush them at every outpost.

However, if they repent, establish prayers and give in charity, then leave them to their way, for Allah is forgiving and merciful. [5]

If an individual idol-worshipper asks you for security, then grant safe passage to him so he can have the opportunity to hear the word of Allah. Then escort him to a place where he can be safe.

(They deserve this gracious treatment), for they're a people who don't know (about Allah's way of life). [6]

Those Who Break Treaties willfully must be Opposed

How can there be a treaty with idol-worshippers in the sight of Allah and His Messenger, other than with those with whom you've made a treaty near the Sacred Masjid?

As long as they're true (in their word) to you, then stay true (in your word) to them, for Allah loves those who are mindful (of their honest obligations). [7]

Again, how can (there be treaties with idol-worshippers), especially given the fact that if they overpowered you, they would neither respect family ties nor treaty obligations?

They say what you want to hear, but their hearts are filled with hatred towards you, for most of them are disobedient wrongdoers. [8]

They've sold the signs of Allah for a miserable price and have hindered people from His way. What they've done is utterly criminal! [9]

Truly, when it comes to a believer, they neither respect family ties nor obligations, and thus they'll go beyond all bounds! [10]

Yet, despite all of that, if they repent, establish prayer and give in charity, then they'll become your brothers in religion. That's how We explain the verses for people who understand. [11]

However, if they betray their agreements after giving their word and then taunt you about your religion, then fight the leaders of rejection, for they have no beliefs that would constrain them. [12]

And *shouldn't* you fight against people who betray their agreements and plot to drive away the Messenger and who take aggressive action against you first? Are you scared of them? By all rights, you should fear Allah, if you truly believe. [13]

So fight against them, and Allah will punish them by your hands and humiliate them. (He'll) help you against them and heal the (bruised) feelings of the believers by calming the sense of outrage within their hearts.

Allah turns toward whomever He wants, and Allah is full of knowledge and wisdom. [14-15]

Did you think you were just going to be left alone before Allah could distinguish who among you has striven hard (in His cause) and who has restrained himself from taking others as close intimates in preference to Allah, His Messenger and (the community of) believers? Allah is well-informed of all that you do. [16]

Only the Righteous Must Control Places of Worship

Background Info... v. 17-22

This passage was revealed in response to the ongoing sayings of many of the Meccans that they were sincere custodians of Allah's holy shrine in Mecca. The words of the Prophet's uncle 'Abbas, who was captured several years before this revelation at the Battle of Badr, show the influence of this viewpoint.

When he was brought to Medina, many of his relatives who had become Muslim and who had migrated with the Prophet began scolding him for believing in idols and cutting off family ties.

'Ali ibn Abi Talib was especially hard in his accusations. 'Abbas said in his defense, "What's wrong with you, for you're only mentioning our shortcomings and not our strong points?"

When 'Ali asked what those were, 'Abbas replied, "We (pagans) fill the sacred shrine with pilgrims; we serve the Ka'bah, and we give water to the pilgrims while freeing those in debt." (Asbab ul-Nuzul)

Later on, after 'Abbas had accepted Islam, he had a discussion with 'Ali ibn Abi Talib and Talhah ibn Shaybah in which he and Talhah boasted of their services to the Ka'bah. 'Ali replied that he had been praying facing the Ka'bah six months before any of them, and he also was striving with the Prophet all along, and so his service to Allah was more valuable than their services to the Ka'bah. (Ma'ariful Qur'an)

It's not the place of idol-worshippers to maintain the prayer-houses of Allah, for they've given proof against themselves that they reject (Him). Their efforts are useless, and they're going to dwell in the Fire. [17]

Allah's prayer-houses must be maintained only by those who believe in Allah and the Last Day and who establish prayer, give in charity and fear none but Allah.

They're the ones who (can be considered) to be rightly guided; (so,

255

they'll treat those places of worship with proper respect). [18]

Are you (idol-worshippers of the opinion) that merely giving water to pilgrims and maintaining the Sacred Masjid (in Mecca) is somehow equal to (the sacrifices made for Allah's sake) by those who (truly) believe in Allah and the Last Day and who struggled in the cause of Allah?

They're not equal in Allah's sight, and Allah doesn't guide an oppressive people. [19]

Those who believed (in Allah), who migrated and who struggled in the cause of Allah with their wealth and their lives, are more valuable in the sight of Allah, and they are the ones who will be successful. [20]

Their Lord has given them the good news of MERCY from His Own Self, of His satisfaction and of gardens filled with everlasting delights that will (be theirs) forever!

They will live within them forever, and with Allah are the greatest rewards! [21-22]

Making the Choice

Background Info... v. 23-24

When new converts to Islam in Mecca were asked to migrate to Medina, they were often inundated with requests from their non-Muslim relatives to stay where they were. Even after the Conquest of Mecca, converts from the pagan tribes of the countryside continued to face this familial pressure to remain at home. This passage asks such converts to make a choice: either remain with the pagans for worldly reasons or migrate for the sake of Allah. (*Ma'ariful Qur'an*)

O you who believe! Don't take your fathers or your brothers as close friends if they love concealing (the truth of Allah) more than having faith (in Him). Anyone who does that is doing wrong. [23]

Say (to the believers, who may be inclined to remain among their pagan relatives):

"*If your fathers, brothers, spouses, relatives, financial gains, trade deals that you're afraid will suffer or the lovely homes you live in are more beloved to you than Allah, His Messenger or in struggling in His cause, then you just wait until Allah's command comes to pass. Allah doesn't guide people who are rebellious.*" [24]

Allah Helps the Righteous

As it is, Allah has already helped you on many battlefields. On the day of (the Battle of) Hunayn, however, when your great numbers made you feel overconfident - *that by itself did nothing for you.*

The wide earth hemmed you in (as you passed through the narrow valley and were suddenly taken by surprise in ambush). And so you turned back in retreat. [25]

Then Allah sent His tranquility down upon the Messenger and upon the believers, and He sent forces (of angels) you couldn't even see. And so He punished the faithless, and that's how He repays those who cover (the light of faith within their hearts). [26]

Then after that, Allah accepted the repentance of whomever He wanted to from among those (who fled after the initial ambush), for Allah is the forgiving and merciful. [27]

> **Background Info... v. 28**
>
> After the conquest of Mecca, pagan pilgrims continued to enter Mecca, and they continued to perform their religious rites, sometimes naked, often clapping and whistling, as they were wont to do. So after a short time had passed, the Prophet forbade the future entry of idolaters into Mecca, and this verse was the source for his ruling. (*Ma'ariful Qur'an*)

O you who believe! The idol-worshippers are impure, so don't let them come near the Sacred Masjid after this year of theirs has passed.

If you're afraid of becoming poor (on account of the financial losses that this ban might cause), then Allah will enrich you as He wills from His Own bounty, for Allah is full of knowledge and wisdom. [28]

Be Prepared to Defend Yourselves

> **F.Y.I.**
>
> In the context of history, this verse was revealed after the Byzantine Empire had already become openly hostile to the Muslims of Medina and a war footing was in place. The purpose of this verse is to give a powerful call for the Muslims to face a declared enemy that happened to be culturally Christian (the Byzantines).

(Don't be afraid to) fight against those who don't believe in Allah and the Last Day, who don't forbid what Allah and His Messenger have forbidden, and who don't accept the true way of life.

(If) those who received the scripture (before you make war upon you, then fight them) until they (agree) to pay (an annual) tax from their own hand, understanding that they've been subdued. [29]

257

When a Holy Man is Overly Magnified

The Jews call (the ancient scholar) Ezra a son of God, and the Christians call ('Esa) the Messiah a son of God, but those are just phrases from their mouths.

They do nothing more than copy what the faithless in ancient times used to say. Allah's curse is upon them, and they're greatly deceived! [30]

They've taken their theologians and saints as lords in place of Allah (by obeying them in everything), and also the Messiah, the son of Maryam, as well, even though they were ordered to serve none but the One God alone – *there is no god besides Him!* He is far more glorified than the partners they attribute to Him! [31]

This is the True Religion and it will Win in the End

They want to put out the light of Allah's (truth) with their mouths, but Allah won't allow anything but the perfection of His light to be completed, no matter how much the faithless hate it. [32]

He's the One Who sent His Messenger with guidance and the true way of life so that it can prevail over all other ways of life, no matter how much the idol-worshippers hate it. [33]

Beware the Corruption of "Men of God"

O you who believe! Truly, there are many theologians and saints who falsely eat up the wealth of the people, and thus they divert them from Allah's path.

There are those who stow away (untaxed) gold and silver without spending it in Allah's way, so give them the news of a painful punishment. [34]

(That will be) a day when (their wealth) will be made burning hot in the fires of Hell, and it will be used to brand their foreheads, their sides and their backs.

"This is what you stowed away for yourselves! Now experience (the value) of what you stowed away!" [35]

Don't Alter the Calendar to Gain an Advantage

There are twelve numbered months in Allah's sight, and this was recorded by Him on the day He created the heavens and the earth.

Four of them have sacred restrictions, and that's the established custom, so do no wrong against yourselves within them (by violating this rule).

Fight against the idol-worshippers in a united front, even as they fight against you in a united front (even during the restricted months,) but know that Allah is with those who are mindful (of Him). [36]

Suddenly postponing (restricted months) is an added degree of (trying) to cover over (Allah's truth), and those who cover over (their awareness of the truth) are led into doing wrong on account of it.

They make it lawful one year (to violate a restricted month) and forbidden another year. They adjust the number of months restricted by Allah, so (in their eyes) restricted months become lawful!

The evil of their actions seems good to them, but Allah won't guide a people who cover over (their faith). [37]

Answer the Call to Fight

Background Info... v. 38-42

In the year 630, the Prophet received word from visiting Syrian olive traders that the Byzantines had amassed an army and were preparing an attack on Medina.

Apparently, word of the success of Islam had reached the Byzantine emperor Heraclius, and he was not one to allow a new power to rise, especially since he had recently concluded a terrible war with the Persians in the year 627.

And so the Byzantines mobilized and began operations against any Arab tribes that were inclined towards Islam in southern Iraq and Syria.

The Prophet organized his followers to march northward to meet this new challenge. The Expedition to Tabuk, as it came to be called, saw no combat, as the Byzantines withdrew unexpectedly. Yet, the Prophet's hand was strengthened in southern Syria and Iraq when he contracted alliances with local rulers all over the area.

A faction of hypocrites decided to remain in Medina and thus weakened the potential size and resources of the expedition. Their cowardice is what this passage is referencing.

O you who believe! What's wrong with you? When you're called to go out and fight in the cause of Allah, suddenly you hold tightly to the earth?

Do you love the life of this world more than the next life? But the life of this world provides such little comfort when compared to the life of the next! [38]

If you don't go out, then He'll punish you severely, and then He'll just replace you with another people. You bring no harm upon Him at all (by refusing to answer His call), for He has power over all things. [39]

If you don't help (Muhammad against the Byzantine Romans,) then (you should know that) Allah helped him when the faithless drove him away (from Mecca and tried to hunt him down).

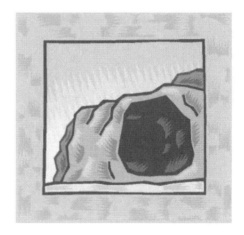

He was just one of two (men hiding out) in a cave when he said to his companion, (Abu Bakr, who was afraid that the Meccans would capture them), *"Don't be afraid, for Allah is with us."*

Then Allah sent His peacefulness down upon him, and (later, at the Battle of Badr,) He strengthened him with forces (of angels) that you couldn't even see.

He brought down the (boasting) claims of the faithless completely, for Allah's

260

word is the highest of all. Allah is indeed powerful and wise. [40]

March out, whether lightly or heavily equipped, and strive with your wealth and your persons in the cause of Allah. That's best for you if you only knew. [41]

If there were going to be a guaranteed profit and an easy journey, then they would all follow you, but it's going to be a far distance, (and it will be hard) on them, so much so that (many of them are falsely) swearing, "*If only we could make it, then we would certainly accompany you.*"

They're destroying themselves (with their false assertions), for Allah knows that they're lying. [42]

On those Who Made Excuses and Remained at Home

Background Info... v. 43

The Prophet, being soft-hearted, began granting exemptions to people from the general mobilization he had called for earlier for the two-week march northward to Syria. (Many of these exemptions were granted to people who were otherwise fit for service.)

May Allah forgive you (Muhammad)! Why did you grant anyone exemptions (from joining the Expedition to Tabuk) before you even had the opportunity to see clearly which of them were honest (in their petitions) and which of them were liars? [43]

Those who (really) believe in Allah and the Last Day would never ask to be excused from striving with their wealth and their persons, and Allah knows best who's mindful (of their duty to Him). [44]

The only ones who ever ask to be excused are those who don't believe in Allah and the Last Day and whose hearts are filled with doubts - leaving them hesitant in their misgivings. [45]

If they had really intended to march out, then they would've made some kind of preparations for it. Therefore, Allah didn't like that they should march out (anyway, due to the mischief they would've caused along the way), so He hindered them further, and they lagged behind. So they were told, "*Sit with those who stay and sit (at home).*" [46]

If they would've marched out with you, they wouldn't have augmented (your strength). Rather, they would've caused indiscipline (among your men) as they scurried about in your midst, sowing seeds of sedition among you. Some of you would have listened to them, and Allah knows who the corrupt ones are. [47]

As it is, they had already plotted sedition before, and they made your situation unsettled (in the past), even until the truth arrived and the order of Allah became clear, though they hated it. [48]

Hypocrites are Unreliable

Background Info... v. 49

This was the statement of Jadd ibn Qays, who was a leader among the Banu Salamah tribe. The Prophet had asked him, "Would you like to go and fight the yellow ones (the Romans) this year?"

Ibn Qays replied, "Messenger of Allah! Grant me an exemption, and don't put me in turmoil, for by Allah, my people know that there isn't a man who is more attracted to women than I, and I'm afraid that if see the women of the (Romans) that I wouldn't have any patience (to control myself)."

So the Prophet granted him an exemption on such a flimsy excuse. Then the Prophet advised the rest of the Banu Salamah tribe to chose another chief. 'Abdullah ibn Ubayy of the Auws tribe also (predictably) asked for an exemption. (Asbab ul-Nuzul)

Among them are some who said, "*Grant me an exemption, and don't give me a hard trial to face,*" but hadn't they already been tried before (during previous battles)!

Truly, Hellfire surrounds all those who cover over (their faith)! [49]

If something good happens to you, it bothers them, but if some disaster strikes you, they say, "*We prepared ourselves (for this setback) beforehand,*" and then they turn away self-satisfied. [50]

Say to them, "*Nothing happens to us except what Allah has already recorded for us, and He's our Protector.*" So let the believers trust in Allah! [51]

Then say to them, "*Are you expecting anything else for us other than one of two good possibilities, (either victory or martyrdom)? All the while we're expecting that you'll receive a punishment from Allah, either from His Own Self or from our hands. Just wait and see, and we'll be waiting, too.*" [52]

Tell them, "*Spend whatever you want or whatever you feel compelled to (spend to support the northern expedition,) but it won't be accepted (as a good deed by Allah), for you're a rebelliously disobedient people.*" [53]

Their contributions won't be accepted because they rejected Allah and His Messenger.

They come to prayers lacking motivation, and they spend (in charity) only reluctantly. [54]

262

So don't be impressed by their money or their sons. Allah wants to punish them with these things in the life of this world, so they'll leave (this life) with souls that have rejected (Allah). [55]

They swear to Allah that they're on your side, but they're not on your side. They're constantly nervous (that they might be singled out)! [56]

If they could find some place to escape to, either a cave or a hideout, they would turn towards it straightaway in a rush. [57]

Hypocrites are never Satisfied

> **Background Info... v. 58-59**
>
> When the Prophet was distributing some charity, a recent convert from among the bedouins named Hurqoos ibn Zuhayr was unsatisfied with his share, and he said, "Be fair! Be fair!"
>
> 'Umar got angry and asked the Prophet for permission to kill the disrespectful man, but the Prophet stopped him and replied to Hurqoos, "Woe to you! Who is fairer than I am?" Then the Prophet said, "If I weren't fair, then I'd be truly lost!"
>
> After Hurqoos left, the Prophet told his companions, "Among this man's descendants will be some whose prayer, when one of you sees it, would make his own prayer seem lacking, and his fast will seem the same as compared to their fast, but they will be rebels in religion, just like an arrow goes through the body of a hunted animal. Wherever you find them, fight them, for truly they're the worst (spiritually) dead people under the cover of the sky." (Bukhari)

> This passage was then revealed about Hurqoos. Years after the Prophet's passing, Hurqoos joined an extremist group of ultra-purists known as the Kharajites, and he fell in the Battle of Nahrawan against the caliph's forces.
>
> Extremist groups to this day generally follow this deviant ideology, which is based on the notion that all Muslims besides themselves are hopeless sinners in need of correction.

Among them are some who talk against you with regards to (how you're distributing) charity. If they're given some, then they're happy, but if they're not (given any), *then they're upset!* [58]

If only they would've been satisfied with what Allah and His Messenger had given them and had said, "*Allah is enough for us! Allah and His Messenger will give us something from His bounty soon enough, and we place our hopes (for material blessings) in Allah.*" [59]

Those Deserving of Charity

> **Background Info... v. 60**
>
> This verse was revealed after a man had approached the Prophet, asking for some goods to be given to him out of the funds for distribution. The Prophet replied, "Allah, the Most High, never allowed any prophet to distribute the sadaqah by his own decision, nor did He give this power to anyone who was not a prophet. He determined from His Own Self eight categories (of people who are to receive it.) If you fall under one of those eight categories, then I can let you have some." (Abu Dawud)

Charity is meant for the poor, for the needy, for those whose profession it is to distribute it, for encouraging (recent converts), for the (freeing) of bonded servants, for those (straining under a load) of debt, for use in the cause of Allah, and also (to help stranded) travelers.

These are the stipulations set by Allah, and Allah is full of knowledge and wisdom. [60]

Don't Annoy the Prophet

> **Background Info... v. 61**
>
> Some hypocrites were slandering the Prophet, and when they were told to stop, one of them said, "He'll listen to anybody." This meant that they felt they could lie to the Prophet's face and convince him that they didn't say anything wrong. This verse references that. (*Ibn Kathir*)

Among them are some who upset the Prophet when they say, "*He'll listen to anybody.*"

Reply to them, saying, "*He listens to what's best for you. He believes in Allah. He believes in the (integrity of) the faithful, and he's a mercy for those who believe.*"

Whoever upsets the Prophet will have a painful punishment. [61]

They swear to Allah in front of you to impress you, but it would be more appropriate for them to impress (both)

Allah and His Messenger, if they're (sincere) believers. [62]

Don't they know that the fire of Hell is reserved for all who oppose Allah and His Messenger and that that's where they'll have to stay? That's the worst humiliation of all! [63]

The Headache of the Hypocrites

> **Background Info... v. 64**
>
> During the Expedition to Tabuk, some hypocrites were ridiculing the Prophet for daring to march an army northward, saying, "This man wants to conquer all of Syria – its palaces and fortresses, and it's just not possible." Others took to belittling the sincere believers and making fun of them. This verse was revealed in response. (*Asbab ul-Nuzul*)

The hypocrites are afraid that a chapter might be revealed about them, exposing what's really in their hearts.

Say to them, "*Go ahead and make fun of (this message)! Allah will bring out whatever you're worried about (and make it known)!*" [64]

> **Background Info... v. 65**
>
> A hypocrite said in a gathering while encamped during the Expedition to Tabuk, "I've never seen any (oral) reciters like ours! They have the hungriest stomachs, the most deceitful tongues, and they're the most cowardly in battle." A sincere Muslim spoke out, saying, "You lie! You're a hypocrite, and I'm going to tell the Messenger of Allah." When the Prophet was informed, he summoned the

If you ask them (what they were talking about), they say, "*We were just talking nonsense, all in good fun.*"

Ask them, "*Were you poking fun at Allah, His verses and His Messenger?*" [65]

Make no more excuses, you people who rejected (faith) after (supposedly) having accepted it!

Although We may forgive some of you, We're still going to punish others among you on account of their wickedness. [66]

Hypocrites Protect Each Other

Hypocrites, both males and females, are all alike with each other. They call (people) towards bad conduct and discourage good behavior, while closing their hands tight (to avoid giving in charity).

They've forgotten Allah, so He's forgotten them. The hypocrites are certainly rebellious wrongdoers. [67]

Allah has made a promise to the hypocrites, both male and female, and to those who cover over (their faith in Him), that they will have the fires of Hell in which to dwell.

That will be enough for them, for Allah's curse and a relentless punishment are what they're going to get! [68]

"*(All you hypocrites!) You're just like those who came before you. Yet, (the ancient peoples) had more (worldly) power, wealth and sons than you. They had their time to enjoy their share, even as you and those who came before you did, also.*

"*You even speak the same kind of* nonsense *that they did! Yet, their actions were useless, both in this world and the next, and they're going to be the losers (in the end, just as you will be, if you don't repent).*" [69]

Haven't they heard the stories of those who went before them, of the people of Nuh, the (tribes) of 'Ad and Thamud, the people of Ibraheem, the companions of Madyan, and of the overthrown (towns of Sodom and Gomorrah)?

Messengers went to all of them with clear evidence (of the truth). It wasn't Allah who did them any wrong, for they wronged their own souls. [70]

265

The Unbreakable
Bonds of Brotherhood

The believers, both male and female, are the close protectors of one another. They command what is recognized (as good) and forbid what is unfamiliar (to Allah's way of life).

They establish prayer, give in charity, and obey Allah and His Messenger. Allah will pour His mercy down upon them, for Allah is powerful and wise. [71]

Allah has made a promise to the believers, both male and female, of gardens beneath which rivers flow in which to dwell, and beautiful mansions in everlasting gardens of delight. However, the greatest delight of all is to please Allah, and that's also the greatest success! [72]

Be Firm against Hypocrites
and their Wily Ways

O Prophet! Strive hard against the faithless and the hypocrites.

Be firm with them, for their home is in Hellfire – *the worst destination!* [73]

Background Info... first part v. 74

The first part of this verse is about what a hypocrite named Julas said while on the expedition. Julas had just finished hearing a speech by the Prophet in which he had warned the hypocrites that their opposition to Allah was tearing them apart inside and that Allah would punish them in the next life.

Julas then returned to his friends and said, "By Allah! If what Muhammad says is true, then we're worse than donkeys." A dependent of his named 'Amr ibn Qays retorted, saying, "What Muhammad says *is* true, and so you are worse than donkeys." Then he told Julas, "By Allah! Julas, you're the closest person to me; you've been the most favorable to me, and I would never want any harm to touch you more than anyone else! But you've said something that, if I told on you, then you would be exposed (as a hypocrite), but if I hid it, it would destroy me. One of them is the lesser of the two evils."

After the Muslims returned to Medina from Tabuk, 'Amr went and told the Prophet what Julas had said. The Prophet summoned him to the masjid and asked him why he said what he did. Julas invoked the curse of Allah upon himself if he was lying, and then he swore to Allah facing the pulpit of the masjid that he never said anything like that.

'Amr swore he was truthful, as well, and then said, "O Allah! Prove the truth of the honest and expose the lies of the liar." Then this verse was revealed to the Prophet, and he recited it. Thereafter, Julas repented of his words, and it is said that his repentance was sincere. He was never known to indulge in hypocrisy again. (Ibn Kathir)

They swear to Allah that they've never said anything (against you), but indeed they've uttered words of rejection, and they're rejecting (Allah) even after (they claimed) to have submitted (to Him).

Background Info... last part v. 74

On the journey back from the Tabuk expedition, a faction of hypocrites who had wanted 'Abdullah ibn Ubayy to be crowned king plotted to assassinate the Prophet by surrounding him slowly with their numbers and then pushing him off his mount down a cliff, if ever one appeared on the trail.

However, their plot unraveled due to the vigilance of two companions who never left the Prophet's side and warned him when the men began to converge on his intended path.

The Prophet shouted at them, and they fled. He asked the two men who had been watching over him, Hudhayfah and 'Ammar, if they knew who the men were. Hudhayfah replied, "No, Messenger of Allah. They were wearing masks, but we do recognize their horses."

The Prophet then said, "They're going to be hypocrites until the Day of Judgment. Do you know what they wanted to do?" The two men answered in the negative, and the Prophet said, "They wanted to surround the Messenger of Allah and throw him (down into) the valley." Hudhayfah said, "Messenger of Allah! Should you ask their tribes to send their heads to you?"

The Prophet answered, "No, for I wouldn't want it to be said by the Arabs that Muhammad used some people for fighting and, after Allah gave him victory with their help, that he commanded them to be killed." Then he said, "O Allah, throw a *dubaylah* at them."

The men asked the Prophet what that was, and he replied, "It's a fiery dart that falls into the heart of one of them and brings about his end." Later on someone asked Hudhayfah about those assassins, and Hudhayfah mentioned that the Prophet told him the names of all of them, and he told no one else. So Hudhayfah had the nickname, *"The Keeper of the Secret."* (At-Tabari)

They tried to (murder the Prophet), though they were unable to carry it out. *This was their response to the bounty with which Allah and His Messenger had enriched them!*

If they repent, it would be the best for them, but if they persist (in their rebellious ways,) then Allah will punish them with a painful penalty, both in this life and in the next.

In that case, no one on earth would be able to protect them or help them! [74]

On Those Who Betray their Pledge

Background Info... v. 75-78

A man named Tha'labah went to the Prophet and asked for him to beseech Allah to make him rich. The Prophet said to him, "Woe to you, Tha'labah, a little thanks that you can give is much better than what you won't be able to handle."

Then the Prophet told him that if he really wanted riches, then he could invoke Allah to give them to him.

Thereupon, Tha'labah swore the oath that is contained in verse 75. The Prophet then gave Tha'labah a herd of sheep, and within a short amount of time the herd expanded greatly, causing Tha'labah to become very wealthy.

Because of the size of his herds, though, he also had to move progressively farther from Medina, resulting in his more and more infrequent visits to worship in the masjid. Later on, when the Prophet sent people to collect the charity tax from Tha'labah, he put off the tax collectors on two separate occasions.

This passage was then revealed about him, and someone went to him and told him, "You're ruined! A passage has been revealed about you!" So Tha'labah hurried to the Prophet and begged him to accept his charitable contribution, but the Prophet told him that Allah has forbidden him from accepting his charity. Then Tha'labah began throwing dust on his own head in sorrow, and the Prophet told him, "It's because of what you did. I gave you an order, and you disobeyed it."

After the Prophet's passing, Tha'labah went to Caliph Abu Bakr and begged him to accept his charity, and Abu Bakr refused, saying the Prophet never accepted it.

The same thing happened during the rule of 'Umar ibn al-Khattab and Uthman ibn Affan and Tha'labah passed away in despair during Uthman's reign. (*Ibn Kathir*) It is said that Allah did not accept his repentance because he harbored hypocrisy in his heart. (*Ma'ariful Qur'an*)

Among them are some who made a deal with Allah that if He gave them (great riches) from His Own bounty, then they would (reciprocate) by giving (richly) in charity (in the cause of Allah), and further that they would be among the righteous. [75]

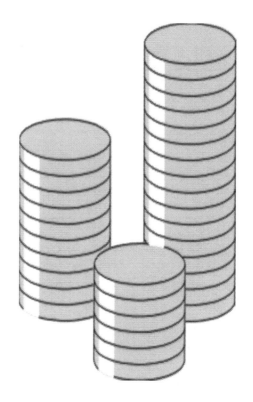

Yet, when He *did* give them (riches) from His bounty, they became greedy and turned back, hesitant (to support the cause). [76]

So He let hypocrisy grow in their hearts (as a result,) and it will remain there until the day when they're going to meet Him (for judgment), and that's because they broke their deal with Allah and also because they lied. [77]

Don't they realize that Allah knows all their secrets and their veiled schemes and that Allah knows what's hidden (in the deep recesses of their hearts)? [78]

Don't Ridicule the Donations of the Poor

Those who make fun of the believers when they give in charity from their own convictions, or who (make fun of those who have) nothing more to give than their own work due to their poverty, and then who further make fun of them (for donating huge sums of their resources to Allah's cause, should know) that Allah will throw their teasing back at them and that they're going to have a painful **PUNISHMENT**. [79]

Whether you ask for their forgiveness or not – even if you asked seventy times for their forgiveness, Allah won't forgive them because they rejected Allah and His Messenger. Allah will not guide a people who are rebellious and corrupt. [80]

About Those Who Remained behind in Medina

> **Background Info... v. 79**
>
> The Prophet made a public call one day for donations to support the cause. A poor man named Abu 'Aqil came and donated a small amount of dates, explaining that he worked all night drawing water, earned two measures of dates for his pay and was thus donating half of what he earned.
>
> Some hypocrites laughed and said, "Allah and His Messenger don't need this (small amount), for what benefit could it bring." The Prophet then picked up the dates with his own hands and placed it atop the pile of donated money and goods.
>
> Then a man named 'Abdurrahman ibn 'Awf came forward and asked if anyone else was going to give in charity, and the Prophet replied, "No one except you." Thereupon 'Abdurrahman declared he was donating a huge sum of gold in charity. 'Umar ibn al-Khattab said, "Are you crazy?" 'Abdurrahman said that he wasn't and explained that he really did have that much money, and he donated it. The hypocrites defamed him and said he just wanted to show off.
>
> This verse was revealed regarding this incident and is meant to show that even a little given sincerely can mean a great deal in Allah's sight and that a lot given in Allah's cause should be praised and not ridiculed. (Asbab ul-Nuzul)

> **Background Info... v. 81-83**
>
> There was a heat wave and famine in Medina, and the journey north to Syria was going to be a long, hard trek of two weeks.
>
> The Prophet warned his followers of this and asked for donations to cover the expenses of the mission. Many Muslims came forward, men and women, and huge sums of money were donated.

Those who remained behind (in Medina) rejoiced in their inaction behind the back of the Messenger of Allah.

They hated (even the mere thought) of striving in the cause of Allah with their wealth and their persons, and they said, *"Don't go out (on the Expedition to Tabuk) because it's far too hot (in the desert)!"*

Say to them, *"The fires of Hell are even hotter!"* If they would only realize it! [81]

So let them laugh a little now, for soon they will cry much more as a payback for what they've earned (for themselves on their record of deeds.) [82]

If Allah brings you back to any of them and they ask you for (permission) to venture out (with you on some future expedition), tell them, *"You're never going to venture out with me, nor will you ever fight an enemy by my side, for you chose to sit and be inactive the first time, so now keep sitting with those who get left behind."* [83]

Don't Honor a Hypocrite

> **Background Info... v. 84-85**
>
> This passage was revealed concerning 'Abdullah ibn Ubayy, the leader of the hypocrites of Medina. He passed away, and his son, who was a committed believer, went to the Prophet and asked if he could bury his father in one of the Prophet's robes.
>
> The Prophet gave it to him, and then the son asked the Prophet to pray for his departed father. The Prophet was about to pray for him when 'Umar ibn al-Khattab objected, saying that the dead man had been a hypocrite and an enemy of Allah.
>
> The Prophet replied, "I've been given the choice of whether to pray for him or not. I know that if I pray for the forgiveness of (a hypocrite) seventy times, he won't be forgiven. Yet, if I knew that he'd be forgiven if I prayed for forgiveness more than that, then I'd do it." *(Bukhari)*
>
> The reports differ as to whether the Prophet actually offered a funeral prayer for him or merely a supplication, but this passage was revealed sometime later, forbidding funeral prayers for known hypocrites.
>
> Why did the Prophet give his robe for the funeral? After the Battle of Badr, many years before, one of the prisoners taken was the Prophet's pagan uncle 'Abbas. He had no shirt, and because he was a tall man, the Prophet asked for the equally tall 'Abdullah ibn Ubayy to give one of his shirts to clothe 'Abbas. He did so. The Prophet then was returning the favor. *(Qurtubi)*
>
> The Prophet said of the robe that was used to bury Ibn Ubayy: "What good will

270

Never offer a (funeral) prayer for any of them that dies, nor stand by their grave (as they're being lowered down into it), for they rejected Allah and His Messenger, and thus died in a state of defiant rebellion. [84]

So neither be impressed by their money nor their (numerous) sons, for Allah wants to punish them through these things in this world so that they'll leave this life with souls that have lost (their ability to believe in Allah). [85]

When a chapter came down (asking them) to **BELIEVE** in Allah and to strive alongside His Messenger, the eligible ones from among them came to you and asked for exemptions, saying, "*Leave us, for we'd rather stay with those who sit (at home)*." [86]

They preferred to be with those who stayed behind! Their hearts are sealed shut, and they understand nothing! [87]

However, the Messenger and the believers with him **STRIVE** with their wealth and their persons. Therefore, they shall have the best (reward), even as they'll be the most successful. [88]

Allah has prepared gardens for them beneath which rivers flow, and there they shall remain - *and that's the ultimate success!* [89]

The Bedouins Offered their Excuses

Some of the (bedouin) Arabs also came to you in order to offer their excuses and to claim exemptions. And so those who were dishonest to Allah and His Messenger sat idly by.

It won't be long before a painful punishment overtakes those among them who covered over (their awareness of the truth). [90]

There's no blame, however, on those who were too weak or ill or who couldn't find the resources to spend (for the journey), as long as they're sincere to Allah and His Messenger.

There are no grounds of complaint against the good (people who wanted to come, but who couldn't find a way), for Allah is forgiving and merciful. [91]

No Blame for those who could not be Accommodated

> **Background Info... v. 92**
>
> A group of men volunteered for the Expedition to Tabuk, but when the Prophet explained he had insufficient resources to equip any more men, they left weeping bitterly.
>
> The Prophet later told his companions after they returned from the journey, **"Some people were left behind in Medina, but it was like they were with us all the time in every valley and every mountain pass we crossed. They were left behind only for legitimate reasons."** (Bukhari, Abu Dawud)

(There are also no grounds of complaint) against those who came to you for transportation and to whom you had to say, "*I have no transportation for you.*"

They turned back with tears overflowing from their eyes at their inability to spend (money to arrange their own way). [92]

There are, however, legitimate grounds (for complaint) against those who claimed exemption even though they were independently wealthy. They preferred to remain with those who stayed behind. So then their hearts were sealed shut, and they understood nothing. [93]

They're going to make their excuses to you when you return to them, but say to them, "*Don't make any excuses (for your cowardice), because we're not going to believe you.*

"*Allah already told us about your situation, and it's what you do that Allah and His Messenger will consider. In the end, you're going to be brought back to the One Who knows the hidden and the clear, and then He's going to show you the true meaning of all that you did.*" [94]

When you return back to them, they're going to swear to you in Allah's (name) that you should leave them alone - so go ahead and leave them alone (by shunning them), for they're stained (by their very own sins), and Hellfire is their destination. That's the reward they deserve for what they've done. [95]

They're also going to swear to you (as to the validity of their excuses), trying to make you pleased with them.

If you do become pleased with them, (then you should know) that Allah is not pleased with those who were rebelliously disobedient. [96]

The (bedouin) Arabs are the **worst** when it comes to rejection and hypocrisy and are thus more likely to be ignorant of the command that Allah has sent down to His Messenger. Allah is full of knowledge and wisdom. [97]

Some of the (bedouin) Arabs consider what they spend (in charity) to be a financial penalty.

They keep looking for disasters to come upon you, but let the worst disasters fall upon them, for Allah listens and knows (all about their treachery). [98]

Some of the (bedouin) Arabs, however, do believe in Allah and the Last Day.

They look upon what they spend (in charity) as a way to bring themselves closer to Allah's presence and to (be worthy) of the Prophet's prayers (for their forgiveness and success.)

They truly are brought closer (to Allah by their charity and sincerity), and soon

Allah will admit them to His mercy, for Allah is forgiving and merciful. [99]

Forgiveness is Offered Freely to those who Desire It

The forerunners (in faith) are those who were the first to migrate (from Mecca), then those who helped them (in Medina) and finally those who followed (closely behind) them in doing what was good.

Allah is pleased with them and they with Him, and He's prepared for them gardens beneath which rivers flow to live within forever. That's the ultimate success! [100]

Some of the (bedouin) Arabs (that live) around you (in the countryside) are hypocrites, even as there are (hypocrites) among the people of Medina.

They're persistent in hypocrisy, and although you don't know (who they are), We know who they are. We're going to punish them twice (through fear and humiliation), and then they're going to be sent into an even more severe punishment after that! [101]

Conflicted Actions

Background Info... v. 102-103

Ten men who failed to respond to the mustering of the militia to march toward Tabuk felt ashamed. Some time after the army left, seven of them swore to their wives that they would tie themselves to their fence posts or to pillars in the masjid until the Prophet forgave them.

(There are) some other (people) who've admitted to their sins. They had mixed moral deeds with evil ones, but Allah may yet turn to them (in forgiveness), for Allah is forgiving and merciful. [102]

Take charity from their wealth so you can cleanse and purify them, and pray for them, for your prayers are truly a source of tranquility for them. Allah hears and knows (about all things). [103]

Don't they know that Allah accepts the repentance of His servants and that He accepts their charitable contributions? Allah is the One Who Accepts Repentance, and (He truly is) the Merciful. [104]

Say (to the people who want to repent of their sins), "*Do (good deeds), for Allah will soon see the results of your efforts, even as the Messenger and the believers (will see them, as well). Soon you're going to be brought back to the One Who knows the hidden and the plainly seen, and He's going to show you the meaning of all that you did.*" [105]

(Indeed, among this group of people) are some who are waiting nervously for Allah's command, so they can know whether He's going to punish them or turn towards them (in forgiveness). Allah is full of knowledge and wisdom. [106]

The Masjid of Mischief

from Abu Amir to the hypocrites were also intercepted – letters that encouraged sedition and rebellion! When some of the hypocrites invited the Prophet to enter Quba first before Medina and to pray in their masjid, this passage was revealed.

The Prophet then ordered some of his companions to go to the *Masjid of Mischief*, as it was called, and have it torn down. One man named Thabit ibn Arqam later built a house on the site, but he had no children survive him – ever - and thus the seemingly cursed plot fell into disuse.

After that, the site became a garbage dump. Abu Amir did die far from home in southern Syria among strangers. (*Ma'ariful Qur'an*)

Only a masjid built for sincere devotion to Allah can be called a masjid of Allah. No house of worship should be used to plot against the religion to which it is supposed to be dedicated.

There are those who built a masjid (for no other purpose) than to promote mischief and rejection (of Allah), seeking to divide the believers and to set up a rallying place for those who previously made war on Allah and His Messenger.

They're going to swear that they meant nothing but good by it, but Allah declares that they're all liars. [107]

Never set foot within (their masjid), for there's (another) masjid (nearby in the town of Quba) whose foundations were laid from the first day upon mindfulness (of Allah).

It's far more appropriate for you to stand within that one, for there are people inside of it who love to be purified, and Allah loves those who make themselves pure! [108]

Whose (place of worship) is better: the one who lays his foundation upon mindfulness of Allah and the seeking of His pleasure, or the one who lays his foundation upon a weak sand dune that's ready to crumble at any moment?

It will crumble – *along with him* – and topple into the fires of Hell. Allah doesn't guide people who are in the wrong! [109]

Such a (weak) building site could never be anything more than a cause for nervousness in their hearts - even until their hearts are shattered (by stress)! Allah is full of knowledge and wisdom. [110]

This is Allah's Deal

Background Info... v. 111-112

These two verses were revealed in the Meccan Period after the last Pledge of 'Aqabah, in which some seventy visitors from Medina pledged themselves to the Prophet and invited him to resettle in their city.

(There were two prior such pledges by smaller groups of six and then twelve persons respectively.)

At this last pledge, taken some months before the Prophet left Mecca for the safety of Medina, one of the new converts asked the Prophet, "Messenger of Allah, we're making a deal right now. If there are any requirements from either your Lord or you, let them be enumerated at this time clearly."

The Prophet said, "As for Allah, I lay down the condition that you all shall worship Him and only Him. As for myself, the condition is that you should protect me as you protect your selves, wealth, property and children." Someone asked him, "If we fulfill these two conditions, what will we get in return?"

The Prophet replied, "Paradise." The people exclaimed then that they accepted that deal and that they would never cancel this agreement. Then these two verses were revealed, and the Prophet recited them.

The people then lined up to place their hands in his to make their solemn oaths. (*Ma'ariful Qur'an*)

Allah has bought from the believers their lives and their wealth, and in return (He'll give them) Paradise.

They will fight in His cause; they will kill and be killed – and this is a promise that He's bound by in the Torah, the Injeel and the Qur'an.

Who is more faithful to his agreement than Allah? So be pleased with the bargain you've made, for that's the ultimate success! [111]

(The true believers are those who) turn (to Allah) in repentance, serve Him, praise Him, wander abroad (in His cause), bow down in prostration before Him, command what is recognized (as good), and forbid what is unfamiliar (to Allah's way of life).

They are the ones who observe Allah's limits, so now give good news to the believers! [112]

Faith and Falsehood have a Clear Divide

Background Info... v. 113

After the Prophet's beloved uncle, Abu Talib, passed away, affirming his allegiance to idolatry even as he breathed his last, the distraught Prophet vowed to continue to pray for his forgiveness.

Later on, in the early Medinan Period, 'Ali heard a man loudly praying for his deceased pagan parents to be forgiven.

When 'Ali asked the man why he was praying for his pagan parents, he explained that Ibraheem also prayed for his pagan father. (Based on verse 19:47.) 'Ali informed the Prophet about this, and some time later, this verse was revealed prohibiting Muslims from praying for relatives who had died while still believing in idols. (*Tirmidhi, Bukhari, Muslim*)

It's not right for the Prophet and the believers to pray for the forgiveness of idol-worshippers, even if they're close relatives, after it's been made clear to them that they're going to be companions of the raging blaze. [113]

Ibraheem only prayed for his father's forgiveness because of a PROMISE he had made to him. However, when it became clear to him that (his father) was an enemy of Allah, he distanced himself from him.

It was just that Ibraheem was accustomed to invoking (Allah frequently), and he was forbearing. [114]

Allah will never let a people go astray after He's (begun to invite them to)

guidance, until after He's made clear to them that of which they should be aware, for Allah knows all about everything. [115]

The control of the heavens and the earth belongs to Allah. He gives life, and He brings death. You have neither any protector nor helper apart from Him. [116]

Allah Tested the Believers

And so it was that Allah turned towards the Prophet, the Immigrants, and the Helpers who followed Him during a difficult time (on the Expedition to Tabuk, for the journey was long and **HARD**).

However, a segment of them let their hearts become crooked, (influencing them away from their duty,) but He turned towards them, as well, for He was kind and merciful towards them. [117]

The Case of the Three Who were Forgiven

Background Info... v. 118

There were three men named Ka'b ibn Malik, Hilal ibn Umayyah and Murarah ibn ar-Rabi' who were otherwise perfectly able-bodied and fit to answer the call for the Tabuk Expedition.

They had been among the earliest converts, but they failed to muster with the rest of the militia when it was time to march northward. (Murarah was talked out of participating by, among other things, his concern for the harvest time, and he became interested in his comfort and prosperity. Hilal was having a family reunion. K'ab was wealthy and couldn't bear to leave his fortune behind!)

When the Prophet returned, these men were shunned for about fifty days, and they felt miserable, so much so that it seemed (as one of them later described it) that the earth and their own souls were closing in upon them.

The Christian king of the Ghassanid tribe in Syria, Suhrabil ibn Amr, received reports of the shunning of these men, and he sent a letter to Ka'b offering to take him in to his kingdom if Ka'b would renounce Islam, but Ka'b threw the letter in his cooking fire.

In time, the Prophet accepted the remorse of these men, and they were welcomed back into the community upon the revelation of this verse. Ka'b left a rather lengthy story about his experience and he told how joyful both he and the community were when it was all over.
(Bukhari, Muslim)

(He also turned in mercy) to the three (men) who remained behind (without a valid excuse). (They were so remorseful) that the vast earth, itself, seemed to close in upon them, and their souls seemed to strangle them (with guilt), as well.

They understood that there was no **running away** from Allah, unless (it was on a path) that led back to Him. So He turned towards them so they could repent, for Allah is the Acceptor of Repentance and the Merciful. [118]

Reflections on the Lessons of Tabuk

O you who believe! Be mindful of Allah, and be among those who are truthful (to their vows). [119]

It wasn't right for (some of) the people of Medina and the local desert Arabs to refuse to follow the Messenger of Allah, nor was it right that they preferred their own lives over his.

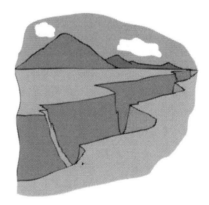

That's because there was (no sacrifice) they could've made, whether it was thirst, fatigue or hunger in the cause of Allah, nor any step (they could've taken) to raise the ire of the faithless, nor any injury they could've received from the enemy,

278

(without being generously repaid for it by Allah).

For sure, Allah never lets the reward of those who do good become lost. [120]

They also could not have spent anything, whether a little or a lot, or trekked across a valley without having that deed recorded to their credit, and that was so Allah could reward their actions with good (in return). [121]

The believers, however, should not march out all together (leaving no one behind to guard the home front).

If a certain number remains behind during every expedition, then they could exert themselves in learning the religion.

And then they could remind the people when they return (home) that they should be on their guard (against immorality). [122]

O you who believe! Fight the faithless who are all around you, (ready to strike at you). Be resolute against them, and know that Allah is with those who are mindful (of Him). [123]

Stay Strong with the Faith

Whenever a chapter comes down, some (of the hypocrites) say (in a disrespectful way), "*So who among you feels their faith has been strengthened by it?*'

Oh, but those who (truly) believe *do* have their faith strengthened by it, and they rejoice besides! [124]

Those who are sick at heart find that (newly revealed verses) add nothing but doubts to their doubts; so they're going to die in a state of rejection. [125]

Don't they see that they're being tested at least once or twice every year.

Yet, not only *do they not repent,* they don't even pay attention to the reminders! [126]

279

Whenever a chapter comes down, they look at each other (and say), "*Is anyone looking at you?*"

Then they turn away, even as Allah has turned their hearts away, for they're a people who don't understand at all. [127]

Now a messenger has come to you from among yourselves, and he's worried sick that you might be harmed (in the cause of Allah).

In fact, he's distraught over your (welfare), for he's truly kind and merciful to the believers. [128] If they turn away, just tell them:

> "*Allah is enough for me.*
> *There is no god but He.*
>
> *"On Him do I trust;*
> *He's Lord of the throne supreme.*" [129]

Jonah

10 Yūnus

Late Meccan Period

☞ Introduction

This chapter is the first in a series of six late Meccan chapters that continue to address the core theological concepts of Islam. Nature and its complexity are proof of Allah's handiwork for those who care to look into it deeply. Allah communicates with humanity through messengers who receive His messages and teach them to their fellows. The reality of life is that it's a short time filled with temptations, tests and trials that we must weather.

In the end, if we are successful in negotiating the storms of this world, with full faith in Allah, then we can achieve permanent success in the Hereafter, or if we fall into bad deeds, evil and dishonesty, we may suffer punishment in Hellfire. Like a big exam, our conduct in this world ultimately decides our fate. Allah will punish injustice, though He is more merciful to us than we could ever deserve.

In the Name of Allah,
the Compassionate, the Merciful

Background Info... v. 1-2

Ibn 'Abbas (d. 687) explained the pagan position alluded to in this verse by saying, "When Allah sent Muhammad as a messenger, most of the Arabs denied him and his message, saying, 'Allah is too exalted to send a mere human being like Muhammad.'" So then this passage was revealed, commenting upon their objection. (*Ibn Kathir*)

*A*lif. *Lām. Rā.*

These are the verses of the Book of Wisdom. [1]

Is it so strange to people that We've sent Our inspiration to a man from among themselves, so he could warn people (of Allah's judgment) and give the good news to the believers that they can achieve confirmed status in the sight of their Lord?

Yet, the faithless say (of it), "*This is obviously just magic!*" [2]

Your Lord is Allah, the One Who created the heavens and the earth in six time periods. Then He established Himself upon the throne (of power) and began issuing commands.

There are no intercessors other than those whom He allows. That's your Lord Allah, so serve Him. Won't you take a reminder? [3]

All of you will return back to Him, and Allah's promise is true.

He's the One Who began the process of creation and then repeats it, so that He can justly reward those who believe and do what's morally right.

281

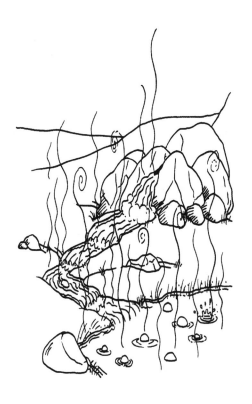

the heavens and the earth are proofs for those who are mindful (of Him). [6]

Those who don't look forward to their meeting with Us, who are satisfied with the life of this world and who disregard Our (revealed) verses - they're going to have their home in the Fire on account of what they've earned for themselves. [7-8]

However, those who believe and do what's morally right will be guided by their Lord on account of their faith – rivers will flow beneath them in gardens of delight! [9]

Their supplication within (the garden) will be, "*Glory be to You, O Allah!*"

Their greeting within will be, "*Peace,*" and they'll end their supplications by saying, "*Praise be to Allah, the Lord of All the Worlds!*" [10]

The Fickle Nature of Humanity

Those who reject Him will be forced to drink boiling muck, and they'll have a painful punishment on account of their rejection. [4]

He's the One Who caused the sun to glow brightly with multiple (colors in splendor) and the moon to be illuminated. He measured out (the moon's) stations, so you could keep track of the years and the passage (of time).

Allah didn't create (all of these things) except for a true purpose, and He explains His verses to people who understand. [5]

Truly, in the alternation of night and day and in everything that Allah created in

If Allah were to rush forward for people the evil consequences (of their deeds) in the same way that they (want) Him to rush forward the good (things that they think they

deserve), then their (time) would come to an end immediately, but We leave those who don't look forward to their meeting with Us wandering in their willful blindness. [11]

Background Info... v. 15

Five leaders among the Quraysh went to the Prophet and asked him to alter the teachings of the Qur'an so that they could keep worshipping their idols. This verse references their request.
(*Asbab ul-Nuzul*)

Yet, when Our clear verses are recited to them, those who don't look forward to their meeting with Us say, "*Bring us some other Qur'an, or change this one (to suit us)."*

Say to them, "*It's not my place to change it, for I follow only what's being revealed to me. If I ever disobeyed my Lord (by making up verses on my own), then I would be in utter fear of the punishment of a momentous day."* [15]

Then say to them, "*If Allah had wanted, then I wouldn't be reciting (this message) to you, nor would He have made it known to you.*

"I've lived with you for a whole lifetime before this (message came to me, and I've never spoken of religious issues before), so won't you realize (that it came suddenly and that it must be from Allah)?" [16]

Who's more wrong than the one who invents a forgery and then attributes it to Allah or who denies (the truth of) His (authentic) verses?

The bad people will **never** succeed! [17]

When misfortune comes upon a human being, he cries out to Us while lying down on his side, sitting or standing.

However, when We've removed his misfortune, he passes on his way <u>as if he had never cried out to Us</u> when hardship befell him before!

That's why the extravagant think their (pointless) deeds are beneficial for them. [12]

And so it was that We destroyed generations that came before you when (their people) turned into oppressors. Their messengers went to them with clear evidence; yet, they still wouldn't believe! That's how We repay the bad people. [13]

Now We've caused you (Arabs) to inherit the land after them to see how you would act. [14]

283

They serve in place of Allah things that can neither harm them nor benefit them, but then they (try to justify their idol-worship by) saying, "*These (idols) intercede for us with Allah.*"

So ask them:

"*Are you really informing Allah about something in the heavens and the earth about which He doesn't know?*"

Glory be to Him! He's so high above the partners they're assigning to Him! [18]

And what were people other than one community (in the beginning); yet, they fell into disputes (with each other and scattered away all over the world).

If it wasn't for a word (of command) that your Lord previously issued (to let people have free will and then be judged by what they chose), then their differences would've been settled between them (immediately). [19]

Then they ask, "*So why isn't a miracle being sent down to him from his Lord?*"

Answer them, saying, "*The unseen (realm of the supernatural) belongs to Allah, so wait (and see), for I'll be waiting with you.*" [20]

Many don't Understand the Reality of their Lives

When We give people a taste of mercy after they had been suffering from some hardship – then look - they start plotting against Our signs straightaway!

Say to them, "*Allah's plan is even faster than that! Our (angelic) envoys are keeping track of whatever you're planning.*" [21]

He's the One Who makes it easy for you to travel over the land and sea. You board ships and sail along on them with favorable winds, and (the sailors) are pleased with their (progress).

However, when a storm arises and the waves begin to assault them from all sides, they feel as if they're going to perish.

Then (they realize) that all religion belongs to Allah, so they cry out to Him, (pledging to serve Him) sincerely, saying, "*If You save us from this, then we'll be forever grateful!*" [22]

Then, when He saves them, they act outrageously throughout the earth (once more) against all right! O people! Your rebellion is against your own souls!

(There's only a) short time to enjoy the life of this world – and then you're going to come back to Us, and that's when We're going to tell you the meaning of everything you ever did. [23]

The example of the life of this world is like the water that We send down from the sky. It mingles with the various plants of the earth and causes them to sprout (to life).

(These plants) then provide food for both people and animals. (The plants keep on growing) until the earth is clothed with their (blossoms and flowers), and then it's made (beautiful).

The people who own (the land around them) think that they're in control of it, but then Our command comes upon it by night or by day.

Then We reduce it to dry stubble, as if there had never been any luxurious growth there just the day before! That's how We fully explain (Allah's) signs for those who think. [24]

The Final End is Where the Outcome will Be Decided

Allah is calling (you) to the Realm of Peace, and He guides whomever He wants towards a straight path. [25]

Those who do good will have good (in return) – *and even more than that!* There will be neither darkness nor shame upon their faces, for they're the companions of the Garden, and there they shall remain! [26]

Those who've earned evil against themselves will be rewarded similarly with evil, and they'll further be covered in disgrace.

They'll have no one to defend them against Allah, and their faces will be shrouded in the darkest shades of night. They're the companions of the Fire, *and that's where they're going to stay!* [27]

One day, We're going to gather them all together, and We'll say to those who made partners (with Us), "*Go to your places! You and the idols you've made!*"

Then We're going to separate them, and their partners will say, "*It wasn't us you were worshipping! Allah is enough of a witness between you and us that we knew nothing of your worship of us.*" [28-29]

Then and there every soul will be tried for what it had earned (in its life) before, and they'll be turned over to Allah, their rightful guardian. Whatever they invented will leave them to languish! [30]

The Sentence is Proven
True against Them

Ask them, "*Who provides resources for you from the sky and the earth? Who has power over hearing and sight? Who brings life out of death and death out of life, and who governs the course of all matters?*"

(After they've thought about it), they'll be sure to say, "*Allah.*" Then ask them, "*So won't you then be mindful (of Him)?*" [31]

That's Allah for you, your true Lord. What is there after truth except mistakes? So how is it that you're turning away? [32] And so it is that the sentence will be proven true against those who rebel, for they won't believe. [33]

Ask them, "*Is there any (idol) from among your (false gods) that can begin creation and then renew it?*" Say to them, "*Allah began the creation, and He renews it. So how are you deceived away (from the truth)?*" [34]

Ask them, "*Are there any among your (idols) that can guide someone to the truth?*"

Then say to them, "*Allah guides to the truth. So isn't the One Who guides to the truth more worthy of being followed than (an idol or false god) that will remain lost unless it's guided (itself)?*"

Just how do you figure things? [35] Most of them follow nothing but guesses; yet, guessing can never win out over the truth, and Allah knows what they're doing. [36]

About those who Say
the Prophet Invented It

This Qur'an isn't something that could've been produced by any other besides Allah. On the contrary, it confirms (the truth of those revelations) that came before it, and it's a detailed explanation of the Book (of Allah).

There's nothing doubtful within it, (for it's a scripture revealed) from the Lord of All the Worlds! [37]

Are they saying, "*He made it all up?*" Then (challenge them by) saying, "*So bring a chapter just like it, and then call upon anyone you can besides Allah (to compare the two), if you're being so honest.*" [38]

But no! They're denying what they can't even comprehend even before it's been fully clarified for them.

In the same way, those who came before them also denied (the truth of their revelations,) but just see how the wrongdoers came to an end! [39]

Among them are some who believed in (their scriptures), while others did not, and your Lord knows best who the immoral are. [40]

If they accuse you of lying, then tell them, "*My deeds belong to me, even as your deeds belong to you. You're not responsible for what I'm doing, nor am I responsible for what you're doing.*" [41]

Now among them are some who merely **pretend** to listen to you, but can you force the deaf to hear, even while (those uncaring people) have no intellect? [42]

There are others among them who stare at you, but can you guide the blind, even as they refuse to see? [43]

Allah is never unjust to people in the least. Rather, it's people who are unjust to their own souls. [44]

One day, He's going to gather them all together, and it'll seem (to them) as if they had passed only a single hour of a day (in their earthly lives).

They're going to recognize each other's (faces), and so it will be that those who denied their meeting with Allah and who refused guidance will be lost. [45]

Whether We show you now some of what We've promised them or We take your soul (before that), they're all going to come back to Us (in the end). Then Allah will be the witness over what they've done. [46]

A messenger was sent to every community (in the world). When their messenger comes before them (as a witness on the Day of Judgment), the issue will be decided between them with justice, and they won't be treated unfairly. [47]

(Now your people are) asking you, "*So when will this promise come to pass, if you're being so honest?*" [48]

Say to them, "*I have no power to bring harm or benefit to myself, except as Allah wills.*

287

"Every community has its own (predetermined) time limit. And when its deadline is reached, it can neither prolong it by an hour nor accelerate it." [49]

Ask them, *"Do you see? If His punishment were to come upon you (suddenly) during the night or during the day, which part of it would the bad people want to hurry on? Would you then finally believe in it at last?"*

"What! Will you now (believe it's real when it happens), even though you wanted to hurry it on! Then the wrongdoers will be told, 'Suffer the unending punishment! You're only getting what you deserve!'" [50-52]

Now they're asking you to confirm it by saying, *"Is that the truth?"* Tell them, *"Absolutely! By my Lord, it's the truth, and you can't escape from it!'* [53]

Answer Allah's Call and be Saved

For every soul that sinned, if it had everything on earth to offer as a ransom (to save itself), it would offer it.

(Nonetheless, such bribes won't be accepted,) so they're going to be filled with regret when they see the punishment. They'll be judged with justice, however, and they won't be treated unfairly. [54]

Isn't it (a fact) that whatever is in the heavens and on the earth belongs to Allah? Isn't it (a fact) that Allah's promise

is a true one? Yet, most of them don't understand. [55]

He's the One Who gives life and death, and you're going to return back to Him. [56]

O people! An earnest appeal has now come to you from your Lord, as well as a healing for your hearts and guidance and mercy for the believers. [57]

Say to them, *"Let them celebrate in Allah's bounty and in His mercy."* That's better than (all the money) that they hide away. [58]

Ask them, *"Have you seen (and considered) all the resources that Allah sends down for you, (so you can survive in this world)? Yet, you make some of those things forbidden (to eat) and other things lawful (to eat, for no logical reason)."*

Then ask them, *"Has Allah given you permission (to do that), or are you making things up and assigning them to Allah?'* [59]

So what do those who invent lies against Allah think about the Day of Assembly? Allah is the master of endless favor towards the people (of earth); yet, most of them are thankless. [60]

288

Allah is always Watching Over You

There isn't a single thing that you're involved with, nor any portion of the Qur'an that you recite, nor any deed that you do without Us being there to see it, even while you're still in the middle of it!

There's nothing on the earth nor in the heavens that's hidden from your Lord – *nothing even as small as a speck* - and nothing smaller or greater than that exists without its being recorded in a clear record. [61]

Without a doubt, the closest allies of Allah will have neither fear nor sorrow! [62] They're the ones who believed and who were mindful (of their duty to Him). [63]

So there's good news for them in the life of this world, as well as (good news for them) in the next - *Allah's words (of prophecy) never change* - and that

(promise which is from Him is indeed the signifier of) the greatest success! [64]

Don't let what (the pagans) are saying bother you, for all combined powers belong to Allah. He's the Hearing and the Knowing. [65] Without a doubt, (all creatures) within the heavens and the earth belong to Allah.

So what are they following, those who call upon 'partners' in place of Allah? They're following no more than conjecture and inventing lies. [66]

He's the One Who made the night for you to rest in and the day to make things clearly seen. There's evidence in these things for any who care to listen. [67]

Addressing an Outrageous Claim

Now they're claiming, "*Allah has begotten a son!*" Glory be to Him! He's the Self-Sufficient! Everything in the heavens and on the earth belongs to Him!

You have no proof to make such a claim! Are you saying things about Allah about which you know nothing? [68]

Say to them, "*Those who invent a lie against Allah will never succeed.*" [69]

Just a bit of fun in the world (for them) - *and then they'll come back to Us!* Then We'll make them suffer a terrible punishment on account of their covering (over the truth). [70]

All Prophets had to Struggle

Recite for them the story of Nuh, when he said to his people, "*My people! If my continued presence among you is a burden for you, even as I've been reminding you of the signs of Allah, (it doesn't matter) for I'm depending on Allah.*

"*So join together, both you and your idols, and gather your plans (against me). Don't second guess your plans. Then sentence me (to death), and give me no chances.*" [71]

"*If you (do decide) to turn away (from my preaching, then consider this): I haven't been asking you for any reward (for my efforts). My reward is due from none other than Allah, and I've been commanded to be with those who submit (to His will).*" [72]

(His people ultimately) rejected him, but We saved him and whoever was with him in the boat. We let them inherit (the land), even as We overwhelmed in the flood those who rejected Our signs. Now go and see how those who were warned were brought to an end! [73]

Then after him We sent messengers (all over the world) to their individual nations.

They brought clear signs to them, but their (people) wouldn't believe in what they had already (decided to reject) beforehand. That's how We seal the hearts of the defiant. [74]

Musa and the Sorcerers

Then after them We sent Musa and Harun with Our signs to Pharaoh and his nobles, but (the Egyptians) were an arrogant and wicked people. [75]

When the truth came to them from Us, they said of it, "*This is obviously magic!*" [76]

Musa said to them, "*Are you saying this about the truth when it's come to you? Is this what magic is like? Mere sorcerers are never successful!*" [77]

(The Egyptians responded,) saying, "*Have you come to turn us away from the traditions of our ancestors, so you and your brother can become powerful in the land? (Well, it won't work) because we're never going to believe in you!*" [78]

Then Pharaoh commanded, "*Bring me every skilled sorcerer (that we have)!*" [79]

When the sorcerers arrived, Musa said to them, "*Cast down whatever (spell) you wish to cast!*" [80]

After they had their turn to cast, Musa said, "*What you've brought is wizardry, but Allah will render it useless, for Allah never lets the work of the immoral triumph.*

"By His words, Allah will prove the truth, no matter how much the bad people hate it!" [81-82]

None of (the Egyptians) believed in Musa except for some of the offspring of (Pharaoh's) people, for they feared persecution from Pharaoh and his nobles. Pharaoh certainly was a tyrant in the land whose cruelty knew no bounds. [83]

The Children of Israel Believe in Musa

Musa announced (to the Hebrews), "My people! If you believe in Allah, then trust in Him, if you're truly submissive (to His will)." [84]

"We trust in Allah," they answered. (Then they prayed,) "Our Lord! Don't make us a test for the oppressors. [85] Save us, through Your mercy, from those who reject (You)." [86]

Then We inspired Musa and his brother, saying, "Make homes for your people in Egypt, and turn your homes into centers

(of worship). Establish prayers, and give good news to the believers." [87]

Musa prayed, "Our Lord! You've given Pharaoh and his nobles fancy trinkets and wealth in the life of this world. Our Lord, they've mislead (many) away from Your path, so obliterate their wealth and harden their hearts so much so that they won't believe until they see the painful punishment." [88]

"Your prayer is accepted," came the answer. "So stand by the straight (path), and don't follow the path of those who have no knowledge." [89]

The Children of Israel Escape from Egypt

We led the Children of Israel across the sea. Then Pharaoh and his hordes brazenly followed after them in (their blind) rage, even until he was overwhelmed and about to be drowned, at which time he said:

"Now I believe - there's no god save for the One in Whom the Children of Israel believe! Now I submit!" [90]

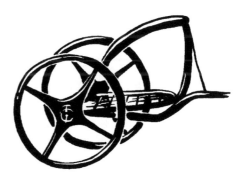

"What! Now (you want to submit)?" (it was said to him.) *"Just a little while ago you were the cause of great turmoil!"* [91]

"We're going to save your body today, so you can become an example to those who will come after you. Yet, still most people are unconcerned with Our signs!" [92]

And so it was that We settled the Children of Israel in an appropriate place and provided them with wholesome resources.

It was only *after* they were given knowledge that they fell into rival groups, but Allah will judge between them as to their differences on the Day of Assembly. [93]

Ask Those who came Before You

If you're ever in doubt about what We're revealing to you, (Muhammad,) then just ask those who've been reading the scripture before you.

The truth has indeed come to you from your Lord, so don't be among the doubtful, nor be among those who deny Allah's (revealed) verses, for then you'll be among the losers. [94-95]

Those who've had the sentence of your Lord proven against them won't believe, even if every proof were presented to them – *that is until they see the painful punishment (right before their eyes)!* [96-97]

Of All the Cities

Why hasn't there been a single settlement that believed, so that by its faith it could have prospered, other than the people of Yunus?

When they believed We removed the punishment of disgrace from them in the life of this world, and We allowed them to enjoy themselves for a (little) while longer. [98]

If Allah had wanted, He could've made everyone on earth into believers, (but He didn't). So how can you make people believe when they don't want to? [99]

No soul can believe except by Allah's leave, and He brings dire consequences down upon those who don't use their reason. [100]

Say to them, "*Look around at all (the wonderful signs) throughout the heavens and on the earth*," though neither proofs nor warners are of any use to a people who have decided not to believe. [101]

Do they really expect any (other fate) than what befell those who passed away before them in former days?

Then say to them, "*You just wait then, for I'll be waiting with you, as well.*" [102]

In the end, We saved Our messengers and those who believed, and it was entirely appropriate for Us to save those who believed. [103]

A Call to those in Doubt

Say to them, "*People! If you have any doubts about my way of life, (then know that) I don't serve what you're serving in place of Allah. And what's more, I serve Allah, the One Who will take your souls (at death), and I've been commanded to be among the faithful.* [104]

"*(I've also been told), 'Set your face upon the pure natural way. Never be an idol-worshipper, nor call upon any other besides Allah, for they're just (material) things that can neither benefit nor harm you. If you did, then you would truly be wrongdoers.'*" [105-106]

If Allah touches you with some harm, no one can remove it besides Him, and if He intends for any good to come your way, then no one can withhold His favor.

He causes it to reach whichever of His servants that He wills, for He's the Forgiving and the Merciful. [107]

Say to them, "*People! Now the truth has come to you from your Lord! Whoever is guided is guided for the good of his own soul, and whoever goes astray does so to his own loss. It's not my place to manage your affairs.*" [108]

Now follow the revelation that's being sent to you, (Muhammad,) and be patient until Allah decides the matter, for He's the best one to judge. [109]

Hūd

11 Hūd

Late Meccan Period

☞ Introduction

This chapter is similar to the last in theme, and it continues the veiled message of separation. In other words, it prepares the Prophet and his followers for the possibility of abandoning their hometown. This is hard for anyone to do, let alone large groups of people. Late Meccan chapters like this continually mentioned episodes from the lives of prophets such as Nuh (Noah) and Musa who had to make a clean break from their people and past lives for the sake of a brighter future.

When the order finally came to the Prophet to lead his followers to Medina, they would've already been well-versed in the principle of migrating for the sake of Allah's faith. Such was the tense atmosphere in the late Meccan period that it even began to show upon the appearance of the Prophet. Abu Bakr, noting that the Prophet seemed to be getting worn down, asked him, "It seems that you've been aging. Why is that?" The Prophet answered, "The chapter of Hūd and others like it have aged me." *(Tirmidhi)*

In the Name of Allah,
the Compassionate, the Merciful

*A*lif. *Lām. Rā.*

(This) Book contains clear teachings that have been categorically explained by One Who is wise and well-informed. [1] Therefore, you should serve none other than Allah.

(Muhammad, say to all people,) *"I've (been sent) to you from Him both to warn and to give good news.* [2]

"So then, seek the forgiveness of your Lord, and repent to Him, so He can provide you with good things to satisfy you (here on earth) for a while and ultimately grant His favor upon those who are worthy of merit. If you turn away, then I'm afraid that you'll be punished on a momentous day. [3]

"All of you will go back to Allah, and He has power over all things." [4]

Background Info... v. 5

Ibn 'Abbas (d. 687) was asked about this verse. He explained that it was about a superstition the pagans had in which they were afraid to expose themselves to the sky if they had to remove any of their clothes, either for answering the call of nature or from sleeping with their wives. *(Ibn Kathir)* This verse is telling them that Allah sees them no matter how much they try to hide.

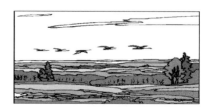

294

As it is, they close up their hearts and try to hide from Him! However, even though they wrap themselves up in their cloaks, He still knows what they hide and what they show, for He knows (all the secrets) of the heart. [5]

The Faithless can't
Hide in their Denials

There isn't a **creature** that moves on the earth without its needing Allah for its food and supplies. He knows where its usual resting place is, even as He knows where it lurks for a while, for everything is recorded in a distinctive ledger. [6]

He's the One Who created the heavens and the earth in six time periods, and His throne was over the water.

(He created you) so that He could test (you in order to bring out) which of you is most noble in conduct.

However, (Muhammad), even if you told them, "*You really are going to be resurrected after death,*" those who cover over (the light of faith in their hearts) would be sure to say, "*This is obviously just magic.*" [7]

Then if We delayed the punishment for some time, they would be sure to say, "*So what's holding it back?*"

Oh, but on the day when it actually comes upon them - *nothing will hold it back from them then* - and they'll be completely surrounded by what they used to laugh at! [8]

Beware the Fickle Heart

If We let a human being have a taste of Our mercy, but then take it away from him, he becomes gloomy and thankless. [9]

If We then let him experience good fortune after a bout of hardship has befallen him, he merely says:

"*My streak of bad luck is over,*" and then he becomes proud and overconfident. [10]

Although that's not the case with those who persevere and do what's morally right, for they're going to be forgiven, and they'll have a great reward. [11]

Stay the Course

Perhaps you've been tempted to abandon some of what's been revealed to you, or perhaps your heart has become filled with anxiety (at the thought that) they might say, "*Why aren't any treasures being sent down to him, or why aren't there any angels coming along with him?*"

You're only a warner, and Allah is the One Who manages all affairs! [12]

(Perhaps you're afraid) they might say, "*He made it all up!*" (If they do say that, then) tell them, "*So bring ten chapters like it, and call whomever you can other than Allah (to judge them as to their similarity), if you're really so honest!* [13]

"*And if your (idols) don't answer you, then know that this revelation is being sent down with Allah's knowledge and that there's no god besides Him. So now will you submit (to Him)?*" [14]

Those who desire the life of this world *and all its glitter* will be repaid by Us for the deeds they did within it, and (they) won't be shortchanged. [15]

They're the ones who will have nothing in the next life - *other than the Fire!* All the plans they made will be useless there, even as all that they did will come to nothing! [16]

Are (such evil people the same as) those who accepted the (revealed scriptural) proof of their Lord, which was taught by a witness sent from Him, even as the Book of Musa (was also sent) before it, as a source of guidance and mercy?

(The believers) put their faith in it, but those factions (from days gone by) who abandoned (their revelations) will have nothing but the Fire as their promised meeting place.

Have no doubt about that, for it's the truth from your Lord, though most people don't believe. [17]

Who can be more wrong than the one who invents a lie against Allah? They're going to be brought back before their Lord, and then the witnessing (angels) will say, "*These are the ones who lied against their Lord!*"

Without a doubt, Allah's curse will befall the corrupt! [18] They're the ones who hinder others from following the path of Allah, trying to make it seem crooked - *all the while they're the ones who are rejecting (the concept) of the next life!* [19]

There's no way they can obstruct Allah (and His purpose) in this world, nor will they find anyone to protect them besides Allah.

Their punishment will be doubled, for they (couldn't bring themselves) to hear (the message) or notice (the signs of Allah). [20]

They're the ones who've lost their own souls, and whatever they invented will leave them to languish. [21] Without a doubt, they're going to be the biggest losers in the next life! [22]

Those who believed, who did what was morally right and who humbled themselves before their Lord, they'll be the companions of the Garden, *and there they get to stay!* [23]

The two classes (of people, both the faithless and the believer), can be compared to the blind and deaf and the seeing and hearing.

Are they the same in comparison? So won't you take a reminder? [24]

Nuh's People Rejected Him

And so it was that We sent Nuh to his people, (and he announced), "*I'm a clear warner (who's been sent) to you (to teach you) that you should serve no one else besides Allah. I'm afraid that you might be punished on a terrible day.*"
[25-26]

The leaders of the faithless among his people said, "*We don't see anything in you more than a mortal man like ourselves, nor do we see anyone following you except the weakest and least sophisticated among us, nor do we see you as any better than the rest of us.*

"*No way (are you a messenger of Allah)! We think you (and your followers) are liars!*" [27]

(Nuh) replied, "*My people! Have you considered that I (just might have) been given clear evidence from my Lord and that He might have indeed sent His mercy down upon me from His Own presence?*

However, if (those things) are unclear to you, then should we force you to accept (Allah's truth) when you're dead set against it?" [28]

"*My people! I'm not asking you for any money in return (for my preaching). My reward is due from none other than Allah, and I'm not going to push away (the poor people) who believe, (just because you look down upon them).*

"They're going to meet their Lord, (even as you will). It's just that I've (come to the conclusion) that you're an ignorant people." [29]

"My people! Who would help me against Allah if I pushed the (poor) away? So won't you take a reminder? [30]

"I'm not telling you that I have the treasures of Allah, nor do I know what's hidden, nor do I claim to be an angel.

"And I won't say about the ones whom you look down upon that Allah won't grant them something good, for Allah knows what's in their souls, and if I ever were to (push the poor away), then I would be acting like a tyrant." [31]

They answered, *"Nuh! You've argued with us and carried on the argument for a long time, so now bring down upon us that with which you've threatened us - that is if you're really telling the truth!"* [32]

"Allah will certainly bring it down upon you," (Nuh) replied, *"but only when He wants to do it, and then you won't be able to stop it!* [33]

"If Allah wants to leave you astray, then my advice won't do you any good, even though I want to advise you, for He is your Lord, and you're going to return back to Him." [34]

(So now are the idol-worshippers of Mecca) saying, *"(Muhammad) has just made (this story) all up"*?

Answer them, saying, *"If I made up (the story of Nuh), then it would be my fault alone, but I'm free of all your (kinds of) corruption.* [35]

The Great Flood

> **F.Y.I**
>
> Nuh preached to his people for many years. After he was finally and completely rejected by his people, as evidenced by his speech contained in chapter 71, Allah ordered that he should build a boat and save the few who believed. This is perhaps the world's oldest story, and we remember it to this day for the many lessons it gives.

Nuh received an inspiration (from Allah) that said:

"No more of your people will believe, except for those who've already believed. So don't feel any more sadness over what they're doing. [36]

"Build a boat under Our sight and by Our direction, and don't ask Me any further about those who do wrong, for they're going to be drowned." [37]

298

So (Nuh) began to build the boat, but every time the leaders of his people passed by him they would ridicule him.

He would say to them in answer, "*If you're making fun of us now, (know that) we're (soon) going to be making fun of you.* [38]

Soon you're going to know who it is that has a humiliating penalty in store, and who it is that will have a lasting punishment." [39]

Then Our command arrived, and the heated banks (of the rivers) began to overflow!

"*Board (the ship),*" We said, "*and take a pair of male and female from every kind (of useful livestock).*

"*Load up your family, all except for those against whom the sentence has already been given, and (load) the believers.*" However, only a few had ever believed along with him. [40]

(Nuh) said to (his followers), "*Set out upon (the boat), for its course and its coming to anchor will be in the name of Allah, and my Lord is truly forgiving and merciful.*" [41]

(Thereafter, the ship) floated with them upon waves (that towered over them) like mountains.

Nuh called out to his son, who had become separated from the rest (of the faithless), "*My son! Come on board with us, and don't (share the same fate) as the faithless!*" [42]

"*I'll climb upon some mountain,*" he called back, "*and that will save me from the (rushing) water!*"

(Nuh looked away in sadness and) said, "*Today, no one is safe from the command of Allah, unless He decides to be merciful to him.*"

Then the waves came between them, and (his son) was just another one of those who had been DROWNED. [43]

Then the saying went out: "*Earth! Swallow your water! Sky! Hold back (your rain)!*" The water went down, and the judgment (of Allah) was fulfilled.

The boat came to rest upon Mount Judi, and the saying went out: "*The wrongdoing people have passed away!*" [44]

Then Nuh called upon his Lord and said, "*My Lord! My son was of my own family. Even still, Your promise is true, and You're the fairest judge of all.*" [45]

"*Nuh!*" (Allah) replied. "*He was no longer part of your family, for his actions were other than moral, so don't ask Me about things you may know nothing about. This is a word of caution that I'm giving to you so you won't be one of the ignorant.*" [46]

"*My Lord!*" (Nuh) answered. "*I seek Your protection so that I won't ask You about things I may know nothing about. Unless You forgive me and show me mercy, then I would surely be among the losers.*" [47]

The call went out (from the heavens):

"*O Nuh! Come down (out of the boat) with peace from Us and also with blessings upon you and upon the people who are with you, (and also upon the communities that will descend) from them - peoples to whom We'll give enjoyment, even though in the end a terrible punishment from Us will befall them.*" [48]

These are some of the hidden stories (that were unknown) to you (Muhammad) and that We're revealing (to you). Neither you nor your people knew them before.

So bear patiently (the persecution of the Meccans), for the final (victory) is only for those who were mindful (of their duty to Allah). [49]

Hūd Calls to His People

We sent to the (people of) 'Ad their brother Hūd. He said (to them), "*My people! Serve Allah! You have no other god than Him. You've been doing nothing but inventing (false gods).* [50]

"*My people! I'm not asking you for any reward for this, for my reward is due from none other than the One Who created me. So won't you understand?*" [51]

"*My people! Ask your Lord to forgive you, and turn to Him (in repentance). Then He'll send abundant rain down upon you and add strength to your strength. Don't turn away in wickedness!*" [52]

"*Hūd!*" they answered. "*You haven't brought us any convincing proof. We're not about to abandon our gods on your word alone, nor will we ever believe in you.* [53]

We'll admit to no more than to say that maybe some of our gods have afflicted you with insanity."

(Hūd) replied, "*I call upon Allah as my witness, even as you are witnesses, as well, that I'm free of your making partners in place of Him, so plot against me all you want, and give me no chance.* [54-55]

"*I'm going to trust in Allah, the One Who is my Lord and your Lord. There isn't a creature that moves without Him having a hold on its forelock, and my Lord is on a straight path.*" [56]

"*If you turn away, then (at least) I've conveyed the message to you with which I was sent. (Now it just might happen that) my Lord will cause another people to rise up in your place.*

"*(No matter how much you resist Allah,) you can't harm Him in the least. My Lord is the guardian of all things.*" [57]

And so when Our command came, We saved Hūd and those who believed along with him by an act of Our Own mercy, and We saved them from a tremendous punishment. [58]

And so that was the (people of) 'Ad. They renounced the signs of their Lord, disobeyed His messengers, and obeyed the commands of every arrogant enemy (of faith). [59]

They were pursued by a curse in this life, and on the Day of Assembly, (oh, how they'll be punished), for the 'Ad rejected their Lord, and so - *away with the 'Ad, the people of Hūd!* [60]

The Thamud Suffer a Similar Fate

We sent to (the people of) Thamud their brother Salih.

He said (to them), "*My people! Serve Allah! You have no other god than Him.*

"*He's the One Who produced you from the earth and settled you upon it.*

"*Ask for His forgiveness, and turn to Him (in repentance), for my Lord is always near and ready to respond.*" [61]

(His people) said, "*Salih! You were one of us, and we had always placed our best hopes in you (that you might one day be our leader).*

"*Are you now forbidding us from worshipping what our ancestors worshipped? We have serious doubts about what you're calling us towards.*" [62]

"*My people!*" (Salih) answered. "*What do you think? If I have evidence from my Lord and if He's given me mercy from His Own Self, then who could help me against Allah if I ever disobeyed Him (by giving up this mission)?*

"*So (the bribes) you're offering me (to quit) are no more than the instruments of my own ruin.*" [63]

"*My people! This camel (you see here is specially blessed) by Allah and is a sign for you. Therefore, leave her to graze on Allah's land, and do her no harm, or a swift punishment will befall you.*" [64]

(Then the arrogant people among them) cut (her legs) and crippled her, so (Salih) told them, "*Enjoy yourselves in your homes for the next three days, (after which you're going to be destroyed), and that's a promise that won't be proven false.*" [65]

When Our command came, We saved Salih and those who believed along with him from the humiliation of that day through an act of Our Own mercy. Your Lord is Capable and Powerful! [66]

The **mighty blast** overtook the wrongdoers, and they lay cowering in their homes by the morning. [67]

(It looked) as if they had never lived or flourished there before! And so it was (their fate), for the Thamud rejected their Lord, and so - *away with the Thamud!* [68]

The Ruin of Lut's People

Our emissaries went to Ibraheem with good news. They said, *"Peace,"* and *"Peace,"* he answered back. Then he hurried to serve them a roasted calf. [69]

However, when he noticed that their hands never moved to partake of (the meal), he became suspicious of them and grew afraid. *"Don't be afraid,"* they said, *"for we're being sent against the people of Lut."* [70]

His wife just stood there and laughed when We gave her the good news of (a son named) Is-haq and (a grandson named) Yaqub. [71]

"Misfortune is mine!" she sighed. *"How could I bear a child now, seeing that I'm an old woman and my husband here is an old man? That would be something amazing, indeed!"* [72]

"Are you amazed at Allah's command?" they asked. *"Allah's mercy and blessings are (invested in) you, the people of (this) house, and He is indeed praiseworthy and full of glory."* [73]

When Ibraheem's sense of unease had left him, and after he had heard the good news (of a son), he began to plead with Us on behalf of Lut's people, for Ibraheem was (by nature) forbearing and prone to beseeching (his Lord as a matter of habit). [74-75]

"Ibraheem!" (the angels said.) *"Put an end (to your pleading). The command of* your Lord has already gone out. They're going to receive a punishment that cannot be turned away."* [76]

When Our emissaries arrived (in the area of the cities of Sodom and Gomorrah and met with) Lut, he became worried about their (safety), for he felt powerless (to protect) them (from his wicked people).

"Oh, what a stressful day!" he cried out, (as he noticed) his people rushing towards his (house), eager (to seize his guests), for they had long been engaged in perverted ways.

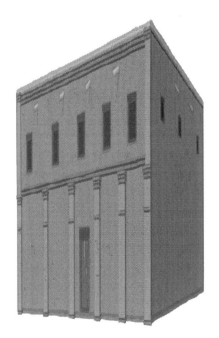

"My people!" he begged them. *"My daughters are here, and they're more appropriate for you! Be mindful of Allah, and don't disgrace me with regards to my guests. Isn't there a single man among you with good sense?"* [77-78]

"You know we want nothing from your daughters," they answered, "and you know quite well what we want (to do with your guests)!" [79]

"If only I had the strength to keep you at bay," (Lut) cried out, "or some strong force to call upon!" [80]

"Lut!" (the angels) said. "We are emissaries from your Lord! They won't reach you, (for we're going to hold them back).

"Flee (this city) with your family while some of the night still remains, and don't let anyone look back. However, your wife (is not going to leave with you).

"And so she's going to suffer the same fate that they're going to suffer. Their time will be up by the morning, and isn't the morning near at hand?" [81]

When Our **COMMAND** came, We turned (their towns) inside out and rained shower upon shower of hard-packed brimstone down upon them - (each blow being) imposed by your Lord, and such (punishments) are never far from those who do wrong. [82-83]

Madyan was also Tested

We sent to (the people of) Madyan their brother Shu'ayb. He said, "My people! Serve Allah! You have no other god than Him! Don't cheat when you measure or weigh (in your business dealings).

"I see that you're in prosperity now, but I'm afraid that you'll be punished on an overpowering day." [84]

"My people! Weigh and measure fairly, and don't withhold from people what rightfully belongs to them. Don't spread corruption in the land with a desire to cause chaos. [85]

"(The fairly earned profits) that Allah has left for you are the best for you, if you only had faith! However, I haven't been given the task of watching over you." [86]

"Shu'ayb!" they answered. "Are the prayers that you're making (to your God) telling you that we should give up worshipping what our ancestors did or give up using our property as we see fit?

"Oh, aren't you the one who is so forbearing and filled with common sense, (especially when you're telling others what to do)!" [87]

"My people!" (Shu'ayb) replied. "Now you just see if I have clear evidence from my Lord (to back up my claim.

"Here, take a look at my own business dealings), for (Allah) has given me good returns (through honest trade as a bounty) from His Own Self.

"I don't want to engage in what I've been forbidden to do, unlike your own practices. My only desire is to improve (your lives) to the best of my ability.

"My success will come only from Allah! I trust in Him and turn to Him (in repentance)." [88]

"My people! Don't let my opposition (to your longstanding practices) cause you to do (more) wrong (in response), for you might suffer a fate similar to that of the peoples of Nuh, Hūd or Salih, and the people of Lut are not so far away from you (that you should claim ignorance). [89]

"Ask your Lord to forgive you, and turn towards Him (in repentance and obedience), for my Lord is full of forgiveness and loving tenderness." [90]

"Shu'ayb!" they answered. *"We don't even understand most of what you're telling us! In fact, we think you're the weakest among us.*

"If it wasn't for your family (connections), we would've stoned you already, because you don't have any power to prevent us." [91]

"My people!" he replied. *"Is my family's (influence) the most important factor for you to consider (in deciding whether to harm me or not), even more than (your fear of) Allah?*

"Are you casting Him aside behind your backs (so easily)? My Lord completely surrounds whatever you're doing!" [92]

"My people! Do whatever you can, and I'll do whatever I can, likewise. You're soon going to know who will have a humiliating punishment befall them and who is lying, so keep on watching, for I'll be watching with you." [93]

When Our command came, We saved Shu'ayb and those who believed along with him through an act of Our Own mercy, but the mighty blast took hold of the corrupt, and they lay cowering in their homes by morning. [94]

(It looked) as if they had never lived and flourished there before! And so it was that the (people of) Madyan were removed - *just like the people of Thamud!* [95]

305

Take a Warning from the Pattern of History

And so it was that We also sent Musa with Our signs - and also with a clear mandate - to Pharaoh and his nobles.

However, (his nobles) obeyed Pharaoh's orders, and (obeying) Pharaoh's orders was not the most rational (thing for them to do). [96-97]

He's going to stand before his people on the Day of Assembly and then lead them into the Fire - *and oh, how terrible is the place into which they'll be led!* [98]

They're followed by a curse in this (life), and on the Day of Standing (for judgment) they're going to get an **awful** gift (in exchange for their awful deeds). [99]

These are some of the stories of the nations (of the past) that We're narrating to you. Some of them still exist, while others have been mowed down. [100]

It wasn't We Who did them any wrong. Rather, they did wrong against their own souls. All those idols that they used to call upon besides Allah were of no use to them when Allah's command went out, nor did they add anything (to their troubles) except for more destruction. [101]

That's what being seized by your Lord is like when He seizes towns steeped in the midst of their own corruption, and His grasp is exceedingly firm! [102]

There is a sign in this for those who fear the penalty of the next life. That will be a day when all people will be gathered together, and that will be a day of giving testimony. [103]

We won't delay it any more than the time that's set for it. [104]

On the day when it arrives, no soul will be allowed to speak unless it's been granted His permission. Some of those (assembled) there will be **wretched**, and others will be HONORED. [105]

The wretched will be in the midst of the Fire, and they'll have nothing but moaning and wailing, and they'll remain there for as long as the heavens and the earth endure, except as your Lord wills, and your Lord does whatever He wants. [106-107]

Meanwhile, those who are held in high esteem will be in the midst of the Garden, and they'll remain there for as long as the heavens and the earth endure, except as Allah wills, and it will be a gift that never ends. [108]

Have no doubts (about the true nature) of what these (Meccans) are worshipping, for they're worshipping nothing more than what their ancestors worshipped before them (out of blind habit).

We're going to pay them back what is due to them without withholding anything. [109]

And so it was that We gave the scripture to Musa, but (later generations) differed about it.

If it wasn't for the statement (of principle) that went out before from your Lord (that people will have time to make their choice as to whether or not to believe), then the matter would've been decided between them. However, they persist in doubts and misgivings about it. [110]

What is a Sincere Believer?

All shall be repaid by your Lord for the result of their deeds, for He's well-informed about everything they're doing. [111]

So stand up firmly (for the truth) as you've been ordered to do, both you and those who are with you who turn (to Allah for guidance).

Don't overstep (Allah's laws). Indeed, He's watching everything you do. [112]

Don't lean towards (being on the side of) wrongdoers, or else the Fire will take hold of you.

You have no other protector than Allah, and you won't be helped (by anyone else if you cross Him). [113]

> **Background Info... v. 114**
>
> A man had kissed a woman to whom he was neither married nor related, and he went to the Prophet in repentance and asked how the sin could be erased.
>
> This verse was then revealed. After the Prophet recited it, the grateful man asked, "Messenger of Allah, is this verse just for me?" The Prophet replied, "This is for all of my community." (Bukhari)

Establish prayer at the two ends of the day and during some hours of the night, for good deeds remove evil deeds.

This is a reminder for those who would be reminded. [114]

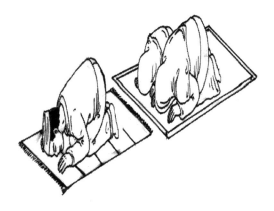

Be patient (with any hardships that befall you), for Allah will never allow the reward of the righteous to be lost. [115]

Parting Thoughts
on the Path of Truth

So now why weren't there - in all the generations that went before you - people with sense enough to prevent others from spreading chaos and disorder in the earth, except for the very few whom We saved (from harm)?

The wrongdoers followed after nothing more than what pleased them, and they were truly wicked. [116]

However, your Lord never destroys a settlement unjustly, (that is) as long as its people are behaving well. [117]

If your Lord had wanted, He could've made all people into a single community. However, they never cease to argue, except for the ones who've been graced with your Lord's mercy, and this is the purpose for which We created them.

The sentence of your Lord will be fulfilled: "*I will fill Hellfire with jinn and people all together!*" [118-119]

(The purpose) of all of these stories of (the ancient) messengers that We're relating to you is to strengthen your heart.

These (stories) that are coming to you contain the truth, as well as warnings and reminders for those who believe. [120]

So say to those who don't believe, "*Do whatever you can, and we'll do whatever we can.* [121] *Wait for some time, and we'll be waiting, also.*" [122]

The (knowledge) of unseen things within the heavens and the earth belongs only to Allah, and all matters will go back to Him (for their resolution), so serve Him, and trust in Him.

Your Lord is not unaware of what you're doing. [123]

Joseph

12 Yūsuf

Late Meccan Period

☞ Introduction

The story of Yusuf (Joseph) has long been considered one of the most engaging and heart-warming accounts in the Qur'an. It is also the single longest chapter with only one continuous theme and story line. It was revealed near the last days of the Prophet's stay in Mecca, at a time when the pagans and enemies of Islam were closing the noose of public enmity around the Muslims from all sides. A group of visiting Jews from the northern city of Yathrib (later to be called Medina) had doubts about the validity of Muhammad's prophethood.

Hoping to expose him as a possible fraud, they suggested to the pagans that they should ask him to narrate a Jewish story that the Arabs knew nothing about. In the main square of Mecca, a pagan man asked him, "What happened to Yusuf and his brothers? How did they come to live in a far-away land among strange people?"

If Muhammad (p) failed to answer, then it could've been said that he was a fake and not a true prophet. Muhammad (p) said that he would wait for revelation from his Lord. A short while later, Muhammad (p) stood out in the public forum and proceeded to recite the entire story of Yusuf and his brothers - without a pause or break - until the entire length of this chapter was finished. (Verses 1-3 were revealed and added later.)

As Muhammad (p) recited the story, the crowd fell silent. When he had finished, the Jewish visitors who witnessed the event left without saying a word. A few weeks later, several more visitors came from Yathrib, this time Arabs, and they accepted Islam at a site called 'Aqabah. The Muslim community now had two great lights to give them hope: the addition of new believers from another city; and *the most beautiful of all stories,* as the Qur'an described the story of Yusuf.

In the Name of Allah,
the Compassionate, the Merciful

*A*lif. *Lām. Rā.*

These are the verses of the clear Book. We've sent it (in the form of) an Arabic Qur'an so you can think (on it) deeply. [1-2]

Now We're going to narra te to you the most beautiful story in Our revealing this portion of the Qur'an to you. You didn't know (this story) before. [3]

309

The Dream

Yusef said to his father, "*O Father! I saw (in a dream) that eleven stars, the sun and the moon were all bowing themselves to me!*" [4]

"*My little son,*" his father answered. "*Don't mention this vision to your brothers for they might plot against you (out of jealousy). Shaytan is the clear enemy of all of humanity!*" [5]

"*(It's my feeling) that your Lord is going to choose you (to be a prophet) and teach you how to interpret (the meaning of passing events).*

"*(By this gift), He will complete His favor upon you and upon the descendants of Yaqub, even as He had already completed it upon your forefathers, Ibraheem and Is-haq. Indeed, your Lord has all knowledge and wisdom.*" [6]

And it just so happens that in (the story of) Yusuf and his brothers, there are definitely lessons for (those) people who asked! [7]

The Brothers Plot against Yusuf

(Yusef's older brothers complained among themselves,) saying, "*Our father loves Yusuf and his (younger) brother (Benjamin) more than he loves us, even though we're just as good! Our father is obviously mistaken!*" [8]

(Then one of the brothers suggested), "*So then let's kill Yusuf or send him away to some far off place. Then our father will give us all his attention. There'll be plenty of time for all of you to reform yourselves later on.*" [9]

However, one of the other (brothers) said, "*Don't kill Yusuf! Why don't you throw him down in the bottom of a well? Then some passing caravan can find him (and take him away).*" [10]

(Later, the brothers approached their father and said,) "*Father! Why don't you entrust Yusuf with us, since (you know) we have his best interests at heart? Send him with us tomorrow to enjoy himself and play. We'll protect him (from any danger).*" [11-12]

"*I'm uneasy,*" their father replied, "*about your desire to take him (along with you). I'm afraid that a wolf might eat him while you're not paying attention.*" [13]

"If a wolf were to eat him," they answered, "while there's so many of us (there to protect him), then we would have perished (first)!" [14]

So, they took Yusuf out with them, (after assuring their father he would be fine), but secretly they had all agreed to throw him down a well.

(Then, as they seized Yusuf and were about to throw him into the deep hole), We revealed (this message to) his (heart), "One day you're going to tell them about their affair when they won't even know (who you are)!" [15]

Then (the brothers) returned home at nightfall in tears. [16] "Oh, Father!" they cried. "We went racing with each other and left Yusuf all alone (to watch) our things. Then a huge wolf (came and) ate him up! Yet, you'll probably never believe us, even though we're telling the honest truth!" [17]

(Then they pulled out his shirt,) which they had secretly stained with false blood. "It can't be!"

Yaqub cried. "You must have made (some kind of plan) amongst yourselves! As for me, I can only wait with gracious patience. Only Allah can (help me) bear (the pain) of what you've described." [18]

Then a caravan of travelers passed by, and when they sent their (water boy) to the well, he let down his bucket and shouted, "Hey! (Look at this!) What a lucky break! Here's a fine young boy!"

Then they stowed him away like a treasure, though Allah knew what they were doing. [19]

(Yusuf's brothers) sold him (to the caravan) for the measly price of (a handful) of silver coins. That's how low of an opinion they had of him! [20]

Yusuf in Egypt

The Egyptian who bought (Yusuf) said to his wife, "Treat him honorably, for he might bring us some benefit, or we could even adopt him as a son."

This is how We settled Yusuf in the land so We could teach him how to interpret passing events.

Allah has complete proficiency over His affairs; yet, most people never realize it. [21]

In time, as Yusuf became fully mature, We endowed him with sound judgment and intelligence, and that's how We reward those who are good. [22]

However, she in whose house he lived (began to feel attracted to him), and she sought to seduce him against his (moral) nature.

She bolted the doors and said to him, *"I'm ready for you now, (so come to me)!"*

"Allah forbid!" Yusuf exclaimed. *"Your husband is my master! He's the one who made my life here tolerable! No good comes to people who do wrong!"* [23]

However, she desired him greatly, and he would've desired her, except that he remembered the proof of his Lord.

And so We turned him away from corruption and (the desire to do) shameful deeds, for He was one of Our sincere servants. [24]

Then they raced each other to the door, and she tore his shirt from behind (as he attempted to get away). When they reached the door they found her noble (husband) standing right there!

(Thinking quickly,) she said, *"What other punishment can there be for someone who wickedly (tried to seduce your wife) except prison or a painful beating!"* [25]

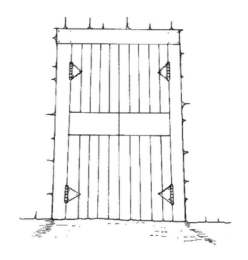

But she's the one who tried to seduce me away from my own nature!" (Yusuf) protested.

Just then, a member of her household who witnessed (the scene as it unfolded), suggested, *"If his shirt is torn from the front, then she's telling the truth, and he's the liar!* [26] *But if his shirt is torn from the back, then she's the liar, and he's telling the truth!'* [27]

When he saw that Yusuf's shirt was, indeed, torn from the back, (he turned to his wife and scolded her), saying, *"Truly, this is your ploy, and your ploy is formidable!* [28]

"Yusuf, forget any of this ever happened!" (Turning back to his wife), he said, *"Apologize for your offense, for you're clearly at fault!"* [29]

The Women of the City Find Out

(When news of the event became known), the (upper class) women of the city (began to gossip), saying, "*The wife of the great minister wants to seduce her own houseboy. He must have stricken her with passionate desire. We can see that she's clearly losing her mind!*" [30]

When she heard of their malicious gossiping, she invited them and prepared a banquet for them. (After they all arrived and were seated,) she gave each of them a (fruit-cutting) knife.

(While they were cutting their food), she called out to Yusuf, saying, *"Come out (Yusuf, and stand here) before them."*

When they saw him, (his handsome features) astounded them, and they cut right through (their fruit) to their hands!

"*Allah save us!*" they cried. *"He's no ordinary man! This is no less than an angelic being!*" [31]

"There before you now," she said, "*is the one you blamed me for! (Yes,) I did try to seduce his very soul, but he eluded me and resisted me in order to preserve his innocence! Now if he doesn't do what I command, he'll surely be thrown into prison and be with the most contemptible!*" [32]

"My Lord!" (Yusuf) cried. *"I desire prison far more than what they're calling me towards, and unless You steer their ploy away from me, I might become attracted to them and act like an ignorant fool."* [33]

Then his Lord heard (his plea) and turned their ploy away from him, for truly He is the Hearing and the Knowing. [34]

Then, after they saw the evidence (of what was going on), it occurred to (the husbands of the women) that it would be best to put him in prison for a while. [35]

The Two Prisoners

Now along with Yusuf there were two other men who were put in (the prison). The first one said, *"I saw myself (in a dream) pressing wine."*

The second one said, *"I saw myself (in a dream) carrying bread on my head with a swarm of birds eating off it."*

(Then they said to Yusuf), *"Tell us the meaning of these (strange dreams), for we can tell that you're a good one (to ask)."* [36]

(Yusuf) answered, *"Even before your next meal comes, I'll explain to you the meaning of (your dreams that will predict) events before they even happen to you. This is part of what my Lord has taught me. I've given up the customs of (these) people who disbelieve in Allah and reject the (punishment) of the next life.* [37]

" I follow the customs of my fathers, Ibraheem, Is-haq and Yaqub, and none of us ever made any partners with Allah. This comes from the grace of Allah that's been bestowed upon us and upon people (in general), though most people are thankless." [38]

Then he said, *"My fellow inmates! Which is better: many lords arguing among themselv es, or the One, Irresistible Allah?* [39] *If you don't serve Him, then you're serving nothing more than names that you and your ancestors made up, and Allah gave no one permission to do that.*

"The right to command is for none save Allah, and He has commanded that you serve nothing besides Him. That's the straight way of life, but most people don't understand." [40]

"My fellow inmates," he continued. *"As for the first of you, he will again pour out the wine for his master to drink. As for the other, he will be hung from a stake, and the birds will eat off his head. The matter you two asked me about has been decided."* [41]

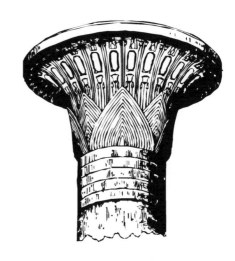

(Then Yusuf) whispered to the one whom he thought would be released, *"Mention me to your master."*

However, Shaytan made (the man) forget all about it, so Yusuf lingered in prison for a few more years. [42]

The Mysterious Dream

The king (of Egypt called to his nobles) and said, *"I saw (in a dream) seven fat cows being eaten by seven skinny ones and seven green shafts of grain and seven others withered. My nobles! Tell me what my vision means if you can explain the meaning of visions."* [43]

314

"Just a confused bunch of symbols," they replied. *"We're not experts at figuring out the meaning (of such cryptic dreams)."* [44]

However, the one who had been released (from prison), and who now remembered (Yusuf) after so long, said, *"I'll tell you what it really means. Send me (to the one who can solve this riddle)."* [45]

(When the wine-server arrived at the prison, he went to Yusuf's cell) and said, *"Yusuf, the one (who predicted the) truth (for me so long before)!*

"Explain for us the meaning of (this new vision): seven fat cows being eaten by seven skinny ones; seven green shafts of grain followed by seven withered ones. Tell me, so I can return to the people (at the royal court) so they can know." [46]

(Yusuf) replied, *"For seven years you'll diligently grow crops like you always do, but when you harvest them leave all the grains in the stalk except for the little that you must eat.* [47]

"Then after this will come seven dreadful years (of bad harvests), in which you will have to live off of what you had stored up in advance, saving only small, guarded supplies. [48]

"Then after that, a year will come in which the people will be delivered (from the drought), and they'll press (wine and oil once more)." [49]

Yusuf in the Court of the King

(When the man returned with the meaning of the dream), the king (was impressed), and he said, *"Bring him to me."*

However, when the messenger (of the king) went (to the prison to release Yusuf, he refused to leave his cell).

He said, *"Go back to your master and ask him, 'How is it with the women who cut their hands?' My Lord is aware of their trap."* [50]

(The king then ordered the women who were involved in the affair to be gathered before him.) Then he asked them, *"What were your intentions when you tried to seduce Yusuf's very soul?"*

The women answered, *"God save us! We don't know anything bad about him!"*

Then the wife of the great minister said, *"The truth has now become clear, for it was I who tried to seduce him, but he indeed remained honorable."* [51]

(When Yusuf was told about what happened, he said,) *"So there it is – (I wanted the truth to come to light so that* my master) would know that I was never unfaithful to him in his absence, and Allah never guides the plans of betrayers! [52]

"I don't deny my own shortcomings, for the soul can descend into corruption unless my Lord is merciful. Certainly, my Lord is forgiving and merciful." [53]

Then the king commanded, *"Bring him to me; I'm going to take him into my personal service."*

When (Yusuf came to the court, the king reassured him), saying, *"Feel confident today in my presence, for your position is secure and established."* [54]

(Yusuf) said, *"Put me in charge of all the granaries in the land. I'll guard them knowing (their full importance)."* [55]

And so it was in this manner that We established Yusuf in the position that he could take anything in the land in whatever quantity he willed.

We parcel out Our Mercy to whomever We want, and We never lose the reward of those who do good. [56] The reward of the next life is much better for those who believe and who are mindful (of Allah). [57]

The Brothers Go to Egypt

(When the foretold famine struck the region), Yusuf's brothers arrived in his presence (to buy food), but they didn't recognize him, although he knew immediately who they were. [58]

After he had provisioned them with what they needed, he told them, *"Bring me (the youngest) brother you have from the same father as yourselves.*

"Don't you see that I give full measure and that I provide the best hospitality? [59]

"Now, if you don't bring him to me, you won't get any more (grain) from me, nor shall you ever come near me again." [60]

They answered, *"We'll certainly get our way from his father. Surely we'll do it."* [61]

Then (Yusuf quietly) told his servants, "Put their trade goods back into their saddlebags, (and do it in such a way) that they won't find out until after they've returned to their families, for that may spur them into returning (for more supplies)." [62]

(When the brothers) returned to their father, they said, *"Father! We won't get any more grain (unless we take our youngest brother with us next time), so send our brother (Benjamin) with us so we can get more (supplies). We'll certainly protect him."* [63]

316

"Should I trust you with him," (Yaqub) replied, *"when I had already trusted you with his brother (Yusuf) so long before? Even still, Allah is the best guardian. He's the most merciful of the merciful."* [64]

Then, when they were unpacking their supplies, they found their trade goods (hidden in the grain).

They said, *"Father! For what more can we ask? Our trade goods have been returned to us so we can go and get more food for our families.*

"We'll protect our brother and get a full load of grain (extra from our host in Egypt). That's like nothing (for him to give)." [65]

Yaqub said, *"I'll never send him with you unless you swear a special promise to me in Allah's name that you'll be sure to bring him back, unless you, yourselves, are trapped."*

After they swore their oath, he said, *"Allah, You be the One Who guarantees what we've said!"* [66]

(Then he gave his sons the following instructions), saying, *"My sons, don't enter the city all from the same entrance, but rather each of you should pick a different entrance, not that I can help you against Allah with my advice.*

"No one can decide (the outcome of events) except Allah. I'll trust in Him, and let everyone who would trust (in something) trust in Him." [67]

When they entered the city in the way their father had instructed, it didn't help them in the least against (the plan of) Allah.

It was just something Yaqub felt he had to say, for he was - *by Our instruction* - very intelligent (and experienced), but most people don't know that. [68]

Who Took the King's Cup?

(When the brothers arrived and) were admitted back into Yusuf's presence, he took his (younger) brother (Benjamin) aside and insisted that he stay with him.

He told him, *"(Benjamin,) surely I'm your own brother, so don't be worried over what the (other brothers) may do."* [69]

Then after Yusuf had given them the supplies they needed, he (secretly) put a drinking cup into his (youngest) brother's saddlebag.

(When the brothers began to leave for the return journey,) an announcer shouted out after them, *"Hey, you there! In the caravan! You're surely thieves!"* [70]

(The brothers turned towards the guards) and said, *"Just what is it that you're missing?"* [71]

"We're missing the great cup of the king," they replied, *"and whoever brings it back will get a camel's load (worth of valuables)."* (Then the captain of the guard said,) *"I can assure you of that!"* [72]

(The brothers protested), saying, *"By Allah! You know we didn't come here to make trouble in this land, and we're certainly not thieves!"* [73]

"So then what should the penalty be (for this crime)," the (Egyptians) asked, *"if you're found to be liars?"* [74]

"The penalty" they answered, *"should be that the owner of the saddlebag in whose possession you find the item should be held (as a slave) to pay for the crime. This is how we penalize criminals (in our country)."* [75]

Then (Yusuf came and) began to search their baggage first, before coming to his brother's (bag). When (he opened) the bag of his brother (Benjamin, he held up the cup), and there it was!

That's how We planned it for Yusuf. He couldn't hold his brother, according to the law of the king, except that Allah willed it.

We increase the status of whomever We want, but over all learned masters is a more knowledgeable One. [76]

(The brothers) cried out, *"If he stole something, then you should know that he had another brother who used to steal before!"*

Yusuf kept his feelings to himself, so as not to give the secret away to them. Instead, he said, *"You're in the worst position, and Allah knows best the truth of what you claim!"* [77]

They begged, *"Great one! He has an old and respected father! Take one of us in his place, instead. We see that you're fair (in your decisions)."* [78]

(Yusuf) replied, *"Allah forbid that we should take anyone besides the one who had our property. If we did that, then we would be acting unjustly."* [79]

What will the Brothers Tell their Father?

When (the brothers) saw no chance of him changing his mind, they discussed the matter among themselves privately.

The oldest one among them said, *"Don't you know that you made a promise to your father in Allah's name and that even before this you failed in your duty to Yusuf? As for me, I won't leave this land until my father allows me or Allah makes a decision about me, and He's the best to decide."* [80]

"Go back to your father and tell (him), 'Father! Your son stole something. We report only what we know, and we couldn't guard against what we didn't expect! [81]

"Ask at the town we passed through and in the caravan in which we returned, and you'll see that we're telling the honest truth." [82]

(When Yaqub was informed), he cried out, *"Not so! You've made up a story to cover yourselves! I can do no more than endure this (tragedy) with dignity. Perhaps Allah will bring them all back to me (somehow), for He's full of knowledge and wisdom."* [83]

Then he turned away from them and cried, *"How sad I feel for Yusuf!"* Then his eyes glazed over and became white. Blinded by his sorrow, he became increasingly despondent. [84]

(The brothers) shouted, *"By Allah! You'll never stop remembering Yusuf until you exhaust yourself or die!"* [85]

(Yaqub answered them), saying, *"I'm only complaining about my sorrow and sadness to Allah, and I know things from Allah that you don't.* [86]

"My sons! Go back to Egypt, and ask about Yusuf and his brother! Never give up hope of Allah's compassion. Truly, no one despairs of Allah's compassion except for those who cover over (their awareness of His power over them)." [87]

(When the brothers returned to Egypt) and entered (Yusuf's presence once again), they said, *"Great one! Grief has come upon our family and us. We only have a few goods left (to trade), so grant us full rations as an act of charity for us. Allah rewards the charitable."* [88]

(Then Yusuf spoke), saying *"Do you remember how you dealt with Yusuf and his youngest brother in your ignorance?"* [89]

(When they realized who the man before them was,) they asked, *"Are you really Yusuf?"*

"(Yes), I am Yusuf," he replied, *"and this is my brother (Benjamin)! Allah has brought the gift (of this reunion) to all of us. Truly, whoever is mindful (of Allah) and who patiently perseveres (through any hardships), Allah will never let the reward of those who were good become lost."* [90]

(The brothers) cried out, *"By Allah! Allah has indeed preferred you over us, and we're guilty of a crime!"* [91]

"Let there be no blame upon you this day," Yusuf replied. *"Allah will forgive you, and He's the most merciful of the merciful.* [92]

"Now, go and take my shirt with you; cast it over my father's face, and he will see again. Then return here all together with your families." [93]

Yaqub's Premonition

Even as the caravan departed (from Egypt, Yusuf's) father exclaimed (to the people around him in his encampment), *"I smell the scent of Yusuf, even though you may think I'm senile."* [94]

"By Allah!" they replied. *"But you have an old, wandering mind."* [95]

However, when the herald of good news arrived and put the shirt over (Yaqub's) face, he immediately regained his ability to see. Then he said (to those around him), *"Didn't I say to you that I know things from Allah that you don't?"* [96]

320

(Then the brothers) cried out, *"Father! Ask forgiveness for our sins; we were truly in the wrong."* [97]

"Very soon will I ask my Lord to forgive you," he replied, *"for He is indeed the Forgiving and the Merciful."* [98]

The Fulfillment of the Dream

(When Yaqub and all the rest of his family) entered into Yusuf's presence, he provided a home for his parents with himself, saying, *"Enter safely into Egypt, if it pleases Allah."* [99]

He raised up his parents onto a high place (of honor), but they all fell down prostrate before him.

(Yusuf) exclaimed (in wonder), *"My Father! This is the completion of the vision I had so long before. Allah has made it all come true!*

"He was good to me when He got me out of prison and then brought all of you here from out of the desert - even after Shaytan had caused conflict between me and my brothers. My Lord is subtle in what He wills, for He is the Knowing and the Wise." [100]

(Yusuf prayed), *"My Lord! You've indeed given me some power and taught me how to interpret passing events. Originator of the heavens and the earth! You're my protector in this world and in the next. Take me as one surrendering (to Your will), and join me with the righteous!"* [101]

This is one of the hidden stories that We're revealing to you by inspiration. You weren't there among (Yusuf's brothers) when they agreed on their affair and made a plot. [102]

Yet, most people won't believe, no matter how hard you wish them to. [103]

The Natural Signs of Allah

You're not asking (the faithless) for any reward for this - *this is no less than a reminder for all the worlds.* [104] Then how many signs in the heavens and on the earth do they pass by?

Yet, they turn (their faces) away from them! [105] Most of them don't believe in Allah without making (others as partners) with Him! [106]

Do they feel safe against the **overwhelming** nature of Allah's wrath coming down upon them or of the sudden arrival of the (final) Hour without their even noticing it? [107]

Say to them, *"This is my way. I'm inviting (you) to (believe in) Allah with evidence as clear as sight. (This is) my (way, and the way of) whoever follows me. Glory be to Allah! I'll never be an idolater!"* [108]

We didn't send before you any beings other than men whom We inspired, and they lived in human communities.

Don't they travel through the earth and see what became of those (disbelieving nations) before them?

(Regardless of what people get in this life), the home of the next life is the best for those who are mindful (of Allah). So won't you understand? [109]

(The forces of darkness will be granted a period of ascendancy), even up to the point when the messengers begin to lose hope (of the success of their mission) and feel they've been denied (utterly by their people).

Then, (without any advance warning), Our help will come and reach them, and We'll save whomever We want, but Our punishment will never be steered away from the bad people. [110]

And so it is that there are lessons in the stories (of past civilizations) for people of understanding.

(This tale of Yusuf) is not a fictional account, but a confirmation of (the message that came) before it. It's a detailed account of all things and a guide and mercy to a believing nation. [111]

Thunder

13 Ar-Ra'd
Late Meccan to Early Medinan Period

☞ **Introduction**

This chapter was mostly revealed in the later portion of the Meccan period, although a few verses date from Medina. It summarizes many of the ongoing themes touched upon in other chapters and introduces some dramatic imagery and unique doctrines related to the next life. The name of the chapter is taken from verse 13 where the very thunder itself is said to sound with the praise of Allah.

In the Name of Allah,
the Compassionate, the Merciful

*A*lif. Lām. Meem. Rā.

These are the verses of the Book, the very one that's being revealed to you from your Lord, and it's the truth. Yet, most people don't believe. [1]

Allah is the One Who **RAISED** the skies without any supports that you can see. Then He established Himself upon the throne (of power).

He tamed the sun and the moon, (causing) each to complete its orbit in a precise amount of time. That's how He regulates all matters.

(The reason why) He explains the proof (of His power) in such detail is so that you can believe confidently in the meeting with your Lord. [2]

He's the One Who spread the earth out wide and placed firm mountains within it and (flowing) rivers, as well.

(He also placed upon the earth) all types of fruit in pairs, two by two, and He draws the night like a veil over the day. In these things are signs for people who think. [3]

There are (distinct) regions adjoining each other on the earth, as well as vineyards, fields of grain and date palms growing from either (multiple root systems) or from only one (root).

They're all watered with the same water; yet, some of them (produce fruits that) are better for eating than others. In these there are signs for those who reflect. [4]

323

If you're amazed (at how they can deny Allah, after seeing how complex the world He made is), even more amazing still is their saying, "*When we're reduced to dust, are we really going to be created as good as new?*"

They're the ones who are blatantly denying their Lord, so they're the ones around whose necks will be shackles! They'll be the companions of the Fire, *and that's where they're going to stay!* [5]

They're asking you to hurry on something awful in preference to something good.

Yet, there have been many humiliating punishments (that struck previous peoples) before them.

However, your Lord is full of forgiveness towards people, even in their corruption, just as He's also harsh in punishment. [6]

And then the faithless ask, "*So why isn't a miracle being sent down to him from his Lord?*" Yet, you're only a warner and a guide for all nations. [7]

Allah Encompasses All Things

Allah knows what every female bears and how much the wombs are early or late, for everything is measured in His sight. [8]

He knows what's beyond sight, as well as what's clearly seen, for He's the Great One, the Highest of All! [9]

So it's all the same whether one of you hides his words or says them openly or whether you lay hidden by night or walk about in broad daylight. [10]

(Every person has angels) following him, both before him and behind him. They guard him by the command of Allah.

Truly, Allah will never change the condition of a people unless they change what's in themselves.

Whenever Allah wants to bring misfortune down upon a people, there can be no averting it, nor will they find any protector besides Him. [11]

Thunder is a Reminder

Background Info... v. 12-13

There is a story that two pagan men from Mecca approached the Prophet just after he arrived in Medina and asked about Islam. One of them named 'Amr ibn at-Tufayl asked what he would get if he accepted Islam, and the Prophet replied that he would have all the rights and duties of an ordinary Muslim.

'Amr then asked if he could be made the ruler of the Muslims after the Prophet passed away, and the Prophet answered him, saying, "That's not your right or your people's right; however, I could appoint you as a cavalry leader." 'Amr said, "I'm already a cavalry leader in the land of Najd. What if you rule the cities and I rule the countryside?"

The Prophet refused this offer, and 'Amr and his friend, a man named Arbad, left in anger, vowing to bring an army back with them to destroy the Muslims.

Before leaving town, however, they hatched a plot to kill the Prophet. While 'Amr was to engage the Prophet in conversation, Arbad would sneak up from behind the Prophet and strike him down. 'Amr returned to the Prophet and accordingly began to distract him. Arbad came from behind, but for some reason he couldn't pull his sword from its sheath.

The Prophet saw Arbad behind him, trying to unsheathe his sword, and he realized what was going on, so he left them in haste.

The two men fled the city, but two companions named Sa'd and Usayd came upon them and ordered them to surrender. The pair fled again, and Arbad was struck by a stray lightning bolt in the desert and died.

'Amr took refuge in a woman's house (she belonged to the tribe of the hypocrite, 'Abdullah ibn Ubayy,) and she noticed he had an ulcer growing on his leg. On his return journey to Najd, he died from that ulcer.

This passage was revealed in comment on this situation. *(Ibn Kathir)*

He's the One Who shows you the lightning as a source of both fear and hope, and He's the One Who raises up the heavily laden clouds (bursting with rain). [12]

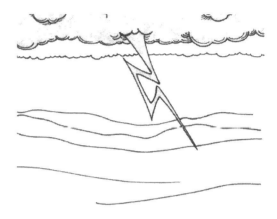

The very thunder, itself, glorifies His praises, as do the angels - wonderstruck (by His power).

He sends booming thunderbolts and strikes whomever He wants. Yet, these (people) are still arguing about Allah, though He's extremely cunning. [13]

Supplications are honestly due to Him alone. Those (idols) whom they call upon besides Him don't hear them any more than if they brought their empty hands to their mouths to take a sip of water and nothing reached them.

The supplications of those who cover (the light of faith within their hearts) are nothing more than blunders. [14]

All who reside within the heavens and the earth bow down before Allah, either willingly or unwillingly, as do their **shadows** in the mornings and the evenings. [15]

Ask them, "*Who is the lord of the heavens and the earth?"*

(Answer for them by) saying, "*Allah.*"

Then say to them, "*So are you taking protectors other than Him, things that have no power to bring either benefit or harm to themselves?*"

Ask them, "*Are the blind and the seeing the same, or is the darkness the same as the light?*"

Are they making partners with Allah – partners who (somehow managed to) create (things by themselves) that are just like what He created, so much so that (the two) creations seem the same?

Say to them, "*Allah created everything, and He's the One and the Irresistible.*" [16]

He sends down water from the sky. The resulting channels flow in a measured way, and the rushing (rapids) carry away the foam that forms on its surface.

Likewise, a similar kind of foam also arises when they heat (ore) in the fire to make jewelry or tools.

That's how Allah distinguishes the truth from falsehood, for the foam is discarded while what is useful for people remains on the earth. That's how Allah lays out His examples. [17]

Two Ways of Life, Two Results

Good things will come to those who respond to their Lord. However, those who ignore Him – even if they had everything in the heavens and on the earth and much more besides to offer as a bribe, (it would be of no use), for a strict accounting will be made of them.

Their final home will be in Hellfire, and what a terrible place to rest! [18]

326

Is the one who knows that what's been revealed to you from your Lord is the truth the same as someone who's blind (to that fact)? Only the thoughtful ever take reminders. [19]

They're the ones who fulfill their agreement with Allah, and they don't break their word. [20]

They (have respect for the family ties) that Allah has commanded to be joined, and they fear both their Lord and the strict accounting (to come). [21]

They're patient and seek Allah's (approving) gaze, even as they establish prayers and spend (in charity) out of what We've supplied to them, both in secret and in public. They also ward off evil with good.

They're the ones who will gain the final home - everlasting gardens that they'll be allowed to enter, along with the righteous among their parents, spouses and descendants.

Angels will enter (upon their presence) from every gate, (saying), "*Peace be upon*

you on account of your patient perseverance! How delightful is the final home!" [22-24]

However, those who break their agreement with Allah after having given their word, who separate what Allah has ordered to be joined, and who cause chaos and disorder in the land – they'll be far removed (from Allah's mercy), and they'll have the most miserable home! [25]

Allah increases or restricts the resources of whomever He wants. (Those who only love this life) revel in the life of this world, but the life of this world is nothing but a passing pleasure compared to the next life. [26]

Believers Know the Truth

Those who cover over (their awareness of the truth) ask, "*So why isn't a miracle coming down to him from his Lord?*"

Say to them, "*Allah leaves astray whomever He wants, and He guides those who repent (of their sins towards the path leading back) to Him.*" [27]

"*(They're the ones) who believe and whose hearts find relief in the remembrance of Allah, for without a doubt, in the remembrance of Allah hearts can find relief.*" [28]

"*Those who believe and do what's morally right will find the deepest satisfaction and the finest homecoming.*" [29]

And so We've sent you to a community that has had many other (civilizations) pass away before it, in order for you to recite to them what We're revealing to you. Yet, they're rejecting the Compassionate!

So say to them, *"He is my Lord; there is no god but He. On Him do I trust, and to Him do I turn."* [30]

This Qur'an is a Serious Message

If there ever was a recital (of scripture) that could move mountains or crack the earth or cause the dead to speak, (then this would be it)! But no! The command over all things rests with Allah. Don't the believers realize that if Allah had wanted, He could've guided all people together?

As for those who cover over (their faith), misfortune will continue to befall them because of their (misguided) actions, or it will settle in near their homes even until Allah's promise comes to pass. Indeed, Allah never fails in His word! [31]

And so it was that messengers who came before you were ridiculed, but I gave the faithless some time before I finally seized them, *and oh how (terrible) was My conclusion!* [32]

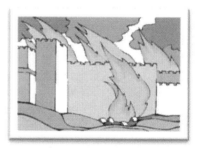

The Final Destination

Is the One Who stands over every soul and what it records for itself (the same as any other)? Yet, they've made partners with Allah!

Ask them, "*So name them! Are you going to tell Him about something that He doesn't know on the earth, or are you just saying something (with no truth to it)?*"

No way! Those who cover over (their understanding of the truth) are pleased with their posturing, but they're really being kept away from the path (by it).

For those whom Allah leaves astray, there can be no one to guide them. [33]

They're going to be punished in this worldly life, but the punishment of the next life is so much more severe, and they'll have no defender against Allah. [34]

(What's the) likeness of the Garden that's been promised to those who were mindful (of Allah)?

Rivers will flow beneath (its trees)! There'll be no end to eating, nor will its shade ever cease!

This is the final (home) for those who were mindful (of Allah), while the final (destination) of those who covered up (their faith) is in the Fire. [35]

Those to whom We've given the scripture (in the past) rejoice in what We've revealed to you, but among the factions (of other religions) are some who reject a part of it.

Say to them, "*I'm commanded to serve Allah and not to join partners with Him. I call to Him, and back to Him is my final goal.*" [36]

> **Background Info... v. 37**
>
> The Prophet was told of some people who had vowed to fast every day, others who vowed to pray all night, and yet others who vowed to remain celibate for their whole lives. The Prophet ordered them not to follow through with their plans and said, "As for me, I fast, and then I break my fast. I stand in prayer at night, but then I sleep. I eat meat, and I marry women, so whoever turns away from my example is not of me." (*Bukhari, Muslim*) This verse was revealed in comment.

So now We've revealed (the Qur'an) as an authoritative (book) in the Arabic (language).

If you were to follow their whims after already receiving knowledge, then you would find neither any best friend nor defender (to help you) against Allah. [37]

The Prophet will be Victorious over His Foes

We sent messengers before you and arranged for them to have wives and children. It was never the place of a messenger to bring a miracle unless Allah allowed it, and for every age (of history) there has been a scripture. [38]

Allah cancels or confirms whatever He wants, for He has the Mother of the Book (with Him). [39]

Whether We show you now part of the (punishment) that We've promised them or take your soul back to Us (before it befalls them), your duty is only to proclaim (the message) to them. It's Our task to call them to account. [40]

Don't (the Meccans) see how We're gradually reducing the lands (over which they hold influence) from their outlying borders?

Allah commands, and no one can hinder His command, and He is quick to settle accounts. [41]

The (faithless) who came before (these people) also made plans, though Allah is the ultimate planner over everything at once! He knows what every soul earns for itself, and the faithless will soon know who will have the final home (of Paradise). [42]

The faithless may say, "*You're not a messenger (from Allah),*" but say to them, "*Allah is enough of a witness between you and me, even as is anyone who knows (of Allah's previously revealed) scriptures.*" [43]

Abraham

14 Ibrâhîm
Late Meccan Period

☞ Introduction

This chapter, which is something of a continuation of the arguments introduced at the conclusion of the last, was revealed during the late Meccan period when it seemed inevitable that some sort of break or separation had to occur between the pagans and the Muslims. Indeed, verses 13-15 foreshadow the ultimate action that the Meccans would take, that of threatening to drive the Prophet and his followers away. Not known to them, however, the Muslims were soon to leave on their own to a sanctuary far to the north known as Yathrib, and later known as *Medinat-un-Nabi,* or the *City of the Prophet* (*Medina* for short).

In the Name of Allah,
the Compassionate, the Merciful

*A*lif. *Lam. Ra.*

(This is) a book that We've revealed to you so you can lead people out of every type of DARKNESS and into **LIGHT**, by Allah's leave, towards the path of the Powerful and Praiseworthy. [1]

Allah is the One to Whom belongs whatever is in the heavens and whatever is on the earth. Those who cover over (their awareness of the truth) are doomed to a harsh punishment! [2]

Those who love the life of this world more than the next life, and who try to hinder others from the way of Allah - *wishing to make it seem crooked* – they're the ones who are far off in error. [3]

The Messengers and Their Missions

*W*e never sent any messenger unless he spoke the language of his own people, so that he could explain things to them clearly.

Allah leaves astray whomever He wants, and He guides whomever He wants, for He's the Powerful and Wise. [4]

And so it was that We sent Musa with Our signs (and told him), "*Lead your people out of darkness and into light, and teach them to remember the days of Allah.*"

Truly, there are signs (in this story) for every extraordinarily patient and thankful person. [5]

Remember when Musa said to his people, "*Recall Allah's favors upon you when He saved you from Pharaoh's people. They mistreated you greatly - butchering your sons while leaving your daughters alive. That was an enormous test from your Lord.*" [6]

And remember when your Lord proclaimed (His promise to you, saying), "*If you're thankful, then I'll grant you even more (than just your freedom), and if you're ungrateful, then (know that) My punishment is harsh.*" [7]

Even Musa had told them, "*If you ever became ungrateful, and if everyone else on the earth likewise became ungrateful, even then Allah would have no need (for any of you), for He would still be praised (by other beings).*" [8]

Ignoring the Messengers

Haven't you heard the stories of those who lived before you – the people of Nuh and 'Ad and Thamud and all those who came after them?

No one knows about them more than Allah. Messengers went to each of them with clear evidence.

However, their (people) invariably put their hands up over their mouths and said, "*We reject whatever you've been sent with, and we're doubtful of the value of what you're calling us towards.*" [9]

Their messengers would ask them, "*Do you have any doubts about (the existence of) Allah, the Creator of the heavens and the earth? He's calling you so He can forgive you your sins and give you an extension on your time limit.*"

(The people would always answer,) saying, "*You're no more than a mortal man like us! You just want to turn us away from what our ancestors worshipped. So bring us a clear and decisive (miracle to prove your mission is true!)*" [10]

Their messengers would answer them, saying, "*While it's true that we're no more than mortals like yourselves, Allah favors whichever of His servants that He wants.*

"*It's not our place to bring a clear and decisive (miracle) without Allah's permission. (True) believers should trust in Allah, (rather than in miracles)!*" [11]

"*We have no reason not to trust in Allah, for He's guided us on our pathways. So then we're going to patiently endure all of your abuse. Those who would trust (in something) should trust in Allah.*" [12]

Then the rejecters (of truth) would tell their messengers, "*We're going to drive you out of our land, unless you return to our traditions!*"

Thereupon, their Lord would inspire (the messengers), telling them, "*We're going to destroy the wrongdoers, though We'll lodge your (bodies) in the earth, (and you shall remain there) long after (they're gone).*

"That's how it is for anyone who fears his meeting (with Me) and who takes My threat (of punishment) seriously." [13-14]

(Even though the wrongdoers) wanted to have victory (over the righteous), each and every stubborn tyrant failed in frustration. [15]

Hellfire is coming up ahead of each one of them. Therein he'll (be forced to) drink boiling, disgusting muck in huge gulps, but he'll never be able to get it past his throat!

Death will confront him from every side; *yet, he'll never die*, for a relentless punishment is what he'll have to face. [16-17]

The Price of Evil

The example of those who reject their Lord is that their deeds are like ashes that are blown around by a strong gust of **WIND** on a stormy day.

They have no power at all over what they've earned for themselves, and that's by far the worst mistake! [18]

Don't you see that Allah created the heavens and the earth for a true purpose? If it were ever His desire, He could remove you and bring about some new kind of creation, and that's not too hard for Allah. [19-20]

(The faithless) will be marched all together before Allah. Then the weak-minded will say to (the influential) and self-assured, *"We were only following whatever you suggested, so can you do anything for us now against Allah's wrath?"*

"If Allah had guided us," they'll reply, *"then we would've guided you. It doesn't matter now whether we're outraged or resigned to our fate, for there's no way for us to escape."* [21]

Once the issue has been decided, Shaytan will say, *"Allah made a true promise to you, but I broke my promise to you, and I had no power over you other than through suggestion.*

"You listened to me, so don't blame me. You only have yourselves to blame.

"I can no more hear your cries than you can hear mine. I don't accept the blame for what you previously did when you joined me (in Allah's power)."

For sure, wrongdoers have a terrible punishment prepared for them! [22]

However, those who believed and did what was morally right will be admitted into gardens beneath which rivers flow, and there they get to stay, by their Lord's leave. They'll be greeted with the word, *"Peace!"* [23]

The Parable of the Two Trees

Don't you see how Allah sets out the example of a good word? It's like a good tree whose roots are strong and stable, with branches jutting up into the sky. [24]

It bears fruit at all times, by its Lord's permission. Allah offers such examples for people so they can be reminded. [25]

Now the example of a rotten word is like a rotten tree that's been torn out of the earth by its roots. It has no way to hold itself up! [26]

Allah will support and uphold those who believe in the good word, both in this life and in the next, while Allah will let the wrongdoers go astray, and Allah does whatever He wants. [27]

The Endless Bounty of Allah

> **Background Info... v. 28-30**
>
> This passage refers to the pagan Arabs of old who transformed Ibraheem's shrine in Mecca over many generations into a house of idolatry and superstition. The Prophet once identified the man who instituted idolatry in Mecca. He said it was a man named Abu Khuza'ah.
>
> Tribal oral history records that he was the son of Luhay ibn Qam'ah of the tribe of Jurhum, which was the ruling tribe of Mecca before the Quraysh invaded the city and drove the Jurhumites away several centuries before the birth of Muhammad. *(Ahmad, Ibn Kathir)*

Haven't you seen those who paid Allah back for His favor by (trying to) cover over (correct knowledge of Him), and who have thus brought their people into the realm of doom - *Hellfire?*

They're going to burn in it, - *and how terrible a place to settle!* [28-29]

They were the ones who set up rivals with Allah, in order to steer others away from the path.

So say to them, *"Enjoy yourselves now, but you're headed straight for the Fire!"* [30]

Tell My servants who believe to establish prayer and to spend (in charity) out of the resources that We've given to them, both in secret and in public, before a day arrives in which there will be neither bargaining nor friendship. [31]

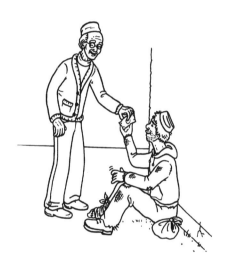

Allah is the One Who created the heavens and the earth. He sends down water from the sky and uses it to produce the fruits that sustain you.

He put at your service the ships that sail through the sea by His command, and He also put rivers at your service, as well. [32]

Likewise, He put the sun and the moon at your service; they both follow their orbits without fail, even as He made the very night and day useful for you. [33]

He gives you everything for which you could ask! If you ever tried to count Allah's favors, you would never be able to enumerate them all! Yet, still humanity is lost in corruption and ingratitude! [34]

The Prayer of Ibraheem

Recall when Ibraheem said, *"My Lord! Make this settlement (of Mecca) tranquil and secure, and keep me and my descendants away from idol-worship.* [35]

"My Lord! So many people have been led astray by them. Whoever follows me is of the same mind as me, and whoever disobeys me – well, You're forgiving and merciful." [36]

"Our Lord!" (he continued,) *"I've settled some of my descendants in this barren valley next to Your Sacred House, so they can, our Lord, establish prayer.*

"So make some people sympathetic towards them, and supply them with fruits so they can learn to be thankful." [37]

"Our Lord! You know what we conceal and what we reveal, for nothing at all can ever be hidden from Allah, neither on the earth nor in the sky. [38]

"Praise be to Allah Who has given me my sons, Isma-il and Is-haq, even in my old age, for My Lord hears all requests! [39]

"My Lord! Make me a prayerful person, and make my descendants prayerful, as well. Our Lord! Hear my request. [40]

"Our Lord! Forgive me and my parents and all those who believe on the Day of Account." [41]

Allah Delays Punishment for a Reason

Don't think for a moment that Allah ignores the actions of the wrongdoers. He's only giving them a break until the day comes when eyes will stare unblinking, when they'll run around in a frenzy with heads raised, not looking at themselves, and feeling a void in their guts! [42-43]

So warn people of the day when the punishment will come upon them, when the wrongdoers will cry, "*Our Lord! Give us more time, even just a little! We'll surely answer Your call and follow the messengers then!*"

(However, they'll be told,) "*Weren't you the ones who swore before that you would never be brought down (from your powerful positions)?* [44]

"You lived (near the ruins of past civilizations) who had done wrong against their own souls!

"You clearly saw how We dealt with them, and We offered so many examples to you!" [45]

They wove their mighty schemes, but their schemes were in Allah's full view (and thus could never succeed) - *even though (their plans) seemed strong enough to shake the mountains!* [46]

So don't ever think that Allah will fail in what He's promised to His messengers, for Allah is Powerful and a master of retribution. [47]

The Promise of a Day of Justice

A day will come when the earth will be transformed into a different earth, even as the skies will be transformed, as well, and then everyone will be marched before Allah, the One, the Irresistible. [48]

That day you'll see the sinners all tied together in chains; their only clothing will be burning, oozing tar, even as their faces will be enveloped in fire. [49-50]

(That'll be their fate), so that Allah can repay every soul with what it deserves, for Allah is quick in settling accounts. [51]

This announcement (is a message) for all humanity, so let them be warned by it, and let them know that He is only One God. Let thoughtful people then be reminded. [52]

The Stony Ground

15 Al Hijr
Late Meccan Period

☞ Introduction

By the late Meccan period the Prophet was feeling continuously fatigued. The constant persecution that he and his followers were facing, the daily insults, the stories of woe that his followers brought to him of their own travails and suffering, and the fact that, despite all the logical arguments he brought to prove that idolatry was false, the majority of his people still clung to ignorant traditions – all of these things began to take a toll on the Prophet. This chapter was revealed to the Prophet partly to console him and partly to convince him to remain steadfast, hoping upon the favor of Allah to change his circumstances and those of his followers who believed in his message and suffered on account of it.

In the Name of Allah,
the Compassionate, the Merciful

*A*lif. Lām. Rā.

These are the verses of the Book and a clear recitation. [1]

It just may happen that (one day) those who covered (the light of faith within their hearts) will wish that they had surrendered (to Allah), but leave them alone to eat and make merry – preoccupied in their false hopes, for soon they'll know (the truth)! [2-3]

We've never destroyed any settlement without setting their time limit in advance, nor can any community know when its term is up, nor can they delay it. [4-5]

The Mocking of the Faithless

(*T*he Meccans) say, "*Hey you, the one who's getting this 'revealed message.' (We think) you're crazy!* [6]

"*So why aren't you bringing angels down to show us if you're really so honest?*" [7]

However, We never send angels down except for a compelling reason, and (if they did happen to come), then the (faithless) would get no relief! [8]

We're sending the message down to you, (Muhammad,) and We're going to protect it. [9]

We sent messengers before your time among the religious sects of the past, but no messenger ever came to them without them mocking him. [10-11]

That's how We (allow the notion) to seep into the hearts of the bad people that they can disbelieve in (the message because it's so easy to insult Allah's prophets).

However, the customs of the ancients have passed away! [12-13]

Even if We opened up a door to the sky for them and they climbed ever farther up into it, they would still say, "*Our eyes are just blurry – no, wait! We've been (the victims) of some kind of sorcery!*" [14-15]

The Signs of Allah

And so it was that We placed the constellations in the sky and made them as decorations for all who see them. We're also guarding them from every outcast devil. [16-17]

If any of them secretly tries to hear something, he's chased away by a brilliant shooting star. [18]

We spread the earth out (wide like a carpet) and placed within it steady mountains.

We developed everything on earth in a **BALANCED** way and provided resources for the survival of both you and the (many creatures) that are not your responsibility. [19-20]

There's nothing (that exists) without its proper resources being (arranged for it) in Our sight, and We release nothing (of those resources) unless it's measured out accordingly. [21]

We send the fertilizing winds and cause water to fall from the sky to provide you with water, even though you're not in charge of its supply. [22]

We're responsible for bringing life and death, and We're going to inherit (all things after they die). [23]

Ibn 'Abbas (d. 687) explained the reason for the revelation of these two verses. He said, "A beautiful woman, among the most beautiful of women, used to come (to the masjid) and pray behind the Prophet.

Some of the men used to intentionally seek out the rows closest to the front so they wouldn't be able to see her (by making furtive glances back at the women's prayer lines).

Other men would pray in the last row (of the men's lines) so they could peek back under their raised arms (when they were prostrating) and look at her. Because of this, Allah revealed this passage." (Ahmad, Tirmidhi, Nisa'i)

As it is, We know who among you moves ahead and who falls behind. [24] Your Lord is the One Who will gather them all together, for He's full of wisdom and knowledge. [25]

The Fall of Shaytan

And so it was that We created human beings from pliable clay - from mere molded mud, and We created the jinns, even before (human beings), from the intense heat (of pure energy). [26-27]

Your Lord said to the angels, "*I'm going to create mortal man from mineral-rich clay, from molded mud.* [28]

"*After I've constructed him and breathed into him (something of) My spirit, you must all prostrate to him (out of respect).*" [29]

The angels fell down in prostration all together, but Iblis didn't (join with the angels), for he refused to be with those who prostrated. [30-31]

Then Allah asked, "*Iblis! What's wrong with you that you didn't join those who prostrated?*" [32]

"*I'm not going to prostrate myself to a mortal man,*" Iblis answered, "*for You created him from mineral-rich clay, from mere molded mud!*" [33]

"*Then get out of here!*" Allah ordered. "*You're an outcast, and you'll be cursed all the way to the Day of Judgment!*" [34-35]

"*My Lord!*" Iblis cried out. "*Give me some time until they're resurrected.*" [36]

"*You'll have your time,*" (Allah said), "*until a day whose arrival is appointed.*" [37-38]

"*My Lord!*" (Iblis) said. "*Since You made me slip up, I'm going to make (immorality and wickedness) seem proper and good to those on earth, and I'm going to deviate all of them (morally) - except, (of course), for Your sincere servants among them.*" [39-40]

"*The path (that they follow) will be the straight one that leads back to Me,*" (Allah) answered, "*and you'll have no power over My servants, except for the ones who put themselves in the wrong and follow you.*" [41-42]

Hellfire is the promised destination of them all! There will be seven gates

340

(leading within it) – one gate for each class (of sinners). [43-44]

Now as for those who were mindful (of their duty to Allah), they will be among gardens and springs. [45]

(They'll be told,) *"Enter within in peace and safety!"* [46]

Then We're going to cleanse their hearts of any lurking sense of bitterness (so they'll truly) be brothers as they face each other, (relaxing) on couches. [47]

They'll feel no exhaustion, nor will they ever be asked to leave. [48]

So announce to My servants that I am *indeed* the Forgiving and the Merciful and that My punishment will be a terrible punishment. [49-50]

The Guests of Ibraheem

Tell them about the guests of Ibraheem. [51]

When they came before him and said, *"Peace,"* he answered them back, saying, *"We're uneasy about you."* [52]

They said, *"Don't feel uneasy, for we're here to give you the good news of a son who will be exceedingly perceptive."* [53]

(Ibraheem) asked, *"Are you coming here to give me this good news now that I'm an old man? So what kind of good news is that!"* [54]

"We're bringing you this good news in all truth, so don't be discouraged!" [55]

(Then Ibraheem realized his folly and) said, *"Who can be discouraged at Allah's mercy except for those who are astray?"* [56]

Then he asked, *"So what's the errand that's brought you here, emissaries (of Allah)?"* [57]

"We're being sent (to destroy) a wicked people," they answered, *"except for the family of Lut, whom we're supposed to save all together, though not his wife, whom we've determined will remain behind."* [58-60]

In the Cities of the Plain

When the messenger (angels) came to Lut's family, [61]

(Lut) said, *"You seem to be strangers (to this city)."* [62]

"Yes," they answered, *"and we've come to you to bring about (the order of destruction from Allah that the faithless) have been doubting. And so we've come here to bring the reality home to you, and we're honest in what we say.* [63-64]

"So travel by night with your family when there's only a little of the night left, and you, yourself, must be the one (who guards) the rear.

"Let no one look back, and keep going onward to where you're told to go." [65]

341

And so, We let him know about the command that the roots of (the bad people) were going to be cut off by the morning. [66]

The local people of the city came running excitedly (when they learned there were strange men in Lut's house). [67]

(Lut) said to them, "*These are my guests, so don't disgrace me. Rather, be mindful of Allah, and don't dishonor me!*" [68-69]

"*Didn't we forbid you from (hiding) anyone at all (from us!)*" they shouted. [70]

"*My daughters are here,*" (Lut) pleaded, "*if you have to do something.*" [71]

By your very life, (Muhammad), they were milling about wildly in their drunkenness!

Then the powerful blast overtook them before morning. [72-73]

We turned (their city) upside down and rained down upon them a shower of hardened stones! [74]

Truly, there are signs in this (incident) for those who consider. Even though the (city) was located on a highly (traveled) road, (now it can no longer be found)! So truly, there are signs in this for those who believe. [75-77]

Destroyed Nations

The Companions of the Thicket were also wrongdoers, and likewise We took vengeance upon them. They were located on a clearly marked route, (but their prominence did nothing to save them). [78-79]

The Companions of the Stony Ground also denied their messengers. We sent Our signs to them, but they kept turning away from them. [80-81]

They used to carve their homes out of mountain cliffs, (thinking they were) secure. [82]

Then the powerful blast seized them one morning, and nothing they prepared was of any use to them. [83-84]

Don't Lose Heart

We didn't create the heavens and the earth and everything in between them except for a true purpose.

The Hour (of Judgment) is certainly drawing near, so excuse (the shortcomings) of others with gracious detachment. [85]

Your Lord is the Most Knowledgeable Creator! And so it is that We've given you the seven frequently repeated verses, (so you can gain inspiration and strength), and a majestic Qur'an. [86-87]

Don't strain your eyes longingly at what We've given certain classes (of people in power and wealth,) nor should you feel sorry for them (because they're blinded by those things).

Rather, you should (focus yourself) on lowering your wing (in kindness) to the believers. [88]

(All you need to) say (to the arrogant ones is), "*I'm the one who's warning you plainly.*" [89]

Background Info... v. 90-91

The pagans would go out and meet incoming caravans to warn the new visitors not to believe in the call of a man among them named Muhammad, and they also warned that he was a sorcerer. They would recite scattered phrases of the Qur'an to the visitors and make fun of its message, and so they 'sectioned' it up. (*Ibn Kathir*)

(And thus, you must continue your preaching,) even as We're directing (Our revelations) to those who are dividing themselves (up into different camps concerning the truth of this message), and who also try to slice this Qur'an up into disjointed sections (by quoting it out of context in order to ridicule it). [90-91]

And so, by your Lord, We're going to question all of them together about what they've done. [92-93] So call to them openly with whatever you're commanded, and turn away from those who make partners (with Allah). [94]

We're enough (of a protector) for you against those who ridicule you [95] and against those who set up a rival god with Allah. Soon they're going to know (the truth)! [96]

We know how your heart aches at what they're saying, but glorify and praise your Lord, be among those who bow down prostrate, and serve your Lord until what is certain comes to you. [97-99]

The Bee

16 An-Nahl
(aka An-Ni'am)
Late Meccan Period

☞ Introduction

This chapter was revealed after the migrations of some of the Prophet's followers to Abyssinia. Although the migrants eventually returned after hearing false reports that Meccan persecution had eased, the situation of the young religious group was uncertain. The mention of plots against the believers of ancient days is also a clear reference to the ongoing plots that the idol-worshippers were always hatching against the followers of the Prophet.

No greater example is there of the ability of otherwise normal people to become oppressors than in the way that the Meccans, who thought so highly of themselves, became so wicked and violent against those who disagreed with the backward superstitions that held sway in that culture. The Muslims were not calling for a violent overthrow of the society. Rather, they called for reforming personal conduct, establishing a safety net to support the weak and poor, and for abandoning idolatry and the many invented superstitions that had no basis in logic or reason.

In the Name of Allah,
the Compassionate, the Merciful

Background Info... v. 1-4

Some of the pagans used to ridicule the Prophet because the foretold punishment from Allah **wasn't** materializing upon them.

A pagan poet named an-Nadr ibn al-Harith even taunted the Prophet, saying, "O Allah! **If it's within Your power, then** throw stones down upon us to hasten **our suffering!**"

This passage was revealed in response to their ridicule, promising that the punishment would come one day, but not when they wanted. (*Asbab ul-Nuzul*)

He sends the angels with the spirit of His command and bestows it upon whichever of His servants that He wants, (saying): "*Warn (people) that there is no god but I, so be mindful of Me.*" [2]

He created the heavens and the earth for a true purpose. He's so high above the partners they assign to Him! [3]

Allah's command will come to pass, so don't seek to rush it. *All glory be to Him!* He's so high above the partners they assign to Him! [1]

He created human beings from a drop of mingled fluids, and look how that same (human) becomes openly quarrelsome! [4]

What has Allah Provided for Us?

He created livestock (animals) for you. You use (their hides) for warmth and make other useful products, even as you eat them, as well. [5]

You feel joyous at their sight as you bring them (in for the evening) and when you lead them out to pasture (in the morning). [6]

They carry your heavy loads to places that you couldn't get to (by yourselves), unless you wore yourself out in the journey!

(Allah provided you with these beasts of burden), for your Lord is kind and merciful. [7]

(He also created) fancy horses, mules and donkeys for you to ride, and for you to parade in exhibitions. He will create other (modes of transportation) that you (currently) know nothing about. [8]

It's Allah's (prerogative) to point out the right path, because there are other paths that swerve aside. If Allah had wanted, He could've guided you all (by giving you no choice but to be believers). [9]

He's the One Who sends **WATER** down from the sky. You drink from it, and from it grows the bushes upon which you graze your cattle. [10]

He also uses (the same water) to produce for you the grains, olives, dates, grapes and all the other types of fruit. There is a sign in this for those who reflect. [11]

He made the night and the day, the sun and the moon and the very stars themselves useful for you by His command. There are signs in these (things), as well, for those who use their reason. [12]

There is also, in all the things that He's multiplied for you in the earth and that encompass every shade of color, a sign for people who remember (the favors of Allah). [13]

He's the One Who tamed the sea for you, so you could eat fresh meat from it and also so that you could harvest (the pearls and shells) that you wear as ornaments.

You see the ships sailing through the waves that allow you to seek out Allah's bounty. (Thus, the many resources that you gain should) give you (further reason) to be grateful. [14]

He set up firm highlands in the earth to minimize the effects of earthquakes upon you, and (He laid out) rivers and passes (in the world), so that you could be guided on your travels. [15]

(He also provided the many natural) landmarks and even the stars above by which (travelers) may orient themselves. [16]

So is the One Who can create (such) things equal to the one who can create nothing at all? Won't you take a reminder? [17]

If you ever tried to add up all of Allah's favors, you would never be able to count them all! Indeed, Allah is forgiving and merciful! [18]

Allah knows what you conceal and what you reveal. The (statues) that they call upon besides Allah can create

nothing, for they themselves are merely created (things) - *dead and lifeless*! They don't even know (if or) when they'll be resurrected! [19-21]

The Two Potential Results

Your God is One God. Those who have no faith in the next life have stubborn hearts, and they're arrogant besides! [22]

Without a doubt Allah knows what they're (doing both) in secret and out in the open, and He has no love for the arrogant. [23]

When they're asked, "*What has your Lord revealed?*" They answer, "*Tales from long ago!*" [24]

On the Day of Assembly they can bear their own burdens in full, as well as the burden (of the crime they committed against) the unsuspecting (people) whom they misled!

Oh, how terrible the burdens they will bear! [25]

And so it was that those who came before (these Meccans) also schemed (against Allah), but Allah knocked out the foundation of their structure, and the roof caved in upon them!

The anger (of Allah) took hold of them from directions they never even expected! [26]

On the Day of Assembly, He's going to cover them in shame and say, "*So where are all My partners about which you used to argue?*"

The people of knowledge will remark, "*Today, those who covered (the light of faith within their hearts) are truly overwhelmed in shame and misery.* [27]

"*They're the ones who had their souls taken by the angels while they were in a state of corruption against their own selves.*"

(Then the doomed sinners) will offer their abject submission, saying, "*We didn't do anything wrong (intentionally).*"

(However, it will be said to them), "*That's not true, for Allah knows what you were doing. So enter into the gates of Hellfire, and stay in there!*" The home of the arrogant is an awful one indeed! [28-29]

When those who are **mindful** (of Allah) are asked, "*What has your Lord revealed?*" they say, "*Only the best!*"

For those who do good, there will be good in this world, and the home of the next life is even better! How excellent is the home of those who were mindful! [30]

They'll be entered into eternal gardens beneath which rivers flow! They'll have everything there they ever wished for, and that's how Allah rewards those who were mindful (of Him). [31]

They're the ones who will be taken by the angels (at death) in a state of purity, and who will be told, "*Peace be upon you. Enter the Garden on account of what you did (in the world).*" [32]

Are (the faithless) just waiting (for the time when) the angels come for them, or (are they waiting) for the arrival of the command of your Lord?

That's what those who went before them did, but Allah never did any injustice to them (when He punished them), for they had been doing injustice against their own souls. [33]

The evil of their deeds overtook them, and the very thing at which they used to laugh closed in upon them from all sides! [34]

Allah Keeps His Promises

Those who make partners (with Allah) say, "*If Allah had wanted to (prevent us), then we would've never worshipped anything besides Him - neither ourselves nor our ancestors - and we would never have prohibited anything in preference to His (laws)."*

That's how others before them behaved. What else is there for the messengers to do other than to convey the message clearly? [35]

And so it was that We sent to every community a messenger (who said), "*Serve Allah, and shun falsehood."*

Among them were some who were guided by Allah, while others among them had (the consequences of) their mistaken ways proven true against them.

So travel all over the world, and see what happened to those who denied (Allah). [36]

If you're anxious for them to be guided, (know that) Allah doesn't guide those whom He leaves astray, and there will be no one to help them. [37]

They swear by Allah – *using their strongest oaths* – that Allah will never raise the dead to life.

But no! It's a **promise** He's going to keep, though most people don't know it, so that He can present to them the meaning of those things in which they differed, and so that those who covered (the light of faith within their hearts) can finally know that they were indeed liars. [38-39]

When We want something to happen, We only need to say, "*Be,*" - and there it is! [40]

Migration for Faith will be Rewarded

> **Background Info... v. 41-42**
>
> This passage refers to the nearly eighty men, women and children who fled Meccan persecution to Abyssinia in the year 615. Later on, the Muslims were settled in lush Medina, a "fine" homeland indeed!

We're going to give a fine (reward) in this world to those who migrated (from their homes in the cause of Allah) after suffering under persecution.

However, the reward of the next life will be even greater, if they only knew! [41]

(They were the ones) who persevered patiently and who placed their trust in their Lord. [42]

O Muhammad,
You are One of the Chosen

The messengers that We sent before you, (Muhammad), were no more than (mortal) men (like yourself) to whom We granted revelation.

Just ask the people who received the message before you, if you don't know about it. [43]

(We sent them) clear evidence and scripture, just as We're also sending the message down to you, so you can convey clearly to people what's been sent for them, and so they can also think about it. [44]

So do those who make evil schemes feel so safe that Allah won't cause the earth to swallow them up or that the punishment won't come upon them suddenly from where they least expect it? [45]

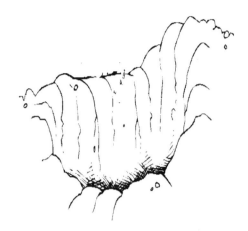

(Do they feel so safe that they don't think) He'll take a hold of them while they're in the middle of their affairs, having no chance to prevent it, or that He won't take a hold of them by gradually eroding (their power)?

Your Lord is kind and merciful, (and He may take that slower route in order to give them time to repent). [46-47]

Don't they look at what Allah has created, even (at the small) things, like the way in which their shadows bend to the right and the left, prostrating themselves before Allah in the most humble way? [48]

Whatever is in the heavens and whatever is on the earth bows down to Allah, from crawling creatures all the way up to the angels.

None of them are too proud (to submit to His will). [49]

(The angels) stand in awe of their Lord Who towers over them, and they do everything they're commanded to do. [50]

On Dual Gods

Allah has said, "*Don't take gods in pairs, (saying there is one god of good and another god of evil), for He is only One God, so be in awe of Me.*" [51]

Whatever is in the heavens and the earth belongs to Him, and sincere obedience is due only to Him. *So should you be mindful of any other besides Allah?* [52]

How do People Disobey Their Lord?

Nothing good ever comes to you except that it comes from Allah. Whenever you're stricken with hardship, you cry out to Him in desperation. [53]

Yet, when He removes your hardship, some of you make partners with their Lord, as if to show their ingratitude for the favors We've granted them. *So enjoy yourselves now, but soon you'll know (the truth)!* [54-55]

The Foolish Teachings of Idolatry

The (Meccans) set aside a portion of the resources that We've provided to them for their survival. (Then they offer that portion) to (their idols), *not even knowing (if they're real or not)!* By Allah!

You're going to be questioned about all of your superstitions! [56]

The Shameful Choice of the Pagans

Then they assign daughters (as offspring) to Allah - *all glory belongs to Him!* – even as they keep for themselves (the sons) that they desire! [57]

When the news is brought to one of them of (the birth) of a female (child), his face darkens, and he's filled with anguish. He hides himself from his fellows in shame, on account of the bad news he's received.

Should he keep (the baby girl) in contempt or bury her in the sand? *Oh, what a terrible predicament on which they must decide!* [58-59]

This is the evil example of those who don't believe in the next life, while the highest example belongs to Allah, for He's the Powerful and the Wise. [60]

If Allah were to seize people (and punish them) for their corruption (according to what they deserve), then He wouldn't leave a single creature alive (on the earth)!

However, He gives them a break for a set amount of time. When that time limit expires, then they have no way to delay (their due punishment) - no, not even for an hour, just as they have no way to advance it. [61]

They attribute to Allah (the daughters) that they hate (for themselves), even as their tongues express the lie that they deserve everything that's good for themselves (like having sons).

Yet, without a doubt the Fire (is all that) they're going to get, and they're going to be among the first to be ushered into it! [62]

By Allah! We sent (prophets) to those nations that went before you, but Shaytan made their (evil) actions seem appropriate and good to them.

He's also the patron (of these Meccans) here today, but they're going to receive a painful punishment. [63]

We didn't send the Book to you for any other purpose than for you to explain to them clearly those things about which they've been arguing, and also so it could be a guide and a mercy for those who believe. [64]

Ponder these Signs of Allah

Allah sends water down from the sky, and He uses it to give life to the earth after it was dead. There is a sign in this for people who listen. [65]

There is another sign in livestock (animals), for We produce (milk) for you to drink from a place within their bodies between the contents of their intestines and blood, a drink pure and tasty for any who drink it! [66]

And from the fruit of the date palm and from grapevines you get alcoholic beverages and fine (non-alcoholic) products, as well. In this is a sign for people who are wise. [67]

Your Lord inspired the bee to build its nests in hillsides, on trees, and in (the structures that people) build. Then (He inspired it) to eat of the many (flowering) fruits and to follow humbly the wide paths of its Lord.

They produce from within their bodies a drink of varying shades of color that is a source of healing for humanity. In this is a sign for those who reflect. [68-69]

Allah creates you, and then He causes you to die. Among you are some who are reduced to a state of senility (in your old age), so much so that you know nothing, even though you had known much before. (Allah can do this) for Allah is full of knowledge and power. [70]

The Foolishness of Idolatry

Allah has favored some (of you) with more (material) blessings than others. Those who've been favored with more resources aren't going to cast them at those whom they control to make them equal with them. Would they so eagerly scorn Allah's bounty like that? [71]

Allah has given you mates of your own kind, and from your mates He's produced for you sons, daughters and grandchildren, even as He's given you so many wholesome resources besides.

Would it then be right for (your descendants) to believe in falsehood and be thankless towards Allah's bounty and to worship others in place of Allah - beings who have no power to provide them with resources from the heavens or the earth, and who could never gain the ability to do so? [72-73]

So don't invent (false) representations of Allah, for Allah knows (what He's really like), and you don't know. [74]

Allah lays out the example of a slave under the control of another. He has no power at all, while another (person) to whom We've given Our favors (freely) spends (of his wealth without restriction) in private and in public.

Are the two equal? Then praise be to Allah, but most of them don't understand. [75]

Allah lays out the further example of two men. One of them is dumb and has no ability to do anything. He's a constant headache to his guardian.

No matter where he sends him, he does nothing right. Is this kind of man equal with someone who commands justice (with full confidence) and is on a straight path? [76]

What Allah has Done for You

To Allah belongs whatever is beyond human perception in the heavens and the earth. What is the command of the Hour (of Judgment) but the twinkling of an eye or even quicker? Truly, Allah has power over all things! [77]

He's the One Who brought you out of the wombs of your mothers when you didn't know a single thing.

352

Then He placed within you the abilities of hearing and sight, as well as intelligence and affection, so you could learn to be grateful. [78]

Haven't they seen the birds held aloft in the midst of the sky? Nothing holds them in place save Allah, and that is a sign for those who believe. [79]

Allah provided you homes as places of rest and tranquility. He provided for you (the knowledge of how to make) tents out of animal skins, which you find so light (and easy to handle) when you travel, as well as when you stop (to make camp).

Out of their wool, their fur and their hair, (you make) things (like clothing and blankets) that you can use for a while for your comfort. [80]

Allah has also provided for you, out of what He's created, things (like trees) that can give you shade. He provided the mountains wherein you can find shelter.

He produced clothing for you to protect yourselves from the heat and armored vests to protect you from violence against each other (in warfare).

That's how He completes His favors upon you, so you can submit (to His will in thanks). [81]

However, if they turn away, (know that) your only duty is to convey the message clearly. [82]

They recognize Allah's favors; yet, then they deny them (by denying the One Who provided them). Thus, most of them are thankless. [83]

The Witnesses Testify

One day We're going to raise a witness from every community. Then there won't be any more excuses accepted from those who covered (the light of faith within their hearts), nor will they be allowed to make up (for their sins). [84]

When the wrongdoers see the punishment (right there before them), it won't be lessened, nor will they receive any break (from it). [85]

When those who associated partners with Allah actually see their partners, they're going to say, "*Our Lord! These are our (idols) whom we used to call upon besides You.*"

However, (the idols) will throw their statement back at them, saying, "*You're all liars!*" [86]

On that day they're going to recognize their total dependence on Allah, and all their inventions will leave them to languish. [87]

Those who rejected (Allah) and who hindered (people) from the path of Allah will have punishment upon punishment, for they used to cause trouble. [88]

One day We're going to raise a witness out of every community drawn from among their own, and We'll bring you out as a witness against these (people of Mecca).

We've sent down to you the Book that explains everything. It's a guide, a mercy and a source of good news for those who've submitted (to Allah). [89]

Fulfill Your Agreement with Allah

Allah commands that justice be done, that good be implemented and that relatives be treated with generosity.

He forbids all shameful acts, as well as criminal behavior and rebellion. This is how He's instructing you so you can be warned. [90]

Fulfill the agreement of Allah after you've agreed to it, and don't break your promises after you've sworn upon them. You've made Allah your guarantee, and Allah knows everything that you do. [91]

Don't be like a woman who pulls apart the yarn she's just spun, even after it became strong, nor use your oaths to deceive each other, just so that one group can have an advantage over the others (through making temporary alliances).

Allah will test you in this, and on the Day of Assembly He's going to clear up for you the matters about which you argued. [92]

If Allah had wanted, He could've made you all into one unified community, but He leaves astray whomever He wants, and He guides whomever He wants, though you will all be questioned about what you've done. [93]

So don't use your promises to deceive each other, for the foot that was firmly planted might begin to slip, causing you to suffer the terrible (consequences) of having hindered others from the path of Allah. You would then have a severe punishment befall you. [94]

Don't sell the agreement of Allah for a miserable price, for there's (a reward) with Allah that's far better for you if you only knew. [95]

Whatever (material goods) you have will vanish, but whatever lies with Allah will last forever.

We're going to compensate those who patiently persevered by rewarding them according to the best of their deeds. [96]

Whoever does what's morally right, whether male or female, and has faith, We're going to give him a new life that's a life of purity. We're going to reward them according to the best of their deeds. [97]

Allah is in Control of What He Reveals

Whenever you read the Qur'an, ask for Allah's protection against Shaytan, the outcast. [98]

He has no authority over those who believe and who place their trust in their Lord. [99]

He only has authority over those who take him as their patron and who make partners (with Allah). [100]

When We substitute one verse for another, and Allah knows what He's gradually revealing, they (object) by saying, "*You're just a lying fraud.*"

Certainly not! Yet, most of them don't understand. [101]

Tell them, "*The Holy Spirit* (Angel Jibra'il) *is bringing the revelation from your Lord in all truth, in order to strengthen (the faith) of the believers, and as a source of guidance and good news to those who've submitted themselves (to Allah).*" [102]

No Man Teaches Muhammad

Background Info... v. 103-105

There were several young foreign slaves in Mecca who were originally from Persian or Byzantine-controlled lands. Two of these young slaves, named Jabr and Yasar, worked as blacksmiths, and it is said that they knew some passages from the Bible and used to say them.

The Prophet sometimes stopped at the young men's workshop to talk to them, perhaps hoping to have an affinity with others who believed in one God, but this made the tongues of the Meccans begin to wag.

Since they couldn't find any other plausible explanation for the Prophet's constant revelations, they began to suggest that these two young slaves were teaching Muhammad about religion and that somehow those boys were the source of Islam!

When one of those boys was asked if he were teaching Muhammad, the boy replied, "No, Muhammad is teaching me!"

This passage was revealed in response. (*Zamakhshari*)

We know that they're saying, "*It's a man who's teaching him*," but the tongue of the (foreign slave) to whom they're pointing is not fluent (in Arabic), while this (Qur'an) is in the purest and most precise Arabic. [103]

Those who don't believe in Allah's (revealed) verses will not be guided by Allah, and they're going to have a painful punishment. [104]

It's those who don't believe in Allah's verses who are frauds, and they're all liars! [105]

Faith Renounced by Force is Still True Faith

Background Info... v. 106-109

When Meccan persecution against the Muslims mutated into murder, some Muslims felt compelled to recant their faith to save their lives, even though they secretly held onto faith.

The worst incident was when the pagans seized a man named Ammar, along with his father Yasir and his mother Sumayah and some others, and took them to a field to be tortured. They tied Sumayah and Yasir to the ground and speared them to death. They then roughed up Ammar and threatened to kill him, like his parents, if he didn't renounce his faith.

Ammar did so weeping and out of fear and then later went to the Prophet in mortal fear of displeasing Allah. The Prophet accepted that Ammar never

356

Whoever rejects Allah after having accepted faith in Him - unless he's been forced to (renounce it) while his heart remains committed - and who has opened his heart to rejection, Allah's wrath is upon (all such people).

They're going to have a **SEVERE PUNISHMENT**, and that's because they love the life of this world more than the next life.

Allah will never guide people who reject (Him by choice). [106-107]

They're the ones who've had their hearts, ears and eyes sealed up by Allah, and they're unconcerned (about it). Without a doubt, they're going to be losers in the next life. [108-109]

However, your Lord – for those who migrated (from their homes) after having been persecuted and who then struggled and persevered – after all of this, your Lord is forgiving and merciful. [110]

One day every soul will come forward to plead for itself. Every soul will then be repaid for what it has done, and none of them will be treated unfairly. [111]

The Example of a Prophet to His People

Allah lays out the example of a society enjoying peace and security, even as it was amply supplied with resources from every quarter. Yet, it was thankless towards Allah's favors.

Therefore, Allah caused it to experience both hunger and panic. (It encircled them) like a cloak (wrapped around them), all on account of (the evil in which its people) used to indulge. [112]

Then a messenger came to them, who arose from among themselves, but they denied him. And so the punishment seized them even as they were still busy in their corruption. [113]

Some Dietary Restrictions

Eat from the resources that Allah has provided for you that are lawful and pure, and be thankful for Allah's favor, if it's Him you really serve. [114]

He's only forbidden you (to eat) dead carcasses, blood, pork, and anything that's had a name other than Allah's name invoked over it.

However, if someone is forced by necessity (to eat of these forbidden things in order to avoid starvation) and does so only reluctantly, without indulging in it more than necessary, then Allah is forgiving and merciful. [115]

(All you people!) Make no statements in support of the lies that your tongues may promote, arbitrarily declaring, "*This is lawful, while that's forbidden*," in order to somehow attribute fraudulent lies to Allah.

Those who invent false claims and then put them on Allah will never succeed. [116]

There's only a slight profit (to be made in promoting such lies), but then they'll have a painful punishment. [117]

Follow the Path of Ibraheem

We prohibited for the followers of Judaism what We already told you about before, and We were never unfair to them. Rather, they were unjust against their own selves. [118]

However, your Lord - to those who do wrong in ignorance and who then thereafter repent and reform (themselves) - after all of that, your Lord is indeed forgiving and merciful. [119]

Ibraheem was foremost in devotion to Allah, for he was a natural monotheist, and he never made partners (with Allah). [120]

He was thankful for Allah's favors, for He chose him and guided him to a straight way. [121]

We gave him good in this world, and in the next life he's going to be among the righteous. [122]

Then We inspired you, (Muhammad,) with the message that you should follow the creed of Ibraheem, the natural monotheist, and he never made partners (with Allah). [123]

358

Wisdom in Dialogue

Background Info... v. 124-125

Although this is a Meccan chapter, these last verses [124-128] were revealed in Medina and were tacked on at the end of this chapter by the Prophet's order.

These few verses in particular make mention of one of the many issues that were coming out in the growing interfaith dialogue between the Muslims and the Jews.

From the context of verses 118-125 we can see that the Arab converts in Medina had probably asked if there was a Sabbath for them as there was for the Jews (or perhaps the Jews had suggested to them that they should have one).

This passage points out that in Ibraheem's original religion there was no Sabbath and that the Jews were given harsh dietary restrictions and difficult Sabbath rules on account of their disobedience to Musa.

The (restrictions) of the Sabbath were only imposed upon (the Jews) who argued (about Allah's commands), but Allah will judge between them in what they've been arguing about. [124]

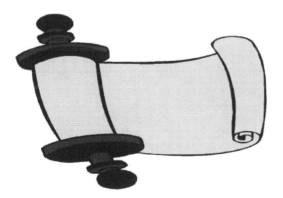

Invite (others) to the way of your Lord with wisdom and beautiful preaching, and reason with them in ways that are best. Your Lord knows best who is straying from His path and who is being guided (towards it). [125]

Take the High Road

Background Info... v. 126-128

This passage is sometimes understood to be a continuation of verses 118-125, in that an interfaith issue involving the status of the Sabbath came up in Medina, and an argument might have ensued, save for the patience of the Muslim side.

Under that line of reasoning, this passage is telling the Prophet to keep on preaching and to be high-minded about it, even if the listeners, who in this case would be Jews, have some objections to his views on the subject.

Then verse 126 would say that if the preacher could score a point, as it were, in the interfaith debate, that he shouldn't go overboard in pressing his advantage, for it would only put the listener on the defensive.

When you score a point of logic, be patient and resist the urge to pounce too eagerly on the weakness in your opponent, that is if you want to make him feel respected and welcomed enough so you can perhaps one day open his heart to faith and not just tear him down.

Other commentators say this passage is not connected with the preceding verses [118-125] at all and that it was revealed after the Battle of Uhud, when the Muslims, who had narrowly escaped destruction, returned to the battlefield the next day to find that the pagans had mutilated the dead Muslim fighters.

When the Prophet saw the body of his beloved uncle Hamza badly cut up, he became very distraught and called for revenge upon the pagans many times beyond what they did to Hamza.

This verse, then, would be telling the Prophet not to go beyond the limits of what was done to him. After he recited it, the Prophet said, "We will be patient. We will not take revenge out on anyone."

Then the Prophet made up for his thoughtless oath as outlined in 5:89. (*Ma'ariful Qur'an*) Given the change of tone in verses 126-128, the second view seems more likely, i.e., that this passage is referring to self-restraint in the face of atrocity, and Allah knows best.

If you can bring consequences against them, don't bring any consequences against them that are worse than what you've suffered.

However, if you persevere patiently instead (and fight against the desire to get back at them), that's the best for those who are patient. [126]

Therefore, be patient, for your patience is due to none other than Allah. Don't feel sorry for them, and don't be worried on account of their scheming. [127]

Allah is with those who are mindful (of Him), and He's with those who (promote) what's good. [128]

The Night Journey

17 Al Isrā'
aka Bani Isrā'il
Late Meccan Period

☞ Introduction

This chapter was revealed mainly in the year 621, with a few portions being revealed earlier. This was about one year before the migration to Medina, and the unmistakable tone of closure presented in this chapter clearly shows that the Muslims were expecting that they would soon abandon Mecca for a safer place.

Already Islam was growing in the northern city of Yathrib, due to the efforts of some very dedicated new converts there, and the Muslims in Mecca were restive as they chafed under Meccan persecution. Some Muslim converts had already been murdered by the pagans, and the tension was apparent and palpable.

With regards to the Night Journey and Ascension, the Prophet's cousin, Hind bint Abi Talib (aka Umm Hani), said, "The Messenger of Allah spent the night in my house. He said his night prayers and went to sleep. Just before dawn, he woke us up, and we all prayed the dawn prayer together. When the prayer was finished, he said, 'Umm Hani. I prayed with you the night prayer in this place, then I went to (Jerusalem) and prayed there, and as you can see, I've just finished praying the dawn prayer here with you.' I said, 'Messenger of Allah, don't tell people about this for they'll ridicule you and hurt you.' He replied, 'By Allah, I'm going to tell them.'" (At-Tabari)

Then the Prophet went out of her family home and told people the following account: "While I was in Mecca, the roof of the house was opened, and Jibra'il descended. He opened my chest and washed it with Zamzam water. Then he brought a golden tray full of wisdom and faith, and having poured its contents into my chest, he closed it. Then a creature that was all white was brought, which was smaller than a mule but bigger than a donkey. The creature's stride was so wide that it reached the farthest point of its eyesight in just one step. I was carried on it."

The Prophet then explained that he was taken to Jerusalem on that mount, which flew at a dazzling rate of speed, and that he was deposited on the Temple Mount. There the spirits of the prophets of old materialized behind him, and he led them in prayer.

Then the Prophet continued his account, saying: "Jibra'il then took my hand and ascended with me to the nearest heaven." The Prophet was then taken into the otherworldly dimension of the *Akhirah*, or Hereafter.

As he passed further through its levels, he saw various prophets from ancient days, including Adam, Ibraheem, Musa and 'Esa. Each of them welcomed him with warm greetings as he went by them. When he was taken into the seventh and highest layer of Paradise, he saw innumerable wondrous sights, including the delights of Paradise and the coming and going of multitudes of angels. The Prophet continued his story, saying, "Then (Jibra'il) took me until we reached the *Sidrat-il-Muntaha* (the Lote Tree of the Furthest Boundary), which was shrouded in colors I can hardly describe." (See Qur'an 53:1-18)

"Then I was (brought close) to the *House of Ma'moor* (in which 70,000 angels visit everyday), and three containers were offered to me. One had wine, the other milk and the third honey. I took the milk. Jibra'il said, 'This is the Islamic way of life, which you and your followers are following.'"

Next, Jibra'il brought Muhammad closer to the highest boundary of Paradise, beyond which the full manifestation of Allah's power exists. The Prophet described that he couldn't even comprehend the wonders of creation that he was witnessing.

In later years when someone asked the Prophet what he saw at that point and if he, in fact, saw Allah, he said, "Only blinding light, how could I then see Him?" (Ahmad) It was during this part of the journey that Muhammad received the direct command from Allah that his followers were to offer prayers *fifty* times in a day.

When the Prophet was being taken back down through the seventh layer of Paradise, Musa stopped him and convinced him to go back to Allah and ask for a reduction. Musa pointed out that he had had a hard enough time with the Children of Israel and that fifty prayers upon his followers would be too much.

The Prophet did accordingly, and Musa convinced him to ask for further reductions. Eventually the prayers were reduced to five times a day, and the Prophet told Musa he was too shy to ask for any further reductions after that. Muhammad was then brought back down to the Temple Mount in Jerusalem, and from there the mysterious steed carried him back to Mecca, where he was finally deposited back in his bed.

Predictably, when the Prophet told his story, the Meccans ridiculed him fiercely. A few converts to Islam actually renounced their faith, thinking that the Prophet was saying something totally preposterous. *How could a man go to Jerusalem and back in one night?*

Some people went to Abu Bakr and told him what had happened, and they asked him if he believed it was true. He replied, "By Allah! If Muhammad, himself, has said it, then it's true. He tells us that the word of Allah comes to him directly from Heaven to Earth at any hour of the night or day, and we believe him. Isn't this a greater miracle than what we're questioning here today."

Then Abu Bakr led a crowd to the Prophet, and they all listened to his story directly. When the Prophet finished describing Jerusalem, a city to which he had never been, and recounted what he had seen of its streets and buildings, those who were present, and who had been to Jerusalem before, agreed that it was an accurate description of the city.

Abu Bakr, who had himself visited Jerusalem many times, declared, "You spoke the truth, Messenger of Allah." Then the Prophet announced that on his way back to Mecca from Jerusalem, he saw a caravan on the road leading towards Mecca. He said that he had called to the leaders of that caravan to point out to them where one of their animals had wandered off in the desert and that he drank from a water jar on the back of one of those camels. He also predicted when that caravan would return (at sunrise on such-and-such day) and that a gray camel would be in the front of the line.

On the appointed day, a caravan did enter Mecca at sunrise, led by a gray camel, and when the leaders of that caravan were questioned, they described how they were led by a stranger's voice to their lost animal in the desert. It was also found that one of their camels was carrying a water jar on its back that had a broken seal.

Due to his affirming the truth of the Prophet's story, Abu Bakr earned the nickname, *As-Sadeeq*, which means the one who affirms the truth.

Glory be to the One Who took His servant on a journey by night from the sacred place of prostration (in Mecca) to the faraway place of prostration (in Jerusalem) - *to an area that We've specially blessed* - so We could show him some of Our signs. Truly, He's the One Who Hears and Observes (all things). [1]

The Children of Israel were Punished for their Sins

We gave the scripture to Musa and made it a source of guidance for the Children of Israel.

So don't take anyone other than Me as your keeper, all you (Jews) who are descended from those whom We carried with Nuh! He was a truly thankful servant! [2-3]

We warned the Children of Israel in (their) scripture that they would twice cause corruption in the earth and be filled with conceited arrogance, (and thus they would be punished twice). [4]

When the first warning came to pass, We sent Our servants, (the Babylonians), against you, *and they were greatly skilled in warfare.* They rampaged through every part of your homes, and thus it was a warning fulfilled! [5]

Then We allowed you to return (to the land of Israel, after your captivity in Babylon), as a kind of (victory for you) over them. We also added to your wealth and sons and allowed your population to increase. [6]

If you were any good at all, you were good for the benefit of your own souls, and if you were evil, it was to the detriment of your own souls.

Then later, when the second warning came to pass, (after you had become disobedient once more), your faces were framed in disgrace as (the Romans) entered into your temple of prayer, even as (the Babylonians) had done (so long before), and they destroyed whatever they laid their hands on. [7]

Perhaps your Lord may show you mercy (yet again, by allowing you to recover and rebuild), but if you return (to sinful ways), then We'll return (with a third penalty).

We established Hellfire as a prison for those who cover (the light of faith within their hearts). [8]

The Reality of History

Background Info... v. 9-11

Some commentators believe this passage is referring to the taunting of an-Nadr ibn al-Harith, when he dared Allah to send down destruction upon him and his fellow pagans. (*Ma'ariful Qur'an*)

This Qur'an certainly guides (people) towards stability (in their lives and societies) and gives good news to the believers who do what's morally right that they shall have a great reward. [9]

Those who don't believe in the next life (should know) that We've prepared a painful punishment for them. [10]

A person (inadvertently) cries out for evil when his cry should be for good, but people are impatient by nature. [11]

We made the night and the day as two (of Our) signs.

We darkened the sign of the night, even as We illuminated the sign of the day, so you can go out and look for the bounty of your Lord, and also so you can keep track of and count the passage of years. And so We explain everything in detail. [12]

We All Have to Make Choices

F.Y.I.

The pagan Arabs used to try and predict the future by looking at which way the birds flew (similar to what the ancient Romans did). This passage is making a play on that by saying that a person's fortune is with them and their own deeds, rather than being determined by something external to them like bird patterns. (*Asbab ul-Nuzul*)

We've tied the bird (of his fortune) around the neck of every human being, and on the Day of Standing (for judgment) We're going to bring out a record that he'll see laid out in the open. [13]

"Read your record! Today your own soul is enough to account against you!" [14]

Whoever finds guidance is guided for the benefit of his own soul, while whoever goes astray does so to the lose of his own soul.

No bearer of burdens can bear the burden of another. We never brought Our punishment down upon any nation unless We raised for them a messenger (to warn them first). [15]

When We decide that a nation is to be destroyed, We send Our command to those who are lost in the pursuit of pleasure, (telling them that they must reform or else face the consequences), so the sentence can be proven true against them (that they deserve their punishment). *Then We destroy them completely!* [16]

How many generations have We destroyed after Nuh? It's a fact that your Lord is well-informed and observant of the sins of His servants. [17]

Whoever desires the temporary things (of this world) will have them in whatever quantity We wish to give, but afterwards We're going to give them Hellfire so they can burn within it in HUMILIATION and disgrace. [18]

Whoever desires the next life, *who makes an effort to achieve it as is required,* and who has faith, their efforts will be appreciated (by Allah). [19]

Both (the believers and the faithless) have Our bounty showered down upon them, for the bounties of your Lord are not withheld. [20]

Have you noticed how We've given more to some than to others? However, the next life is where the higher status and greater bounty awaits. [21]

Your Lord Commands Kindness to Parents

Don't set up other gods alongside of Allah, or you'll end up humiliated and forsaken. [22]

Your Lord has decided that you must serve no one else but Him and that you should be kind to your parents. Whether one or both of them becomes old in your lifetime, never speak to them rudely nor scold them, but rather speak to them in generous terms. [23]

Kindly lower the wing of HUMILITY towards them and say, *"My Lord! Be merciful to them even as they cherished me when I was small."* [24]

365

Your Lord knows what's in your heart, so if you behave in a moral fashion, then He's forgiving to those who repent (of their sins). [25]

Sharing the Wealth

Give what's rightly due to your relatives, the needy and (stranded) travelers.

Don't waste your money like a squanderer. [26]

Squanderers are like the brothers of devils, and Shaytan was ungrateful to his Lord. [27]

Background Info... v. 28

Some people asked the Prophet for a share in some cloth that had been donated, but he had none left to give. This verse was revealed to tell the Prophet what to do in their case. (*Ma'ariful Qur'an*)

If you (don't have any money to give to the poor) and are forced to turn away from them, though in the expectant hope that some *mercy* might come to you from your Lord (that you can later share with them), at the very least say something to put them at ease. [28]

Background Info... v. 29-30

There is a story told that a poor boy went to the Prophet and asked for a shirt and that the Prophet gave his only good shirt to him, leaving him with nothing to wear. As such, he remained in his home without a shirt until someone gave one to him. This passage was then revealed. (*Ma'ariful Qur'an, Asbab ul-Nuzul*)

Don't tie your hand to your neck (like a miser), nor extend it out so far (in donating) that you become guilty (of causing your own) poverty. [29]

Your Lord provides abundant resources to whomever He wants, and He measures (out slimmer resources to whomever He wants, as well). For sure, He is well-informed and watchful (over the needs) of His servants. [30]

The Pillars of Wisdom

Don't kill your children because you're afraid of becoming poor. We'll provide resources for them, as well as for you. Indeed, killing them is an enormous crime. [31]

Don't go anywhere near any unlawful intimate activity for it's a shameful practice and opens the way (to even greater sins and dangers.) [32]

Don't take the life of anyone (whose life) Allah has forbidden (to be taken), except for a just cause (under the law). If anyone is killed wrongfully, then We've given his heir the power (to either demand punishment, take monetary restitution or forgive).

However, don't let him go beyond the limits (in his legal right) to take a life, (as he might bring harm to the innocent), for he's already being supported (by the law and should be satisfied with his options). [33]

Don't (tamper with) an orphan's property before he reaches the age of full strength (at maturity), unless you plan to improve it.

Fulfill every agreement, for every agreement (that you make) will be asked about (on the Day of Judgment). [34]

Give full measure (to your customers) when you measure (for them), and weigh with an accurate scale, for that's best for achieving a good result. [35]

Don't get involved with things about which you know nothing, for every act of hearing, seeing or (feeling in) the heart will be asked about (on the Day of Judgment). [36]

Don't strut through the earth acting like you're so great, for (you're not strong enough) to rip the earth apart, nor can you grow as tall as the mountains. [37]

All sinful practices like those are despicable in the sight of your Lord. [38]

These are among the (pillars of) wisdom that your Lord has revealed to you, so don't take any other god alongside of Allah, or you just might find yourself being cast into Hellfire in disgrace - with (only yourself) to blame! [39]

Pagans don't Understand the Use of Reason

> **Background Info... v. 40**
>
> The pagans believed that the angels were the female daughters of Allah, while they (the pagans) valued sons for themselves above daughters. Thus, by putting on Allah what they didn't want for themselves, they were making Allah seem shortchanged.

Has your Lord chosen to give you sons, while taking daughters for Himself among the angels? You're making an outrageous assertion! [40]

And so it is that We've explained (the issues in) various (ways) in this Qur'an, so

367

they can be reminded, but it only seems to make them distance themselves from it even more! [41]

Say to them, *"If there were (other, lesser) gods (existing) alongside of Him,"* - as they claim – *"then they would surely (be working hard to do those things) that would bring them closer to the Lord of the throne, (in their efforts to win His favor.)"* [42]

Glory be to Him! He is high above all the things that they're saying (about Him) – infinitely higher! [43]

The seven heavens, the very earth and all who (live) within them glorify Him! There isn't anything that exists that doesn't glorify His praise, even if you don't understand how they glorify Him. He is indeed forbearing and forgiving. [44]

What do the Faithless Seek in the Qur'an?

When you recite the Qur'an (Muhamad), We put an invisible screen between you and those who don't believe in the next life. [45]

We put wrappers over their hearts to prevent them from understanding the Qur'an and also a deafness in their ears. When you're remembering your one Lord in the Qur'an, they just turn their backs in disgust. [46]

> ### Background Info... v. 47-48
>
> The Prophet would often recite the Qur'an aloud in his house at night. Even though the Meccan leadership officially disavowed and scorned him, still the verses themselves were often mesmerizing, giving rise to their charges that he was a sorcerer who bewitched men with his verses. One night three prominent idolaters snuck near the windows of the Prophet's house, but each came alone and wasn't aware of the others.
>
> These three men, Abu Jahl, Abu Sufyan and Al-Akhnas ibn Shurayq, stayed listening until the dawn. They noticed each other when they were leaving, and when they each admitted to stealthily listening to the Qur'an, they swore they wouldn't do it again, lest the young men of the tribe start to do the same.
>
> The next night, however, each of the three returned, thinking that he alone would not keep his word.
>
> When they noticed each other again, they took to swearing and vowing to keep his word this time, but the same incident occurred the next night, as well. In the morning Al-Akhnas went to Abu

368

Sufyan and asked his opinion about what Muhammad was saying.

Abu Sufyan replied, "By Allah, I heard some things I recognized and knew what they were about, but I heard other things whose meaning and import I didn't know." Al-Akhnas nodded his agreement and left.

Later on, he went to Abu Jahl and asked his opinion, and Abu Jahl answered, "We've always been in competition with the Bani 'Abd Manaf, (the Prophet's sub-clan). We fed (the poor) when they did, and we gave away (in charity) as they did.

So when we were running neck and neck with them like in a horserace, they said, 'There's a Prophet among us to whom revelation comes from Heaven.' So how can we compete with that? By Allah we will never believe in him nor accept what he says." Then Al-Akhnas left. (Ibn Hisham)

This passage is a reference to this kind of behavior on the part of the Meccans. They would also look for snippets of the Qur'an that could be willfully misinterpreted or ridiculed publicly to make Islam seem like something it was not.

We know what they're really listening for when they listen to you, (for they merely wish to find something to criticize) so they can talk about it in their private conversations, saying, "*You (Muslims) are following nothing more than a man who's been bewitched!*" [47]

Do you see what kind of an example they're making of you! However, they're the ones who've gone astray, and they'll never find a way (out of their mistaken beliefs). [48]

The Faithless Object to the Resurrection

"*What!*" they exclaim. "*When we've rotted away to dust and bones, are we really going to be made like new?*" [49]

Say to them, *"(Yes, indeed), even if you were made of stone or iron, or some other created material that's even harder than (the hearts) in your chests!"*

Then they ask, "*So who's going to bring us back (to life)?*"

Tell them, "*The One Who created (you) the first time!*" However, they just bob their heads towards you and say, "*So when will all this come to pass?*"

Tell them, "*The time might be close at hand, and it will be a day when He calls you, and you'll (be forced to) answer with His praise, even as you'll think you only stayed (in the world) for a little while.*" [50-52]

Beware of Your Constant Enemy

> **Background Info... v. 53**
>
> It is said that this verse was revealed after some of the Prophet's companions asked him how they should respond to the insults of the pagans. (*Asbab ul-Nuzul*)

Tell My servants that they should only speak of good things, for Shaytan tries to make divisions among them.

Shaytan is the obvious enemy of humanity! [53]

Your Lord knows you best. If He wants to be merciful to you, then He'll do so, and if He wants to punish you, then He'll do so. We haven't sent you to be their guardian. [54]

Your Lord knows (all about every creature) that (exists) within the heavens and the earth.

We gave some prophets more gifts than others, even as We gave the Zabur to Dawud. [55]

There is no Escaping the True Conclusion

Say to them, "*(Go ahead and) call upon all those whom you pretend (to be gods) besides Him! They have no power to solve your troubles, nor can they ward them off.*" [56]

Those upon whom they're calling (for favors) are themselves trying to find their own way to their Lord, even if they're already close (to Him)!

They greatly desire to receive His mercy, even as they're in mortal fear of His punishment, *for your Lord's punishment is truly something to think about!* [57]

There's not a single settlement that will escape Our annihilation, or at the very least (have a taste of) a strong punishment, before the Day of Assembly (arrives), and that (statement has been) recorded in the Book (of Decrees). [58]

We never withhold sending miracles for any other reason than the fact that ancient peoples (so frequently) called them lies.

We sent a (special) camel to the (people of) Thamud for them to see, but they treated her badly.

And so it is that We only send miracles (in order to make people) afraid (of the coming punishment). [59]

(Remember) when We told you, *"Your Lord surrounds people (in His power)!"*

We didn't send the vision (of the next life) down upon you for any other purpose than to be a test for people.

(The mention of) the cursed tree (of Zaqqum) in the Qur'an (was for the same purpose), as well.

We (only use such symbols) to instill fear in them (so that they'll perhaps be inclined to listen), but it only adds to their immense denial (of faith). [60]

Shaytan's Challenge to Allah

When We told the angels, *"Bow down (in respect) to Adam,"* they all bowed down.

Iblis, however, (who was a jinn in their company, did not bow along with them).

"How can I bow down to a creature that You made from mud?" he asked. [61]

"Look at that!" he continued. *"This (human) is the one whom You're honoring over me! If You give me a chance until the Day of Assembly, I'll make his descendants blindly obedient (to me), all but a few!"* [62]

"Go away," (Allah) replied, *"and if any of them follow you, then Hellfire will be enough of a reward for you all! [63]

"Dazzle any of them that you can with your (alluring) voice (of temptation). Attack them with your cavalry and with your infantry.

"Share in their wealth and children, and make promises to them - even though the promises of Shaytan are nothing more than deception. [64]

"As for My servants, however, you will have no power over them. Your Lord is quite enough to take care (of them)."* [65]

Your only Safety Lies with Allah

Your Lord is the One Who makes ships sail smoothly through the sea so you can seek of His bounty (through fishing or trade), for He is merciful to you. [66]

When a disaster strikes you at sea, however, all those (false gods) that you call upon besides Him leave you to suffer! Though when (Allah) returns you safely to land once more, you turn away (from Him), for human beings are thankless! [67]

Do you feel so safe then that He won't make a part of the earth swallow you up when you're back on (dry) land?

(Do you feel so safe) that He won't send a windstorm against you that'll leave you helpless to take care of yourself? [68]

Do you feel so safe that He won't send you back out to sea (on a subsequent voyage) and then send a heavy gale against you to drown you on account of your ungratefulness?

Even still, you won't have anyone to avenge yourself against Us! [69]

(So be grateful), for We've been generous to the sons of Adam by providing them with transportation on both land and sea, by giving them resources that are wholesome and by granting them favors more advantageous than most of the rest of creation ever received. [70]

The Record will be Complete

One day, We're going to call out the leaders of every people. Those who receive their records in their right hand will read their records, and they won't be wronged in the least. [71]

However, those who were blind (to the truth) in this world will be blind (to it) in the next life, for they had veered off the path. [72]

Background Info... v. 73-77

This passage was revealed in response to some idol-worshippers who asked the Prophet to give them special treatment in exchange for their conversion.

One report says that it refers to the leaders of Mecca who told the Prophet they would be more inclined to follow him if he drove away his poor underclass followers. (*Ma'ariful Qur'an*)

Another report says that members from the tribe of Thaqif visited the Prophet and offered conversion if he would exempt them from charity and prayer, exempt them from having to cancel the interest owed to them, even as they could continue to charge interest, and that their sacred trees would be protected and inviolate.

According to this report, the Prophet was in the midst of having his secretary write this contract for the tribe, when this verse was revealed telling him not to cave in to their demands. (*Zamakhshari*)

Yet, a third incident attributed to this revelation is that the Quraysh asked **Muhammad** to alter a verse of the Qur'an to their liking. In desperation he almost agreed with them, but this passage told him to stand firm and warned him to be on his guard against the subtle suggestions of those who would have him compromise. (*Zamakhshari*)

Their plan was to tempt you away from what We were revealing to you and to get you to substitute in Our name (principles) that were quite different. (If you had done so), then (those evil people) would've become your closest friends! [73]

If We hadn't given you strength, then you probably would've inclined a little towards (their requests). [74] In that case, We would've made you suffer equal amounts (of punishment), both in this life and after death, and you wouldn't have had anyone to help you against Us! [75]

Their (ultimate) plan was to try and frighten you into fleeing from (your) hometown, so they could keep you away in exile.

If they (had succeeded in driving you away), then they would've remained (safe in their homes) only a little while longer after you (left, before We destroyed them). [76]

This has been our way with the messengers We sent before you, and you will never find any change in how We operate. [77]

Strengthen Yourselves for What Lies Ahead

Establish prayers after the sun begins to decline (at noon) until the onset of nightfall, and recite (the Qur'an) at dawn, for reciting (the Qur'an) at dawn is witnessed (by the angels). [78]

Pray in the late hours of the night, as well, as an extra bonus for you (above and beyond what's required), for your Lord will shortly raise you to a highly regarded position. [79]

Now utter (this supplication, and then prepare yourself to migrate to Medina), "*My Lord! Let my entrance be an honest entrance, let my exit be an honest exit, and bestow upon me power from You to help me.*" [80]

373

And also declare (this phrase in order to strengthen your resolve for the coming migration), "*The truth has arrived, and falsehood will vanish, for falsehood always vanishes!*" [81]

We're sending down in this Qur'an that which is a source of healing and mercy for the believers, even as it causes nothing but loss to the wrongdoers. [82]

Each will Act according to His Nature

Whenever We bestow Our favors upon a human being, he turns away and becomes aloof, but when calamity strikes him, he descends into deep despair. [83]

Say to them, "*Everyone acts according to his own disposition, but your Lord knows best who is being guided on the way.*" [84]

What is the Nature of the Human Spirit?

Background Info... v. 85

'Abdullah ibn Mas'ud (d. 653) reported the following incident that caused the revelation of this verse: "While I was strolling with the Prophet through a desolate patch, he stopped to rest on a palm leaf stalk.

Some Jews passed by, and one of them said to the others, 'Ask him about the spirit.' Another one said, 'Why do you want to ask him about that?' A third man among them said, 'Don't ask him, or you might get an answer you won't like.' Finally they agreed on: 'Let's all ask him.'

Then they asked the Prophet, but he didn't answer, and then I knew he was receiving revelation, so I stayed where I was. Then the new revelation was received, and the Prophet recited (this verse)." (Bukhari)

Now they're asking you about the spirit (Angel Jibra'il).

Tell them, "*The spirit is under the command of my Lord, and no knowledge of it has ever come to you except for a little.*" [85]

If We ever wanted, We could take away (this message) with which We've been inspiring you, and then you wouldn't have anyone to represent you in your claim against Us. [86]

However, (the extent of) your Lord's mercy and His favor towards you is indeed tremendous! [87]

Say to them, "*If the whole of humanity and all the jinns were to gather together to produce something similar to this Qur'an, they could never produce the like of it, even if they all worked together and pooled their resources.*" [88]

And so it is that We've explained for people in this Qur'an every type of example (so they can ponder over them). Yet, most people are unwilling to accept it and are thankless. [89]

Answering a Bunch of Objections

Background Info... v. 90-93

This passage recounts a relentless assault from the pagans, who said all of these things to the Prophet in a huge outdoor gathering that they arranged.

After they asked for many miracles to benefit their city and themselves, the Prophet told them, "I won't do any of that, and I won't ask my Lord for these things. I wasn't sent for this reason; rather, Allah sent me to you to bring you good news and warnings. If you accept what I've brought you, then it will be good fortune for you in this world and in the next, but if you reject it, then I will wait patiently for the command of Allah until Allah judges between me and you."

So that's when they asked the Prophet to make the sky fall upon them. The Prophet then said, "That's for Allah to decide, and if He wants to, He will do that to you." These verses were revealed about that incident. (*Asbab ul-Nuzul*)

They say, "*We're never going to believe in you until you make a spring gush forth for us from the earth, or until you have a garden filled with date palms and grapevines and rushing streams flowing abundantly in their midst, or until you make the sky shatter and fall down upon us, as you pretend will happen, or until you bring Allah and the angels here in front of us, or until you have a house decorated with gold, or until you have a ladder that can reach right up into the sky!*

"*Even then, we won't believe you ever climbed up there, unless you send a book down to us that we can read (for ourselves).*"

Say to them, "*Glory be to my Lord! Am I not a messenger who's just a mortal man?*" [90-93]

Nothing prevented the people (of former nations) from believing when guidance came to them, except for their saying, "*Has Allah really sent a mortal man as a messenger?*" [94]

Say to them, "*If the earth were populated by angels, going about their business quietly, then We would've certainly sent an angel down from the sky to be a messenger for them.*" [95]

Then say, "*Allah is enough of a witness between you and me, for He's well-informed and watchful over His servants.*" [96]

For the one who is guided by Allah, such a one is truly guided, but for the one whom He leaves astray – *you won't find any protector for him in place of (Allah)!*

On the Day of Standing (for judgment), We're going to gather them together, flat on their faces – *blind, mute and deaf* - and then their destination will be in Hellfire.

Every time (the heat of the fire) seems to die down, *We'll stoke the fire back to its full intensity!* [97]

That's the compensation that they're going to receive because they rejected Our (revealed) verses and said, "*What! When we've rotted away to dust and bones, are we really going to be made like new once more?*" [98]

Don't they see that Allah, the One Who created the heavens and the earth, has the power to create them as they were (before)?

It's only because He's set a specific time-limit for them - *and there's no doubt about that* - but still the wrongdoers do

nothing more than thanklessly refuse (the invitation of salvation). [99]

Say to them, "*If you had control over all the treasures that (emanate from) the mercy of my Lord, you would be unwilling to share them (with others) out of the fear of spending too much, for human beings are tightfisted!*" [100]

Take the Example of Musa

And so it was that We gave nine evident miracles to Musa when he came (before Pharaoh and his nobles) – just ask the Children of Israel!

Pharaoh said to him, "*Musa! I think you've been bewitched!*" [101]

"*You know full well,*" (Musa) replied, "*that these (miracles) have been sent down by none other than the Lord of the heavens and the earth, as clear evidence for all to see. I think that you, Pharaoh, are doomed to perish!*" [102]

Thus, (Pharaoh) resolved to wipe (the Hebrews) off the face of the earth, but We drowned him and all those who were with him, and We said to the Children of Israel, "*Dwell upon the earth, but when the final*

376

promise comes to pass, We're going to gather you in a mixed crowd (on the Day of Judgment)." [103-104]

The Qur'an is the Truth

We sent (the Qur'an) down for a true purpose, and it has, indeed, been sent down for that true purpose. We didn't send it to you for any other reason than to give good news and also to warn. [105]

We divided this Qur'an (into sections) so you could recite it to people in intervals, and (that's why) We've been revealing it in successive stages. [106]

Tell (the idol-worshippers of Mecca), "*Whether you believe in it or not, the (Jews and Christians) who were given knowledge (of Allah's revelations) before you fall down on their faces humbly when they hear it being recited to them, and they say, 'Glory be to our Lord!*

*"Our Lord's promise has been fulfilled!' They fall down on their faces weeping, and it increases their humble (submission)." *[107-109]

Background Info... first half v. 110

The Prophet was prostrating and calling upon Allah, saying, "O Compassionate, O Merciful," when a pagan man happened by. The ignorant pagan said out loud, "He claims to pray to one (Allah), but he's praying to two!" Then this verse was revealed mentioning that Allah has many holy names by which He can be invoked. (*Ibn Kathir*)

Also tell them, "*Call upon Allah, or call upon the Compassionate, for regardless of whatever name you use to invoke Him, the most beautiful names belong to Him.*"

How should we Recite the Qur'an?

Background Info... v. 110

This verse was revealed in Mecca at a time when the pagans would ridicule the Qur'an whenever they heard it being recited. The Prophet used to recite it in a strong and clear voice, but it would often attract needless heckling from the pagans. However, if he recited it too softly, his companions and also interested pagans wouldn't be able to hear it from him and learn it, so this verse tells him to take a middle ground.

After the migration to Medina, these restrictions were no longer as essential and didn't apply, though the commentators say it remains as a general principle for the believers not to shout or whisper in their prayers, but to take a middle course. (*Ibn Kathir, Bukhari*)

(Muhammad!) Don't recite (the Qur'an) in your prayers too **LOUDLY** or too *softly*, but recite in an even tone in between the two extremes. [110]

Then say, "*Praise be to Allah, Who doesn't give birth to children, nor does He have any partner in His kingdom, nor does He need anyone to protect Him from weakness, so magnify Him greatly!*" [111]

The Cave

18 Al Kahf
Late Meccan Period

☞ Introduction

This chapter holds a special place in the imagination of Muslims. The Prophet once said of this chapter: "Whoever recites the Chapter of the Cave on Friday, it will illuminate him with light from one Friday to the next." *(Al-Hakim)* On another occasion he said, "Whoever recites the first and last verses of this chapter, there will be a (spiritual) light from his feet to his head, and if he were to recite the entire chapter, for him there is light from the earth to the sky." *(Ahmad)*

This portion of revelation came during a particularly difficult time. Due to relentless Meccan persecution, a large number of Muslims had migrated to Abyssinia for safety. Meanwhile, back in Mecca, the leaders of the Quraysh sent two messengers (an-Nadr ibn al-Harith and 'Uqbah ibn Abi Mu'ayt) to Yathrib (Medina) to ask the Jews about Muhammad and to get their opinion as to whether he was a true prophet or not.

The Jews sent back a suggested list of three topics about which they could ask him. "Ask him," the rabbis said, "about the reason for why the young men left their city and sought refuge in a cave and then what happened next, for this is a unique event. Ask him about the man who traveled both to the east and the west of the earth and what happened to him. Finally, ask him about the spirit and what it was." *(at-Tabari)* Those three questions are the reason for revelation of some of the portions of this chapter.

When the Meccan messengers returned, they asked the Prophet about these issues. At first Muhammad said that he would have the answer right away, but he forgot to say, "As Allah wills." To teach him a lesson - that he could not order Allah to reveal things - no new revelation came for fifteen days. The Prophet realized his mistake and repented. Then verses 18:23-24 were revealed to explain the reason for the delay, and then finally the answers came.

Be that as it may, the Meccans were unfazed by the fine answers given in this chapter. They decided to punish Muhammad and the two clans to which he was most closely related, and from which many of his followers came, by forcibly ejecting them from the city and isolating them in a barren desert valley. They wrote their decree on vellum and hung it in the Ka'bah for effect. This was known as the Boycott, and for three years the Meccans refused to trade with the exiles, sell them food or allow them to leave the valley. The Muslims suffered deprivation on an appalling scale. If it wasn't for secret food deliveries smuggled in by sympathetic Meccans in the night, the Muslims would surely have perished.

Visiting Arab chieftains from the countryside eventually shamed the Meccans into lifting their cruel policy. When the document hung within the Ka'bah, wherein was written the decree, was examined, it was found that ants had eaten away all the ink, leaving the sheet blank. It was little consolation for the Prophet, however, for in the same year the Boycott was lifted, his beloved wife and soul-mate Khadijah passed away, a death no doubt hastened by the many years of suffering in the open desert during the Boycott.

The Prophet's uncle and only political protection, Abu Talib, also passed away, leaving the Prophet more vulnerable to violence than ever before. Perhaps the story of the Sleepers of the Cave contained within this chapter is a veiled note of hope for the Prophet that persecution doesn't last forever and that eventually the truth will prevail over ignorance.

In the Name of Allah,
the Compassionate, the Merciful

Praise be to Allah, the One Who sent down to His servant a Book in which He allowed no crookedness. [1]

(It's a Book that's) straightforward (and clear), so He can warn (all people) of a terrible penalty from Him, and so that He can give good news to the believers who do what's morally right that they're going to have an excellent reward - (a reward) that will stay with them forever. [2-3]

(It's also a message that's been revealed) so He can warn those who say, *"Allah has begotten a son."*

They have no knowledge (that could justify their claim), nor did their forefathers (have any certain proof), either.

It's really an outrageous statement that's coming out of their mouths, for what they're saying is no more than a lie! [4-5]

Perhaps you'll worry yourself to death as you follow after them, distressed that they're not believing in this narration. [6]

Whatever (riches and distractions) that We've placed in the earth are but a dazzling display by which We test them, in order to bring out those whose conduct is the best. (In the end), We're going to reduce whatever is upon (the earth) to dry dust. [7-8]

The Companions of the Cave

> **Background Info... v. 9-22**
>
> Jewish visitors from Yathrib (Medina) were trying to help the Meccan idol-worshippers expose Muhammad as a fraud by providing them with questions that they could ask him, hoping he would stumble.
>
> They told the Meccans to ask Muhammad about the Companions of the Cave, and this story contained in verses 9-22 was revealed in response.

Have you ever considered that the Companions of the Cave and the inscribed writings might be among Our wondrous signs? [9]

When the young men fled (from persecution) to the cave, they said:

"Our Lord! Be merciful to us, and resolve our situation in the most appropriate way." [10]

Then We boxed up their ears for a number of years while they were in the cave, (so they would have no news of the outside world). [11]

Then, (after some time had passed), We awakened them to test which of the two sides (among them) would be better able to calculate the length of their stay. [12]

We're telling you their story truthfully, for they were young men who believed in their Lord. Therefore, We increased them in guidance. [13]

Indeed, We fortified their hearts when they had confronted (their people), saying to them, *"Our Lord is the Lord of the heavens and the earth, and we're never going to call upon any god besides Him. If we did that, then we would be saying something blasphemous.* [14]

"These people of ours have taken other gods in place of Him, so why don't they bring some clear authority to justify what they've done? Who can be more wrong than the one who invents a lie against Allah?" [15]

(Then they made a plan to escape the wrath of their people, saying to each other), *"After you've turned away from them and all that they serve besides Allah, then seek refuge in the cave. Your Lord will shower His mercy upon you and make your situation easy to bear."* [16]

The World Transforms

(If you were looking out from) the cave's entrance, you would've seen the sun as it rose away leaning to the right. When it set, it would move away from them and then down to the left, all the while they remained there, lying in the middle of the cave.

These are among the signs of Allah. Whomever Allah guides is guided (to the straight path), while whomever Allah leaves astray – *you won't find any right-minded best friend for him!* [17]

You would have thought they were awake (if you saw them), but they were asleep! We turned them on their right sides and their left, while their dog stretched out his two forelegs at the entrance.

If you would have come upon them, you would have run away in abject terror of them! [18]

That's (how they were) when We awakened them, so they could ask each other (about their situation.)

One of them asked, *"How long have you all been here?"*

"We've been here a day or maybe part of a day at most," (they answered, but after a long discussion), they (all agreed that they weren't sure).

So they said, *"Allah knows best how long you've been here. Let's send one of you with his money to the city to see which is the best kind of food he can bring, so you can at least satisfy (your hunger) with it.*

"Let him be discreet, and let him not talk to anyone about (the rest of us), because if they come upon (you), then they'll stone you or force you to return to their traditions. Then you'll never succeed." [19-20]

It was (on account of his antique coins and dress) that We made people aware of their situation.

(This was so) they could know that Allah's promise is true and that there can be no doubt about the Hour.

Later on, (after the youths grew old and died, the people) disagreed among themselves about how (best to commemorate) their case.

"Let's build a (monumental) structure over (their graves)," (some people suggested), but their Lord knew about them (and their less than honest intentions).

However, those who won the decision said, *"We're going to build a house of prayer over (their graves)."* [21]

(Christians differ over the details of the story, with some) saying that there were three (young people in the cave) and that their dog was the fourth among them.

(Others) said they were five, with their dog being the sixth, but they're just GUESSING about what they haven't seen. (Others even assert that) they were seven, with their dog being the eighth.

Say to them, *"My Lord knows best what their exact number was, and only a few (people) know for sure (how many they were)."*

So don't get drawn into arguments with them (on such speculative issues), but rather (talk to them) only on topics that have clear resolutions, and don't consult any of them at all about (such obscure topics). [22]

Don't Forget to Account for the Will of Allah

Never say of anything, *"I'll do it tomorrow,"* without adding, *"If Allah wills."*

If you forget (to add this phrase), then remember your Lord (when you recall your lapse) and say:

"I hope that my Lord guides me closer to the rightly guided way." [23-24]

(Some people say that the Companions of the Cave) stayed in their cave for three hundred years, and (others) add nine (more years to that figure). [25]

Tell them, *"Allah knows better how long they stayed, for the unseen (secrets) of the heavens and the earth belong to Him.*

"He sees them and listens (to all things). (Nothing that exists) has any protector besides Him, and He never shares His rule with anyone." [26]

Choose Your Side

Recite what's been revealed to you of the Book of your Lord. No one can change His words (of command), and you'll never find anyone who can save you besides Him. [27]

Keep your soul content with those who call upon their Lord in the morning and in the evening, seeking His face. Don't let your eyes pass beyond them, desiring the flashy glitter of this world's life.

Don't obey anyone whose heart We've allowed to become careless of Our remembrance, who follows his own whims and whose purpose (in life) is lost. [28]

Say to them, *"The truth (has now come to you) from your Lord."* Whoever wants to believe (in it), will do so.

Whoever wants to reject it, will do so. We've prepared for the wrongdoers a fire whose (flames) will surround them like walls.

Every time they ask for relief (from the heat), they'll have scalding water poured over them as hot as molten brass!

It'll sear their faces! *Oh, how awful a drink and how horrible a place to rest!* [29]

As for those who believed and did what was morally right, *We're never going to lose track of the reward of anyone who did good!* [30]

For them are everlasting gardens beneath which rivers flow. They'll be adorned with gold bracelets while wearing embroidered robes of green silk.

They'll relax on couches within (the garden) - *oh, how wonderful a payment and how excellent a place to rest!* [31]

The Story of the Gardener who Bragged

Lay out for them the example of two men. We gave one of them two gardens of grapevines, surrounded them with date palms, and then placed grain fields in between. [32]

Both of the gardens produced abundantly, and there was never a bad harvest, and in their midst We let a gentle stream flow. [33]

His harvests were truly grand, so (one day) he had a tense conversation with his companion during which he boasted, "*I have more wealth than you, and I have more (influence in society than you on account of my) many followers!*" [34]

Then he went into his garden in a state of injustice against his own soul. (Looking around, he then said to himself,) "*I don't think any of this will ever perish, nor do I think the Hour (of Judgment) will ever come.*

384

"Even if I was brought back to my Lord, I'm sure I'll find something there even better in exchange." [35-36]

His companion had told him, when they had talked before, "*Are you going to reject the One Who made you from dust, then from mingled fluids, and then crafted you into a man?* [37]

"As for me, (I believe) that He's my Lord Allah, and I'll never make any partners with Him." [38]

"Whenever you go into your garden, why don't you say, 'It is as Allah wills,' and 'There is no strength except with Allah?' If you've noticed that I have less money and fewer children than you, maybe it's because my Lord will give me something better than your garden.

"Perhaps He might send thunderbolts from the sky (down upon you) and turn (your garden) into shifting sand, or maybe your water supply will sink in the earth so deep that you'll never be able to recover it." [39-41]

And so it came to pass that the fruits (of his labor) were encompassed (in utter destruction).

He just stood there, wringing his hands in worry over what he had invested on his property, which was now destroyed down to its very foundations!

All he could say was, "*I'm ruined! If only I had never made partners with my Lord!*" [42]

He had no group of supporters (to help him) against Allah, nor was he even able to save himself! [43]

(On the Day of Judgment), the only protection that will be available will be from Allah, the Ultimate Reality. He's the best One to reward and the best One to bring matters to a close. [44]

What is this World Really About?

Lay out for them the example of what this world is really like. It's like the water that We send down from the sky. The plants of the earth absorb it, but soon afterwards they become as dry stubble to be blown about by the winds. Allah is the only One Who prevails over all things! [45]

Wealth and children are merely the glitter of the life of this world, but the moral deeds that endure are the best in the sight of your Lord, and the best on which to hope (for the future). [46]

One day We're going to send the mountains away, and you're going to see the land as a level plain. Then We're going to gather all of them together, leaving no one behind. [47]

They'll all be standing at attention before your Lord in rows, (and they'll be told), "*So now you've come back to Us (as naked) as (the day) We created you the first time. But no! You never thought We would bring about your appointed meeting!*" [48]

(Each person's) record (of deeds) will be placed (before him), and you'll see the wrongdoers in a state of panic on account of what (their records) contain.

"*We're doomed!*" they'll cry out. "*What kind of book is this! It leaves out nothing small or great, and it makes mention of everything!*"

And so they'll find out about everything they ever did, for it will all be right there, laid out before them, and your Lord won't treat anyone unfairly. [49]

When We are Questioned

We told the angels, "*Bow down to Adam,*" and they all bowed down, except for Iblis, who was one of the jinns.

He broke away from his Lord's command. So are you now going to take him and his descendants as protectors besides Me?

They're your enemies, so it's a truly bad deal that the wrongdoers are making! [50]

I didn't let them witness the creation of the heavens and the earth - *no, not even their own creation* - nor would I take such misleaders as assistants. [51]

One day (Allah) will say, "*Call upon those whom you assumed were My partners.*"

They'll call out to them, but they won't answer back. Then We'll erect a dreadful prison wall between them. [52]

The bad people will see the Fire and feel themselves falling into it, and they'll find no way out. [53]

Many will Turn Away

We've given detailed explanations in this Qur'an, using every kind of example for people (to ponder). Yet, human beings argue over most things. [54]

There's nothing to prevent people from believing – especially now since guidance has come to them - nor from asking for their Lord's forgiveness, except that they've followed the pattern of ancient peoples (who denied that Allah would ever send His revelations to a mortal man) or that they would suffer from the onslaught of (Allah's) punishment. [55]

We only send messengers to give good news and to warn, but the faithless argue over foolish points in an effort to weaken the truth (in the eyes of their fellows). They take My (revealed) verses and what they've been warned with as a joke. [56]

Who's more wrong than the one who's reminded of the signs of his Lord but then turns away from them in forgetfulness because of what his hands have done?

(As a penalty), We've wrapped veils over their hearts to prevent them from understanding and placed a deafness in their ears. Even if you called them to guidance, they'd never agree to be guided. [57]

Even still, your Lord is the Forgiving and a master at showing mercy. If He were to take a hold of them (immediately and punish them) for what they've earned for themselves (on their record of deeds), then He would've certainly hurried their punishment forward.

However, they have their time limit, and after that they'll have no place to be safe. [58]

(This is the pattern of previous) generations that We destroyed. When they were immersed in corruption, We fixed a final date for their destruction. [59]

Musa Seeks a Teacher

Background Info... v. 60

Musa was often disobeyed by his people, and they were prone to arguing with him. After one such episode, Musa lost his temper and said, **"Who's the smartest man among the people? It's me - I'm the smartest!"**

Because Musa **didn't** say Allah was the most knowledgeable of all, Allah made him go on a quest to learn patience. Allah told him to go to the coast (of the Red Sea) where the Gulf (of 'Aqabah) and the Gulf (of the Suez) meet at the bottom tip of the Sinai Peninsula and look for a person there who was more learned than even he. Musa asked Allah, **"How can I find him?"**

Allah told him, **"Take a fish in a container, and you will find him where you lose that fish."**

So Musa set out with his servant, bringing a fish in a container, on the journey to find the wisest man in the world. (Condensed from *Bukhari*)

By Allah's command, Musa (set out on a journey to seek a man wiser than himself).

He said to his servant, "*I won't give up until I've reached the junction of the two seas or until I've spent years traveling.*" [60]

When they finally did reach the junction, (they made camp for the night), but they forgot all about their fish, (which then leapt out of its container) and made its way into the sea through a tunnel. [61]

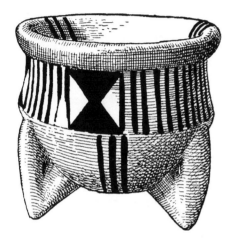

After they (arose the next morning and) traveled (some distance farther), Musa said to his assistant, "*Bring us our breakfast, for as it is we've endured so much fatigue on our journey.*" [62]

"*Did you see (what happened) when we were resting on that boulder (the night before)?*" (the servant exclaimed).

"*I forgot (to tell you about) the fish, and only Shaytan could've made me forget to mention it. It (leapt out of the container) and made its way back into the sea in an amazing way!*" [63]

"*That was it!*" Musa cried. "*That was (the sign) for which we were looking!*"

Then they retraced their footsteps and found one of Our servants upon whom We had granted mercy from Our Own presence and whom We had taught from Our Own knowledge. [64-65]

"*Can I follow you,*" Musa asked, "*so you can teach me something of the good sense that you've been taught?*" [66]

"*You won't be able to have patience enough (to learn) from me,*" (Khidr) replied, "*for how could you have patience in situations where your knowledge is incomplete?*" [67-68]

"*Allah willing, you'll find me patient,*" (Musa) replied, "*and I won't disobey your commands.*" [69]

"*If you really want to follow me,*" (Khidr) said, "*then don't ask me about anything until I've spoken about its meaning first.*" [70]

The Mysterious Journey

Then they proceeded on (and took passage on a ship), but then (Khidr) damaged (the boat and caused it to take on water).

(Musa) cried out, "*Have you damaged it in order to drown those within it? What an awful thing you've done!*" [71]

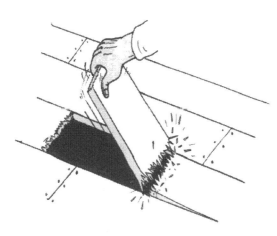

"*Didn't I tell you,* "(Khidr) intoned, "*that you would have no patience with me?*" [72]

"*Don't hold my forgetfulness against me,*" (Musa) cried, "*nor be hard on me in my position.*" [73]

So then they proceeded on until they met a young man, but then (Khidr) killed him.

"*Have you killed an innocent person,*" (Musa) cried out, "*who hasn't murdered anyone! What a horrible thing you've done!*" [74]

"*Didn't I tell you,* "(Khidr) answered, "*that you would have no patience with me?*" [75]

Then (Musa) begged him, saying, "*If I ever ask you about anything after this, then you have every right to part ways with me, and you would be fully justified as far as I'm concerned (to make me leave).*" [76]

Then they traveled farther until they came to some people in a town. They asked them for food, but the (townspeople) refused to give them any hospitality.

(As they passed through the town,) they came upon a wall that was about to collapse, but then (Khidr) repaired it.

"*If you want,*" (Musa) remarked, "*you could ask them for some payment for (your labor).*" [77]

"*This is where you and I will go our separate ways,*" (Khidr) announced, "*but first let me tell you the full meaning of those things for which you had no patience.*" [78]

"*As for the boat, it belonged to some poor (sailors) who used it on the sea, and I only desired to make it (temporarily) unserviceable, for there was a certain king coming up from behind them, seizing every boat by force.*" [79]

"*As for the young man, his parents were believers, and we were afraid that he was going to bring sorrow down upon* them due to his rebellious and thankless nature. [80]

"So we only desired that their Lord give them (a better son) in exchange, one who would be purer and nearer to a merciful disposition." [81]

"As for the wall, it belonged to two young orphans of the town. Below it was a buried treasure that was their due right.

"Their father had been a moral man, so your Lord desired that they should reach maturity and find their treasure, as a mercy and favor from your Lord.

"I didn't (do all those things) from my own motivations. This is the meaning of (all of those things) for which you had no patience." [82]

The Master of Two Horns

Background Info... v. 83

The following subject, that of the story of the "Master of the Two Horns," is one of the topics that visiting Jews from Medina told the Meccans to ask Muhammad about. Who was the Master of Two Horns?

It was hoped by the Arabs and Jews that Muhammad (p) would stumble on this issue and expose his lack of knowledge. Yet, when the revelation of this story came to him, the Jews realized that Muhammad (p) was a man with which to be reckoned, and the pagans were further dumbfounded.

The Master of Two Horns refers to King Cyrus the Great of Persia, who was spoken about in glowing terms in the Jewish scriptures in the book of Daniel (8:20) and also in the book of Isaiah (verse 45:1).

Now they're asking you about the Master of the Two Horns. Say to them, "I'll narrate for you something of his story." [83]

We established him in the earth and gave him the means to reach every (place he wanted). [84]

He followed one way until he reached the setting of the sun, and it appeared to him to set (behind) a murky body of water.

Near it he found a people (who were given to misbehavior, but who had no power to resist him). We said, "Master of the Two Horns! Either punish them or treat them well." [85-86]

390

"The one who does wrong shall be punished," he announced. *"Then he'll be sent back to his Lord, and He'll punish him with a harsh penalty.* [87]

However, the one who has faith and does what's morally right will be well rewarded, and we'll issue easy commands to him." [88]

Then he followed another way until he came upon the rising of the sun. He found it rising upon a people who had not been provided by Us with secure shelter. [89-90]

(He left them alone) as they were, for We knew better what he had there before him. [91]

Then he followed another way until he came upon (a land) between two mountain (ranges).

He found beneath them a people who could barely understand a word (of his language). [92-93]

They told him, *"Master of the Two Horns! The Yajuj and Majuj (tribes) cause great destruction in the land. Could we pay tribute to you so you can build a strong barrier between us and them?"* [94]

"(The wealth and power) that my Lord has granted me is better (than any tribute you could give).

"Help me instead with your strength (and labor), and I will build a barrier between you and them. Now bring me pieces of iron!"

(Then he ordered the people to build) until he had filled the space between the steep mountains (with strong fortifications).

"Blow (with your bellows!" he then commanded), and when he had made it as hot as fire, he said,

"Now bring me molten copper so I can pour some of it over (the iron to reinforce the defenses)." [95-96]

391

And so the (enemy) was rendered helpless to climb over (the walls of the forts), nor could they penetrate them from below. [97]

(When he saw that the enemy was powerless to invade the valley,) he remarked, "*This is a mercy from my Lord, but when my Lord's promise comes to pass, then He'll reduce (the deterrent) to dust, and my Lord's promise is a true one.*" [98]

On that day, We're going to let (the barbarians) surge forward like waves, one after the other. Then the trumpet will be blown, and We'll collect them all together. [99]

We'll present the full expanse of Hellfire for the faithless to see - *those whose eyes had been under a veil against remembering Me* – even more they were (unwilling) even to listen (to the message)! [100-101]

A Day of Winners and Losers

Do the faithless think that they can take My (created) servants as protectors besides Me? Well then, We've made Hellfire ready to entertain all those who covered over (their ability to believe)! [102]

Say to them, "*Should we tell you about those who are going to lose the most in their deeds?* [103]

"*(It's) those whose life's work has been wasted, even as they thought they were getting something good for their efforts.*" [104]

They're the ones who denied the (revealed) verses of their Lord and their meeting with Him.

Their works will be rendered void, and on the Day of Assembly We'll give them no weight (in the balance of deeds). [105]

That's their reward – *Hellfire* – because they rejected (their Lord) and took My (revealed) verses and messengers as a joke. [106]

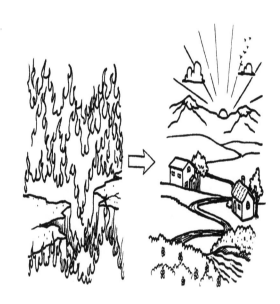

Those who had faith, however, and did what was morally right will be entertained in an exclusive garden in Paradise.

There they get to stay, never wishing for anything to change! [107-108]

Allah is without Limit

Background Info... v. 109

This verse was revealed in response to a Jewish man who boasted to the Prophet that the Old Testament was a lengthy text; thus, his people could claim a greater amount of knowledge and legitimacy on account of its massive size. (*Asbab ul-Nuzul*)

Say to them, "*If the ocean were made of ink (and it was used to write out) the words of my Lord, the ocean would run dry first before the words of my Lord would be exhausted, even if we added another ocean just like it to help!*" [109]

Muhammad (p) is no More than a Man

Background Info... v. 110

Apparently this verse was revealed in the Medinan Period in response to a Muslim man who told the Prophet that he did good deeds for the sake of both Allah and his reputation and that this dual purpose of his was good enough for him to satisfy his own sense of duty. (*Ma'ariful Qur'an*)

This verse warns against adding any 'partners' in one's service to Allah, even if that 'partner' is one's own sense of self-satisfaction or pride in one's reputation.

Say to them:

"I'm just a man like yourselves. I've received inspiration (that commands me to inform) you that your God is One God and that whoever expects to meet his Lord, let him do moral deeds and let him not join any partners at all in the service of his Lord." [110]

Mary

19 Maryam
Middle Meccan Period

👉 Introduction

This chapter was revealed in approximately the year 614. By that time, the Meccan leaders had failed in their initial efforts to break the will of the Prophet and his followers. Their next major policy initiative involved open persecution and economic pressure.

After some months passed, and the travails and suffering of the Muslims of Mecca became unbearable, the Prophet told his followers that they could migrate to Abyssinia if they chose, that the government there was overseen by a just king, a Christian king, and that they could stay there until Allah had made a better situation for them in their homeland.

The first migration was of eleven men and four women, who narrowly eluded capture. A few months later, in the year 615, a much larger group of refugees, consisting of over eighty men and eleven women, escaped Mecca, leaving only about forty or fifty Muslims behind in Mecca with the Prophet. The migration of so many people caused a great amount of consternation in Mecca, as every family had at least one member who left, even close relatives of Abu Jahl, Abu Lahab and Abu Sufyan had migrated.

The leaders of the Quraysh decided to send a delegation to Abyssinia to petition the king to return the refugees to Mecca. The two men they chose soon arrived at the court of the king of Abyssinia, bearing expensive gifts. At first they lavished offerings upon the king's officials, and then they met with the king in person and asked for the return of the Meccans who had taken refuge in his kingdom. They explained the refugees were religious rebels who gave up the religion of their people and didn't embrace Christianity, either.

The king, being a fair man, decided to let the Muslims plead their case, saying, "I'm not going to give them back without a proper hearing, for these people have put their trust in my country, rather than in any other country. They've come here to seek shelter, and I won't betray them. Thus, I'll send for them first and investigate the charges that these people have made against them. Then I'll make my final decision."

The leaders of the Muslim migrants were brought to the king, and their spokesman was Ja'far ibn Abi Talib, who said, "O King! We were a people lost in ignorance and had become very corrupt. Then Muhammad came to us as a Messenger of Allah. He did his best to reform us, but the Quraysh began to persecute his followers, so we've come to your country in the hope that here we will be free from persecution."

Then Ja'far was asked to recite some of the Qur'an, and he recited verses from this chapter that relate to Maryam (Mary), 'Esa (Jesus) and Yahiya (John the Baptist). The king began to weep, and he said, "Most surely this revelation and the revelation of 'Esa have come from the same source. By Allah, I will not give you up into the hands of these people."

The Meccans weren't about to give up so easily, however, and the next day they met with the king once more to press him to turn over the Muslims. They told the king that the Muslims denied the divinity of Christ and thus hoped to inflame hatred in his heart towards the Muslims.

When the king summoned Ja'far again and asked him what the Qur'an said about 'Esa, Ja'far answered, "He was a servant of Allah and His Messenger. He was a spirit and a word of Allah, which had been sent to the virgin Maryam."

In the Name of Allah,
the Compassionate, the Merciful

Kāf. Hā. Yā. 'Ayn. Sād. [1]

(This is) a reminder of the mercy of your Lord to His servant Zachariah. [2]

He called out to his Lord in private prayer, saying, "*My Lord! My bones are weak, and my hair is filled with grey. However, I've never been left without blessings when I've called upon You, my Lord.*" [3-4]

"*Now I'm worried about what my relatives (will do) after me, and my wife is barren, so grant me an heir from Yourself, one who will inherit (the mantle of righteousness) from me and from the family of Yaqub. Make him, My Lord, someone with whom You'll be pleased.*" [5-6]

"*Zachariah,*" (a voice called out to him), "*we've come to give you the good news of a son who shall be called Yahiya. We've never called anyone else by that name before.*" [7]

"*My Lord!*" (Zachariah) replied. "*How can I have a son, seeing that my wife is barren and I'm weakened by old age?*" [8]

"*And so it shall be,*" (the voice) answered, "*for your Lord says, 'That's easy for Me, for I already created you before when you were nothing.'*" [9]

"*My Lord,*" (Zachariah) cried out, "*give me a sign!*"

(The voice) replied, "*Your sign shall be that for three nights you won't be able to speak to anyone, even though you're not mute.*" [10]

Then Zachariah left his private chamber and came out among his people, inspiring them (through hand motions) that they should glorify Allah in the morning and at night. [11]

The Nature of Yahiya

"*Yahiya! Take hold of the scripture firmly!*"

We made him wise, even from his youth, and (gave him) sympathy from Us towards (every living thing), for he was pure-hearted and mindful (of Allah). [12-13]

He was also kind to his parents and was neither aggressive nor rebellious. [14]

So peace be upon him the day he was born, the day that he died and the day that he's raised to life again. [15]

Mary Receives Her News

Mention in the Book (the story of) Maryam when she withdrew from her family to a place in the east. [16]

She set up a curtain (to screen herself) off from (her family), and then We sent Our angel to her, who appeared like a mortal man in all respects. [17]

"*I seek the protection of the Compassionate from you!*" she cried out (when she saw the stranger approaching).

"*If you're mindful (of Allah, then you'll leave me alone)!*" [18]

"*Truly, I am a messenger from your Lord,*" he answered, "*(sent to tell) you about the gift of a pure boy.*" [19]

"*But how can I have a son,*" she asked (in surprise), "*when no man has ever touched me, and I'm not a loose woman?*" [20]

"*And so it will be,*" he answered, "*for your Lord says, 'That's easy for Me.' (Your son) will be appointed as a sign for people, as well as a (source of) mercy from Us, and thus it's been decided!*" [21]

Then she conceived him and withdrew with him to a far off place (outside the city). [22]

The labor pains soon drove her to the trunk of a palm tree, and she cried out, "*Oh! If only I had died before this and become something forgotten or lost to sight!*" [23]

"*Don't be distressed!*" a voice called out from under her. "*Your Lord has provided a spring for you. Now shake the palm tree towards you, and it will shower ripe dates upon you.*" [24-25]

"So eat, drink and rest your eye, and if you happen to see any man, tell him, 'I've vowed a fast for the Compassionate, and I won't talk to any person at all today.'" [26]

'Esa Spoke as a Baby

In time, she went back to her people, carrying (the baby, but when they saw her) they cried out, *"Maryam! You've come to us with something bizarre!*

"O Sister of Harun! Your father wasn't a bad man, and your mother wasn't a loose woman!" [27-28]

(Maryam was speechless and frightened), and she merely pointed to the baby.

(Her family looked surprised) and asked, *"How can we talk to a baby in a cradle?"* [29]

(Then the baby 'Esa spoke out), saying, *"I am a servant of Allah. He's given me (knowledge of) the scripture and made me a prophet.* [30]

"He's placed blessings upon me wherever I may be and has made me prayerful and charitable for as long as I live. [31]

"(He also) made me gentle towards my mother, being neither aggressive nor rude. So peace be upon me the day that I was born, the day that I die and the day that I'll be raised to life again." [32-33]

This was 'Esa, the son of Maryam, and that's an exposition of the truth about which they're arguing. [34]

It's not right (to say) that Allah has taken a son. All glory be to Him! Whenever He decides something, all He has to do is say, *"Be,"* and it is! [35]

('Esa, himself, said), *"Allah is my Lord and your Lord, so serve Him, for that's the straight path."* [36]

However, the various factions (among the Christians) differed amongst themselves (about the true nature of 'Esa).

Those who cover up (the truth) will be doomed at the sight of a momentous day. [37]

Oh, how they're going to hear and see (the truth) on the day when they appear before Us!

As of today the wrongdoers are clearly mistaken, but warn them still of the stressful day when the issue is going to be decided once and for all.

They're careless, and they don't believe (in the truth). [38-39]

(In the end, however,) We're going to inherit the earth, as well as whoever's upon it, and then they're all going to come back to Us. [40]

Ibraheem and His Father

Mention in the Book (something about) Ibraheem, for he was an honest man and a prophet. [41]

He said to his father, *"My father! Why are you worshipping things that can neither hear nor see nor bring you any benefit at all?* [42]

"My father! Some teachings have come to me that haven't reached you, so follow me, and I'll guide you to an even path. My father! Don't be in the service of Shaytan, for Shaytan is a rebel against the Compassionate. [43-44]

"My father! I'm afraid that a punishment might befall you from the Compassionate that might cause you to be included among Shaytan's allies." [45]

"Are you talking against my gods?" (his father) demanded. *"Ibraheem! If you don't back off, then I'll stone you! Now get yourself away from me!"* [46]

"So peace (and good bye) to you then," (Ibraheem) answered. *"However, I'm still going to pray to my Lord for your forgiveness, because He's always been kind to me."* [47]

"Now I'm going to turn away from you and from those whom you call upon besides Allah. All I can do is call upon my Lord and hope my prayer to my Lord doesn't go unanswered." [48]

And so he turned away from (his people) and from those (false gods) that they worshipped besides Allah. (In time), We granted him Is-haq and then Yaqub, and We made each one a prophet. [49]

We granted Our mercy to them and gave them high honors that are (still spoken of by the) honest tongues (of those in later generations). [50]

Other Prophets also had their Commission from Allah

Mention in the Book (something about) Musa, for he was selected (by Allah) and was both a messenger and a prophet. [51]

We called out to him from the right side of the mountain and brought him close to Us for an intimate conversation. [52]

Out of Our mercy, We granted (him the help of) his brother Harun, and he was made a prophet (alongside of him). [53]

Also mention in the Book (something about) Isma-il, for he was true to his word, and he was a messenger and also a prophet. [54]

He used to order his people to pray and to give in charity, and his Lord was pleased with him. [55]

Mention further in the Book (something about) Idrís. He was an honest man and a prophet whom We exalted to a high place. [56-57]

Those were some of the prophets from Adam's offspring who were favored by Allah, and (who were descended) from those whom We carried (in the boat) with Nuh, and some of whom (were descended) from Ibraheem and from Israel.

They were among those whom We guided and selected. Whenever verses (revealed from) the Compassionate were recited to them, they would bow down prostrate in tears. [58]

After them came generations (of people) who missed their prayers and followed their own **desires**. Soon enough they're going to be lost in disillusion, but that's not the case with those who repent and believe and who do what's morally right.

They're going to enter the Garden, and they won't be wronged in the least. [59-60]

(For them) are gardens of delight - the same ones that the Compassionate promised to His servants in the realm beyond human perception. His promise will surely come to pass! [61]

They'll hear no useless chatter (in Paradise), but rather the greetings of peace. They'll have whatever they need there for their survival every morning and evening. [62]

That's what the Garden will be like, and that's the place We're going to give as an inheritance to those servants of Ours who were mindful (of their duty to Allah). [63]

The Statement of the Angels

Background Info... v. 64-65

When the idol-worshippers were asking the Prophet questions about the Companions of the Cave, the Master of the Two Horns and other topics, the Prophet said that he would answer them the next day, but he failed to say, "As Allah wills", (and so the reminder in 18:23-24).

A full fifteen days passed, during which the pagans began taunting the Prophet for his lack of response from Allah to their questions. When Jibra'il finally did go to the Prophet with the new revelations of most of chapter 18, the Prophet expressed his gratitude at finally seeing him. He also asked why he didn't come sooner.

This passage here was revealed to him to explain that the angels only go where they are commanded and serve at Allah's pleasure – not at the pleasure of a mere human being. (*Asbab ul-Nuzul*)

(Angel Jibra-il told Muhammad), "*We don't come down (to the earth) without your Lord's command.*

"Whatever is in front of us and behind us and all things in between belong to Him, and your Lord never forgets - the Lord of the heavens and the earth and everything in between!

"So serve Him, and be constant in your service to Him! Do you know of any other who can be named (as an equal) with Him?" [64-65]

The Bridge over Hellfire

Background Info... v. 66-70

This passage was revealed in response to Ubayy ibn Khalaf, a pagan leader who picked up an old bone in his hand and said, "Muhammad is pretending that we're going to be raised up after death!" (*Asbab ul-Nuzul*)

The human says, "*So then when I'm dead, am I really going to be raised back to life again?*" [66]

Doesn't the human recall that We created him from nothing already once before? [67]

By your Lord, We're certainly going to gather them back together, along with all the devilish (jinns). Then We'll bring them forward on their knees and gather them all around Hellfire. [68]

We'll then drag out from every faction all those who were the most rebellious against the Compassionate. *We know best who deserves to be burnt in (the fire)!* [69-70]

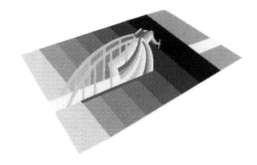

400

There's not one among you except that you're going to have to pass over (the bridge than spans over Hellfire).

This is an outcome that your Lord will bring about, but We're going to save those who were mindful (of their Lord), even as We're going to leave the wrongdoers on their knees. [71-72]

Allah Gives Us All a Chance

> **Background Info... v. 73-76**
>
> These verses echo the common **Meccan objection to the Prophet's** preaching. Muhammad was attracting converts mostly from the lower classes in society, and the wealthy Meccan leaders mocked this trend, pointing out that they dressed better and looked more refined due to their affluence.

When Our clear verses are recited to them, the (well-to-do among) the faithless say to the (common) believers, "*Which of these two sides is in a better position? Which group seems more impressive in the public forum?*" [73]

Yet, how many generations before them have We destroyed who were better equipped and more impressive in their appearance (than they)? [74]

Say to them, "*If anyone goes astray, the Compassionate will hold out (the rope of salvation) to them, up until the point they see the promised (penalty of Allah coming to pass), whether it be the punishment (of destruction) or the coming of the Hour. Then they're going to realize who it was*

that was in the worst position and who it was that had the weakest influence (among men)!" [75]

Allah increases the guidance of those who seek to be guided.

Moral deeds that endure are the best in your Lord's sight for repayment and the best for profitable returns. [76]

Allah Records Everything

> **Background Info... v. 77-87**
>
> A follower of the Prophet named Khabab ibn al-Aratt, who was a blacksmith, went to a pagan named Al-As ibn Wa'il to collect payment for a sword he had made for him, but Ibn Wa'il refused to pay him what he owed unless Khabab renounced his faith in the Prophet first.
>
> Khabab refused, saying he would never do that even until the day Ibn Wa'il died and was raised to life again. Ibn Wa'il then asked Khabab if he really believed that there would be a heaven filled with gold and silver after death.
>
> When Khabab nodded in the affirmative, Ibn Wa'il then boasted, "And so after I've been brought back to life and been given wealth and children, then I'll repay you your money!" This passage was revealed in comment on this episode. (Bukhari, Muslim)

Have you seen the type (of person) who rejects Our (revealed) verses; yet, he has (the audacity) to say, "*I'm certainly going to be blessed with abundant wealth and children.*" [77]

Has he looked into what's beyond human sight or made a deal with the Compassionate? [78]

No way! We're going to record what he's said, and We're going to increase his allotted share of punishment! [79]

Everything that he's said will come back to Us, and he's going to appear before Us bare and alone. [80]

They've taken other gods in place of Allah and expect to get power (from them)? [81]

No way! Those (false gods) are going to reject the service they offer to them, and they're going to be their opponents (on the Day of Judgment)! [82]

Haven't you seen how We've riled up the devils against the faithless to make them furious with anger? [83]

So don't be in a hurry against them, for We're merely counting down (the days they have left before We punish them). [84]

One day We're going to gather the righteous before the Compassionate like an honored delegation, even as We're going to drive the bad people into Hellfire like a thirsty herd (of cattle) being driven to a well. [85-86]

No one will have any power to intercede, except for the one who has permission from the Compassionate. [87]

Ascribing Children to Allah

They're claiming that the Compassionate has taken a son! They've said an outrageous statement! [88-89]

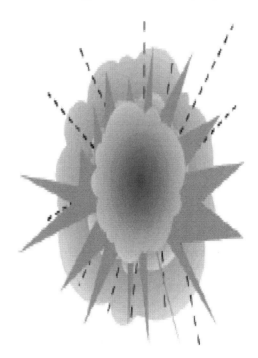

It's as if the skies are ready to explode, as if the earth is ready to crack apart, as if the mountains are ready to crumble to pieces that they should call for the Compassionate to take a son! It's not imaginable for the Compassionate to take a son! [90-92]

There isn't a single being in the heavens nor on the earth except that it must come as a (humble) servant to the Compassionate. He's counted them and numbered them all precisely! [93-94]

Everyone of them will come before Him alone on the Day of Assembly, and

He'll bestow His love upon those who believed and did what was morally right. [95-96]

And so We've made (this Qur'an) easy on your tongue, so you can use it to give good news to those who are mindful (of their duty to Allah), as well as warn those people who are given to senseless opposition. [97]

How many generations before them have We destroyed? Can you find a single one of them (still surviving) or hear so much as a whisper from them? [98]

This Concludes Volume 1

Please Go to Volume 2 to Continue

When you finish the reading of the Qur'an, you should say:

And indeed, Allah, the Exalted, has spoken the truth...

Then the reader should return to the beginning of the book
and read the first chapter along with a few verses of chapter two.

This Shows that the cycle of searching for Allah's guidance never ends
but begins anew until the day we return to meet our Lord.

Don't Miss

In the Gardens of Delight!

**A huge anthology of stories, poems,
novellas and inspiring writings to build your Islamic Faith**

**Over 500 pages each!
Collect all 10 volumes!**

Go to www.amirahpublishing.com

for a complete list of books by Yahiya Emerick

A version of this work for teenagers is also available:

"The Holy Qur'an As If You Were There"

See it on our website or at your favorite Online Bookstore